8
AF181441

Patent Pledges

Patent Pledges

Global Perspectives on Patent Law's Private Ordering Frontier

Edited by

Jorge L. Contreras

Associate Professor, S.J. Quinney College of Law, University of Utah, USA

Meredith Jacob

Assistant Director, Program on Information Justice and Intellectual Property, American University Washington College of Law, USA

Edward Elgar PUBLISHING

Cheltenham, UK • Northampton, MA, USA

© The Editors and Contributors Severally 2017

All rights reserved. No part of this publication may be reproduced, stored in a retrieval system or transmitted in any form or by any means, electronic, mechanical or photocopying, recording, or otherwise without the prior permission of the publisher.

Published by
Edward Elgar Publishing Limited
The Lypiatts
15 Lansdown Road
Cheltenham
Glos GL50 2JA
UK

Edward Elgar Publishing, Inc.
William Pratt House
9 Dewey Court
Northampton
Massachusetts 01060
USA

A catalogue record for this book
is available from the British Library

Library of Congress Control Number: 2016957230

This book is available electronically in the **Elgar**online
Law subject collection
DOI 10.4337/9781785362491

MIX
Paper from
responsible sources
FSC® C013056

ISBN 978 1 78536 248 4 (cased)
ISBN 978 1 78536 249 1 (eBook)

Typeset by Columns Design XML Ltd, Reading
Printed and bound in Great Britain by TJ International Ltd, Padstow

Contents

List of contributors vii
Acknowledgements xvi

Introduction 1

PART I LANDSCAPE OF PATENT PLEDGES

1 A patent pledge taxonomy 7
Jorge L. Contreras
2 Unilateral patent pledges: motivations and key principles 37
Duane R. Valz
3 Patent sharing in biotechnology 56
Dov Greenbaum
4 Patent pledges in green technology 82
Bassem Awad

PART II LITIGATION INVOLVING PATENT PLEDGES

5 Patent pledge enforcement theories 101
Jorge L. Contreras
6 Patent pledges at the U.S. International Trade Commission 117
Elizabeth I. Winston
7 Voluntary patent pledges: enforcement in Germany 137
Catharina Maracke and Axel Metzger

PART III COMPETITION LAW AND PATENT PLEDGES AROUND THE WORLD

8 Is patent reform via private ordering anticompetitive? An analysis of open patent agreements 151
Matthew W. Callahan and Jason M. Schultz
9 Enforcing patent pledges under EU law 168
Rafal Sikorski

10 Patent pledges and antitrust law in Brazil 189
Ricardo Sichel
11 Patent pledge enforcement in China 197
Elizabeth Xiao-Ru Wang
12 Patent pledges: Korean perspectives 209
Sang-Seung Yi and Yoonhee Kim

PART IV PATENT PLEDGES AND INNOVATION

13 The informational effects of patent pledges 227
Clark D. Asay
14 Open innovation and patent pledges 248
Mariateresa Maggiolino and Maria Lillà Montagnani
15 The role of patent pledges in the cloud 260
Liza Vertinsky
16 Patent pledges and developing countries: the tryst with India's destiny 277
Tania Sebastian

PART V PATENT PLEDGES MOVING FORWARD

17 How to make and keep a patent pledge 285
Timothy S. Simcoe
18 A registry for patent pledges 290
Jorge L. Contreras
19 Overcoming information asymmetry in patent pledge records 301
Nicole Shanahan
20 Best practices for making patent pledges 317
Meredith Jacob

Appendix 323

Index 337

Contributors

Clark D. Asay is an Associate Professor of Law at Brigham Young University (BYU) Law School. Before coming to BYU, Professor Asay was a Visiting Assistant Professor and Shughart Scholar at Pennsylvania State University's Dickinson School of Law. Prior to entering legal academia, Professor Asay worked at Amazon's Lab126 and supported the Kindle, Kindle Fire, Amazon Fire, and Amazon Echo teams. Professor Asay also worked at the law firm of Wilson Sonsini Goodrich & Rosati, where he practiced in the field of technology transactions and intellectual property licensing. Professor Asay's research and teaching interests focus on intellectual property law, technology, and innovation. He has published papers relating to patents, copyright, open source software licensing, and information privacy. He has taught courses on intellectual property law, information privacy, and contracts. Professor Asay is a graduate of Stanford Law School, where he was an Executive Editor for the *Stanford Law Review*. Professor Asay also earned an MPhil from the University of Cambridge and a BA, summa cum laude, from Brigham Young University.

Bassem Awad is the Deputy Director and theme leader of intellectual property law and innovation at the International Law Research Program, Canadian Center for International Governance Innovation (CIGI). He is an adjunct professor in the Faculty of Law, University of Western Ontario and a head tutor of the distance learning courses for the Academy of the World Intellectual Property Organization (WIPO). Mr. Awad served for several years as a judge and head of the intellectual property (IP) tribunal at the Appeal Court in Egypt and the United Arab Emirates, and as a consultant for the African Union. His current research at CIGI focuses on the role of intellectual property rights in addressing the global challenge of climate change and sustainable development under the international trading system. Dr. Awad received his PhD and LLM degrees in IP from the University of Montpellier and the University of Paris 1 Panthéon-Sorbonne. His research interests include patent law, comparative IP, and governance of IP rights. He is a member of the International Association for the Advancement of Teaching and Research in Intellectual Property and the Editorial International Committee of the journal *Cahiers de Propriété Intellectuelle*.

Matthew W. Callahan practices civil litigation as an associate in the San Francisco office of a national law firm. Previously, Mr. Callahan was a Technology and Civil Liberties Fellow at the ACLU of Northern California. His work focused on data privacy, online free speech, and government surveillance, as well as litigation under the U.S. and California Constitutions. Mr. Callahan holds degrees from New York University School of Law (JD) and Harvard University (AB).

Jorge L. Contreras is a Professor of Law at the University of Utah, and a Senior Policy Fellow at American University Washington College of Law. He has written and spoken extensively on the institutional structures of intellectual property, technical standardization, and biomedical research. He currently serves as a member of the National Institutes of Health's (NIH) Council of Councils, and previously served as Co-Chair of the National Conference of Lawyers and Scientists (NCLS) and a member of the National Advisory Council for Human Genome Research (NACHGR), and the Advisory Council for NIH's National Center for the Advancement of Translational Sciences (NCATS). Professor Contreras's work has appeared in a range of scientific, policy, and legal publications including *Science*, *Nature*, *Georgetown Law Journal*, *North Carolina Law Review*, *Journal of Competition Law and Economics*, *Telecommunications Policy*, *Jurimetrics*, *Arizona State Law Journal*, *American University Law Review*, *Utah Law Review*, *Antitrust Law Journal*, *Berkeley Technology Law Journal*, and *Harvard Journal of Law and Technology*. He is the founding editor of SSRN's *Law, Policy and Economics of Technical Standards* eJournal, and the editor of the *Cambridge Handbook of Technical Standardization Law* (2 vols., Cambridge University Press forthcoming). Prior to entering academia, Professor Contreras was a partner at the international law firm Wilmer Cutler Pickering Hale and Dorr LLP, where he practiced technology and transactional law in Boston, Washington, and London. He holds degrees from Rice University (BA, BSEE) and Harvard Law School (JD).

Dov Greenbaum is the Director of the Zvi Meitar Institute for Legal Implications of Emerging Technologies at the Interdisciplinary Center (IDC) Herzliya, Israel. Concurrently, he is also an Assistant Professor in the Department of Molecular Biophysics and Biochemistry at Yale University (adj.). Dr. Greenbaum has degrees and post-doctoral fellowships from Yeshiva University, Yale University, University of California Berkeley, ETH Zurich, and Stanford University. In addition to his academic affiliation and training, he is also an intellectual property attorney (California and United States Patent and Trademark Office (USPTO)), with particular experience in the fields of biopharmaceutical litigation, and high tech patent drafting and prosecution, including drafting in the fields of biotech, robotics, software, computer hardware, and defense.

Meredith Jacob serves as the Assistant Director for Academic Programs at the Program on Information Justice and Intellectual Property at American University Washington College of Law. Currently her work includes research and advocacy focused on: open licensing and open innovation models, open access to federally funded research, flexible limitations and exceptions to copyright, and public interest international intellectual property. Previously, Ms. Jacob worked with state legislators on a variety of intellectual property and regulatory issues affecting pharmaceuticals and the privacy of prescription records. She has a JD from American University Washington College of Law and a BA in Chemistry and Political Science from Williams College.

Yoonhee Kim is a licensed Korean patent attorney and currently an Associate at Finnegan, Henderson, Farabow, Garrett & Dunner, LLP. He received a JD magna cum laude from American University Washington College of Law and a BS in Chemical Engineering from Seoul National University. His experience includes working as a Dean's Fellow to Professor Jorge Contreras at American University Washington College of Law, where he researched patent and competition issues surrounding the standard-setting process and FRAND commitments. While in law school, Mr. Kim also worked in the Office of Policy Planning at the U.S. Federal Trade Commission where he assisted the staff with the policy projects involving standard-essential patents and patent assertion entities. Mr. Kim regularly writes and has been published on international and comparative patent law and on the topics at the intersection of patent and competition laws. His recent topics of interest include the Korea Fair Trade Commission's antitrust investigation into Qualcomm's FRAND licensing practices (co-author, published in *CPI Antitrust Chronicle*) and the comparative aspects of a patent law doctrine in the United States, Korea, and Japan (published in *Journal of Patent & Trademark Office Society*).

Mariateresa Maggiolino is an Associate Professor of Commercial Law at Bocconi University of Milan and Research Fellow at the Bocconi ASK Research Center. She has been a visiting professor at Fordham law school, where she taught antitrust law, her main field of interest. She has extensively published in international journals and edited books.

Catharina Maracke is an Associate Professor at the Graduate School for Media and Governance, Shonan Fujisawa Campus, at Keio University. Her current work and research interests include intellectual property law and policy, standardization efforts for public licensing schemes, and the general interaction between law and technology. Professor Maracke is also a faculty affiliate at the Berkman Klein Center for Internet and Society and a Visiting Professor at the Berlin School of Library and Information Science at Humboldt University, Berlin. She graduated from the University of Kiel and the Hamburg Court of Appeal, Germany, with the First and Second State Examination. While studying, Prof. Maracke obtained a scholarship from the Max-Planck Institute for Intellectual Property, Competition and Tax Law in Munich to write her PhD thesis on the history of the German Copyright Act of 1965. As international Director at Creative Commons she has overseen the international license porting projects for more than three years. Professor Maracke has served as a board member for iCommons and the Open Course Ware Consortium and as a member of the Global Agenda Council on the Intellectual Property System at the World Economic Forum. She is admitted to the bar in Germany.

Axel Metzger is Professor of Law at Humboldt University, Berlin, where he teaches civil law and intellectual property. Professor Metzger graduated from the University of Hamburg and passed the First and the Second State Examination at the Hamburg Court of Appeals. He received a Doctor juris from the Universities of Munich and Paris II (Panthéon-Assas), an LLM from Harvard and finished his Habilitation in Hamburg in 2008. Professor Metzger was full professor at the University of Hannover, Germany (2008–2014) and visiting professor at Basle University (2011) and Bucerius Law School (2012). He is author and editor of numerous books and articles on intellectual property and information technology law.

Maria Lillà Montagnani is Associate Professor of Commercial Law at Bocconi University, where she teaches courses on intellectual property law, and is Director of the ASK Research Center. She has been a faculty associate at the Berkman Center for Law and Society of Harvard University and visiting scholar at Centre for Commercial Law Studies, Queen Mary University of London, and a scholarship holder at Max Planck Institute for Intellectual Property, Competition and Tax Law of Munich. Her research interests are in the field of copyright law, patent and trademark law, and competition law. She has published in leading international law journals, including *World Competition*, *IIC International Review of Industrial Property and Copyright Law*, and *Cardozo*

Art & Entertainment Law Journal. She co-edited several books including *Intellectual Property and Social Justice: A Law and Economics Approach*, published by Edward Elgar in 2010. In 2012 she published the book *Il diritto d'autore nell'era digitale: la distribuzione online delle opere dell'ingegno* (Giuffrè).

Jason M. Schultz is a Professor of Clinical Law and Director of New York University's (NYU) Technology Law and Policy Clinic. His clinical projects, research, and writing primarily focus on the ongoing struggles to balance intellectual property and privacy law with the public interest in free expression, access to knowledge, and innovation in light of new technologies and the challenges they pose. Prior to joining NYU, Professor Schultz was an Assistant Clinical Professor of Law and Director of the Samuelson Law, Technology & Public Policy Clinic at the University of California Berkeley School of Law (Boalt Hall). Before joining Boalt Hall, he was a Senior Staff Attorney at the Electronic Frontier Foundation (EFF), one of the leading digital rights groups in the world and before that practiced intellectual property law at the firm of Fish & Richardson, PC. He also served as a clerk to the Honorable D. Lowell Jensen of the Northern District of California. He is a member of the American Law Institute.

Tania Sebastian is an Assistant Professor at Vellore Institute of Technology Law School, VIT University Chennai Campus, Chennai, India. She has also held the position of Assistant Professor of Law at Gujarat National Law University in Gujarat, India. She received an LLM degree in Intellectual Property Rights and Cyber Law from the Indian Law Institute, and her undergraduate degree from Bangalore University.

Nicole Shanahan is an attorney in California and a Residential Fellow at CodeX, the Stanford Center of Legal Informatics, a joint center between Stanford Law School and Computer Science. She is the founder and CEO of ClearAccessIP, an integrated patent management technology, and a legal technologist who specializes in the utilization of structured databases, APIs, UI/UX, automation and SaaS. Her research at Stanford is entitled "Smart Prosecution," an ongoing, multi-disciplinary project applying data science to the prosecutorial process and involving partnerships with district attorneys and police departments.

Ricardo Sichel is a Professor of Civil and Commercial Law at the Federal University of the State of Rio de Janeiro. In addition to his academic role, Professor Sichel has also worked in the Legal Department of the Brazilian Patent and Trademark Office since 1984. He received his law degree from the Federal University in Rio de Janeiro. Professor

Sichel also attended the Westfälische Wilhelms University in Münster, Germany, where he received Master of Laws and Doctor of Law degrees. While at the Westfälische Wilhelms University, he wrote an essay on "European Patent Law" and completed a thesis on "Communitarian Patent Agreement and TRIPS."

Rafal Sikorski graduated from the Faculty of Law and Administration of Adam Mickiewicz University in Poznań in 1999. In 2000, he received an LLM in International Business Transactions from the Central European University in Budapest. Since 2005 he has held a PhD in Legal Science awarded by the Faculty of Law and Administration of Adam Mickiewicz University in Poznań, where he currently works as an assistant professor at the Chair of European Law. He has also been a scholar at the TMC Asser Institute in The Hague. His academic accomplishments include a number of publications on copyright law, industrial property law, unfair competition law, competition law, and private international law. Within his academic work he mainly focuses on relations between competition law and intellectual property law, with a particular emphasis on standardization and patent pools. Additionally, Professor Sikorski deals with issues in determining the governing law for intellectual property law contracts and infringements of such.

Timothy S. Simcoe is an Associate Professor of Strategy and Innovation at the Boston University Questrom School of Business, and a Research Associate at the National Bureau of Economic Research. From 2014 to 2015, he served as a Senior Economist on the President's Council of Economic Advisers. Professor Simcoe's research focuses on standards, innovation and technology policy, intellectual property and corporate strategy. His research has been published in the *American Economic Review*, *Management Science*, the *RAND Journal of Economics*, *Organization Science* and the *Journal of Applied Econometrics*. He is an editor at *Management Science* and the *Journal of Industrial Economics*. In 2012 he served on a National Academy of Sciences Committee to evaluate Intellectual Property Management in Standard-Setting Processes. Professor Simcoe holds a BA in Applied Mathematics from Harvard, and an MA in Economics and a PhD in Business Administration from the University of California, Berkeley.

Duane R. Valz is General Counsel of Zymergen, Inc., an emerging growth company operating at the intersection of bioscience, automation, data analytics, and machine learning. Prior to Zymergen, Mr. Valz was Senior Patent Counsel for strategic IP initiatives at Google. He led a team managing a variety of projects directed towards present and future risk mitigation, spanning targeted patent development, licensing, acquisitions, standards, and open source patent strategy. Among other projects, Mr. Valz architected and published Google's Open Patent Non-Assertion (OPN) Pledge. He also served on the Board of Directors for the Open Invention Network on Google's behalf. Mr. Valz has counseled a wide range of emerging growth, private, and publicly held companies on IP and technology matters in various capacities. Before joining Google in 2011, Mr. Valz practiced at Chadbourne & Parke LLP, where he was twice named in *IAM Strategy 300: The World's Leading IP Strategists*. His past experience includes serving as Head of Patent Development at Yahoo! and as Director of Intellectual Property at Quantum Corporation. He received his JD from the University of California at Berkeley, School of Law where he served as submissions editor of the *Berkeley Technology Law Journal*. He earned his BA with honors and distinction in general scholarship from the University of California Berkeley.

Liza Vertinsky is an Associate Professor at Emory School of Law. She came to Emory in 2007 after a decade of legal practice focusing on intellectual property transactions. Her areas of expertise include intellectual property, innovation, the intersection of IP and global health, and law and economics. Her research program is motivated by a deep interest in how legal rules – particularly patent law and contract law – influence the ways in which individuals and groups organize their economic activities. She is particularly interested in exploring the institutional environments within which alternative forms of intellectual production take place, with a focus on biomedical innovation. Professor Vertinsky clerked for Judge Stanley Marcus, first for the U.S. District Court in the Southern District of Florida and then for the Eleventh Circuit Court of Appeals. Education: BA, Oxford University, 1991; JD, Harvard Law School, 1997; MA, Economics, University of British Columbia, 1992; PhD, Economics, Harvard University, 1997.

Elizabeth Xiao-Ru Wang is a Senior Research Fellow and Economist at the Competition Law Centre at the University of International Business and Economics in Beijing, China. Dr. Wang has a PhD in economics from the University of Chicago and a BA in economics from Peking University. She provides economic analyses on issues of merger review, intellectual property rights, vertical restraints, exclusionary conducts, price fixing, and assessment of damages, especially in cross-border matters. She has been involved in casework in a variety of industries, including health care, high tech, financial markets, pharmaceutical, airlines, and consumer products. Dr. Wang has submitted reports to antitrust government agencies in the U.S. and in China and has testified at a U.S. congressional hearing on antitrust issues. Dr. Wang has extensive experience working on antitrust matters with Chinese regulators. Dr. Wang has submitted reports and presented economic analysis in front of the Ministry of Commerce (MOFCOM), and advised clients on merger reviews, antitrust investigation, and private litigation in China.

Elizabeth I. Winston is an Associate Professor of Law at the Catholic University of America, Columbus School of Law. She is a frequent writer and speaker on a range of intellectual property topics, with a particular interest in the intersection of contract law and patent law. Professor Winston has presented at dozens of conferences and has authored numerous legal articles, including in *Wisconsin Law Review*, *Tennessee Law Review*, *George Mason Law Review*, *Missouri Law Review*, *Michigan State Law Review*, *Temple Law Review*, *Intellectual Property Law Review*, *Lewis and Clark Law Review*, *Akron Journal of Intellectual Property*, and *The John Marshall Review of Intellectual Property Law*. She earned her JD at University of Virginia School of Law, and an SB from the Massachusetts Institute of Technology. After law school, Professor Winston served as a clerk to the Honorable James T. Turner of the United States Court of Federal Claims and to the Honorable Paul R. Michel of the United States Court of Appeals for the Federal Circuit. Prior to entering academia, Professor Winston was in private practice with the law firm of Covington & Burling.

Sang-Seung Yi is a Professor in the Department of Economics, Seoul National University (SNU). Professor Yi received his PhD from Harvard University in 1992. He taught at Dartmouth College from 1992 to 1998, at Sogang University from 1998 to 2001, and at SNU from 2001. Professor Yi is the first recipient of the Kim Taesung Memorial Prize in 1998, awarded annually by the Korean Econometric Society to a Korean economist under 40 for academic excellence. In 1984, while a junior at SNU, he was the youngest successful contestant in the Higher Senior Civil Service Examination. Instead of joining the government when he graduated summa cum laude from SNU, Professor Yi enrolled in the PhD program at Harvard University to pursue his interests in economics. Professor Yi's academic research focuses on applied microeconomic theory, industrial organization, and the economic analysis of antitrust. He has published highly cited papers in academic journals such as the *RAND Journal of Economics*, *International Journal of Industrial Organization*, *Games and Economic Behavior*, and the *Journal of International Economics*. Professor Yi's current research focuses on the economic analysis of competition law, with particular interest in the interface between antitrust and intellectual property laws. He has authored numerous papers (including a publication in *Competition Policy International*) and consulted on several key antitrust cases in Korea, including abuse of dominance, horizontal and non-horizontal mergers, and damages estimation from collusion. Professor Yi gratefully acknowledges financial support from the Center for National Competitiveness in the Institute of Economic Research of Seoul National University.

Acknowledgements

This book would not have been possible without the hard work and dedication of many individuals. Among those to whom we extend our gratitude are the participants at the 2014 meeting "Patent Pledges: Developing a Research Agenda": Jonas Anderson, David Blonder, Michael Carrier, Michael Carroll, Tom Cotter, Carter Eltzroth, Sean Flynn, Richard Gilbert, John Harkrider, Drew Hirshfeld, Brian Kahin, Jay Kesan, Lisa Kimmel, Anne Layne-Farrar, Daryl Lim, Rob Mahini, Joe Miller, Suzanne Munck, Bill Page, Allan Shampine, Danny Sokol, and Henry Wixon; all of the presenters and participants at the 2015 Patent Pledges meeting at American University Washington College of Law; Michael Palmedo, who maintains the Patent Pledges Database; our research assistants Nick Doyle, Angela Silvers, Jordan Bledsoe, Michael Eixenberger, and Connor Scholes; Google, Inc., which provided valuable funding for our patent pledges projects; the Program on Information Justice and Intellectual Property (PIJIP) at American University Washington College of Law; the University of Utah S.J. Quinney College of Law and the Albert and Elaine Borchard Fund for Faculty Excellence; and our editors at Edward Elgar, Karissa Venne and Stephen Gutierrez.

Introduction[1]

In 2014, Elon Musk, the outspoken founder of Tesla Motors, surprised the automotive industry by pledging that his company would no longer "initiate patent lawsuits against anyone who, in good faith, wants to use our technology."[2] Tesla's announcement prompted a flurry of media and industry attention. But most importantly, six months later it prompted automotive giant Toyota to pledge that it, too, would permit the royalty-free use of nearly 5,700 Toyota hydrogen fuel cell patents.[3]

It is commonly believed that Tesla and Toyota elected to sacrifice otherwise valuable patent assets in order to pave the way for the fledgling electric vehicle industry, and to ensure that their own vehicle platforms remained integral to the development of this industry. But making such "patent pledges" is not unique to the electric vehicle industry. Beginning in the 1990s, large firms in the computing and software industries began to champion open source code platforms such as Linux and Android. They demonstrated that business models based on tight control over intellectual property are not the only viable pathways to innovation and product development. To support the growth of these emerging open source platforms, firms like IBM and Google each pledged not to assert hundreds of patents against open source products.[4] In recent years, the number of firms venturing into this new ground has grown. For example, Monsanto, the world's leading producer of genetically modified seeds, has publicly committed not to enforce its patents against farmers

---

[1] This chapter is based, in part, on Jorge L. Contreras, *Patent Pledges*, 47 ARIZ. ST. L.J. 543 (2015), with permission of the author.

[2] Elon Musk, *All Our Patents Are Belong to You*, TESLA BLOG (June 12, 2014), http://www.teslamotors.com/blog/all-our-patent-are-belong-you. Tesla Motors has since revised and clarified this initial pledge. *See* Appendix.

[3] *Toyota Opens the Door and Invites the Industry to the Hydrogen Future*, TOYOTA CORP. (Jan. 5, 2015), http://www.toyotanewsroom.com/releases/toyota+fuel+cell+patents+ces+2015.htm.

[4] *IBM Statement of Non-Assertion of Named Patents Against OSS*, IBM CORP. (Jan. 11, 2005), http://www.ibm.com/ibm/licensing/patents/pledgedpatents.pdf; *Open Patent Non-Assertion Pledge*; GOOGLE, INC., http://www.google.com/patents/opnpledge/pledge/.

when trace amounts of patented genetic material appear in their fields by "inadvertent means."[5] And dozens of firms ranging from home-swapping website Airbnb to cloud storage giant Dropbox have committed not to enforce their software patents against businesses with 25 or fewer employees.[6] In fact, over the past decade, hundreds of major patent holders across a broad range of industries have made pledges limiting their ability to assert thousands of patents.

The *patent pledges* made by all of these firms share several key characteristics: they are commitments made voluntarily by patent holders to limit the enforcement or other exploitation of their patents. They are made not to direct contractual counterparties, but to the public at large, or at least to large segments of certain markets. And they are made without any direct compensation or other consideration.

Patent pledges represent a middle ground between full exploitation of a patent's exclusive rights and ceding the patent to the public domain. Unlike patent holders that willingly commit their rights to the public domain, firms making patent pledges retain ownership of, and the ability to exercise at least some rights in, their patents. Their voluntary commitments thus occupy a largely uncharted middle ground between the full commercial exploitation of patent rights and the abandonment of those rights to the public domain.

The best-known category of patent pledge today is the so-called FRAND commitment, in which patent holders promise to license their patents to manufacturers of standardized products on terms that are "fair, reasonable and non-discriminatory." Patents covering well-known standards such as 4G LTE, Wi-Fi, H.264, and hundreds of others are subject to such pledges. To date, courts, governmental agencies, and commentators have devoted substantial attention to FRAND commitments and the potential legal issues that they raise. But patent pledges have been appearing in fields and settings well beyond technical standard-setting, and are impacting widening swaths of the global technology economy. As a result, this increasingly prevalent private ordering mechanism is reshaping conventional notions regarding the role and function of patents in the economy.

In 2012, Jorge Contreras, while at American University, began to collect and categorize patent pledges made by different organizations and to make them publicly available through an online database known as the

---

[5] *Monsanto's Commitment: Farmers and Patents*, MONSANTO, http://www.monsanto.com/newsviews/pages/commitment-farmers-patents.aspx.

[6] THE PATENT PLEDGE, http://thepatentpledge.org/.

Patent Pledge Database.[7] As of this writing, more than 150 different pledges covering thousands of patents have been cataloged in the Patent Pledge Database.

The Patent Pledge Database led to significant interest within academia, industry, and government. In 2014, we convened a workshop in Washington, DC, in which experts in patent law, economics, and technology commercialization gathered to chart a research agenda for patent pledges. This workshop led to a worldwide call for papers and an academic symposium in 2015 focused on the impact, characteristics, and implications of patent pledges in a wide range of industries and regions of the world.

This volume collects the results of this public dialog and academic inquiry into patent pledges, and will hopefully inspire further discussion and research into this phenomenon. Part I offers an overview of the landscape of patent pledges today. In Chapter 1, Contreras offers a descriptive survey of patent pledges by industry sector, and then outlines some common structural characteristics of pledges. He then introduces an analytical taxonomy of pledges based on the motivations driving pledgors to make these commitments, including *inducement*, *collective action*, *voluntary restraint*, and *philanthropy*.

The remainder of Part I is devoted to a series of descriptive accounts of patent pledges in specific market and industry sectors. Valz addresses open source software and other technology issues from an industry perspective. Greenbaum explores the relative scarcity of patent pledges in the biomedical sector. Awad discusses patent pledges intended to foster environmental and "green" technology development.

Part II turns to legal issues that arise with patent pledges. Contreras addresses a range of contemporary theories relating to the legal enforceability of patent pledges. Winston focuses on the treatment of patent pledges at the U.S. International Trade Commission, and Maracke and Metzger offer a perspective on legal enforcement in Germany. In Part III, antitrust and competition law issues are addressed from a range of international perspectives. Callahan and Schultz offer a US antitrust analysis of the Open Patent Agreement. Sikorski offers perspectives on competition law and patent pledges in Europe, and Sichel, Wang, and Yi and Kim provide perspectives from Brazil, China, and Korea, respectively.

---

7 Program on Info. Justice & Intell. Prop. – Am. Univ. Wash. Coll. L., Non-SDO Patent Statements and Commitments, http://www.pijip.org/non-sdo-patent-commitments/.

In Part IV, the authors focus on the impact of patent pledges on innovation and development. Asay addresses issues relating to the informational value of patent pledges. Maggiolino and Montagnani write about the impact of patent pledges on open innovation networks and structures. Vertinsky offers a case study of the use of patent pledges in cloud computing, and Sebastian addresses patent pledges from the perspective of developing countries.

Part V offers thoughts on the future of patent pledges. Simcoe provides a general framework for thinking about the making and enforcement of private commitments. Contreras proposes a governmental or private registry of patent pledges. Shanahan offers suggestions for the rationalization of electronic records of patent pledges. Finally, Jacob provides a best practices framework for making patent pledges in the future.

We hope that this collection offers scholars, legal practitioners, policy makers, and industry representatives new insights and inspiration regarding patent pledges, the newest frontier of intellectual property private ordering.

The Editors

PART I

Landscape of patent pledges

1. A patent pledge taxonomy[1]

Jorge L. Contreras

I. INDUSTRIES AND MARKETS

Generally speaking, four broad industry categories are represented by firms making patent pledges: information and communication technology (ICT), open source software, environmental/green technologies and bio-pharma, pharmaceutical and chemistry technologies (life sciences).

A. Information and Communication Technology (ICT)

Patent pledges, particularly those associated with standards-development activities, arise frequently in the information and communication technology (ICT) sector. This broad industry category includes markets such as wireless telecommunications, networking, computing, consumer electronics, and data exchange. Many of the product categories typically associated with patent pledges are consumer-oriented devices such as smartphones, computers, game players, and home entertainment products manufactured by multinational firms such as Intel, Apple, Samsung, Huawei, Cisco, Microsoft, Ericsson, Verizon, AT&T, IBM, Sony, and Dell. But patent pledges also appear in numerous smaller business-to-business market segments such as avionics electronics, automotive engineering, and semiconductor fabrication. And the firms that participate in ICT standardization are not exclusively large multinationals, as they also include many small- and medium-sized businesses, as well as research institutions and government agencies.

The firms that design and manufacture ICT products often collaborate to develop technical standards within standards-development organizations (SDOs). SDOs are typically organized as non-profit trade associations or consortia, and range from small groups of firms focusing

[1] This chapter is based, in part, on Jorge L. Contreras, *Patent Pledges*, 47 ARIZ. ST. L.J. 543 (2015), with permission of the author.

on a single product category to large, international bodies that produce standards in a broad range of industries. An illustrative group of international SDOs operating in the ICT sector is listed in Table 1.1.

Table 1.1 Selected standards-development organizations (SDOs) in the ICT sector

SDO	Area(s)	Well-known Standards
European Telecommunications Standards Institute (ETSI)	Wireless telecommunications	GSM (2G), UMTS (3G), LTE (4G)
IEEE Standards Association (formerly the Institute of Electrical and Electronics Engineers)	Networking	802.11 (Wi-Fi) Ethernet
International Organization for Standardization (ISO)	Various	ISO 9000, ISO 14000
International Telecommunications Union (ITU)	Telecommunications	H.264
Internet Engineering Task Force (IETF)	Internet	IP, TCP, HTTP
World Wide Web Consortium (W3C)	Worldwide web	HTML, WWW, XML

In addition to these large SDOs, hundreds of smaller consortia and associations actively develop and promote standards in the ICT sector. Participation in these organizations can range from just a few individuals to thousands.

B. Open Source Software

Open source software differs from typical commercial software not with respect to its technical features, but with respect to the legal rights associated with it. That is, software that is released on an open source basis is characterized by the availability, usually at no cost, of the software programmers' code (source code), and the user's right to modify that code, typically with no obligation to the original developer.[2] Open source code first gained a following in the early 1990s with the GNU suite of software tools, but has since come to encompass widely adopted

[2] *The Open Source Definition*, OPEN SOURCE INITIATIVE, http://opensource.org/docs/osd.

platforms and applications including the Linux and Android operating systems, the Firefox web browser, and the Apache web server.

Patent pledges relating to open source software have become increasingly common. In 2004 and 2005, a group of firms including Nokia, Novell, Sun, and others publicly announced that they would not assert patents against use of the Linux operating system.[3] Around the same time, several large patent holders issued blanket assurances covering substantial portfolios of patents and products. Among these were IBM's commitment not to assert approximately 500 patents against open source software products[4] and Google's more recent "Open Patent Non-Assertion Pledge" covering 241 patents.[5] Others, under the umbrella of the non-profit Open Web Foundation, have committed to license patents covering a wide range of open source software interfaces, tools, and specifications.[6]

In addition to these pledges, which have been made independently by patent holders, more than a thousand firms participate as "licensees" in the Open Invention Network (OIN). OIN was formed in 2007 as a vehicle for the promotion of the Linux open source operating system, and has since been expanded to OpenStack and other cloud computing technologies.[7] With funds that it receives from a small group of founding members,[8] OIN acquires patents and then licenses them on a royalty-free basis to all OIN licensees.[9] Licensees, in turn, pledge not to assert their

---

[3] *See*, e.g., *Legally Binding Commitment Not to Assert Nokia Patents Against the Linux Kernel*, NOKIA CORP., http://nokia.com/iprstatements; *Patent Policy: Novell's Statement on Patents and Open Source Software*, NOVELL, INC., http://www.novell.com/company/legal/patents/; *Sun Opens Access to 1,600 Patents*, SUN MICROSYSTEMS (Jan. 25, 2005), http://sys-con.com/story/?storyid=47906.

[4] *IBM Statement of Non-Assertion of Named Patents Against OSS*, IBM CORP. (Jan. 11, 2005), http://www.ibm.com/ibm/licensing/patents/pledgedpatents.pdf.

[5] The Google pledge is a commitment not to assert such patents against users of "free or open source software." *Open Patent Non-Assertion Pledge*, GOOGLE, INC., http://www.google.com/patents/opnpledge/pledge/.

[6] *See Users of OWF Agreements*, OPEN WEB FOUNDATION, http://www.openwebfoundation.org/faqs/users-of-owf-agreements.

[7] Press Release, Open Invention Network, *Open Invention Network Extends its Linux-Protective Network to Cover OpenStack Technologies* (Dec. 30, 2013), http://www.openinventionnetwork.com/pressrelease_details/?id=3.

[8] As of November 1, 2014, the founding members of OIN were Google, IBM, NEC, Novell, Philips, Red Hat, and Sony. *FAQ*, OPEN INVENTION NETWORK, http://www.openinventionnetwork.com/press-room/faqs/.

[9] Id.

own patents against the Linux/OpenStack community.[10] As such, OIN is one of the largest patent pledge communities on record.[11]

C. Green/Clean Technology

Patent pledges have increasingly been used to promote environmentally friendly "green/clean" technologies. While the recent pledge made by Tesla Motors may have grabbed headlines, it is by no means the first such initiative in the area of green/clean technology. One prominent green patent pledge was the Eco-Patent Commons (EPC), a coalition of 13 large firms including IBM, Nokia, Sony, DuPont, Dow, HP, and Xerox, that pledged not to assert specific patents against any technology that "reduces/eliminates natural resource consumption, reduces/eliminates waste generation or pollution, or otherwise provides environmental benefit(s)." The group, which was managed by the Environmental Law Institute in Washington, DC, reported that over one hundred "eco-friendly patents" were pledged by its members while EPC operated from 2008 to 2016.[12] Patent pledges intended to support environmental objectives are discussed more broadly in Chapter 4.

D. Life Sciences

To date, technical standardization in the life sciences has advanced largely without the patent disputes that have emerged in the ICT and software sectors.[13] Several reasons have been proposed for this divergence, including the origin of many life science standards in academic and governmental settings without a strong emphasis on patenting or strong private sector engagement.[14] Some of these factors are discussed in greater detail in Chapter 3.

---

10 *OIN License Agreement*, §§ 1.1–1.2, OPEN INVENTION NETWORK, http://www.openinventionnetwork.com/joining-oin/oin-license-agreement/.

11 *See infra*, Table 1.6.

12 *Frequently Asked Questions*, ECO-PATENT COMMONS, http://ecopatentcommons.org/frequently-asked-questions#QA14.

13 *See* NAT'L RESEARCH COUNCIL, INTELLECTUAL PROPERTY CHALLENGES FOR STANDARD-SETTING IN THE GLOBAL ECONOMY 18–19 (Keith Maskus & Stephen A. Merrill eds., 2013) [hereinafter NAS Report].

14 *See* id.

Nevertheless, patent pledges have begun to emerge in the life sciences. For example, in 2006 four major research institutions led by the Massachusetts Institute of Technology (MIT) committed not to assert patents covering certain RNA-based technology "in order to facilitate widespread distribution of an important class of research reagents."[15] Chemical and agricultural giant Monsanto has pledged that it will not assert its genetically modified seed patents against farmers when trace amounts of Monsanto genetic material appear in their crops through "inadvertent means" (e.g., windborne seeds that contaminate a field).[16] And genetic diagnostics firm Myriad Genetics has pledged that it will not assert patents to "impede non-commercial, academic research."[17] These and other patent non-assertion pledges in the biosciences, especially when coupled with the green technology pledges discussed above, suggest that the phenomenon of patent pledges has moved well beyond its roots in the ICT sector.

II. CHARACTERISTICS OF PATENT PLEDGES

A. Identifying Pledged Patents

Patent pledges may cover one to hundreds or thousands of patents, depending on how the pledged patents are identified. These patents may be identified either specifically (e.g., by patent number) or non-specifically (e.g., by describing a category into which such patents fall). In either case, in order for the pledge to be meaningful, the patents subject to the pledge must be able to be identified unambiguously and without undue effort on the part of the parties relying on the pledge. Table 1.2 illustrates the range of mechanisms by which patent pledges may identify the patents subject to the pledge.

---

[15] Anatole Krattiger, *The Use of Nonassertion Covenants: A Tool to Facilitate Humanitarian Licensing, Manage Liability, and Foster Global Access*, MIHR HANDBOOK OF BEST PRACTICES 1739 (2007).

[16] *Monsanto's Commitment: Farmers and Patents*, MONSANTO, http://www.monsanto.com/newsviews/pages/commitment-farmers-patents.aspx.

[17] *The Myriad Pledge*, MYRIAD, http://www.myriad.com/myriad-cares-2/the-myriad-pledge/.

Table 1.2 Number and identification of patents included in patent pledge

Patents	Example
Single specified patent	Southern California Edison's pledge to grant royalty-free licenses of a single patent covering a method of communicating between a utility and its customer locations
Multiple specified patents	Google's pledge not to assert 241 listed patents against open software implementations
Unspecified patents covering a single specification or standard	Open Web Foundation's Final Specification Agreement OWFa 1.0, covering all patents reading on the DMARC specification
Unspecified patents covering multiple specifications or standards	IBM's pledge not to assert patents against 27 standard specifications related to web services, electronic forms, or open document formats when implemented in the healthcare or education sectors
Unspecified patents covering a single class of products or entities	Multiple firms commit not to assert software patents against companies having fewer than 25 employees
All standards-essential patents	Ericsson's pledge to license all standards-essential patents on FRAND terms
All patents	Cisco's pledge not to transfer patents to non-practicing entities

Though the examples in Table 1.2 are drawn from non-SDO patent pledges, each of these means of identifying patents can also be found within SDO pledges. In smaller SDOs operating in industries that are not heavily patented, a patent pledge may cover only a single patent relevant to a standard being developed.[18] In SDOs serving more heavily patented industries, however, the number of patents pledged by some firms can number in the hundreds, with some standards reportedly covered by thousands of patents.

B. Subject and Scope of Pledge Commitments

The crux of any patent pledge is the commitment that the patent holder makes with respect to the pledged patent(s). Pledge commitments fall

[18] *See* Jorge L. Contreras, *Technical Standards and Ex Ante Disclosure: Results and Analysis of an Empirical Study*, 53 JURIMETRICS 163, 173 (2013) [hereinafter Contreras, *Ex Ante*] (noting that most patent disclosures at VITA, an SDO operating in the avionics and military electronics sector, relate to a single patent).

into three general categories: (1) the primary commitment to license patents, either on royalty-free or FRAND terms, or not to assert patents at all (primary access commitments), (2) more detailed commitments relating to the royalty rates or other amounts that will be charged (secondary royalty commitments), and (3) non-royalty commitments. Some patent pledges may contain one, two, or all three types of commitments. Table 1.3 illustrates the types and frequency of patent pledges found in the Patent Pledge Database.

Table 1.3 Coverage of non-SDO patent pledges (as of Jan. 1, 2015)

Type	Occurrences
1. Primary Access Commitments	
Non-assertion/royalty-free licensing	128
FRAND licensing	20
2. Secondary Royalty Commitments	
Maximum royalty/cap	16
Royalty calculation	10
3. Non-royalty commitments	
Non-injunction	10
No non-practicing entity transfers	3
Binding patent transferees	3
Prior art	4

1. Primary access commitments

The primary access commitment of a patent pledge is generally a broad statement indicating the nature of the access to its patent that the patent holder wishes to give to the public.[19] That is, will the patent holder (1) refrain from asserting the patent against a specified class of potential infringers (i.e., manufacturers of products complying with a standard, small businesses, etc.), (2) license the patent on FRAND terms, or (3) license the patent on royalty-free terms? As among these three

---

19 Patent pledges made within SDOs generally cover only patents that are "essential" to a particular standard. *See*, e.g., ABA COMM. ON TECH. STANDARDIZATION, SECTION OF SCI. & TECHN. LAW, STANDARDS DEVELOPMENT PATENT POLICY MANUAL 11 (Jorge L. Contreras ed., 2007) [hereinafter ABA PATENT POLICY MANUAL].

options, the frequency with which each option is selected varies according to context. For example, some SDOs require that *all* participants license their standards-essential patents on FRAND terms. Others, including the World Wide Web Consortium (W3C), require royalty-free licensing or non-assertion in most cases.[20] And in some SDOs, such as the Internet Engineering Task Force (IETF), participants are free to select which primary access commitment, if any, they wish to make.[21]

2. Secondary royalty commitments

When a patent holder makes a FRAND commitment, it pledges that it will license the covered patents under terms that are "fair, reasonable and non-discriminatory." These general descriptors, of course, do not specify royalty rates or other contractual terms, and numerous disputes have arisen over conflicting views of the level of "reasonable" royalty rates.[22] In an effort to avoid such disputes and provide greater visibility and predictability to potential manufacturers of standardized products, some firms have elected, outside the SDO process, to make additional commitments regarding the royalty rates that they will charge for standards-essential patents.

a) Maximum royalties A number of firms have pledged that they will cap royalty rates for certain product-patent configurations. Maximum royalties may be specified in terms of a percentage royalty rate (e.g., 2.5% of the product sales price), or a per-unit charge (e.g., $0.05 per unit). To date, such approaches have been adopted primarily in the wireless telecommunications sector. Table 1.4 illustrates a number of maximum royalty commitments that have been made and proposed in this sector.

---

20 *W3C Patent Policy*, Sec. 5, W3C, http://www.w3.org/Consortium/Patent-Policy-20040205/ [hereinafter W3C Patent Policy].

21 INTERNET ENG'G TASK FORCE, RFC 3979: INTELLECTUAL PROPERTY RIGHTS IN IETF TECHNOLOGY § 8, at 13 (2005), http://tools.ietf.org/pdf/rfc3979.pdf.

22 *See*, e.g., Microsoft Corp. v. Motorola, Inc., No. C10-1823JLR, 2013 WL 2111217, at *1–4 (W.D. Wash. Apr. 25, 2013); Apple, Inc. v. Motorola Mobility, Inc., 886 F. Supp. 2d 1061, 1087 (W.D. Wis. 2012).

Table 1.4 Maximum royalty pledges in the wireless telecommunications sector

Year	Pledge	Pledgor(s)	Maximum Royalty
2002	Cumulative royalty for W-CDMA (proposed)	Nokia	Cumulative cap of 5% on all royalties covering patents essential to the W-CDMA standard
2008	Framework for LTE technology IPR licensing	Alcatel-Lucent, Ericsson, NEC, NextWave, Nokia, Nokia Siemens Networks, Sony Ericsson	Handsets: single-digit percentage of the sales price Notebooks: single-digit dollar amount
2010	Licensing policy on LTE and service architecture evolution essential patents	Nokia	1.5% of the sales price of end-user devices that deploy LTE as the only wireless communication standard 2.0% for devices in which other standards are utilized in addition to LTE
2012	Letter to IEEE clarifying FRAND commitments	Motorola Mobility	2.25% of net product selling price*
2013	LTE/WiMax pricing statement	Qualcomm	3.25% of the wholesale sale price of devices that implement the LTE/WiMax standards, but not any 3G CDMA standards

Note: * Despite this commitment, Motorola and Microsoft disagreed significantly regarding the appropriate product base pricing to which this 2.25% royalty should be applied, leading to proposed royalties that differed by a factor of 1,000. Microsoft Corp. v. Motorola Mobility, No. C10-1823JLR, 2013 WL 2111217.

b) Royalty calculations Some patent pledges, rather than establishing a maximum royalty, instead specify the methodology that the patent holder will use to calculate royalties. Such commitments often seek to clarify issues such as the royalty "base" that the patent holder intends to use to calculate royalties,[23] or the manner in which products covered by multiple patents will be addressed (i.e., the well-known issue of royalty "stacking").[24] Like maximum royalty commitments, these pledges occur most frequently in the wireless telecommunications sector. Table 1.5 illustrates selected royalty calculation pledges in this sector.

Table 1.5 Selected royalty calculation pledges in wireless telecommunications sector

Year	Pledge	Pledgor(s)	Royalty Calculation
n/d	Patent licensing practices for industry standards	Intel	Royalty base should not exceed the cost of the smallest unit that practices the standard, the technical value of the patented feature compared to alternatives available during the standard-setting process, and the overall royalty that could reasonably be charged for all patents essential to the standard
2002	Modest royalty rates for W-CDMA	NTT DoCoMo, Ericsson, Nokia, Siemens, Fujitsu, NEC, Mitsubishi Electric, Panasonic, Sony	Royalty to be proportional to the number of essential patents held by each company
2008	Framework for LTE technology IPR licensing	Alcatel-Lucent, Ericsson, NEC, NextWave, Nokia, Nokia Siemens Networks, Sony Ericsson	Each patent holder will charge a proportional share of all standard essential IPR for the relevant product category

Like maximum royalty commitments, royalty calculation pledges have largely been made outside the SDO setting. However, at least one major SDO, the IEEE Standards Association, has recently adopted amendments

[23] The royalty base is the price on which a percentage royalty is calculated. For example, if the royalty rate is 5% of net selling price, and the applicable product has a sale price of $100 (the royalty base), then the royalty would be $5.

[24] *See*, e.g., Jorge L. Contreras, *Standards, Royalty Stacking and Collective Action*, 3 CPI ANTITRUST CHRON. (2015); Mark A. Lemley & Carl Shapiro, *Patent Holdup and Royalty Stacking*, 85 TEX. L. REV. 1991 (2007).

to its policies seeking to clarify and circumscribe the manner in which its members must calculate FRAND royalties.[25]

3. Non-royalty commitments

In addition to pledges offering a primary access commitment or relating to the royalties that patent holders will charge, other types of patent pledges have emerged outside the SDO setting. These pledges limit the patent holder's ability to enforce and otherwise maximize rents from its patents, but in ways that are not directly tied to licensing royalties. Two principal examples of these pledges are discussed below.

a) No injunctions One of the most contentious issues facing participants in standard-setting activities is whether a patent holder that has made a FRAND commitment may seek an injunction preventing the use of standardized technology after the parties have failed to agree on FRAND licensing terms. Commitments not to seek such injunctions have been sought and obtained by both the Federal Trade Commission (FTC) and European Commission in actions brought against large patent holders involved in standards-development activities.[26] The question has also been considered by the U.S. federal courts[27] and the International Trade Commission.[28] While courts, administrative agencies, and SDOs continue to wrestle with this issue, several firms including Apple, Google, Intel, and Microsoft have voluntarily pledged to reduce the circumstances under which they may seek to enjoin the use of standards as to which they have made FRAND commitments.[29]

b) No NPE transfers A small but growing number of patent pledges seek to address issues that may arise in connection with the sale or transfer of patents. First, due to the highly publicized increase in lawsuits

---

[25] *See* Michael A. Lindsay & Konstantinos Karachalios, *Updating a Patent Policy: The IEEE Experience*, CPI ANTITRUST CHRON. (Mar. 2015).

[26] In the Matter of Robert Bosch GmbH, FTC File No. 121-0081 (Nov. 26, 2012); In the Matter of Motorola Mobility LLC and Google Inc., FTC File No. 121-0120 (July 23, 2013); Press Release, European Comm'n, Samsung: Enforcement of ETSI Standards Essential Patents (SEPs) (Dec. 21, 2012).

[27] Apple Inc. v. Motorola, Inc., 757 F.3d 1286, 1331–32 (Fed. Cir. 2014).

[28] In the Matter of Certain Elec. Devices, Including Wireless Comm'n Devices, Portable Music and Data Processing Devices, and Tablet Computs., USITC Inv. No. 337-TA-794, 2013 WL 2453722 (June 4, 2013).

[29] *See* Patent Pledge Database.

brought by non-practicing entities (NPEs),[30] a number of firms have expressly pledged not to transfer their patents to NPEs. In a similar vein, the Defensive Patent License (DPL), which does not outright prohibit the transfer of patents to NPEs, allows all DPL pledgors to terminate their licenses if such a transfer occurs.

III. FORM OF PATENT PLEDGES

Patent pledges may be divided into two principal categories in terms of their origin: *coordinated pledges* and *unilateral pledges*. Coordinated pledges are typically made by members of a defined group, according to some predetermined form or formula, with respect to a defined technology or set of patents. All coordinated pledges made by the members of the group need not be identical, but at least the set of pledges within any such group share some basic characteristics. The best-known coordinated pledges are FRAND commitments made in SDOs, but several other important varieties are discussed below. *Unilateral* pledges, on the other hand, are one-off commitments made independently and voluntarily by patent holders.

A. Coordinated Patent Pledges

As noted above, *coordinated* patent pledges are made by members of a specific group according to some predetermined form or formula, usually with respect to a defined technology or set of patents. The group may be the participants in an SDO, or a less formal group of like-minded firms working toward the promotion of a common technology platform or architecture.

1. Pledges made in standards-development organizations

As noted above, the structures of SDOs are diverse, ranging from small groups of firms focusing on a single product category to international bodies that produce standards in a broad range of industries.[31] Thus, even

---

[30] NPEs generally acquire patents for the primary purpose of asserting them in licensing negotiations or litigation, without producing products. They are also known as "patent assertion entities" and, more pejoratively, "patent trolls." *See*, e.g., Colleen Chien, *Of Trolls, Davids, Goliaths, and Kings: Narratives and Evidence in the Litigation of High-Tech Patents*, 87 N.C. L. REV. 1571 (2009).

[31] *See supra* note 13 and accompanying text.

within the SDO context, patent pledges take on a number of different formats and structures. These include the following:[32]

(i) *Contractual*: Some pledges are included in contractual documents signed by SDO participants, either among participants or between each participant and the SDO.[33]

(ii) *Bylaws/Policy*: Many SDOs include patent licensing commitments in their corporate bylaws or policy documents. In some cases, participants must agree to comply with such bylaws and policies when they submit a membership application (often done online) to the SDO, or join a particular technical subgroup.[34] In other cases, the binding effect of these policies is assumed, based on a participant's membership in, or engagement in activities within, the SDO.[35]

(iii) *Letters of Assurance (LOAs)*: Some SDOs require participants to submit a written document (referred to variously as a "letter of assurance," "licensing declaration," or "written assurance") stating their intentions, if any, regarding the licensing of patents. Different SDOs require such LOAs to be submitted at different times during the standardization process. Often, LOAs are template documents that only permit the participant to check a box to indicate whether its licensing approach will be FRAND, royalty-free, non-assertion, or otherwise.

2. Other pledge communities

Not all coordinated patent pledges are made within SDOs. The structures of such pledges vary, but all are characterized by two common elements:

---

[32] A more detailed analysis of the different forms in which SDO patent pledges are made can be found in Jorge L. Contreras, *A Market Reliance Theory for FRAND Commitments and Other Patent Pledges*, 2015 UTAH L. REV 479, at Part I.D.2 (2015) [hereinafter Contreras, *Market Reliance*].

[33] *See* Brad Biddle, Frank X. Curci, Timothy F. Haslach, Gary E. Marchant, Andrew Askland, and Lyn Gaudet, *The Expanding Role and Importance of Standards in the Information and Communications Technology Industry*, 52 JURIMETRICS 177, 186–87 (2012) (describing such "contractual consortia" and examples of the same).

[34] *See* Rudi Bekkers & Andrew Updegrove, *A Study of IPR Policies and Practices of a Representative Group of Standard Setting Organizations Worldwide*, U.S. NAT'L ACAD. OF SCI., 28 (Oct. 3, 2012), http://sites.nationalacademies.org/xpedio/groups/pgasite/documents/webpage/pga_072197.pdf, (noting that in such cases, the SDOs have a relatively narrow technical scope).

[35] *See* ABA PATENT POLICY MANUAL, *supra* note 19, at 82.

the existence of a uniform format in which pledges are made, and some organized community that supports and makes the pledge.

These communities vary in formality and degree of organization. For example, the Eco-Patent Commons (EPC), discussed above, was a relatively well-organized group administered by the Environmental Law Institute (ELI). Participants in the EPC were required to apply to join,[36] and members were required to comply with a detailed set of "Ground Rules" that included the terms of the pledge and other details regarding membership.[37]

Less formal arrangements exist, in which standardized pledge terms are made available by organizations such as the Open Web Foundation (OWF) for adoption by any group that wishes to use them. OWF publishes a Final Specification Agreement that firms involved in the development of a standard outside an SDO can use to make commitments regarding their patents.[38] Table 1.6 offers examples of non-SDO coordinated patent pledges found in the Patent Pledge Database.

3. Unilateral patent pledges

Unlike coordinated patent pledges, *unilateral* pledges are made by firms acting independently. They may vary in their level of formality and specificity, but in each case the firm making the pledge does so on its own terms, without the express involvement of others.

a) Unilateral pledges in SDOs Despite the fact that most SDOs require participants to use standardized forms when making patent pledges, some SDOs permit participants to make pledges on terms of their own choosing. The most prominent example of this pledge type arises in the Internet Engineering Task Force (IETF), which develops standards for the Internet. IETF requires that its participants disclose patents and patent applications that are likely to claim technologies implementing IETF standards and specifications.[39] However, there is no

---

36 *Eco-Patent Commons: Joining or Submitting Additional Patents to the Commons*, ECO-PATENT COMMONS, http://ecopatentcommons.org/join.

37 Eco-Patent Commons Ground Rules 6, WORLD BUS. COUNCIL FOR SUSTAINABLE DEV., http://www.wbcsd.org/pages/adm/download.aspx?id=314&objecttypeid=7 [hereinafter EPC Ground Rules].

38 *Open Web Foundation Final Specification Agreement (OWFa 1.0) (Patent and Copyright Grants)*, OPENWEB FOUNDATION, http://www.openwebfoundation.org/legal/the-owf-1-0-agreements/owfa-1-0.

39 Scott Bradner, *Intellectual Property Rights in IETF Technology BCP79*, BEST CURRENT PRACTICE (March 2005), https:// tools.ietf.org/html/bcp79.

Table 1.6 Non-SDO coordinated patent pledges

Name	Pledgors (Community)
Open Invention Network (OIN)	More than 1,000 firms
Eco-Patent Commons	Bosch, Dow, DuPont, Fuji-Xerox, Hitachi, HP, IBM, Nokia, Pitney Bowes, Ricoh, Sony, Taisei, Xerox
The Patent Pledge	33 firms including Airbnb and Dropbox
OWF Final Specification Agreements	
DMARC	AOL, Bank of America, Cloudmark, Comcast, eCert, Facebook, Fidelity, Linked-In, Microsoft, PayPal, ReturnPath, TrueDomain, Trusted Domain, Yahoo!
Simple Identity Cloud Management	CANAIRE, Cisco, Ping Identity, SailPoint, Salesforce.com, Technology Nexus, Unbound ID
JSON	Citizen Agency, IBM, Mozilla, StatusNet, VMWare
GeoServices REST	ESRI
Leap2A	Pebble Learning
Open Compute Project Battery Cabinet Hardware	Facebook
Oauth WRAP	Facebook, Yahoo!
Motherboard hardware	Facebook
Open Graph Protocol	Facebook
MASHSSL Core	SafeMashups
MediaRSS	Yahoo!
Wireless Industry Leaders LTE pledge	Alcatel-Lucent, Ericsson, NEC, NextWave, Nokia, Nokia Siemens Networks, Sony Ericsson
Modest Royalty Rates for W-CDMA	NTT DoCoMo, Ericsson, Nokia, Siemens, Fujitsu, NEC, Mitsubishi Electric, Panasonic, Sony
Leading Tech Companies United to Support OSGi Technology	Gatespace Telematics, IBM, Nokia, ProSyst, Samsung
Non-Assert for Tuschi I siRNA patent applications	MIT, Whitehead, U. Mass, Max Planck

formal requirement that participants license these patents and patent applications to others on any particular terms (i.e., IETF imposes no FRAND commitment). As a result, firms involved in standards development at IETF frequently make voluntary patent licensing commitments along with their patent disclosures. These commitments, which are predominantly non-assertion or royalty-free licensing commitments,[40] take a variety of forms, and each IETF participant is free to develop its own style and language for such pledges.

b) Web site postings and press releases Many unilateral patent pledges are made by firms outside the context of an organized standard-setting activity, though the pledges themselves may relate to one or more technical standards. Most such unilateral pledges are made (or at least published) through posting on corporate web sites, often accompanied by a press release or other announcement. Microsoft, for example, maintains a web site dedicated to patent pledges that it has made over the years.[41] Though Microsoft's pledges are relatively detailed and legally robust, their content is determined solely by Microsoft as the pledgor. Other firms take a less formal approach, exemplified by the short pledge initially posted in Tesla Motors' online blog.[42]

c) Statements to government officials Some patent pledges are made in the form of statements to governmental officials, which may later be memorialized in correspondence, official announcements, or agency orders. The manner in which such pledges are made varies. In some cases, pledges are made during negotiations with an agency, and they are only referenced in the agency's subsequent order or announcement in the case.[43] In other instances, a patent holder may direct the agency to an existing document, whether an online statement or correspondence with

---

40 *See* Contreras, *Ex Ante*, *supra* note 18, at 178.

41 *Open Specifications Dev Center*, MICROSOFT CORP., https://msdn.microsoft.com/en-us/openspecifications/default. *See also infra* notes 71–74 and accompanying text (discussing Microsoft pledges in greater detail).

42 Some months after Elon Musk of Tesla Motors posted his now-infamous blog *All Our Patents Are Belong to You*, the company revised and clarified its patent pledge substantially. *See* Tesla Motors, Appendix.

43 *Statement of the Department of Justice's Antitrust Division on Its Decision to Close Its Investigations of Google Inc.'s Acquisition of Motorola Mobility Holdings Inc. and the Acquisitions of Certain Patents by Apple Inc., Microsoft Corp. and Research in Motion Ltd.*, U.S. DEPT. JUSTICE (Feb. 13, 2012) [hereinafter *DOJ 2012 Approval Statement*].

an SDO, as embodying its pledge.[44] Finally, in some cases, pledges made to regulatory authorities may appear in formal consent decrees or judicial orders.[45]

d) Other public statements In addition to the forms described above, patent pledges can be made in a variety of less formal settings including speeches, press releases, interviews, and testimony. For example, in 2013, Mark Chandler, the General Counsel of Cisco Systems, wrote an online article in *Forbes* that criticized firms that had sold patents to non-practicing entities (so-called "patent trolls").[46] In the article, Chandler admitted that Cisco had itself sold a small number of patents to a non-practicing entity, but in the next breath pledged that the company "won't do it again."[47] Randy Milch, the General Counsel of Verizon, made a similar admission and pledge verbally during a recorded public symposium,[48] and Yahoo! made a similar statement in testimony that it submitted to the House Committee on the Judiciary.[49]

The apparent informality of some of these statements may give one pause. Nevertheless, it appears that at least some subset of these statements are intended to function as binding commitments, and should be treated as such.

---

44 Id.

45 *See* Jorge L. Contreras, *A Brief History of FRAND: Analyzing Current Debates in Standard Setting and Antitrust Through a Historical Lens,* 80 ANTITRUST L.J. 39 (2015) (detailing a long lineage of antitrust consent decrees containing patent licensing commitments).

46 Mark Chandler, *Good News for the Innovation Economy: The Tide's Turning Against Patent Trolls*, FORBES (Oct. 20, 2013, 5:30 am).

47 Id.

48 Randy Milch, General Counsel, Verizon, *Software Patents and Their Challenges Conference at Colorado Law: Panel* 3 (Oct. 9, 2013), http://www.youtube.com/watch?v=j_jgV6UKnp8&list=PLwFq2GL-i5UjaeZNyVOGbSKaJ5rPmvVNc&index=3 (oral statement at 41:44: "[w]e have sold patents to non-practicing entities. That's wrong. I shouldn't do it. … I have made it clear that we are not selling anymore to non-practicing entities").

49 *Improving the Patent System to Promote American Innovation and Competitiveness: Hearing Before the H. Comm. on the Judiciary*, 113th Cong. 5 (2013) (testimony of Kevin T. Kramer, VP and Dep. Gen. Counsel, IP, Yahoo! Inc.) ("[W]e act responsibly when selling patents. Our policy has been to sell patents only to operating entities rather than to non-practicing entities. We do not want our patents to be obtained by a troll and irresponsibly asserted against others in the Internet industry").

IV. CLASSIFYING PATENT PLEDGES: A TAXONOMY

The analysis of patent pledges as a general phenomenon requires an understanding of the rationales that motivate patent holders to give up important patent rights without consideration. Four basic motivations emerge from the range of pledges that are made across industries and organizational structures: *inducement, collective action, voluntary restraint*, and *philanthropy*. These motivations are by no means exclusive, and patent holders may seek to achieve a number of complementary goals by making particular pledges. However, the taxonomy developed below serves as a useful framework for assessing the optimal legal effect of different types of pledges.

A. Inducement

The most common form of patent pledge is made in order to induce other market participants to do something. The action that the pledgor seeks to induce in others can vary, but it is generally related to third parties' adoption of certain technology choices that are favored by the pledgor. There are three principal sub-categories of Inducement pledges: those intended to induce other firms to adopt and make investments in products that comply with one or more interoperability standards, those intended to induce other firms to adopt a particular technology platform favored, if not actually sold, by the pledgor, and those intended to induce market participants to adopt a broad platform technology. In each of these cases, the pledgor calculates that it is likely to derive greater benefit from the behavior that it seeks to induce in others than from using its patents to exclude others from the market.

1. Interoperability

Interoperability standards such as USB, Wi-Fi, 3G/4G, DVD, and HTTP enable devices manufactured by different vendors to communicate and interoperate with each other without the need for customized interfaces or translation. The market-wide benefits and efficiencies generated through product interoperability are known as "network effects," and often increase as the number of compatible devices in a given network grows.[50] Interoperability also opens markets for new products and services, thus fostering innovation, competition, consumer choice, and

---

[50] *See* Carl Shapiro & Hal R. Varian, Information Rules: A Strategic Guide to the Network Economy 45–46 (1999).

economic growth.[51] The public welfare benefits of standards that enable product interoperability have been recognized widely by courts, regulators, and commentators.[52]

a) Pledges promoting interoperability through SDO standards Despite the acknowledged benefits of interoperability standards, concerns have been raised that opportunistic patent holders could obtain and then assert patents against products complying with a standard after manufacturers have made significant investments in the standardized technology (e.g., plant, inventory, labor, product design, and training). Once a manufacturer has made such investments, it is considered to be "locked-in" and cannot switch to an alternative technology without incurring a substantial cost.[53] Not surprisingly, after a manufacturer is locked-in, a patent holder would have substantial leverage in negotiating a license with the manufacturer, and could charge a super-competitive royalty based, in part, on the manufacturer's high cost of switching.[54] This phenomenon is sometimes referred to as patent "hold-up" and is discussed extensively in the literature.[55]

To alleviate the risk of hold-up, to encourage the broadest adoption of standards, and to induce manufacturers to make the investments necessary to develop and deploy standardized technologies, many SDOs have adopted policies requiring their participants to make patent pledges. One of the most common of these policies imposes a licensing commitment,[56]

---

51 *See* FED. TRADE COMM'N, THE EVOLVING IP MARKETPLACE: ALIGNING PATENT NOTICE AND REMEDIES WITH COMPETITION 191 (2011) [hereinafter FTC EVOLVING IP MARKETPLACE].

52 *See* U.S. DEPT. OF JUSTICE & FED. TRADE COMM'N, ANTITRUST ENFORCEMENT AND INTELLECTUAL PROP. RIGHTS: PROMOTING INNOVATION AND COMPETITION 33 (2007) [hereinafter DOJ/FTC Antitrust and IP Report] ("Industry standards are widely acknowledged to be one of the engines driving the modern economy. Standards can make products less costly for firms to produce and more valuable to consumers").

53 *See* SHAPIRO & VARIAN, *supra* note 51, at 103–16.

54 Id. at 116–30.

55 *See*, e.g., Jorge L. Contreras, *Technical Standards, Standard-Setting Organizations and Intellectual Property: A Survey of the Literature*, in 2 RESEARCH HANDBOOK ON THE ECON. OF INTELLECTUAL PROP. LAW: ANALYTICAL METHODS (Peter S. Menell & David Schwartz eds., 2017, forthcoming) (reviewing literature).

56 Another common, and related, SDO policy requires patent holders to disclose to the SDO and other participants any patents that may be essential to a standard. Disclosure policies often work side by side with licensing policies, but

which requires each SDO participant to promise that it will not use patents to block the use of a standard. Licensing commitments come in several different flavors. Patent holders can commit to license their essential patents on terms that are "fair, reasonable and non-discriminatory" (FRAND), they can commit to license these patents on reasonable terms without a royalty, or they can commit not to enforce these patents at all (non-assertion).[57]

While the market-wide benefits of patent pledges in the standardization context are relatively well understood, the motivation for individual patent holders to make such pledges is more nuanced. Many patent holders, of course, are manufacturers of products that will benefit from standardization. These patent holders are likely to profit directly from the interoperability enabled by standards, and may thus determine that their potential product-related profits will outweigh any loss of revenue attributable to the constraints imposed by the pledge.[58] In some cases, they may determine that the benefits of broad, rapidly available interoperability are so great that they prefer all patent holders to license their essential patents on a royalty-free basis, thus eliminating any patent-related barrier to adoption of the standard. But whether the patent holder's pledge is to license its patents on FRAND or royalty-free terms, its primary motivation is to induce other market participants to adopt the relevant standard and make complementary investments.

b) Pledges promoting interoperability outside of SDOs Patent pledges pertaining to industry standards do not arise exclusively within SDOs. In fact, many such pledges are made outside of the SDO process, either with respect to SDO-developed standards as to which firms have elected to make supplemental pledges, or with respect to standards that were not developed within SDOs. Nevertheless, as explained below, the motivations and goals for non-SDO Interoperability pledges are nearly the same as those applicable to SDO-based Interoperability pledges.

In some cases, firms may elect to make pledges with respect to interoperability standards that were developed within SDOs and as to

---

are not required to make licensing policies effective. *See* ABA PATENT POLICY MANUAL, *supra* note 19, at 15; Bekkers & Updegrove, *supra* note 35, at 13.

57 *See* ABA PATENT POLICY MANUAL, *supra* note 19, at 23.

58 Recent litigation results have demonstrated that patent royalties subject to a FRAND commitment may, indeed, be far less than the patent holder initially sought or desired. *See* Jorge L. Contreras, *Fixing FRAND: A Pseudo-Pool Approach to Standards-Based Patent Licensing*, 79 ANTITRUST L.J. 47, 79–80 (2013) [hereinafter Contreras, *Fixing FRAND*].

which additional SDO-based pledges may already exist. As discussed above, the pledges required by SDOs are usually primary access commitments, in which the patent holder must commit either to license its standards-essential patents on FRAND or royalty-free terms, or not to assert those patents at all. However, individual firms or groups of firms may sometimes wish to offer additional assurances to the market to further encourage use of the standards. For example, in 2002 NTT DoCoMo, Ericsson, Nokia, Siemens, and several Japanese manufacturers pledged that they would license their patents that were essential to the W-CDMA 3G wireless telecommunications standard at rates proportional to the number of such patents held by each company.[59] Similar pledges have been made by these and other industry participants with respect to subsequent wireless mobile device standards.

There are several reasons why firms may wish to make pledges above and beyond their SDO commitments. With respect to maximum royalty commitments (Table 1.5), they may wish to alleviate market concerns regarding potential patent stacking when patent-heavy technologies are concerned.[60] Likewise, royalty calculation pledges reduce uncertainty surrounding the royalty base to be used when calculating royalties for multi-component products. In both of these cases, SDOs, which can only act by consent of their membership, may be unable to achieve sufficient consensus to implement these requirements in their official policies. Thus, to the extent that individual SDO participants determine that it is in their best interest to take additional steps to induce the market to adopt a particular standard, these firms may elect to make such pledges unilaterally.

2. Platform leadership

Interoperability considerations lead firms to make patent pledges when they wish their products to be interoperable with other products adhering to the same standard. It is often the case that no single firm controls such

---

[59] Press Release, Nokia, Industry Leaders NTT DoCoMo, Ericsson, Nokia and Siemens, and Japanese Manufacturers Reach a Mutual Understanding to Support Modest Royalty Rates for the W-CDMA Technology Worldwide (Nov. 6, 2002).

[60] Several commentators have theorized that maximum royalty commitments of one kind or another can avert many of the potential problems inherent to patent stacking. *See* Contreras, *Fixing FRAND*, *supra* note 59, at 67; Mark A. Lemley, *Ten Things to Do About Patent Holdup of Standards (and One Not To)*, 48 B.C. L. REV. 149 (2007); Josh Lerner & Jean Tirole, *A Better Route to Tech Standards*, 343 SCI. 972 (2014).

standards, and the pledging firm's principal benefit derives from being part of a network or ecosystem of interoperable products.

Sometimes, however, a single firm does exert control over a particular technology platform, whether through ownership of proprietary interfaces often referred to as "de facto" standards, or other market forces.[61] In some cases, de facto standards have emerged after "standards wars," such as the contest between Sony's Betamax and Matsushita's VHS video tape formats. In standards wars, the champions of competing formats generally use all weapons at their disposal, including patents, to gain market share.[62] But de facto standards need not emerge through warfare. They can also emerge naturally, based on the market's recognition of a particular technology's benefits and superiority over the competition.[63]

Firms that control particular de facto standards can gain significant market advantages if other firms develop products that operate with or depend on their technology.[64] Such "platform" technologies can become the basis for entire industries.[65] Firms thus often strive to persuade product developers, service providers, and end users to adopt and develop products compatible with their proprietary technology platforms.

This is what happened in the 1980s when Philips and Sony offered attractive licenses of their new compact disc (CD) media format to both disc and player manufacturers worldwide.[66] Their openness to all potential market entrants enabled CD technology to overtake competing home

---

61 ABA Section of Antitrust Law, Handbook on the Antitrust Aspects of Standard Setting 6 (2d ed., 2011) [hereinafter ABA Antitrust Manual]; Michael Carrier, Innovation for the 21st Century: Harnessing the Power of Intellectual Property and Antitrust Law 325 (2009); Timothy F. Bresnahan & Pai-Ling Yin, *Standard Setting in Markets: The Browser War*, in Standards and Public Policy 18 (Shane Greenstein & Victor Stango, eds., 2007).

62 Shapiro & Varian, *supra* note 51, at 261–96 (discussing standards wars over AM radio, wireless phones, 56k modems, and Internet browsers); *see generally* DOJ/FTC Antitrust and IP Report, *supra* note 53, at 34.

63 *See* Shapiro & Varian, *supra* note 51, at 261–62.

64 The owners of proprietary platforms often enable developers to create products that are compatible with or run on the platform through application programmer interfaces (APIs) and other means. *See* David S. Evans, *The Antitrust Analysis of Rules and Standards for Software Platforms*, Coase-Sandor Working Paper Series in Law and Economics, Nov. 8, 2014, at 5–6.

65 *See* id. at 7 (collecting data on prevalence of users and applications written for particular software platforms, including Microsoft Windows (1.35 billion devices and 4 million applications) and Apple iOS (800 million devices and 1.2 million applications)).

66 *See* Shapiro & Varian, *supra* note 51, at 261–62.

audio technologies (cassette tape, 8-track tape, phonograph) within a short period of time.[67] By the same token, it has been argued that Matsushita's flexibility in licensing its VHS video cassette recorder (VCR) technology led to greater market adoption of VHS than Sony's technically superior, but more tightly controlled, Betamax technology.[68]

Patent pledges in which the owner of a proprietary platform assures the market that it will make its patents available to those who wish to develop compatible products and services may help the patent holder achieve market acceptance of its platform.[69] These patent pledges are termed Platform Leadership pledges, as they are made to induce the market to adopt the patent holder's proprietary technology platform.

Microsoft has arguably made a number of such Platform Leadership pledges relating to its product interfaces and specifications.[70] Among the most significant of these are Microsoft's Interoperability Principles, in which it pledges to license all patents that cover certain open protocols on FRAND terms at "low" royalty rates.[71] Microsoft's Interoperability Principles cover hundreds of different standards and protocols.[72] Among these is the Microsoft Exchange ActiveSync suite of protocols, which enable the synchronization of email messages between corporate email accounts and mobile devices. Microsoft claims that ActiveSync has become "the industry standard for mobile messaging synchronization."[73] John Harkrider has argued that the emergence of ActiveSync as a de facto

---

[67] Id.

[68] *See* Oren Bar-Gill & Gideon Parchomovsky, *The Value of Giving Away Secrets* 11 (2003) ("facilitating rather than excluding cumulative innovation will often be in the best interest of the initial patent holder").

[69] *See* Anne Layne-Farrar, *Moving Past the SEP RAND Obsession: Some Thoughts on the Economic Implications of Unilateral Commitments and the Complexities of Patent Licensing*, 21 GEO. MASON L. REV. 1093, 1098 (2014) ("[V]oluntary intellectual property … licensing announcements offer an important tool for persuading other industry participants to buy into a firm's technology option, thereby facilitating its acceptance as a de facto standard").

[70] *The Microsoft Patent Pledges for Implementations of Microsoft Workgroup Server Protocol Program Technical Specifications*, MICROSOFT CORP., https://msdn.microsoft.com/en-us/openspecifications/dn646763.

[71] *Interoperability Principles Program*, MICROSOFT CORP., https://msdn.microsoft.com/en-us/openspecifications/dn646764.

[72] *Patent Promises and Patents*, MICROSOFT CORP., https://msdn.microsoft.com/en-us/openspecifications/dn750984.

[73] Julia White, *Exchange ActiveSync: The Industry Standard for Mobile Messaging*, TECHNET BLOGS: THE MICROSOFT LYNC BLOG (NOV. 16, 2010, 9:12 am).

standard can be attributed, at least in part, to Microsoft's patent pledge covering the protocol. He explains:

> Unlike many other *de facto* standards, which emerged solely from technical superiority or unfettered marketplace competition, Microsoft encouraged the industry to standardize on ActiveSync by promising to license its ActiveSync-essential patents on FRAND terms, at 'low royalty rates.' In doing so, Microsoft hoped both to encourage widespread implementation and, as a corollary, to discourage the development of alternative technologies.[74]

3. Market development

Market Development pledges are made to promote the broad adoption of a nascent or emerging platform technology, generally one in which the patent holder is a leader. These pledges, unlike Interoperability and Platform Leadership pledges, are generally directed to a broad technology category rather than a single standard or product. For example, a patent holder making an Interoperability pledge might commit not to assert its patents against any product implementing the Bluetooth short-range wireless networking standard, whereas a patent holder making a Market Development pledge might commit not to assert its patents against any product using short-range wireless networking. In the first instance, the pledgor wishes to promote the adoption and use of the Bluetooth standard over competing standards, whereas in the second instance, the pledgor wishes to promote the widespread use of short-range wireless networking products, more generally, over competing technologies such as in-home optical fiber.

Market Development pledges are most likely to be made when there is competition among different technology platforms, or when the backers of a new technology platform seek to displace an existing platform.[75] For example, as discussed in the Introduction, in 2014 Tesla Motors pledged not to assert its portfolio of more than a hundred electric vehicle power management patents against electric vehicle manufacturers.[76] Though

---

74 John D. Harkrider, *REPs Not SEPs: A Reasonable and Non-Discriminatory Approach to Licensing Commitments,* COMPETITION POL'Y INT'L ANTITRUST CHRON. (Oct. 2013).

75 *Cf.* Dorothy Gill Raymond, *Benefits and Risks of Patent Pooling for Standard-Setting Organizations*, 16 ANTITRUST 41, 45 (observing that firms forming patent pools are likely to offer royalty-free licenses only when "there is the economic expectation of opening up new markets").

76 *See* Tesla Pledge, Appendix. *See also* Jorge L. Contreras, *Tesla Motors and the Rise of Non-ICT Patent Pledges*, PATENTLY-O (June 16, 2014).

Tesla's announcement was perplexing to some,[77] and viewed as a mere publicity stunt by others,[78] Tesla CEO Elon Musk professed a desire to create a "safe space" in which the embryonic electric vehicle industry could grow, particularly in the face of massive competition from conventional automobiles. He explained that "Tesla, other companies making electric cars, and the world would all benefit from a common, rapidly-evolving technology platform" for electric vehicles.[79]

Market Development pledges, including Tesla's, are similar to Interoperability and Platform Leadership pledges in that they seek to promote the adoption of a particular technology architecture or platform. In Tesla's case, the platform is a national electric vehicle infrastructure including charging stations, parts suppliers, and automobiles, all conforming to Tesla's standards and design choices.[80] Though Tesla does not own every aspect of this infrastructure, nationwide adoption of an electric vehicle platform could yield huge dividends to Tesla as a first mover and supplier of vehicles, parts, batteries, charging stations, and the like, and could also help the fledgling electric vehicle industry to compete more effectively against conventional automobile manufacturers.

In some cases, firms may seek a more direct payoff in exchange for their open source patent pledges. For example, Yochai Benkler explains IBM's support for the Linux operating system as motivated by its desire both to facilitate the development and improvement of the operating system run by its own hardware servers and to expand its own Linux-based service business.[81] He observes that "[w]ithin a span of four years, [IBM's] Linux-related services category moved from accounting for

---

[77] *See* Ashlee Vance, *Why Elon Musk Just Opened Tesla's Patents to His Biggest Rivals*, BLOOMBERG BUSINESS (June 12, 2014) (noting Tesla's advances in battery design, software, and power management).

[78] *See* Paul Nunes & Joshua Bellin, *Elon Musk's Patent Decision Reflects Three Strategic Truths*, HARV. BUS. REV. BLOG NETWORK (July 1, 2014) (discussing possible rationales for Tesla's pledge, including a "mere bid for publicity").

[79] Tesla Pledge, Appendix.

[80] *See* Nunes & Bellin, *supra* note 78.

[81] YOCHAI BENKLER, THE WEALTH OF NETWORKS: HOW SOCIAL PRODUCTION TRANSFORMS MARKETS AND FREEDOM 46 (2006). *See also* CYNTHIA CANNADY, TECHNOLOGY LICENSING AND DEVELOPMENT AGREEMENTS § 2.3 (Matthew Bender, rev. ed. 2015) (IBM's non-assertion pledge "is a licensing strategy to promote IBM products using Open Source … not an anti-IP strategy"). *See also* Robert P. Merges, Colloquium, *A New Dynamism in the Public Domain*, 71 U. CHI. L. REV. 183, 186 (analysing IBM's Linux strategy as an essentially anti-Microsoft strategy).

practically no revenues to providing double the revenues from all patent-related sources."[82] Similar conclusions have been drawn about Google's support for the Android mobile operating system and other corporate support for open source platforms.[83]

B. Collective Action

Markets are routinely confronted with collective action challenges in which each market participant understands that it will benefit from some action if taken by a large number of participants, but the participant itself is unwilling to incur the cost of taking the action. Collective action problems often manifest themselves in the environmental arena, as all firms will likely benefit from taking measures to reduce emissions, conserve energy, and use sustainable materials, but few are willing to incur substantial costs to advance these goals independently. Patent pledges made by groups of firms, such as the participants in the Eco-Patent Commons, can help to address such collective action problems and achieve common ends without excessive individual expenditures.

Others have observed collective action issues in the area of patent litigation, inasmuch as firms that sell patents to non-practicing entities (NPEs) understand that by doing so they fuel potentially disruptive and costly NPE litigation, but are unwilling to forego the compensation that NPEs are willing to pay for their underutilized patents. Pledges not to transfer patents to NPEs, or to terminate licenses upon such transfers, are useful to the pledgor only to the extent that others make similar pledges. Thus, like Inducement pledges, Collective Action pledges are made primarily in order to encourage action by others. However, the action that the pledgor seeks to induce is not the adoption of a particular standard or technology platform, but the making of a similar patent pledge.

Coordinated pledges such as the Defensive Patent License (DPL) (discussed in Chapter 8) expressly depend on the participation of

---

[82] BENKLER, *supra* note 81, at 46.

[83] *See* Brian Behlendorf, *Open Source as a Business Strategy*, in OPEN SOURCES VOICES FROM THE OPEN SOURCE REVOLUTION 149 (Chris DiBona, Sam Ockman & Mark Stone eds. 1999); Robert Young, *Giving It Away: How Red Hat Software Stumbled Across a New Economic Model and Helped Improve an Industry*, in OPEN SOURCES VOICES FROM THE OPEN SOURCE REVOLUTION 113–14 (Chris DiBona, Sam Ockman & Mark Stone eds. 1999); Bradley M. Kuhn, *The State of Free Software in Mobile Devices*, TECH. INNOV. MANAGEMENT REV. (Mar. 2010).

multiple parties. But even individual non-NPE transfer pledges derive most of their value from their ability to inspire, cajole, and shame other like-minded firms and executives to make similar commitments. Thus, Collective Action pledges are made largely to induce imitative behavior by other firms in order to provide the pledgor with the benefits of a collective action.

C. Voluntary Restraint

In some cases, a patent holder may make a pledge in order to persuade the market, or particular market actors, that it will not assert its patents in a particular manner or against particular classes of infringers. In effect, the patent holder, by making the pledge, voluntarily ties its own hands to prevent itself from undertaking certain actions. This approach is often adopted when a fear exists, either across the market or among particular actors, that the patent holder is both able and likely to exert its patents in a manner that is viewed as undesirable.

The market actors to whom such pledges are often directed are governmental authorities, and the pledges are made to persuade such authorities to approve a transaction under review or to discontinue an investigation of the patent holder's activities. Patent pledges, and FRAND commitments in particular, limit the ability of firms participating in standards development to exclude competitors from the market for standardized products and to charge excessive prices for access to essential patents. As a result, antitrust and competition enforcement agencies in both the U.S. and Europe have found FRAND commitments to be one of the principal means by which firms can mitigate antitrust risk arising from collaborative standards development.[84]

While FRAND commitments, and most other forms of patent pledge, can generally be viewed as Voluntary Restraint pledges, there are more specific instances in which firms have made patent pledges to influence the decisions of antitrust enforcement agencies. For example, in early 2012, Apple, Microsoft, and Google each made assurances to the U.S.

---

[84] *See* Fiona M. Scott-Morton, Deputy Assistant Att'y Gen. for Econ. Analysis, U.S. Dep't of Justice, The Role of Standards in the Current Patent Wars, Address Before the Charles River Associates Annual Brussels Conference: Economic Developments in European Competition Policy 5 (Dec 5, 2012) ("FRAND commitments are designed to reduce occurrences of opportunistic or exploitative conduct in the implementation of standards. It is these commitments, along with other things, that make competition authorities more comfortable with these collective decisions").

Department of Justice (DOJ) that it would not seek injunctive relief against implementers of certain wireless telecommunications standards.[85] The impetus for these voluntary declarations was the pending review by the DOJ and the European Commission of three significant patent-based transactions: the $12 billion acquisition of Motorola Mobility by Google, the $4.5 billion purchase of a large patent portfolio from the estate of bankrupt Nortel Networks by Rockstar Bidco (a coalition including Microsoft, Apple, Research in Motion, Sony, and Ericsson), and the acquisition by Apple of Novell's Linux patents.[86] The DOJ cited the pledges made by these three firms as key factors in its decision to approve the proposed acquisitions.[87] The European Commission, which also received such pledges, approved Google's acquisition of Motorola Mobility on the same day.[88]

Not all Voluntary Restraint pledges are made to appease enforcement agencies. In some cases, the intended audience for a Voluntary Restraint pledge may be a court. For example, Myriad Genetics recently came under intense public pressure for the pricing of its BRAC Analysis genetic diagnostic tests and threatening to assert its patents against academic institutions offering similar tests to the public.[89] Myriad's pledge not to assert its DNA patents against academic researchers,[90] a pledge that cost the firm relatively little in terms of real competitive ground, enabled it to represent to the court that it was not an aggressive enforcer of its patents, and that it broadly supported biomedical research.[91]

---

85 *DOJ 2012 Approval Statement*, *supra* note 44.

86 *See* Jorge L. Contreras, *The February of FRAND*, PATENTLY-O (Mar. 6, 2012).

87 Joseph F. Wayland, Acting Assistant Att'y Gen., U.S. Dep't of Justice, Antitrust Policy in the Information Age: Protecting Innovation and Competition, Remarks as prepared for the Fordham Competition Law Institute 7 (Sept. 21, 2012) ("The commitments made by Apple and Microsoft substantially lessened the Antitrust Division's concerns about potential anticompetitive use of FRAND-encumbered standard-essential patents"); *see also DOJ 2012 Approval Statement*, *supra* note 44.

88 Press Release, European Commission, Mergers: Commission approves acquisition of Motorola Mobility by Google (Feb. 13, 2012).

89 Ass'n for Molecular Pathology v. Myriad Genetics, Inc., 133 S. Ct. 2107, 2114 (2013).

90 The Myriad Pledge, MYRIAD GENETICS, INC., https://www.myriad.com/myriad-cares-2/the-myriad-pledge/.

91 Brief for Respondents at 10, Ass'n for Molecular Pathology v. Myriad Genetics, Inc., 133 S. Ct. 2107 (2013) (No. 12-398) ("[S]ince the [Myriad]

D. Philanthropy

Finally, a growing number of patent pledges are made with the outward goal of advancing social causes and public welfare. For example, the Eco-Patent Commons (EPC) explained that "[s]haring environmental patents can help others become more eco-efficient and operate in a more environmentally sustainable manner—enabling technology innovation to meet social innovation."[92] Likewise, numerous firms have pledged not to assert software patents against businesses having fewer than 25 employees in an effort to promote entrepreneurship and the growth of small businesses.[93]

All of these pledges can be characterized as supporting broad social welfare goals, either by promoting the unencumbered development of socially valuable technologies or by reducing the cost burden of patent litigation on an industry. The firms making such Philanthropic pledges are motivated by a range of factors, few of which are purely philanthropic. First, pledging firms themselves may benefit from the effects of their pledges. Thus, whether it is because the increased use of green technology will create a healthier environment and population, or because the growth of small businesses is believed to have a beneficial effect on the marketplace, workforce, and economy, the pledging firm may benefit directly from the collective effect of pledges supporting the same cause.[94]

Another, more direct, justification for Philanthropic pledges is the public relations (PR) benefit that often accompanies their announcement. If the value of the patents to the pledging firm is low, this PR benefit may actually exceed the value that is given up through the pledge. For example, the EPC acknowledged that the patents pledged by its members

---

patents issued, over 18,000 researchers have conducted studies on BRCA1/2 genes, published over 8,000 papers, and conducted over 130 clinical trials. Indeed, one named plaintiff conceded that she may 'sequence the BRCA1 and BRCA2 genes for purely research purposes,' and has been doing so without impediment" (citations omitted)).

92 *Overview*, World Bus. Council for Sustainable Dev., http://www.wbcsd.org/work-program/capacity-building/eco-patent-commons/overview.aspx.

93 The Patent Pledge, http://thepatentpledge.org/.

94 Note, however, that the potential to benefit from the collective effect of philanthropic pledges does not render such pledges Collective Action pledges, as discussed in Section IV.A.2, above. The difference being that the maker of a Philanthropic pledge does not make the pledge primarily to induce other market actors to make the same pledge and thereby achieve some mutually desired result, such as the reduction of NPE litigation.

are not necessarily strategic to their primary businesses,[95] and that these firms receive positive publicity by supporting environmentally friendly initiatives. In a related vein, firms that become the subject of *negative* publicity may seek to improve their public images by making pledges that seemingly benefit the public. The cost-benefit analysis in this case is relatively simple: a firm is better off pledging low-value patents in exchange for a PR benefit than allowing them to gather dust.

Some pledges that fall predominantly into other categories may have some attributes of Philanthropic pledges. For example, Voluntary Restraint pledges, which are primarily intended to assuage public or governmental concerns regarding the patent holders' use of patents, may also be characterized as actions taken for the public good, with concomitant PR benefits for the pledgors.

Likewise, Inducement pledges directed toward the growth of industries perceived to promote social benefits can sometimes share attributes of Philanthropic pledges. The open source "movement" had ideological origins and has long been associated with ideals of volunteerism, transparency, sharing, and openness. Thus, though many patent pledges made with respect to open source code may be classified as Market Development pledges, elements of altruism and community spirit may also influence a firm's decision to make such pledges.

CONCLUSION

Patent pledges are made in a wide variety of industries and contexts. Yet careful analysis of these pledges identifies both commonalities and differences among them. The four-part taxonomy developed in this chapter classifies patent pledges based on the economic and other motivations that lead patent holders to make them. Classification on this basis sheds light on the anticipated effect that these pledges have on other market actors.

---

[95] In 2011, investigators studying the value of patents pledged to the Eco-Patent Commons (EPC) found that the number of patents that firms pledged to the EPC was very small in comparison to their overall patent portfolios, yet the patents did not appear to be substantially less valuable than other patents in the firms' portfolios. Bronwyn H. Hall & Christian Helmers, *Innovation and Diffusion of Clean/Green Technology: Can Patent Commons Help?*, 66 J. ENVTL. ECON. & MGT. 33, 47 (2013).

2. Unilateral patent pledges: motivations and key principles

Duane R. Valz[1]

I. BACKGROUND: THE INCEPTION OF UNILATERAL PATENT PLEDGES

This chapter offers perspectives on unilateral patent pledges made outside of the context of a standards development organization.[2] As described in Chapter 1, some of the earliest such patent pledges have concerned standards essential patents (SEPs), patents covering commercially essential technologies (CEPs)[3] and patents relating to open source software (OSS).[4] What these pledges have in common is the offering by a patent holder to provide rights under its patents relating to commercially important technology used by a broad array of market participants. Some unilateral pledges offer fair, reasonable and non-discriminatory (FRAND) (i.e., monetary) terms for licensing pledged patents. Such pledges are

[1] The views expressed herein are those of the author and not necessarily of his current or former employers.

[2] As described in Chapter 1, patent pledges come in many varieties. This chapter is particularly focused on the two species of unilateral pledges. I also discuss the relation of non-SDO unilateral patent pledges to what I refer to as "community patent licenses." Within the framework of Chapter 1, community patent licenses are coordinated pledges made outside of an SDO context.

[3] For purposes of this chapter, I use the term commercially essential patents or CEPs to denote patents related to a de facto industry standard for which a unilateral patent pledge may have been made by the sole or critical patent holder. *See generally* John Harkrider, *REPs Not SEPs: A Reasonable and Non-Discriminatory Approach to Licensing Commitments*, COMPETITION POL'Y INT'L ANTITRUST CHRONS. (OCT. 2013).

[4] *See Non-SDO Patent Statements and Commitments*, PROGRAM ON INFO. JUSTICE & INTELLECTUAL PROP., http://www.pijip.org/non-sdo-patent-commitments/. In particular, see items attributable to Ericsson (SEPs), Microsoft (CEPs) and IBM (OSS) patent pledges.

usually very short, as they embody a promise to enter into a contractual license agreement, the terms of which still remain to be negotiated with particular licensees who wish to engage with the patent holder. Others—particularly those involving open source software (OSS)—offer rights under pledged patents for free.[5] Such pledges are typically more elaborated, as the pledges themselves set forth the terms and conditions concerning the scope of rights provided and any conditions to which the pledge itself is subject.

Most free patent pledges have been focused on OSS, and many continue to have that focus. OSS had been in existence for many years prior, but by the early 2000s it had gained a critical mass of quality and enterprise adoption, particularly in the operating system domain as exemplified by Linux. For certain players in the proprietary software world at that time, what had started as a nuisance was quickly becoming a possible business threat.[6] Those who saw the promise of OSS and the rapid collaborative innovation that it unlocked, also saw that patents could be used to disrupt more widespread commercial adoption of OSS. New ways of positioning patents to support and protect OSS were desired.

Some of the earliest OSS pledges were made by Red Hat (May 2002),[7] Novell (Oct. 2004)[8] and IBM (Jan. 2005).[9] Red Hat, a company that has built a durable business around installing open source-based enterprise computing systems, took the bold step of pledging non-enforcement of all of its patents for implementations made under prominent OSS licenses by other parties, subject to defensive termination. Novell's pledge was more a statement of values, but did provide strong suggestions that, like Red Hat, it would use its patent portfolio only in defense of OSS

---

5 As discussed in greater detail below even free pledges typically come with conditions or some other form of quid pro quo. Worth noting too is that, beyond OSS, free patent pledges have been made in fields as disparate as power transmission, bioscience, genetically modified organisms, green technology and electric vehicle technology.

6 For instance, Microsoft's Steve Ballmer in 2001 famously stated that "Linux is a cancer that attaches itself in an intellectual property sense to everything it touches." *See* Thomas C. Greene, *Ballmer: "Linux is a Cancer,"* THE REGISTER (June 2, 2001 6:19 PM).

7 *Statement of Position and Our Promise on Software Patents*, RED HAT, INC., http://www.redhat.com/legal/patent_policy.html.

8 NOVEL, *Novell Statement on Patents and Open Source Software*, MICRO FOCUS, https://www.novell.com/company/legal/patents/.

9 *IBM Statement of Non-Assertion of Named Patents Against OSS*, IBM, http://www.ibm.com/ibm/licensing/patents/pledgedpatents.pdf.

technology, and not offensively. IBM, long known for its proprietary patent licensing practices, took the approach of identifying 500 patents and pledging non-assertion against software qualifying as OSS under the Open Source Definition maintained by the Open Source Initiative.[10] All three companies subsequently contributed to the formation in 2005 of the Open Invention Network (OIN), an industry organization offering a patent pool and networked community cross license covering all software files and packages adduced over time to the organization's "Linux System Definition."[11]

II. MARKET IMPACT OF UNILATERAL PATENT PLEDGES

Typically, the motivations for unilateral FRAND pledges made outside a standards development organization is to encourage licensee adoption of covered technologies as well as provide a signal that the pledging party will seek a fair, modest return for patent licenses. Technologies where patent rights coverage is either known and determined to be significant, or else unknown but suspected to be significant, can face a number of marketplace challenges. One such challenge is reluctant adoption. Customer companies typically view use of or reliance on third party technologies covered by third party patents as posing significant risk, particularly if the expectations of the various patent holders are unknown. Another challenge is reluctant license engagement. Even if adoption of covered technologies cannot be avoided, product-making companies may be reluctant to seek out licenses if it is unclear that relevant patent owners will offer them commercially reasonable terms. Pledges are marketplace signals that, at least with respect to the pledge maker, the commercial terms of taking a license are meant to be reasonable and that adoption of the covered technology may not pose as much risk.[12]

---

[10] OPEN SOURCE INITIATIVE, *The Open Source Definition*, OPEN SOURCE, http://opensource.org/osd.

[11] The OIN Linux System Definition, which defines the field of use protected by the OIN license, was initially focused on the Linux operating system but has since been expanded to include many other OSS platforms, applications and utilities. *See* OPEN INVENTION NETWORK, *Linux System*, OPEN INVENTION NETWORK LLC (June 25, 2015), http://www.openinventionnetwork.com/joining-oin/linux-system/.

[12] As recent case law has demonstrated, what constitutes a FRAND license is subject to much dispute and can be very situation specific. *See*, e.g., Ericsson,

The motivations for fee-free and royalty-free (free) patent pledges have similarities to, but a few noteworthy differences from, FRAND pledges. Because no license returns are expected, supporting technology adoption has been a key driver of free pledges. At the time Red Hat and IBM made their pledges concerning OSS, the Linux operating system was just beginning to enjoy more traction with enterprise customers as an alternative to proprietary operating systems such as Microsoft Windows. Both IBM and Red Hat had embraced OSS platforms—such as Linux—as key drivers of their software licensing and consulting businesses.[13] While each company was convinced concerning the value proposition of using Linux and other OSS tools and platforms, many of their customers had to be convinced that the intellectual property (IP) risks posed were not too great. While OSS came with forms of copyright licenses that minimized IP risk, such licenses could not address the risk posed by an unknown quantity of third party patents held by an unknown number of third parties. By making the pledges that they did, IBM and Red Hat accomplished several things: (1) they made their own motivations clear to the marketplace concerning key OSS technologies, (2) they de-risked to the public a significant quantity of relevant patents that they owned (or, in the case of Red Hat, were actively developing), and (3) they established normative values around patents and OSS for other companies to consider, if not aspire to.

Until recently[14] most free pledges concerned OSS.[15] Like all those pledges concerning OSS, pledges such as those made by Tesla Motors

---

Inc. v. D-Link Sys., Inc., 773 F.3d 1201 (Fed. Cir. 2014); Case C-170/13 Huawei Techs. Co. v. ZTE Corp., 2013 EUR-Lex CELEX LEXIS 0170 (Nov. 20, 2014). Accordingly, a pledge to license patents on FRAND terms may offer only limited assurance until a would-be licensee actually enters negotiations with a patent holder. Additionally, as discussed below regarding free networked cross licenses, concern regarding the risk posed by non-pledging parties holding patent rights relating to third party technology can still be an impediment to adoption. This concern is also presented by SEP-related patent pools that offer rights to patents held by some but not all market participants.

13 Indeed, Red Hat is one of the success stories of the first dot-com boom, enjoying growth to this day with its entire business oriented around adapting and installing Linux-based computing systems for its customers.

14 *See* Contreras, Chapter 1, for an overview of the development of patent pledges in other industries.

15 *See Non-SDO Patent Statements and Commitments*, *supra* note 4 (noting the other subject matter coverage of pledges). Many royalty-free pledges have been made to SDOs such as the Internet Engineering Task Force (IETF) and

are similarly geared toward encouraging broader adoption of electric drive technologies and fostering an open innovation environment in that industry segment.

III. PLEDGES COMPARED TO COMMUNITY LICENSING

Alongside patent pledges, community license arrangements have also emerged over the past 15 years.[16] Patent pools are, roughly speaking, the community analog of FRAND patent pledges.[17] Both involve the exchange of money for license rights and both offer such license rights on typically market-sensitive, terms. Similarly, fee- and royalty-free community license arrangements are the community analog of free patent pledges. Both involve the compensation-free exchange of patent rights for freedom of action within a stated product technology field of use and subject to certain conditions.

Community licensing offers a dual benefit: patent holders work co-operatively with one another, and technology adopters may obtain a license to the community's aggregated patents. In the case of OIN, an initial group of six founding companies launched a community license and free patent pool around the Linux System, with licensee membership now well over 1,700 companies and organizations worldwide.[18] OIN thus has had a broad impact on the community of adopters embracing the

---

World Wide Web Consortium (W3C), but such pledges are outside the scope of this chapter.

[16] Such community license arrangements include those maintained by the Open Invention Network and the License on Transfer Network. *See* OPEN INVENTION NETWORK, http://www.openinventionnetwork.com; LOT NETWORK, http://www.lotnet.com. *See also* Contreras, Chapter 1.

[17] Google, for instance, has placed its patents relating to LTE (4G) mobile communications technology into a patent pool organized by Via Licensing. The Via LTE Patent pool offers "transparent and nondiscriminatory access to LTE essential patents in a fair and cost-effective license." *See* VIA LICENSING, *Long Term Evolution: LTE*, VIA LICENSING CORP., http://www.vialicensing.com/lte/index.aspx. Of course, patent pools do not always involve the offer of FRAND licenses as such, and the policies of patent pools involving SEPs may vary from those of the SDOs through which the associated standards were developed.

[18] The six OIN founder companies were IBM, Red Hat, Novell, NEC, Philips and Sony. Google is now a seventh full board member of the organization and SUSE (now a division of MicroFocus) is a successor in interest to Novell. *See* OPEN INVENTION NETWORK, *The OIN Community*, OPEN INVENTION NETWORK LLC, http://www.openinventionnetwork.com/community-of-licensees/.

Linux System. The OIN Linux System Definition includes technologies that collectively support much of the innovation in the technology industry today, from the smartphones that are now ubiquitous in the hands of everyday consumers to critical but more obscure systems that run in the depths of data centers around the globe. The trick with community licensing is that it can often be very difficult to get a diverse array of companies to agree on the precise terms and conditions of the license around which they wish to build a coalition. Even if all participants ultimately share the same values and goals around a particular technology area to be protected, reasonable minds reflecting different business interests can disagree regarding the precise contours of what should be provided for (or not) within the scope of the license. While ultimately successful, it took considerable time and effort to get OIN off the ground. The same holds true of the LOT Network, which took a few years to plan and launch with its original six founding members.[19]

In contrast, patent pledges reflect the interests, as well as the terms and conditions, that make sense to the pledge-making company. Because they are unilateral, patent pledges lack the networked community-of-interest dimension of community license arrangements, except to the extent they complement other unilateral pledges made by other companies. Nonetheless, to the extent that a pledge-making company includes terms and conditions that make sense for the technology field it covers and to those who stand to benefit from the pledge, a unilateral promise can also have a significant market impact. Without the transactional difficulties of obtaining cooperation from other patent holders, or for technology areas in which the pledge maker has a concentrated or singular patent position, a single firm can more easily take a stand and grant patent rights in a meaningful area of interest. In this way a single actor can extend rights to innumerable beneficiaries without the need to identify and convince each one to sign up for a license on a piecemeal basis.

Neither patent pledges nor community licenses provide all-encompassing solutions, whether one's aim is to enter licenses for money or to offer freedom to operate in an open innovation area. Patent pledges are often pursued alongside community licenses, in an effort to enhance the number of arrangements that allow participating firms both to project their values to the marketplace and broaden their points of impact. As mentioned, companies such as IBM, Red Hat and Google are engaged in a number of community license arrangements and as well have made free patent pledges. Patent pledges and community licenses are, and should be

[19] *See* LOT NETWORK, *supra* note 16.

seen as, complements rather than alternatives to each other. Neither type of effort should be seen as incomplete ones standing in isolation without a careful understanding of the entire landscape to which they relate, which may comprise a mosaic of efforts supporting freedom of action and open innovation.

IV. THE OPN PLEDGE

Google initially launched its Open Patent Non-assertion (OPN) Pledge in March 2013.[20] The OPN Pledge was designed to build upon previous free patent pledges directed to OSS, while addressing some of the ways such prior pledges were not well tuned to emerging marketplace dynamics. The patents pledged by Google during its initial launch of the OPN Pledge all concerned MapReduce, a proprietary technology for efficiently analysing large data sets that Google pioneered a decade prior for its own internal uses.[21] In the intervening years, open source variants of MapReduce were developed based at least in part on an academic article published by MapReduce inventors Jeff Dean and Sanjay Ghemawat.[22] Adoption of such open source variants has played a key role in the development of the so-called Big Data analytics industry, which has been accelerating over the past few years. Rather than go on a licensing campaign, Google elected to establish the OPN Pledge.

In years prior to the OPN Pledge launch, Google and its partners, particularly those within the Android ecosystem, faced increasing enforcement litigation as mobile computing became a high growth global phenomenon.[23] Google built up its patent position in the mobile computing and related technology areas. The OPN Pledge was designed to affirm Google's inward and outward views concerning (1) the value of OSS innovation, (2) the responsible use of patents, especially in open

---

[20] *See* Duane Valz, *Taking a Stand on Open Source and Patents*, GOOGLE OPEN SOURCE BLOG (Mar. 28, 2013).

[21] Google has since *expanded* the scope of the OPN Pledge to include many more patents and areas of technology coverage. *See Open Patent Non-Assertion Pledge: Pledged Patents*, GOOGLE, http://www.google.com/patents/opnpledge/patents/. Google continues periodically to increase the number of patents included in the OPN Pledge.

[22] *See* Jeffrey Dean & Sanjay Ghemawat, *MapReduce: Simplified Data Processing on Large Clusters* (Dec. 6, 2004) (paper presented at the Sixth Symposium on Operating System Design & Implementation).

[23] Android, of course, is an open source software platform. *See Welcome to the Android Open Source Project!*, ANDROID, https://source.android.com/.

innovation areas, and (3) the need to maintain a robust defense of its own business, even as Google practiced patent non-aggression in the face of heightening industry conflict. Especially in relation to point (3), Google saw a need to expand the defensive conditions included in a patent pledge, alongside a need by pledging companies to make clearer assurances concerning their intent to be bound by the pledges they have made or will make.[24] Transparency and reliability, not a ready hallmark of the patent licensing industry, were the main guiding principles for the OPN Pledge.

One of the emerging marketplace dynamics that Google undertook to uniquely address through the OPN Pledge was "privateering." Privateering generally refers to the outsourcing of patent enforcement by a patent owner. Typically, the enforcer and owner split whatever returns are obtained from settlements or litigation judgments won by the enforcer. But the patent owner, usually a large operating company, gets to avoid direct involvement in the messy business of patent litigation against other operating companies. The OPN Pledge addresses privateering in two respects. First, Google's OPN Pledge makes clear that the pledge may be terminated with respect to any parties having a financial interest in a patent lawsuit filed against either Google, its subsidiaries, or against a third party based on products or services provided by Google or its subsidiaries.[25] Second, the pledge makes explicit that Google will bind any subsequent owners of its pledged patents to adhere to the terms and conditions of the pledge.[26]

More generally, the OPN Pledge addresses many of the leading critiques of patent pledges, reflected for instance in a 2012 article promoting the Defensive Patent License, a form of community license that has not attracted a licensee network, but which inspired a variant that

---

24 *See Open Patent Non-Assertion Pledge: FAQ*, GOOGLE, at question nos. 13–14, http://www.google.com/patents/opnpledge/faq/ [hereinafter *Google OPN FAQs*] (describing how the OPN Pledge expands upon the defensive termination provisions of OSS licenses, addressing a broader range of patent aggression); id. at question nos. 8–9 (discussing the durable nature of the pledge and Google's express intent that it be binding on Google and any successors in ownership of pledged patents).

25 *Open Patent Non-Assertion Pledge*, GOOGLE, http://www.google.com/patents/opnpledge/pledge/.

26 Id. ("Google will require any person or entity to whom it sells or transfers any of the Pledged Patents to agree, in writing, to abide by the Pledge and to place a similar requirement on any subsequent transferees to do the same").

eventually became the LOT Network.[27] The OPN Pledge itself affirms the intent that it be binding and also that it endure, even if pledged patents are assigned to other parties.[28] Concerns about the enforceability of pledges more broadly are addressed below.

V. KEY NORMATIVE PRINCIPLES

Recent discussions concerning patent pledges have raised a number of issues concerning the degree to which they might be enforceable.[29] Such issues are presented because there is no jurisprudence involving the enforcement of unilateral patent pledges, and therefore no guidance on questions of first impression. This chapter does not undertake to address all of the issues others have raised, but simply to address a number of the more salient issues presented when designing a patent pledge. These salient issues include: (1) reliance, (2) treatment of retracted or disappearing pledges, (3) valuation of pledged patents, and (4) exhaustion (aka the first sale doctrine).

A. Reliance

Non-SDO patents pledges are often unilateral promises made by a patent holder. As discussed in Chapter 1, there is often no formal contractual basis for the scope of the rights and obligations that may flow from the patent holder to a given pledge recipient.[30] Thus, the law has historically

---

[27] *See* Jason Schultz & Jennifer Urban, *Protecting Open Innovation: The Defensive Patent License as a New Approach to Patent Threats, Transaction Costs, and Tactical Disarmament*, 26 HARV. J.L. TECH. 1, 30–33 (2012) (describing the key benefits of patent pledges as "transparency and inexpensive applicability to all who are engaged in innovation covered by the pledge," despite uncertainties regarding whether the doctrines of estoppel or implied license would be enforceable with respect to such pledges); *see also Royalty-Free Patent Licensing: Comparison Table*, GOOGLE, http://www.google.com/patents/licensing/comparison/ (comparing several variants of the Defensive Patent License, including the License on Transfer).

[28] This is one of the reasons why Google elected to identify specific patents as being subject to its OPN Pledge, instead of simply providing a high level characterization of which patents may be included.

[29] *See* Contreras, Chapter 5.

[30] *Cf.* Microsoft Corp. v. Motorola, Inc., 696 F. 3d 872, 885 (9th Cir. 2012) (affirming lower court finding that promises made to an SDO, by patent holders who contribute to a technology standard specification as coordinating SDO members, are binding contracts and adopters of those specifications are third

treated unilateral promises of this kind under equitable principles, namely those of promissory estoppel. Under a theory of promissory estoppel, if a party receiving a unilateral promise has formed a reasonable basis upon which to rely on that promise, then the promisor may be estopped from recanting the promise and thereby held legally bound to fulfill its terms.[31] Even so, cases involving promissory estoppel have typically involved promises made by one person to another, or at most to a discrete set of promise recipients. As pointed out in Chapter 18, patent pledges made more broadly to the public may or may not be specifically apprehended by all parties who stand to benefit from them.[32] Should a patent holder making a pledge be permitted under equitable principles to enforce covered patents in a manner inconsistent with the terms of that pledge, particularly to the extent a given defendant or counterparty did not know of or specifically rely upon the pledge prior to the enforcement event?

For the reasons discussed below, the answer is clearly no. The basic issue presented is one of violating settled marketplace expectations, particularly to the extent a pledge maker has even marginally altered marketplace behavior in response to the pledge having been made. Consistent with the "market reliance" theory described by Contreras in Chapter 5, it should be presumed that a patent holder making a pledge sought to induce certain behavior by market participants standing to be pledge beneficiaries. If it has received the benefit of the pledge by inducing only one or a few parties to engage in that behavior (e.g., paying for a license), the patent holder has altered marketplace dynamics.

---

party beneficiaries). Without the coordinating role of an SDO intermediary, to whom patent assurances are specifically made by member patent holders, a contract theory whereby implementers of covered patents are deemed third party beneficiaries breaks down if applied to unilateral pledges made in broad terms to the public.

[31] The OPN Pledge was designed with this equitable theory in mind. *See Google OPN FAQs*, *supra* note 24, at question no. 9 ("Licenses are typically contractual agreements between two or more parties. In the OSS context licenses typically accompany source or object code distributions or development efforts. Google is not at this stage distributing any software under the OPN Pledge, so in that context Google chose the vehicle of simply extending a broad non-assertion promise in connection with open source implementations that practice Pledged Patents. The Pledge states very explicitly Google's intent that it be legally binding on Google").

[32] Most patent pledges are posted on Internet websites, typically those maintained by the patent holders. Such pledges are not always promoted actively by their makers, so can escape notice by some parties in a position to benefit from them.

It thereafter would be inequitable for the patent holder to selectively comply with the patent pledge, except to the extent that the terms and conditions of the pledge itself set forth the basis for differential treatment of certain pledge recipients. Arguably, the market risks posed by the uncertainty of whether or not a proffered patent pledge may be relied upon is worse than the baseline uncertainty of not having any indications whatever of a patent holder's intents. The OPN Pledge addresses these risks by specifically providing it should be deemed enforceable with respect to any member of the public, regardless of whether there was knowledge of or specific reliance upon the pledge by particular persons.[33] As discussed, patent pledges serve an important role in conveying patent rights and complement other market mechanisms for doing so. There are sound reasons to bias in favor of their enforceability. For instance, allowing even tenuously made pledges to be broken without consequences undermines the value and reliability of all other pledges.

Patent pledges are somewhat analogous to OSS copyright licenses, at least in respect to how their terms and conditions are propagated. A single author of code may post that code for distribution under one or another form of open source license. That author may never meet or specifically negotiate with the parties who download and use her code. Similarly, the parties who download that code may overlook or simply choose to ignore the associated open source license agreement that accompanies it. To what degree, one might ask, was there a meeting of the minds between the author and such adopters of her work? Were the main precepts upon which legally binding contracts are typically presumed to rest ever in place? While such nuances were not explored, more than one Federal Court of Appeals has affirmed the enforceability of open source licenses that are subject to these very vagaries.[34] The

---

33 *See Google OPN FAQs*, *supra* note 24, at question no. 8 ("Our Pledge extends to each and every user, distributor and developer of Free or Open Source Software, regardless of whether each is aware of the Pledge or otherwise would have taken steps to sign on to a document embodying its principles"); id. at question no. 9 ("the Pledge is self-operative. No further action is required for users, distributors or developers of Free or Open Source Software to enjoy the benefits of the OPN Pledge").

34 Jacobsen v. Katzer, 535 F.3d 1373 (Fed. Cir. 2008) (upholding the conditions imposed by the Perl Artistic License on downstream users of covered code, noting that "[o]pen source licensing has become a widely used method of creative collaboration that serves to advance the arts and sciences in a manner and at a pace that few could have imagined just a few decades ago"); Wallace v. IBM Corp., 467 F.3d 1104 (7th Cir. 2006) (ruling that the GNU General Public License 2.0 and the free software distribution mechanism that it permits is not

overriding concern for the courts in each instance is that the substance of the OSS agreements be given legal effect in light of the positive marketplace benefits conferred by the technologies covered by those agreements. Patent pledges have played a significant role in providing patent rights exchange and promoting adoption of innovative product technologies in many fields of interest.

B. Retracted or Disappearing Pledges

Closely related to the issue concerning reliance discussed above, is the issue raised by Contreras in Chapter 18 concerning retracted or buried pledges. The basic issue concerning reliance discussed above relates to pledges that remain in force, and pledge makers electing to enforce their covered patents on terms inconsistent with the pledge against parties who did not know of or specifically rely on the pledge. Some variants of this scenario include pledges that may be retracted by patent holders, or more ambiguously, pledges that disappear from public view without any formal retraction or acknowledgement by the patent holder.

In the case of pledge retractions, it makes sense that those standing to benefit from a particular retracted pledge *at minimum* be allowed to enjoy rights under the terms and conditions of the pledge during the period prior to retraction. For the reasons previously discussed, there should be no requirement that a pledge recipient has specifically relied on the pledge pre-retraction in order to claim coverage under the pledge during that period. Moreover, in specific instances, a particular pledge recipient may have been induced to enter a market or expand its product exposure within one or more markets based on its knowledge of a pledge (e.g., the party determines that receiving a license on FRAND terms makes market entry or expansion economically sensible, whereas entry or expansion on more onerous terms would not make sense). A pledge recipient in such instance should be permitted to establish the extent of its actual reliance on the pledge and the economic harms that it would sustain following retraction were the patent holder able to immediately insist upon different terms. Accordingly, patent holders should be permitted to retract pledges, but only if (1) such a retraction is done explicitly, and (2) includes an explicit date upon which the retraction is being made effective, as well as

anticompetitive, noting that "Linux and other open-source projects have been able to cover their fixed costs through donations of time; as long as that remains true, it would reduce efficiency and consumers' welfare to force the authors to levy a charge on each new user").

(3) a statement as to when the pledge was initially made.[35] In this manner periods of actual and constructive reliance may be determined and applied appropriately to establish the rights of particular pledge recipients against whom a pledge maker is attempting to enforce previously covered patents.

In the case of disappearing pledges, a patent pledge may be de-published or quietly retracted without any specific notice, as described by Contreras in Chapter 18. As such, there is no indication that the pledge maker specifically intended to retract the pledge, but, having been made at one point in time, the pledge is no longer explicitly ascertainable by beneficiaries. The possibilities include purposefully quiet retraction by the patent holder, unintended de-publishing based on website redesign/ reorganization or an intent that the pledge be relied upon only for the period that it was published. In none of these instances would it be fair for a patent holder to be permitted to enforce its pledge-covered patents on terms varying from those offered in the pledge. Having once been made with the intent to influence market dynamics and to induce certain conduct, the quiet disappearance of a pledge leaves tremendous uncertainty. Many pledge recipients may simply assume the pledge is still in force, as they may hear of the pledge from third parties or may have seen it once and not assumed that it would disappear.

Pledges, once made, should generally not be retracted, except upon terms stated or allowed for in the provisions of the pledge itself. Making a pledge is a considerable decision for a company or organization. Pledges should not be made without due deliberation by company management. Similarly, once made—with the implicit assumption or explicit assurance that third parties rely on them—it is simply wrong to silently retract them, or otherwise make the pledge difficult to find, such that the pledge's existence or whether or not it has formally been retracted is left entirely uncertain. When a party to a bilateral license agreement fails to honor an obligation it has incurred, there are consequences: the other party can seek redress in court for breach of contract and any manner in which it has been harmed by such breach. If a pledge is retracted, the consequences of that retraction should be in keeping with the principles previously set forth.[36] To the extent patent pledges provide useful patent rights transfer mechanisms and help establish both community expectations and community norms, it would be unfair and

[35] These principles should similarly apply to pledges whose terms have been materially modified.

[36] *See also* Contreras, Chapter 18.

inequitable to leave those harmed by conduct inconsistent with the explicit terms of the pledge without a legal defense.

C. The Value and Valuation of Pledged Patents

The willingness of a pledger to offer rights under pledged patents for free should not be used to undermine the value or potency of such patents should they ever get asserted, particularly where the pledge has been made subject to clear and reasonable conditions. Patents subject to a free pledge should be evaluated according to their objective market value in the event that the patent holder is given grounds to enforce the patents against a party who has violated the explicit conditions of the pledge (or against a party who is not a pledge recipient). Unilateral pledges are not licenses. Accordingly, that a pledge is made without an expectation of payment should not be used (or usable) as evidence that the license or enforcement value of the patents are minimal or even adversely impacted by their being subject to the pledge.[37] In order for pledge recipients to realize the quid pro quo of offering free rights to the public, the patents must maintain "their teeth" upon being legitimately enforced, and not treated differently than patents never made subject to a pledge. This applies both to the determination of damages as well as whether injunctive relief is available to the patent holder.[38] Especially when

[37] In patent cases, prior licenses are factored into damages awards in a number of ways. Ga.-Pac. Corp. v. U.S. Plywood Corp., 318 F. Supp. 1116, 1120 (S.D.N.Y. 1970), *modified and aff'd*, 446 F.2d 295 (2d Cir. 1971). The first factor is what royalties the patentee has received for licensing the patent-in-suit; the second factor is what royalties licensees have paid to license similar (comparable) patents; the fifteenth factor is what royalty the parties would have agreed to at the time the infringement began if they had reasonably and voluntarily tried to reach agreement. Id. Because a pledge is not a license, and the quid pro quo for a free pledge is non-monetary, the first factor is simply inapposite (unless, of course, the patent holder has separately licensed pledged patents to parties not covered by the pledge). The second and fifteenth factors remain pertinent and should be used in determining damages awards in the enforcement of patents subject to free pledges against non-compliant pledge recipients.

[38] The availability of injunctions under patent law is flexibly determined by applying four equitable principles to the specific facts and circumstances presented in each case. *See* eBay Inc. v. MercExchange, LLC, 547 U.S. 388, 391 (2006) (holding that to obtain injunctive relief in a patent case a "plaintiff must demonstrate: (1) that it has suffered an irreparable injury; (2) that remedies available at law, such as monetary damages, are inadequate to compensate for that injury; (3) that, considering the balance of hardships between the plaintiff and defendant, a remedy in equity is warranted; and (4) that the public interest

provided for in the terms and conditions of the pledge itself, allowing pledge makers to return to a status quo—as if their pledges were never made in the first instance—with non-compliant pledge beneficiaries supports the value of the pledge for all beneficiaries and the value of pledges more generally.

D. Exhaustion

The first sale or exhaustion doctrine in patent law provides a limit on a patent holder's ability to license or enforce its patent(s) reading on a particular patented article that it has sold or authorized another to sell. The state of the law of exhaustion is somewhat in flux, with many nuanced issues presented by modern economic practices and the complexity of modern products, which may incorporate dozens, hundreds or even thousands of patented inventions or which may be self-replicating. That being so, the general doctrine prohibits a patent holder from enforcing its patents against multiple parties in a distribution chain who, respectively, use, sell or otherwise convey a particular article of commerce covered by the patent. A modern formulation of the doctrine holds that "the initial authorized sale of a patented article terminates all patent rights to that item."[39] Historically, the doctrine was understood to prevent a patent holder from collecting monetary consideration more than once concerning a particular patented article. But a recent decision by the Federal Circuit has suggested that even an initial free conveyance of a patented article by a patent holder can give rise to exhaustion, whereby the free conveyance is deemed "an authorized sale."[40] If this case was correctly decided, it is limited to scenarios where a patent holder is the one who chooses to give away its patented product in the hopes of collecting a monetary reward in some other manner downstream.[41]

would not be disserved by a permanent injunction"). The enforcement of patents subject to free pledges against non-compliant pledge recipients should be treated no differently.

39 Quanta Comput., Inc. v. LG Elecs., Inc., 553 U.S. 617, 625 (2008).

40 *See* LifeScan Scot., Ltd. v. Shasta Techs., LLC, 734 F.3d 1361, 1374 (Fed. Cir. 2013) (elaborating on precedent in a manner never explicitly allowed by the High Court, stating "despite frequent references to 'sales' and 'purchasers,' the [Supreme] Court has more fundamentally described exhaustion as occurring when the patented product 'passes to the hands' of a transferee and when he 'legally acquires a title' to it").

41 *See* id. at 1375 ("[A] patentee cannot evade patent exhaustion principles by choosing to give the article away rather than charging a particular price for it. Where a patentee unconditionally parts with ownership of an article, it cannot

Exhaustion can apply in two basic scenarios relative to a patent holder, following (1) its sale of products embodying or incorporating a patented invention, or (2) the sale by one of its licensees of products embodying or incorporating a patented invention.[42] For purposes of considering the exhaustion doctrine in relation to patent pledges, scenario (2) is more pertinent. Patent pledge makers can certainly sell items covered by pledged patents. Those articles would doubtless be covered by the patent exhaustion doctrine under scenario (1). Under scenario (2) the patent pledge maker can independently choose to license another party to sell patent articles covered by pledged patents. If this was done pursuant to a contractual license, outside of the pledge context, then articles sold by the patent holder's licensee would also certainly be covered by the patent exhaustion doctrine. The question presented is whether a patent pledge recipient should be treated in the same manner as a patent licensee, such that a free pledge maker's patents are deemed unenforceable against customers of a pledge recipient or anyone else downstream of both the patent holder and recipients of its pledge.

For many good policy reasons discussed below, the answer to that question is no. One of the key principles animating the exhaustion doctrine is the notion that a patent holder should not enjoy "double recovery" from its patent rights relative to a particular product incorporating those rights. That is, once a patent holder sells a product embodying its patent, or else licenses someone else to sell products embodying the patent, a fair recovery has been had, one that the patent holder can negotiate *ex ante*. To permit the patent holder thereafter to enforce the patent or otherwise seek additional rents from the purchasers of a product embodying the patent(s), or someone else downstream of that purchaser, has been deemed inequitable.[43] In the case of a free unilateral patent pledge, however, there is no recovery by the patent holder of up-front license fees or revenue from product sales. Rather, the benefits from making the pledge may be each pledge recipient abiding by

later complain that the approach that it chose results in an inadequate reward and that therefore ordinary principles of patent exhaustion should not apply").

[42] *See,* e.g., Intel Corp. v. ULSI Sys. Tech., Inc., 995 F.2d 1566, 1569–70 (Fed. Cir. 1993).

[43] *See* Quanta, 533 U.S. at 1766; United States v. Univis Lens Co., 316 U.S. 241, 251 (1942) ("Our decisions have uniformly recognized that the purpose of the patent law is fulfilled with respect to any particular article when the patentee has received his reward for the use of his invention by the sale of the article, and that once that purpose is realized the patent law affords no basis for restraining the use and enjoyment of the thing sold").

some conditions or stated expectations, such as refraining from patent aggression against the pledge maker. The only "reward" for a patent pledge maker is that each pledge recipient benefitting from the pledge abide by the terms and conditions of the pledge itself. Each such pledge recipient may be differently situated in the marketplace, whether as a developer, distributor, intermediate or end user of a product covered by the pledge maker's patent(s). However, each pledge recipient receives a non-assertion assurance directly from the patent holder, without having to rely on a particular upstream party having obtained formal license rights from the patent holder prior to receiving and exploiting an otherwise infringing product. Such a non-assertion promise is offered outside of any privity of contract, and so is based only on equitable principles rather than contractual ones, such as those which are the hallmarks of patent licenses. It would severely undermine the pledge maker's bargain with the public—freedom from suit without any monetary payment—were a pledge beneficiary able to violate material conditions of the pledge, but still claim immunity under the pledge because someone upstream was still in good standing under the pledge.

The patent exhaustion doctrine is subject to limitations, based on a patent holder's ability to segment which of its several rights to exclude under the patent laws it wishes to relinquish with a particular licensee.[44] Fundamentally, all scenarios in which patent exhaustion has been found to apply (i.e., those not involving the conveyance of a patented article by the patent holder itself) have involved a contractual relationship between the patent holder and another party authorized to sell products covered by the patent(s). In recent instances where courts have found that a covenant not to sue provided by a patent holder can give rise to exhaustion, there was still a direct contractual relationship between the patent holder and the recipient of the covenant not to sue.[45] The contractual negotiation between two or more parties is the process whereby a patent holder can

---

[44] *See*, e.g., Helferich Patent Licensing v. N.Y. Times Co., 778 F.3d 1293 (Fed. Cir. 2015) (affirming that a patent holder is permitted to authorize sales of a licensee's products only within certain fields of use and patent claims covering uses outside of those fields are not exhausted, even if those other uses arise from third party use of the licensee's sold products).

[45] *See* TransCore LP v. Elec. Transaction Consultants Corp., 563 F.3d 1271 (Fed. Cir. 2009) (holding that sales of products may be "authorized" under a written covenant not to sue between a patent holder and the party selling such products in the same manner as they might under a patent license between the parties).

convey rights to practice its patent(s) and receive a direct quid pro quo that, in turn, is contractually binding. Depriving a patent pledge maker the ability to seek recourse against any pledge recipient who violates explicit terms and conditions of the pledge by reason of the exhaustion doctrine would be inequitable, both because the premise of the doctrine would not have been fulfilled (no "reward" to the patent holder has been received) and there has been no contractual basis for the conveyance of patent rights in the first instance.[46]

CONCLUSION

Unilateral patent pledges made outside of a standards development organization are a relatively new development. They are nonetheless an important part of the patent landscape concerning the conveyance of patent rights and the conferment of freedom of action around product technologies of interest. Unilateral pledges complement community licenses and are part of a mosaic of marketplace freedoms that market participants can grant in support of various innovation areas. Unilateral pledges are not creatures of contract, but are nonetheless governed by equitable principles. These equitable principles, such as promissory estoppel, should be given legal effect and such pledges deemed enforceable, even if subsumed principles such as reliance may require adaptation to the context of how and why unilateral pledges are made. In a similar vein, equitable principles suggest that free pledge makers not be left in a worse position by virtue of making pledges that are legally enforceable. Particularly, should a pledge maker need to license or enforce its patents consistent with the terms of its pledge (or outside the coverage of the

---

46 *See Google OPN FAQs*, *supra* note 24, at question no. 9 ("Licenses are typically contractual agreements between two or more parties. In the OSS context licenses typically accompany source or object code distributions or development efforts. Google is not at this stage distributing any software under the OPN Pledge, so in that context Google chose the vehicle of simply extending a broad non-assertion promise in connection with open source implementations that practice Pledged Patents. The Pledge states very explicitly Google's intent that it be legally binding on Google. Our Pledge extends to each and every user, distributor and developer of Free or Open Source Software, regardless of whether each is aware of the Pledge or otherwise would have taken steps to sign on to a document embodying its principles. This makes the Pledge different than more conventional licenses or covenants not to sue").

pledge) the fact that the pledge was made should not be used to devalue the pledged patents or render them unenforceable owing to contract-based legal theories.

3. Patent sharing in biotechnology

Dov Greenbaum

Conventional wisdom would suggest that efforts to develop a patent pool, and to share intellectual property and know-how, are somewhat unique within the biopharmaceutical and biotechnology industries. While many large stakeholders in varied hi-tech industries—including Google, Tesla, Toyota, LG, Samsung, Hyundai, Panasonic, Daewoo, and others—and even NASA, have pledged to share their patents more willingly, participated in patent pools, and/or otherwise made licensing of the technology easy and/or free (collectively, "sharing"), the biotechnology industry seems to be relatively unsympathetic to such efforts.[1]

There may be any number of reasons to support these assumptions; this chapter seeks to tease them out, particularly looking to patent assertion entities (commonly called patent "trolls") as a proxy to better understand why biotechnology firms in particular tend not to share.

I. THE TERM BIOTECHNOLOGY

Throughout this chapter, the term biotechnology will be representative of the life sciences industries. While granted the many sub-sectors within represent relatively vastly different areas of technology, for the purposes of this chapter, which contrasts biotechnology innovation with hi-tech innovation, the conflating of industries like biotechnology and pharmaceuticals does not necessarily pose a problem. Similar arguments can be made for the use herein of the catchall term "hi-tech".

This chapter also assumes that generally the field of biotechnology, with its significant barriers to entry,[2] is typically dominated by strong and

[1] *Collaborative Mechanisms for Intellectual Property Management in the Life Sciences*, ORG. FOR ECO. CO-OPERATION AND DEV. (2011).

[2] ANDREW J. HACKLING, ECONOMIC ASPECTS OF BIOTECHNOLOGY 1 (1987).

important players in both industry and academic science,[3] perhaps more so than hi-tech industries in which anyone who can code, could potentially code.[4] This supposition makes the seeming lack of open source options, patent pools and clearinghouses potentially that much more significant in the biotechnology industry.

II. OPEN SCIENCE

Although this chapter presupposes that intellectual property sharing is rare in biotechnology, there have been some elements within the biotechnology industries that have at least toyed with the possibility of sharing their IP and know-how in one form or another, these typically include open science methodologies, patent pooling and clearinghouses, as described below.

Much of the underlying code in the software used by many industries is often open source.[5] However, while the open source *weltanschauung* (i.e., their worldview) is very popular in hi-tech and particularly in software, its overall notion of openness has been slow to translate into other areas of technology, particularly the non-software areas of biotechnology. Here, even though researchers often share techniques, methods, reagents, results, and eventually their discoveries through various publication systems, many in the industry and academia are still stingy in sharing their underlying raw data.[6]

This absence of a grassroots open source revolution in biotechnology might relate to fundamental industry-wide differences in information

---

[3] *The Industry Handbook: Biotechnology*, INVESTOPEDIA.

[4] Michael Rosen, *Software Patents: Reform, Not Repeal*, AM. ENTERPRISE INST. (December 9, 2011).

[5] Steven J. Vaughan-Nichols, *It's an Open-Source World: 78 Percent of Companies Run Open-Source Software*, ZDNET (Aug. 16, 2015).

[6] Geertrui Van Overwalle, *Uncorking Trade Secrets: Sparking the Interaction Between Trade Secrecy and Open Biotechnology*, in THE LAW AND THEORY OF TRADE SECRECY: A HANDBOOK OF CONTEMPORARY RESEARCH 246 (Rochelle C. Dreyfuss & Katherine J. Strandburg eds., 2011); Mark Ware, *Access vs. Importance*, PUB. RES. CONSORTIUM (Oct. 2010); Caroline J. Savage & Andrew J. Vickers, *Empirical Study of Data Sharing by Authors Publishing*, PLoS ONE (Sept. 2009), at 1; Eric Campbell & Eran Bendavid, *Data-Sharing and Data-Withholding in Genetics and the Life Sciences: Results of a National Survey of Technology Transfer Officers*, 6 J. HEALTH CARE L. & POL'Y 241, 241 (2002).

transfer. In contrast to the underlying concerns that pushed Richard Stallman to launch the open source movement in the 1980s, that is, the lack of accessibility to computer software information tied up in undecipherable machine code (famously put as "free speech," not "free beer."),[7] biotechnology (its sharing problems notwithstanding) has not experienced any substantial inhibitory limitations on the free flow of information, at least none that has been so significant as to force a redirection of research.[8] Even the highly contested legal issues relating to access to BRCA gene testing for predispositions to breast and ovarian cancer[9] did not prevent substantial research in this area;[10] PubMed, a medical literature database, lists thousands of BRCA research papers.[11]

In the most recent biotechnology patent brouhaha, CRISPR—the innovative technology that allows for genetic editing *in vivo*, potentially worth billions of dollars and a Nobel Prize[12]—where the two sides are claiming patent priority, MIT/Broad and the University of California have even resorted to using the academic literature to bolster their arguments of inventorship,[13] both parties are still keen on making the technology publicly available.

Without any real indication that information is not made available, there have not been any noteworthy grassroots efforts to demand access to the proprietary information of the larger and biopharmaceutical stakeholders. Moreover, in contrast to open source hi-tech where coding skills figure prominently and can be relatively easy to learn, many of the relevant skills in much of biotechnology still remain more art than science and can take years of apprenticeship to master. This creates significant barriers to entry which limit the number and types of

---

[7] Richard Stallman, *Viewpoint: Why Open Source Misses the Point of Free Software*, 52 COMMUNICATIONS OF THE ACM, NO. 6 (2009), at 31–33.

[8] Tabrez Ahmad, Alimpan Chatterjee & Deya Bhattacharya, *Split Wide Open: Biotechnology and the Open Source Movement*, SSRN (Jan. 8, 2012), at https://ssrn.com/abstract=1981645.

[9] Ass'n for Molecular Pathology v. Myriad, 133 S. Ct. 2107 (2013).

[10] *See* Appendix—Myriad Genetics' patent pledge; Contreras, Chapter 1.

[11] E. Richard Gold & Julia Carbone, *Myriad Genetics: In the Eye of the Policy Storm*, 12(4) GENETICS IN MED. S39–S70 (April 2010).

[12] Michael Specter, *The Gene Hackers*, THE NEW YORKER (No. 16, 2015); Jennifer Kahn, *The Crispr Quandary*, NY TIMES (Nov. 9, 2015).

[13] Eric S. Lander, *The Heroes of CRISPR*, 164(1-2) CELL, at 18–28 (2016); Tracey Vance, *Heroes of CRISPR Disputed*, THE SCIENTIST (Jan. 16, 2016).

practitioners. Any useful open science in biotechnology would need to be more than just the sharing of data through scientific journals; open science in biotechnology requires the actual sharing of know-how, innovation and proprietary tools.

All this notwithstanding, there have been a few areas in biotechnology where open science and the sharing of data and know-how seem to be making some inroads.[14] However, even the smattering of companies involved in open science remain responsible to their shareholders and are, as such, rarely wholly philanthropic; they expect to gain from open science, including learning from academic collaborators, enhancing their absorptive capabilities, attracting high quality star talent, increasing trust-levels with academia resulting in more sharing of theoretical and practical knowledge, and signaling scientific competence.[15]

Moreover, typically, when open science does exist in biotechnology, it tends to favor neglected diseases or other diseases of the less affluent parts of the world as research in these areas tends to be underfunded or the gains of hopefully lower cost therapies are more apparent.

Notably though, open source, often colloquially associated with the lack of intellectual property rights, does not necessarily imply no intellectual property rights, or the withholding of IP enforcement. The specialized licenses that define open source by necessity piggyback on intellectual property rights to make open source work. Open source is in contrast to just dumping all innovation into the public domain. As such, in many open science projects, biotechnology companies still retain often substantial intellectual property rights over their innovation and actually closely control who they grant open access to, this exclusivity that might favor competent partners more likely to succeed can promote, rather than hinder, innovation.[16]

Any minimal inroads in open source notwithstanding, many of the original champions of open science have been disappointed as to the

---

[14] Murray N. Robertson, Paul M. Ylioja, Alice E. Williamson, Michael Woelfle, Michael Robins, Katrina A. Badiola, Paul Willis, Piero Olliaro, Timothy N.C. Wells & Matthew H. Todd, *Open Source Drug Discovery: A Limited Tutorial*, 141(1) PARASITOLOGY, at 148–57 (2014).

[15] Simcha Jong & Kremena Slavova, *When Publications Lead to Products: The Open Science Conundrum in New Product Development*, 43 RESEARCH POLICY, at 645–54 (2014).

[16] Christine Årdal & John-Arne Røttingen, *Open Source Drug Discovery in Practice: A Case Study*, 1827 PLOS NEGLECTED TROPICAL DISEASES (2012).

power and innovation associated with open source science,[17] and with the lack of any revolutionary new models and projects.[18] Perhaps other alternatives to strong assertions of patent rights might also help in biotechnology, for example, patent pools.

III. BIOTECHNOLOGY PATENT POOLS

Patent pools are thought to be a useful method to overcome patent thickets and to otherwise easily share knowledge and innovation.[19] Generally, patent pools are best at minimizing transaction varied costs associated with licensing, minimizing license stacking, and limiting litigation associated with clearing patent rights. This is particularly the case when industry-wide standards read on numerous patents.[20]

This is also particularly the case when products may read on tens if not hundreds of potentially distinct IP rights such as in hi-tech. However, while hi-tech patent pools abound, particularly in areas of public consumer goods that rely on broad standards for interoperability (MPEG, DVD, etc.[21]) patent pools are thought to be a poor fit to biotechnology,[22] and as such remain rare in biotechnology, the academic interest and

---

[17] Stephen M. Maurer, Rai Arti & Andrej Sali, *Finding Cures for Tropical Diseases: Is Open Source an Answer?*,56 PLoS MEDICINE 1.3 (2004).

[18] Stephen M. Maurer, *Open Source Drug Collaborations: A Rational Design Approach*, 5(8) FUTURE MEDICINAL CHEMISTRY, at 895–906 (2013).

[19] Jeanne Clark, Joe Piccolo, Brian Stanton, Karin Tyson, Mary Critharis & Stephen Kunin, UNITED STATES PATENT AND TRADEMARK OFFICE, *Patent Pools: A Solution to the Problem of Access in Biotechnology Patents?* 4 (2000); *Collaborative Mechanisms for Intellectual Property Management in the Life Sciences, supra* note 1.

[20] Justus Baron & Henry Delcamp, *The Strategies of Patent Introduction into Patent Pools*, 24(8) ECON. OF INNOVATION AND NEW TECHNOLOGY, at 776–800 (2015).

[21] Erik Hovenkamp, *Patent Pools and Related Technology Sharing*, in CAMBRIDGE HANDBOOK ON ANTITRUST AND INTELLECTUAL PROPERTY (Daniel Sokol and Roger Blair eds., 2015).

[22] ORG. FOR ECON. CO-OPERATION AND DEV. (OECD), GENETIC INVENTIONS, INTELLECTUAL PROPERTY RIGHTS AND LICENSING PRACTICES: EVIDENCE AND POLICIES 45, 48 (2002) ("On the other hand, patent pools, consortia and cross licensing were not deemed effective for increasing access to genetic inventions owing to the difficulty of assessing the contributions various parties are likely to bring to such a grouping …").

potential economic benefits in them notwithstanding.[23] Synthetic biology, the cross between the standardization of engineering and the living systems of biology, may become a notable exception given the necessary reliance on standardized parts across the industry.[24] Alternatively, some have suggested that the genetics diagnostic testing industry is also a good fit for patent pools.[25]

Although many biotechnology products—particularly pharmaceuticals —read on only one or a handful of patents at most (which some have still defined as being a thicket, e.g., >2)[26] stakeholders have nevertheless tried to introduce patent pools into biotechnology. However, excluding the recently defunct World Health Organization's SARS pool,[27] the WIPO Re:Search consortium,[28] the BIO Ventures for Global Health (BVGH) pool and UNITAID's Medicines Patent Pool (MPP)[29]—all nonprofit humanitarian projects[30] focusing on non-innovating generic therapeutics

---

[23] Thomas D. Jeitschko & Nanyun Zhang, *Adverse Effects of Patent Pooling on Product Development and Commercialization*, 14 BE J. OF THEORETICAL ECON. 1 (2013).

[24] Jorge L. Contreras, Arti K. Rai & Andrew W. Torrance, *Intellectual Property Issues and Synthetic Biology Standards,* 33 NATURE BIOTECH. 24, 24 (2015).

[25] Birgit Verbeure, Esther van Zimmeren, Gert Matthijs & Geertrui Van Overwalle, *Patent Pools and Diagnostic Testing*, 24 TRENDS IN BIOTECHNOLOGY, at 115–20 (2006); *Patent Pools in Life Sciences*, FENWICK & WEST (2009).

[26] Thomas D. Jeitschko & Nanyun Zhang, *On the Challenges Facing Patent Pooling in Biotechnology*, 19 J. INTELL. PROP. RTS. 113, 118 (2014).

[27] James H.M. Simon, Eric Claassen, Carmen E. Correa & Albert D.M.E. Osterhaus, *Managing Severe Acute Respiratory Syndrome (SARS) Intellectual Property Rights: The Possible Role of Patent Pooling*, 83 BULL. WORLD HEALTH ORG. 707, 707 (2005).

[28] Jennifer Dent, Roopa Ramamoorthi, Katy Graef, Lisa Marie Nelson & Johannes Christian Wichard, *WIPO Re:Search: A Consortium Catalyzing Research and Product Development for Neglected Tropical Diseases*, 2(5) PHARMACEUTICAL PATENT ANALYST, at 591 (2013).

[29] Jorge Bermudez & Ellen T. Hoen, *The UNITAID Patent Pool Initiative: Bringing Patents Together for the Common Good*, 4 OPEN AIDS J. 37, 38 (2010).

[30] *Collaborative Mechanisms for Intellectual Property Management in the Life Sciences, supra* note 1 ("So far, there is relatively little experience in creating and maintaining a life-sciences pool. Further, the best-known life science pools have a clear philanthropic purpose. This confirms the conclusions of the 2002 OECD report casting doubt on whether pools really provide a useful [knowledge transfer] in the life sciences").

(often of soon-to-expire branded drugs or even generics[31])—biotechnology patent pools remain rare,[32] although not unheard of.[33]

And even when the biotechnology industry does develop patent pools, such as in the case of Golden Rice,[34] it is often not the IP holders that are initiating pools internally, rather external (non-business) forces such as non-governmental organizations (NGOs), governments, and others with magnanimous goals, that tend to be the driving forces behind these pools.[35] Additionally, when patent pools are developed, they tend to be established narrowly such that they avoid antitrust regulation, limiting their usefulness.[36,37]

Finally, some of the patent pools that have been proposed and developed are actually the result of business reasoning: to thwart an even lesser desired alternative of being forced into otherwise restrictive government policies that might require IP holders to share their data and intellectual property on unfavorable terms.[38] Arguably, even the humanitarian-oriented pools (i.e., not obviously profit motivated) are populated by firms that fear being forced by developing nations into compulsory licenses to access their technology.[39] These companies would rather cede their intellectual property on their own terms and avoid the

---

[31] Jahan Taubman-Rezakhanlou, *Brief: Medicines Patent Pool Announces Sub-Licensing Agreements for Hepatitis C Generics*, INTELL. PROP. WATCH (January 20, 2016).

[32] Birgit Verbeure, Esther van Zimmeren, Gert Matthijs & Geertrui Van Overwalle, *Patent Pools and Diagnostic Testing*, 24 TRENDS IN BIOTECHNOLOGY 115, 115–20 (2006).

[33] llumina and Sequenom, *Pool Noninvasive Prenatal Testing Intellectual Property and End Outstanding Patent Disputes* (December 3, 2014), at http://sequenom.investorroom.com/press_releases?item=429.

[34] David Serafino, *Survey of Patent Pools Demonstrates Variety of Purposes and Management Structures,* KNOWLEDGE ECOLOGY INTERNATIONAL (June 4, 2007).

[35] Jeitschko & Zhang, *supra* note 26.

[36] Standard Sanitary Mfg. Co. v. United States, 226 U.S. 20 (1912).

[37] Jonathan M. Barnett, *The Anti-Commons Revisited*, 29 HARVARD J.L. & TECH. 127 (2015).

[38] Eric Bond & Kamal Saggi, *International Price Negotiations under the Threat of Compulsory Licensing*, VANDERBILT, https://my.vanderbilt.edu/kamalsaggi/files/2011/08/Bargaining-CL-aug10.pdf.

[39] TRIPS: Agreement on Trade-Related Aspects of Intellectual Property Rights, Apr. 15, 1994, Marrakesh Agreement Establishing the World Trade Organization, Annex 1C, THE LEGAL TEXTS: THE RESULTS OF THE URUGUAY ROUND OF MULTI-LATERAL TRADE NEGOTIATIONS 320 (1999), 1869 U.N.T.S. 299, 33 I.L.M. 1197 (1994) [hereinafter TRIPS Agreement], *Part II: Standards*

possibility of parallel imports and/or hostility from developing nations and their supporters worldwide.[40] Nevertheless, the number of compulsory licenses remains relatively low—and falling—as to arguably not be as substantial a concern to many biotechnology firms.[41]

Even with their huge potential for humanitarian benefits in developing nations, patent pools in biotechnology are still rare,[42] although some have suggested that more can be expected.[43] Additionally, recent efforts have also been made to develop similar minded methods of sharing such as consortia.[44] It is possible that the intricacies of pharmaceutical and biotechnology business development simply do not lend themselves to the creation of patent pools in biotechnology. Alternatively, in the case of the efforts to create a Golden Rice patent pool, it is not clear why that pool failed.[45]

In particular, in biotechnology, the freedom to operate analysis is an early step in product development as upfront research and development and other costs are high.[46] Moreover, there is a very long lead time and inability to engineer around IP conflicts. For these reasons, patent thickets are avoided at the outset of a research plan and IP is seen as the central asset of the business plan. As such, with substantial sunk costs

---

Concerning the Availability, Scope and Use of Intellectual Property Rights, WORLD TRADE ORG.

40 Rachel Chu, *Bristol-Myers Squibb and the Medicines Patent Pool: An Unlikely Marriage? The Role of the Medicines Patent Pool in Stimulating the Development and Availability of Global Health Medicines*, 5 EUR. J. RISK REG. 68 (2014).

41 Duncan Bucknell, *Worldwide: The Global IP Scorecard for Pharma & Biotech Compulsory Licenses*, MONDAQ (Oct. 22, 2007); Reed Beall & Randall Kuhn, *Trends in Compulsory Licensing of Pharmaceuticals since the Doha Declaration: A Database Analysis*, PLOS MED. (Jan. 2012).

42 *See*, e.g., Barnett, *supra* note 37.

43 Mark H. Webbink, *Patents, Standards and Antitrust: Patent Pool*, DUKE L., https://law.duke.edu/sites/default/files/centers/judicialstudies/patentlaw intensive/friday_Webbink_Slides-Day_5-2.pdf.

44 Tania Bubela, Garret A. FitzGerald & E. Richard Gold, *Recalibrating Intellectual Property Rights to Enhance Translational Research Collaborations*, SCI. TRANSLATIONAL MED. (Feb. 2012), at 1, 3–4.

45 Geertrui Van Overwalle, *Patent Pools and Clearinghouses in the Life Sciences: Back to the Future*, in RESEARCH HANDBOOK ON IP AND THE LIFE SCIENCES (D. Matthews & H. Zech eds., 2016).

46 Andrew Moody, Comment, *Patently Obvious: A Dual-Standard Solution to the Diverging Needs of the Information Technology and Pharmaceutical Patent Industries*, 39 GOLDEN GATE U. L. REV. 71 (2008).

and product shelf lives extending past the life of patents, we are unlikely to develop patent pools.

In contrast, in the software industry, research and development costs are relatively cheap.[47] As such, speed to market is crucial, timelines are short, and there is more opportunity to license or engineer around later determined IP conflicts, putting IP/marketability concerns much later in the business development process.

More succinctly: whereas many hi-tech companies that see IP as "the necessary and sufficient condition to allow for product commercialization" will promote patent pools as an industry-wide benefit, biotechnology companies that appreciate that "securing IP-rights is generally required to be done early in the development process"[48] will not be as incentivized.

Additionally, biotechnology companies in particular, with their long lead times, might have their IP as their only tangible asset for a number of years until their product is perfected and comes to market. It would be counterintuitive for these companies to put their one and only asset into a pool.[49] And like open science, innovations and new therapies have unfortunately not yet resulted from patent pools in the biotechnology sector; the tens of partnerships and efforts arising out of these pools have been overwhelmingly disappointing.[50]

IV. CLEARING HOUSES

Closely related to patent pools, clearinghouses represent (sometimes) third party developed platforms for facilitating licensing of patents and know-how particularly in areas in which cross-licensing and/or other bilateral agreements are costly. Clearinghouses range from simple databases of relevant IP holders to actual exchanges or royalty collecting agencies.[51] Although clearinghouses are thought to be important in

---

[47] Peter S. Menell, *A Method for Reforming the Patent System*, 13 MICH. TELECOMM. & TECH. L. REV. 487, 501–02 (2007).

[48] Jeitschko & Zhang, *supra* note 26.

[49] Ed Levy, Emily Marden, Ben Warren & David Hartell, *Patent Pools and Genomics: Navigating a Course to Open Science*, 16 BU J. SCI. & TECH. L. 75 (2010).

[50] *WIPO Research Project Creates Partnerships but No New Drug Candidates Yet*, SCIDEVNET (Jun. 18, 2014), at http://www.scidev.net/global/medicine/news/wipo-s-patent-pool-yet-to-deliver-new-drug-candidates.html.

[51] Esther van Zimmeren, Birgit Verbeure, Gert Matthijs & Geertrui Van Overwalle, *A Clearing House for Diagnostic Testing: The Solution to Ensure*

obtaining freedom to operate, and they have been proposed for some areas of biotechnology, such as synthetic biology,[52] biotechnology companies in general have shied away from their use due to fears of loss of secrecy, exclusivity and/or control over the bargaining process in licensing.[53]

V. OTHER PATENT SHARING IN BIOTECHNOLOGY

Moreover, arguably, the simple existence of statutory methods that can force biotechnology patent holders to share their IP may limit the development of these patent sharing methods. For example, given the assumed overall good associated with biotechnological innovation, and in some cases even the life and death stakes associated with access to some biotechnology products, the need for patent pools and the like may not be necessary, as there exist other methods to access patented technologies.[54] These include, for example, Government Use Rights[55] which attach to government funded projects (as is the case for many biotechnology patents, even in industry). Under 35 U.S. Code § 202(c)(4) the Federal Government "... shall have a nonexclusive, nontransferrable, irrevocable, paid-up license to practice or have practiced for or on behalf of the United States any subject invention throughout the world." Under this statute, the Federal Government can apply its rights as an affirmative defense against patent infringement of technologies it helped fund.

Additionally, as per 35 U.S. Code § 203,[56] as part of the 1980 Bayh-Dole Act[57] that allowed institutions to patent innovations developed through tax payer funded grants, the government retains the rights "to

Access to and Use of Patented Genetic Inventions?, 84 BULL. WORLD HEALTH ORG. 352, 352–59 (2006).

52 Timo Minssen, Berthold Rutz & Esther van Zimmeren, *Synthetic Biology and Intellectual Property Rights: Six Recommendations*, 10 BIOTECHNOLOGY J. 236, 236–41 (2015).

53 Esther Van Zimmeren, Sven Vanneste, Gert Matthijs, Wim Vanhaverbeke & Geertrui Van Overwalle, *Patent Pools and Clearinghouses in the Life Sciences*, 29 TRENDS IN BIOTECHNOLOGY 569, 569–76 (2011).

54 Tania Bubela & Robert Cook-Deegan, *Keeping Score, Strengthening Policy and Fighting Bad Actors over Access to Research Tools*, 33 NATURE BIOTECHNOLOGY 143, 143–47 (2015).

55 Disposition of rights, 35 U.S.C. § 202 (2012).

56 March-in rights, 35 U.S.C. § 203 (2012).

57 Patent and Trademark Law Amendments Act (Bayh-Dole), Pub. L. 96-517, Dec. 12, 1980.

require the contractor, an assignee or exclusive licensee of a subject invention to grant a nonexclusive, partially exclusive, or exclusive license in any field of use to a responsible applicant or applicants, upon terms that are reasonable under the circumstances." Notably, however, although Bayh Dole is over 30 years old, march in rights have only been considered for four products and each time the request to initiate those rights has been denied.[58]

Finally, as per 28 U.S. Code § 1498,[59] the United States government and/or its contractors cannot be enjoined or be required to pay damages or lost profits to a fairly compensated patent holder who has been forced to allow his patent to be practiced.

> Whenever an invention described in and covered by a patent of the United States is used or manufactured by or for the United States without license of the owner thereof or lawful right to use or manufacture the same, the owner's remedy shall be by action against the United States in the United States Court of Federal Claims for the recovery of his reasonable and entire compensation for such use and manufacture.

VI. LEARNING FROM PATENT TROLL DATA

The general lack of patent sharing in biotechnology limits the ability to analyse the factors that could lead to changes in how patents and intellectual property are shared in the biotechnology sector. To this end I suggest that we look to the admittedly also limited body of work relating to patent trolling in biotechnology, and the apparent lack thereof. Perhaps the addition of this area of scholarship will provide a fuller picture of the situation and its underlying reasons.

Specifically, I posit that patent trolling and patent pledging/sharing are two sides of the same coin; that is, many of the same factors that lead to the infestation of patent trolls within an industry would similarly lead to a greater amount of patent pledging and sharing in that industry. And, as is the case in biotechnology, the factors that have resulted in relatively fewer trolls in the biotechnology industry are likely the same factors that tamp down sharing efforts in biotechnology. Pointedly, as long as there is minimal trolling activity in biotechnology, we can expect (arguably due to correlation, not causation) there to be minimal amounts of sharing. For

[58] Carolyn L. Treasure, Jerry Avorn & Aaron S. Kesselheim, *What Is the Public's Right to Access Medical Discoveries Based on Federally Funded Research?*, 331 JAMA 907, 907–08 (2014).

[59] 28 U.S.C § 1498 (2012).

example, it would seem that much of the underlying patenting conventional wisdom associated in one area is mirrored in the other: the same factors that would otherwise promote patent pledging, patent pools and other efforts to make patents broadly available, for example to overcome freedom to operate concerns, are the same factors that typically lead to the emergence of patent trolls.

Or, more specifically, we posit that the patent related factors that have led to trolling in hi-tech, specifically in software, are the same factors that have led to patent sharing in this industry. In contrast, we would expect that the patent related factors that have limited the amount of patent sharing in biotechnology might reflect on why there may be little trolling activity in biotechnology. Given the heretofore lack of substantive troll activity in biotechnology, any uptick in trolling might signal a change in the biotechnology patenting environment. This change in the environment could be arguably described as a leading indicator for biotechnology patent sharing. Further, while for the most part we would consider trolls an indicator not an instigator of patent sharing in biotechnology, it may be that in a few instances, it is possible that an increase in troll activity might also directly lead to an increase in patent pledging, although that may not necessarily be the case.

VII. INTRODUCTION TO TROLLS

Trolls (or, non-practicing entities, coercive patent-holding firms, patent aggregators, and other pejoratives and/or euphemisms) are a hard-to-define group. This is partially why anti-troll legislation in the U.S. Congress has a hard time passing. Reputable companies like Texas Instruments with their large patent portfolios and their business model of aggressively enforcing and licensing their IP and not making their own products could be broadly considered trolls.[60] So could universities with their large patent portfolios and no manufacturing base.[61] Effectively as

---

[60] Spencer Hosie, *Patent Trolls and the New Tort Reform: A Practitioner's Perspective*, 4 ISJLP 75, 75 (2008).

[61] Mark A. Lemley, *Are Universities Patent Trolls?*, 18 FORDHAM INTELL. PROP. MEDIA & ENT. L.J. 611, 611 (2008); Andrew Chung, *Apple Ordered to Pay $234 Million to University for Infringing Patent,* REUTERS (Oct. 16, 2015); Erin Fuchs, *Tech's 8 Most Fearsome "Patent Trolls,"* BUSINESS INSIDER (Nov. 25, 2012) (listing Wisconsin Alumni Research Foundation (WARF) as one of these trolls).

U.S. Representative Darrell Issa (R, California) has said: "… [a] troll is impossible to define unless you've been mugged by one."[62]

Patent trolls have been shown to be responsible for much of all patent litigation in the past couple of years,[63] representing a substantial increase over the last decades[64] and a lion's share of the damage awards,[65] with the overwhelming majority of this litigation in hi-tech and software related fields.[66] These facts notwithstanding, naively, one would have assumed that biotechnology is the perfect target for trolls, particularly those trolls that, as described below, have business methods modeled after "shakedowns" in pursuit of their goal of extracting a license.[67] What makes biotechnology companies such obvious targets for trolls? Not only would biotechnology companies want to avoid the high cost of threatened troll litigation in general, and would likely concede to a license demand that makes the troll go away, but litigation becomes all the more risky when that litigation involves "kamikaze" trolls[68] that are relatively unconcerned with the validity of their asserted, and often overreaching,

---

62 Mario Trujillo, *House Members Renew "Patent Troll" Bill 4222*, THE HILL (Feb. 4, 2015).

63 *2015 Patent Dispute Report*, UNIFIED PATENTS ("2015 saw the Most Patent Disputes in History … NPE [Non Practicing Entity, i.e., trolls] litigation made up two-thirds (66.9%) of District Court cases initiated in 2015, compared to 61% in 2014"); Stephen Kiebzak, Greg Rafert & Catherine E. Tucker. *The Effect of Patent Litigation and Patent Assertion Entities on Entrepreneurial Activity*, 45 RESEARCH POLICY 218 (2016).

64 Sara Jeruss, Robin Feldman & Joshua Walker, *The America Invents Act 500: Effects of Patent Monetization Entities on US Litigation*, 11 DUKE L. & TECH. REV. 357, 358–62 (2012).

65 Chris Barry, Kris Swanson & Ronen Arad, *2015 PWC Patent Litigation Study*, PWC.

66 U.S. GOV'T ACCOUNTABILITY OFFICE, GAO-13-465, INTELLECTUAL PROPERTY: ASSESSING FACTORS THAT AFFECT PATENT INFRINGEMENT LITIGATION COULD HELP IMPROVE PATENT QUALITY 28, 30 (2013).

67 Jeff John Roberts, *CEOs Tell Congress: Patent Trolls Are Giving Us the Shakedown*, FORTUNE (Mar. 26, 2015), ("Overstock's top lawyer, Mark Griffin […] was joined by the CEOs of a credit union and an app company, who told horror stories of patent-based shakedowns …"). *See also* Blair Silver, *Controlling Patent Trolling with Civil Rico*, 11 YALE J. L. & TECH. 70, 79 (2009).

68 John R. Allison, Mark A. Lemley & Joshua Walker, *Patent Quality and Settlement among Repeat Patent Litigants*, 99 GEO. L.J. 677, 680 (2011) (noting trolls typically win an embarrassingly low 10% of the cases that they take to litigation).

weak patents.[69] In particular, with bad facts making bad law, the finding of invalidity of the trolls' weak biotechnology related patent might create biotechnology patent-threatening precedent. This likelihood is further exacerbated by the surprisingly poor success rate of biotechnology patent holders in litigation.[70] (Although contrast Lemley's analysis in this area with Holman's.[71])

Nevertheless, thus far, pharma and biotechnology have been somewhat immune from this scourge.[72] Notably, as a result of this perceived or actual immunity from trolls, the biotechnology industry has historically not staunchly supported, and even in some examples, opposed many of the early and current efforts to reform patent law, ostensibly designed primarily to relieve the threat of trolls.[73]

VIII. TROLL TAXONOMIES

Professors Lemley and Melamed divide the troll world into at least three distinct demographics: (i) Traditional Trolls who try to assert a small number of patents that read on a significant area of a particular technology; (ii) Bottom Feeders who are interested primarily in achieving quick settlements for a variety of typically low quality patents; they have

---

69 Erik Hovenkamp, Predatory Patent Litigation 3 (Aug. 5, 2013) (unpublished manuscript).

70 John R. Allison, Mark A. Lemley & David L. Schwartz, *Our Divided Patent System*, 82 U. Chi. L. Rev. 1073, 1080 (2015).

71 Christopher M. Holman, *Supreme Court Asked to Consider Role of Post-Filing Evidence in Assessing Obviousness of Pharmaceutical Inventions*, 34 Biotechnology L. Report 59, 59–67 (2015).

72 Colleen Chien, *Patent Trolls by the Numbers* (Santa Clara Univ. Sch. of Law, Legal Studies Research Paper No. 08-13, 2013); John R. Allison, Mark A. Lemley & Joshua H. Walker, *Extreme Value or Trolls on Top? The Characteristics of the Most-Litigated Patents*, 158 U. Pa. L. Rev. 1, 20–25 (2009); Brian J. Love, *An Empirical Study of Patent Litigation Timing: Could a Patent Term Reduction Decimate Trolls without Harming Innovators?*, 161 U Pa. L. Rev. 1309, 1329 (2013); Sannu K. Shrestha, *Trolls or Market-Makers? An Empirical Analysis of Nonpracticing Entities*, 110 Colum. L. Rev. 114, 118 (2010).

73 Christopher M. Holman, *Biotechnology's Prescription for Patent Reform*, 5 J. Marshall Rev. Intell. Prop. L. 318 (2006); Biotechnology Innovation Org., *BIO Opposes H.R. 9, The Innovation Act* (June 11, 2015), at https://www.bio.org/media/press-release/bio-opposes-hr-9-innovation-act; Editorial, *Patent Reform Acts Ugly*, 25 Nature Biotechnology 1187, 1187 (2007); Jeff John Roberts, *Patent Reform Inches onwards but Poison Pill Could Kill It*, Fortune (June 5, 2015).

no interest in going to trial but use the threat of expensive litigation contrasted with their relatively cheap licensing offer as blackmail; and (iii) Patent Aggregators who amass huge portfolios of patents and demand a license to the entire portfolio.[74]

Some have suggested that in addition to the Lemley-Melamed trolls, a new troll may arise, depending on the outcome of recent patent actions. In particular, Hedge Fund trolls, arguably a misnomer as they otherwise do not act like trolls, file opportunistic patent challenges, ostensibly in the public's interest of reducing drug prices. Once the patent is challenged, the troll shorts the company's stock, without ever actually outwardly resorting to extortion or blackmail.[75]

As suggested earlier, even though biotechnology has yet to have success in the patent sharing world, I suggest that an influx of bottom feeding patent trolls might presage a shift in biotechnology patent pledging. This shift could even be partially a result of these trolls and the threats to freedom to operation that they bring, or alternatively as I have argued, because the same environments that attract some types of trolls also encourage patent sharing.

Put simply, looking at the economics, we would expect to see more troll behavior in biotechnology: trolls tend to be lean, strategic, unscrupulous, opportunistic and profit-driven entities[76] that seemingly, given the opportunity to make money, should move in to the biotechnology space. The fact that they have not (at least according to conventional wisdom) yet moved in en masse (the constant prediction thereof notwithstanding)[77] I argue is supportive of my position, or at least a strong indicator that freedom to operate is not as big a problem in biotechnology as it is in hi-tech.[78]

Further, this seeming lack of trolls is all the more surprising given the difficulties in inventing around an asserted patent in the biotechnology space. Recent data suggests that while increasing, biotechnology and

---

74 Mark A. Lemley & A. Douglas Melamed, *Missing the Forest for the Trolls*, 113 COLUM. L. REV. 2117, 2117–89 (2013).

75 Joseph Gulfo, *Hedge Funds, "Reverse Trolls" Crushing Biopharma Innovation*, CNBC (Jul. 22, 2015).

76 *See* Lauren Cohen, Umit Gurun & Scott Duke Kominers, *Patent Trolls: Evidence from Targeted Firms* 4 (Harvard Bus. Sch., Working Paper No. 15-002, 2015).

77 Ronald I. Eisenstein, *Why Patent Trolls Threaten Biotech*, THE SCIENTIST (May 1, 2006).

78 Robin Feldman & W. Nicholson Price II, *Patent Trolling: Why Bio and Pharmaceuticals Are at Risk*, 17 STAN. TECH. L. REV. 773, 773 (2014).

pharmaceutical companies still receive far fewer licensing or settlement demands than their hi-tech and software counterparts.[79] The few trolls that are entering the biotechnology sector are likely not bottom feeders, but rather traditional trolls that can turn a profit in biotechnology by asserting strong patents.

Why is this the case?

IX. TROLL-FRIENDLY ENVIRONMENTS: HI-TECH v. BIOTECHNOLOGY PATENTING

Troll-friendly environments, particularly for the subset of bottom feeders, seem to be populated by huge numbers of talented but underfunded startups and corresponding risk averse venture capitalists that might be easily deterred by the threat of litigation.[80] These startups are cannon fodder for trolls that attempt to persuade companies to sign licensing agreements or face expensive, time-consuming and venture capital (VC)-funding-losing litigation.[81] These troll-friendly environments are further characterized by a number of patent related factors. Succinctly these factors result in a patent ecosystem wherein stakeholders rarely possess clear and absolute freedom to operate.

Importantly, patent law, while seemingly nondiscriminatory in its statutory underpinnings, does in fact discriminate between different types of technologies—nominally divided into the predictable (hi-tech) and non-predictable arts (biotechnology)—in the application of the law by the courts.[82] As such, even at its most basic level, without considering outside factors, such aspects of the business, regulatory and innovation environments, the application of the laws relating to patenting in hi-tech are substantively different than their application to patenting in biotechnology.

In practice, in addition to the discriminatory practices of the courts, patenting in hi-tech tends to cover more incremental innovation in which

---

[79] Robin Feldman & Mark A. Lemley, *Does Patent Licensing Mean Innovation?* 27 (Stanford Law Sch. John M. Olin Program in Law & Econ., Working Paper No. 473, 2015).

[80] Robin Feldman, *Patent Demands and Startup Companies: The View from the Venture Capital Community* 49 (UC Hastings Research Paper No. 75, 2013).

[81] Colleen Chien, *Startups and Patent Trolls*, 17 STAN. TECH. L. REV. 461, 461 (2014).

[82] DAN L. BURK & MARK A. LEMLEY, THE PATENT CRISIS AND HOW THE COURTS CAN SOLVE IT (2009).

one patent builds only minimally on its predecessors. Additionally, hi-tech products are the result of multiple components each with their own set of relevant patents. The result of this patenting strategy can be enormous numbers of patents covering hi-tech products. These criss-crossing rights can create patent thickets where many of the largest companies by necessity must cross-license with others in the field to gain freedom to operate.

More specifically, in the hi-tech environment there can be: (i) enormous numbers of patents that make comprehensive searches expensive or even ineffective, many of these patents are not actively practiced or are severely underutilized; (ii) successive cycles of low quality patents[83] that are often sold cheaply and in bulk to patent trolls by (failing) companies seeking to monetize their assets;[84] (iii) patents with unclear property rights and scope,[85,86,87]—that is, ineffectual or purposely obfuscated notice[88,89]—often because the technologies themselves are inherently difficult to describe and are typically drafted using unclear and imprecise terminologies and that, unless resolved through expensive litigation, may or may not cover the products against which the patents are asserted; (iv) claim methods that result in patent scope that is so overly broad as to potentially preempt most other efforts in the area;[90,91] (v) the use of patents for purposes not directly related to innovation and technology transfer, such as: to signal investors, for use in defensive strategies,

---

[83] R. Polk Wagner, *Understanding Patent-Quality Mechanisms*, 157 U. PA. L. REV. 2135, 2135–73 (2009).

[84] *But*, c.f. Timo Fischer & Joachim Henkel, *Patent Trolls on Markets for Technology: An Empirical Analysis of NPEs' Patent Acquisitions*, 41 RES. POL'Y 1519, 1519 (2012).

[85] James Bessen & Michael J. Meurer, *The Direct Costs from NPE Disputes*, 99 CORNELL L. REV. 387, 388 (2014).

[86] Mark A. Lemley & Carl Shapiro, *Probabilistic Patents*, 19 J. ECON. PERSP. 75, 75–98 (2005).

[87] Peter S. Menell, *Promoting Patent Claim Clarity* (UC Berkeley Pub. Law Research Paper No. 2171287, 2012).

[88] FED. TRADE COMM'N, THE EVOLVING IP MARKETPLACE: ALIGNING PATENT NOTICE AND REMEDIES WITH COMPETITION 184 (MARCH 2011).

[89] Peter S. Menell & Michael J. Meurer, *Notice Failure and Notice Externalities*, 5 J. LEGAL ANALYSIS 1, 2 (2013).

[90] Kevin Emerson Collins, *Patent Law's Functionality Malfunction and the Problem of Overbroad, Functional Software Patents*, 90 WASH. U.L. REV. 1399 (2013).

[91] Mark A. Lemley, *Software Patents and the Return of Functional Claiming*, 2013 WIS. L. REV. 905 (2013).

and/or, in seeking preemptive freedom to operate[92] and blocking competitors,[93] and (vi) complicated clearances.[94]

Finally, biotechnology patents tend to be maintained longer in relation to hi-tech patents, where at often times, firms will allow their patents to lapse. Judge Moore argues that this is consistent with business practices wherein hi-tech patents are submitted later in the product development cycle and so are generally maintained longer, whereas in biotechnology, where patents are drafted earlier in the development of the product, patents related to product failures or missteps may be abandoned earlier.[95] With this in mind, there may be a relatively higher number of core-business-irrelevant, albeit salable or sharable, patents within the hi-tech industries, given their longer maintenance lives. On the other hand, any biotechnology patent that makes it into middle age has likely proved its worth to its holder, is highly valued[96] and is unlikely to be sold or shared.

As a result of these and other factors, the hi-tech environment is often characterized by patent thickets comprising hundreds if not thousands of similarly scoped or overlapping patents. The result is a situation in which many in the software and hi-tech sector operate in a state of unavoidable rampant patent infringement.[97]

In contrast, the thicket environment does not yet exist in biotechnology.[98] The academic success of the anticommons theory,[99]

---

[92] HAROLD C. WEGNER & STEPHEN B. MAEBIUS, PATENT FLOODING: AMERICA'S NEW PATENT CHALLENGE (2002).

[93] Theresa Veer & Florian Jell, *Contributing to Markets for Technology? A Comparison of Patent Filing Motives of Individual Inventors, Small Companies and Universities*, 32 TECHNOVATION 513, 513–22 (2012).

[94] Mark A. Lemley & Carl Shapiro, *Patent Holdup and Royalty Stacking*, 85 TEX. L. REV. 2163, 2163 (2006).

[95] Kimberly A. Moore, *Worthless Patents*, 20 BERKELEY TECH. L.J. 1521 (2005).

[96] Thomas H. Kramer, *Proposed Legislative Solutions to the Non-Practicing Entity Patent Assertion Problem: The Risks for Biotechnology and Pharmaceuticals*, 39 DEL. J. CORP. L. 467 (2014).

[97] FED. TRADE COMM'N, TO PROMOTE INNOVATION: THE PROPER BALANCE OF COMPETITION AND PATENT LAW AND POLICY (2003).

[98] Jorge L. Contreras, *Patent Pledges*, 47 ARIZ. ST. L.J. 543 (2015).

[99] Michael A. Heller & Rebecca S. Eisenberg, *Can Patents Deter Innovation: The Anticommons in Biomedical Research*, 280 SCI. 698, 698–701 (1998).

thoughtful reasoning,[100] and anecdotal evidence notwithstanding,[101] numerous studies have failed to find evidence of thickets and anti-commons in biotechnology,[102] or even evidence that patents impede innovation in biotechnology.[103] This is the case even though some rights and necessary tools in the development of biopharmaceutical and biotechnology products may be held by others, including competitors.

Looking at patents in general: In biotechnology, drugs and/or tools tend to be covered by one or only a couple of patents that describe the invention with sufficient detail and specificity that it might be difficult to broadly reinterpret the patent for later assertion by trolls. Often the final marketed product in the pharmaceutical industry is covered by at most a handful of patents.[104] More specifically: (i) the top patenting corporations by far remain those in the hi-tech space, with biotechnology not producing anywhere near the enormous number of hi-tech patents.[105] Even the biggest biotechnology patent holders annually create orders of magnitude fewer patents than their hi-tech counterparts;[106] (ii) unlike hi-tech where the comparison of patent portfolios has been compared to

---

100 Id.

101 Thomas D. Jeitschko & Nanyun Zhang, *On the Challenges Facing Patent Pooling in Biotechnology*, 19 J. INTELL. PROP. RTS. 113, 113 (2014).

102 Stephen HANSEN, MICHAEL KISIELWSKI & JANA L. ASHER, AM. ASS'N FOR THE ADVANCEMENT OF SCI., INTELLECTUAL PROPERTY IN THE AAAS SCIENTIFIC COMMUNITY 3 (2005); JOHN P. WALSH, CHARLENE CHO & WESLEY M. COHEN, PATENTS, MATERIAL TRANSFERS AND ACCESS TO RESEARCH INPUTS IN BIOMEDICAL RESEARCH 1, 6 (2005); David E. Adelman & Kathryn L. DeAngelis, *Patent Metrics: The Mismeasure of Innovation in the Biotech Patent Debate,* 85 TEX. L. REV. 1677 (2007); Dianne Nicol, Jane L. Nielsen, Johnathon E. Liddicoat, Christine Critchley & Tess Whitton, *The Innovation Pool in Biotechnology: The Role of Patents in Facilitating Innovation*, SSRN 2503314 (Sept. 30, 2014).

103 Van Overwalle *supra* note 45; Christopher M. Holman, *The Impact of Human Gene Patents on Innovation and Access: A Survey of Human Gene Patent Litigation*, 76 UMKC L. REV. 295 (2007); Christopher M. Holman, *Learning from Litigation: What Can Lawsuits Teach Us about the Role of Human Gene Patents in Research and Innovation?*, 18 KAN. JL & PUB. POL'Y 215 (2008).

104 Anup Malani & Jonathan S. Masur, *Raising the Stakes in Patent Cases*, 101 GEO. L.J. 637, 637 (2013).

105 *Calendar Year Patent Statistics (January 1 to December 31)*, US PTO (2016), at https://www.uspto.gov/web/offices/ac/ido/oeip/taf/reports.htm.

106 Adelman & Deanglis, *supra* note 102, at 1677.

measuring the height of each stack of papers,[107] biotechnology companies rely heavily on the ability to enforce their few patents against competitors, low quality patents would be less than useful in these instances; (iii) the Federal Circuit has used a number of policy levers in the recent past to reign in patent scope for biotechnology patents,[108] including for example the recent ruling regarding the enablement doctrine;[109] (iv) given the nature of biotechnology innovation and the often tedious regulatory environments, in contrast to hi-tech, patents still signal quality to potential investors;[110] and (v) without empirical proof of patent thickets in biotechnology, clearances are much less difficult to obtain than in hi-tech.

It is this environment that has also resulted in the reported growth of patent pledging and sharing in hi-tech: when freedom to operate is difficult to assess or possess, private ordering solutions such as patent pools and clearinghouses are very helpful. Moreover, this same environment makes smaller companies that much more receptive to patent pledges and covenants not to sue as they appreciate that their technology will likely read on a number of patents.

---

107 Colleen V. Chien, *From Arms Race to Marketplace: The New Complex Patent Ecosystem and Its Implications for the Patent System*, 62 HASTINGS L.J. 297, 304–06 (2010).

108 Dov Greenbaum, *An Analysis of the Evolution of the Written Description Requirement vis-à-vis DNA and Biotechnological Inventions*, 1 RECENT PATENTS ON DNA & GENE SEQUENCES 138 (2007).

109 Promega Corp. v. Life Technologies Corp., 773 F.3d 1338 (Fed. Cir. 2014).

110 Michael B. Heeley, Sharon F. Matusik & Neelam Jain, *Innovation, Appropriability, and the Underpricing of Initial Public Offerings*, 50 ACAD. MGMT. J. 209, 209–25 (2007); Elisa Alvarez Garrido & Gary Dushnitsky, *Are Entrepreneurial Venture's Innovation Rates Sensitive to Investor Complementary Assets? Comparing Biotech Ventures Backed by Corporate and Independent VCs*, 37 STRATEGIC MANAGEMENT J. 819, 819–34 (2015); David H. Hsu & Rosemarie H. Ziedonis, *Resources as Dual Sources of Advantage: Implications for Valuing Entrepreneurial Firm Patents*, 37 STRATEGIC MANAGEMENT J. 761, 761–81 (2013).

X. TROLL-FRIENDLY ENVIRONMENTS: HI-TECH v. BIOTECHNOLOGY PRODUCTS

Hi-tech patents tend to have a short shelf life both in terms of their technological applicability and also in their general ability to be monetized.[111] By the end of their term hi-tech companies might no longer care to enforce their patents, even selling them to trolls, who statistically do tend to enforce patents later in their term.[112] Biopharmaceutical patents, due to the long lead time necessary to develop drugs, tend to have longer shelf lives, and the entirety of that life is often monetizable.[113]

More specifically, the most common and possibly lucrative troll business model is that of the bottom feeders who seek to license weak broad patents and/or portfolios of patents to companies with ready-to-market or nearly mature products that are likely covered by hundreds if not thousands of patents.[114] Moreover, these products typically come to market quickly such that even if the infringing technology is the result of independent invention (as is most often the case), that technology probably developed and was incorporated into products even before the asserted patents were published.[115]

In contrast, biotechnology products, particularly those in the pharmaceutical fields, require expensive, and intensive, long lead times. Problematic patents often come to managers' attention early in the development process—often as the result of extensive due diligence. Moreover, these products are the result of extensive expertise held by a relatively small number of stakeholders, and given the need to hold on to patents for the duration of the product life cycle, there are fewer patents to be snapped up and monetized.

---

[111] Richard A. Posner, *Why There Are Too Many Patents in America*, ATLANTIC MONTHLY (July 12, 2012, 10:20 AM).

[112] Love, *supra* note 72.

[113] Ashley Chuang, *Fixing the Failures of Software Patent Protection: Deterring Patent Trolling by Applying Industry-Specific Patentability Standards*, 16 S. CAL. INTERDISC. L.J. 215 (2006).

[114] U.S. GOV'T ACCOUNTABILITY OFFICE, *supra* note 66.

[115] Lemley & Melamed, *supra* note 74, at 2117–89.

XI. PATENT SHARING: PROMOTING A PERCEPTION OF FREEDOM TO OPERATE IN A TROLL INFESTED WORLD

Reiterating the premise that perceptions regarding freedom to operate play a large part in the necessity for patent sharing, the lack of trolls in biotechnology—the seemingly inviting financial incentives notwithstanding—may be indicative of positive perceptions regarding the ability to discern freedom to operate within biotechnology.

The growth of trolls may not only be a proxy measure for determining whether an environment promotes patent sharing. Perhaps patent sharing in an industry may also be, in some cases, an actual symptom or outcome of the growth of trolls in those particular industries.

In the past, as a result of the perceived and sometimes real threat of competitor lawsuits, technology companies in particular have amassed large and expensive patent stockpiles in the manner of the mutually assured destruction strategies of the Cold War.[116,117] In some recent examples, companies have even spent billions of dollars purchasing, and subsequently millions of dollars in maintaining, seemingly non-core business related patents.[118] Many of these are also problematic or low quality patents,[119,120,121] as described above. However, they do not seem to help.[122] These expensive war chests seem to be ineffective in preventing large scale expensive litigation, and perhaps now more importantly, in defending companies against trolls who do not seem to fear patents being asserted against them: axiomatically trolls tend not to have any products that patents can threaten. And practicing competitors have sued each other despite these patent war chests.[123] As the ongoing smartphone

---

116 Bernard T. Feld, *A Pledge: No First Use*, 23 BULL. OF THE ATOMIC SCIENTISTS 46, 46–48 (1967).

117 Michael J. Meurer & James E. Bessen, *Lessons for Patent Policy from Empirical Research on Patent Litigation*, 9 LEWIS & CLARK L. REV. 1, 1–27 (2005).

118 Lemley & Melamed, *supra* note 74, at 2117–89.

119 Gideon Parchomovsky & R. Polk Wagner, *Patent Portfolios*, 154 U. PA. L. REV. 1, 1–77 (2005).

120 *But*, c.f., Robert P. Merges, *Patents, Entry and Growth in the Software Industry* (Aug. 1, 2006).

121 FED. TRADE COMM'N, *supra* note 88.

122 Chien, *supra* note 107, at 297.

123 Lemley & Melamed, *supra* note 74, at 2117–89.

wars[124] indicate, the theories of mutually assured destruction that at least partially promoted the hoarding of large offensive and defensive patent caches[125,126] did not always prevent onerous and costly litigation, even when litigating against practicing entities and direct competitors.

Further, patents are not cheap to maintain. In some instances, large patent portfolios may require millions of dollars in renewal fees and other patent related costs, particularly when accounting for international filings.[127] With little business value, ubiquitous simultaneous invention,[128] questionable patent validity (considering the changing legal environment)[129] and trends to overly broad patents, and their generally unhelpful nature in fending off aggressive trolls and other lawsuits, technology companies might also forgo troll-like opportunities to monetize their non-core patents, particularly given the negative connotations associated with trolls.[130] Until now most companies shed patents for philanthropic goals, the generation of goodwill, patent related cost cutting,[131] and tax related reasons.[132] However, industries which are otherwise abandoning their patents at unprecedented rates,[133] without a strong financial or other business reason to actively use their patent war chests, might now be incentivized to share these patent stockpiles.

Through sharing, many companies stand to gain reputational points for seeming like good corporate citizens, engendering public trust and goodwill in the company by sharing these less than useful stockpiles, an

---

[124] Michael A. Carrier, *A Roadmap to the Smartphone Patent Wars and FRAND Licensing*, 2 CPI ANTITRUST CHRONICLE (2012).

[125] ROBERT P. MERGES, PATENTS, ENTRY AND GROWTH IN THE SOFTWARE INDUSTRY (2006).

[126] COLLEEN CHIEN, EXCLUSIONARY AND DIFFUSIONARY LEVERS IN PATENT LAW (2015).

[127] U.S. GOV'T ACCOUNTABILITY OFFICE, GAO-03-910, EXPERTS' ADVICE FOR SMALL BUSINESSES SEEKING FOREIGN PATENTS (2003).

[128] Lemley & Melamed, *supra* note 74, at 2117–89.

[129] Alice Corporation Pty. Ltd. v. CLS Bank International, et al., 134 S.Ct. 2347 (2015).

[130] Lemley & Melamed, *supra* note 74, at 2117–89.

[131] Scott Smith, *Top 5 Reasons to Audit Your Patent Portfolio in 2013*, LAW 360 (Mar. 8, 2013).

[132] Nicole Ziegler, Oliver Gassmann & Sascha Friesike, *Why Do Firms Give away Their Patents for Free?*, 37 WORLD PATENT INFORMATION 19, 19–25 (2014).

[133] Clara Guibourg, *Abandoned Patents Jump as Businesses Slash Intellectual Property Costs*, CITYA.M. (Oct. 19, 2015).

important benefit in many industries.[134] Moreover, the alternative—that is, acting like a troll—can result in the loss of reputational points when companies opt to assert their less business relevant patent portfolios against companies. Moreover, sharing, broad licensing and covenants not to sue might end up as more reliable cost-saving measures that promote profitable innovation for all stakeholders. Sharing is just a codification of the underlying strategies behind the mutually assured destruction patent races: self-preservation and seeking freedom to operate. How so? Sharing, which effectively dumps large numbers of accessible patents in the public domain may help create, or often simply be the perception thereof, an environment that allows for freedom to operate in an otherwise troll infested world. That perception may be necessary for many small companies to continue to function and innovate. Notably those small companies are often the source of in-licensed technologies.

Companies like Tesla that ostensibly opened much of their patent portfolio are likely unconcerned that their competitors—the uninterested and established major car manufacturers—will co-opt their research and development efforts when given access to their patent portfolio. Rather, as discussed in Chapter 1, innovative companies like Tesla need to seed and incentivize smaller companies to work toward developing the necessary infrastructure and popular support that will allow for greater adoption of their technology, reducing costs for everyone; the dumping of patents into the marketplace arguably creates the necessary false sense of security for start-ups that they will not be sued, perhaps even masking the threat of trolls.

In this case, Tesla ironically is like a mid- to late-twentieth century IBM, promoting the development of the personal computer clones that will grow IBM's market through making its proprietary innovation open to all. Those areas of technology that are not pledging their patents are like Apple and its smaller closed environment.

Does that mean that outside of the few examples described herein, we are unlikely to see a greater push to share in biotechnology given the dearth of trolls?

Perhaps not. As aspects of hi-tech and biotechnology continue to merge, for example in the areas of medical devices, bioinformatics or synthetic biology, the biotechnology industry would be wise to look to incentivizing the creation of their own patent pools and/or clearinghouses

---

[134] Timothy Caulfield, Edna Einsiedel, Jon F. Merz & Dianne Nicol, *Trust, Patents and Public Perceptions: The Governance of Controversial Biotechnology Research*, 24 NATURE BIOTECHNOLOGY 1352, 1352–54 (2006).

to head off the influx of trolls chased out of the hi-tech space and lured by the promises of enormous profits in biotechnology. While anecdotal evidence has in the past suggested that trolls were industry specific, evidence from the growing emergence of trolls in the energy sector might suggest otherwise, albeit possibly as a result of greater reliance on software and technology in this area.[135] The threat of trolls in biotechnology becomes all the more disconcerting as universities and other research institutions failing to otherwise monetize their growing patent portfolios consider patent aggregators and other non-practicing entities as viable monetization options.

CONCLUSION

Hi-tech patents and patent strategies and the nature of the industry have created an environment in which the limitations on freedom to operate result in a reality in which everyone stands to benefit from patent sharing. Out of the failed theories of Mutually Assured Destruction, a new era of Mutually Assured Sharing creates an ecosystem that can promote freedom to operate and deflate the threat of trolls: even when it does not actually create freedom to operate, in a world infested with trolls, it creates a perception of freedom to operate, a perception potentially necessary to incentivize otherwise fearful startups from innovating.

In contrast, in biotechnology, the nature of their patents and their patent strategies result in a reality where most of these factors do not exist and, as a result, neither do trolls in any significant number. Without these factors, and without the fear of trolls, patent sharing in biotechnology has been mostly limited to humanitarian needs or idiosyncratic corporate strategies.

Given hi-tech's motives and limited options, it will be interesting to see whether Google's heretofore short experiment in buying up patents in a seemingly straightforward and simple process[136] will lead to fewer donated patents and more patents landing in Google's lap,[137] which may or may not be a clearinghouse. Will Google become the anti-troll and create a new environment where patent sharing is not necessary to imply

---

[135] *Are Patent Trolls Now Targeting the Energy Industry?*, MORGAN, LEWIS & BOCKIUS LLP (March 2014).

[136] *Google Patent Programs*, GOOGLE, http://www.google.com/patents/licensing/.

[137] Tam Harbert, *Google Bought 28% of the Patents It Liked during Its Patent Purchase Experiment*, IEEE SPECTRUM (Aug. 3, 2015).

freedom to operate? Even months after the close of Google's Patent Purchase Program, Google has been somewhat circumspect in the release of relevant information. Or alternatively will the continued growth of the lucrative troll industry result in a loss of stigma associated with trolls and a growing trend for even patent practicing companies to resort to troll-like strategies, opting for short term profits over long-term innovation inducing?

4. Patent pledges in green technology

Bassem Awad[*]

Technology lies at the centre of the climate change debate and plays a pivotal role in addressing the global challenge of sustainable development in today's economy. The transfer and timely diffusion of green technologies required for mitigation and adaptation are among the major challenges faced by the international community.[1] Recent reports demonstrate that trade, when accompanied by appropriate regulation, can facilitate the transition to a green economy by fostering the exchange of green goods and services, including technologies, and by increasing resource efficiency and generating economic opportunities and employment.[2] Developing the green economy requires new business models that reduce environmental impacts to transform our world and achieve the United Nations Sustainable Development Goals (SDGs).[3]

Green technologies, also called "environmentally sound technologies" or "climate friendly technologies", cover the full spectrum of innovation that protects the environment. They are less polluting, use resources in a

---

* An earlier version of this chapter was first published by the Centre for International Governance Innovation in November 2015 and the revised version is republished with permission.

1 *See* Carlos M. Correa, *Mechanisms for International Cooperation in Research and Development in the Area of Climate Change*, in TECHNOLOGICAL COOPERATION AND CLIMATE CHANGE: ISSUES AND PERSPECTIVES 37 (2011).

2 *See* UNITED NATIONS ENVIRONMENT PROGRAMME, TOWARD A GREEN ECONOMY: PATHWAYS TO SUSTAINABLE DEVELOPMENT AND POVERTY ERADICATION 1 (2011); THE WORLD BANK, GREEN GROWTH: THE PATHWAY TO SUSTAINABLE DEVELOPMENT 1 (2012); ORGANISATION FOR ECONOMIC CO-OPERATION AND DEVELOPMENT, GREEN GROWTH AND SUSTAINABLE DEVELOPMENT: TOWARDS GREEN GROWTH 1 (2011).

3 On 25 September 2015, the 193 countries of the UN General Assembly adopted the 2030 Development Agenda titled "Transforming Our World". The SDGs goals include the need to ensure access to affordable, reliable, sustainable and modern energy for all while promoting sustainable industrialization and fostering innovation.

more sustainable manner, recycle more of their waste and by-products, and handle residual waste in a more acceptable manner than the technologies for which they were substitutes.[4] Despite their diversity,[5] green technology innovation and its transfer are key components of the fight against climate change, in both mitigating and adapting to its harmful effects.[6]

Since the United Nations Framework Convention on Climate Change (UNFCCC) Bali meeting in 2007, the role of the patent system has been the subject of increased attention in climate change discussions on technology transfer. In particular, how the patent system can foster green innovation and promote dissemination of clean technologies on both the national and international stage. The patent system is essentially based on preserving the balance between the public welfare and private incentives. Public welfare is realized when knowledge is disseminated and widely used by members of society. Private incentives are conferred on inventors and creators by allowing them to exploit their works economically.

---

[4] UN Conference on Environment and Development, June 3–14, 1992, Agenda 21, Chapter 34, U.N. Doc. A/CONF.151/4 (1992).

[5] Green technology includes, according to Eric Lane, various categories and sub-categories: renewable-energy generation technologies such as solar, wind, hydro, wave and tidal, geothermal and biofuels; energy storage technologies such as fuel cells and advanced batteries; transportation technologies such as hybrid and electric vehicles; energy infrastructure technologies including smart grid, energy-efficient power systems, building materials and lighting technologies, bio-based plastics and other materials, water filtration and desalination systems; technologies that reduce pollution and emissions, and even carbon trading schemes and other green policies and investment mechanisms. *See* ERIC L. LANE, CLEAN TECH INTELLECTUAL PROPERTY: ECO-MARKS, GREEN PATENTS, AND GREEN INNOVATION 1 (2011).

[6] Mitigation is about slowing down global warming by reducing the level of greenhouse gases in the atmosphere. Among the many mitigation technologies already on the market are renewable energy sources, such as biofuels, biomass, wind, solar and hydro power; low carbon building materials; and emerging technologies which aim to capture carbon out of the atmosphere and lock it away. Adaptation involves dealing with the existing or anticipated effects of climate change, particularly in the developing, least developed and small island countries, which are most severely affected. In addition to "soft" technologies, such as crop rotation, hard technologies for adaptation include improved irrigation techniques to cope with drought, and new plant varieties which are resistant to drought or to salt water. *See* World Intellectual Property Organization, *Climate Change: The Technology Challenge*, WIPO MAGAZINE, April 2009, at 3.

However, the patent system performance indicates that the core technology that should be disseminated with the patent is not easily accessible in practice. The overlap of patent rights in the hands of multiple owners makes it impractical to use the patented invention. The "tragedy of the anticommons" expressed by Michael Heller and Rebecca Eisenberg in 1998 arises when too many owners with blocking power hold rights on previous innovations that may restrict future research.[7] The blocking of knowledge and research tools through multiple patents has revealed concerns about the effects of the patent system on climate change technology innovation.

Moreover, according to the United Nations Secretariat and many developing countries, there are significant barriers to green technology innovation and its transfer, and chief among them is intellectual property rights.[8] The transfer of green technology is not available at affordable prices for developing countries due to the patent laws that limit the use of knowledge disseminated. Such rights create an exclusive exploitation right for the holder of the invention within a specified territory and period of time, which tends to create a monopolistic situation characterized by high prices and restrictions on the dissemination of knowledge for the use of affordable green technology innovation.[9]

The simple existence of a patent on green technology innovation is not a barrier in itself to the transfer of that technology. Much depends on how the exclusive rights that come with a patent are deployed; and how they can be used in transferring green technology.[10] In recent years,

---

7 *See* Michael A. Heller & Rebecca S. Eisenberg, *Can Patents Deter Innovation? The Anticommons in Biomedical Research*, 280 SCIENCE 698, 698 (1998); TOM MAGERMAN, IMPACT AND CONSEQUENCES OF SCIENCE-INTENSIVE PATENTING: IN SEARCH OF ANTI-COMMONS EVIDENCE USING LATENT SEMANTIC ANALYSIS TEXT MINING TECHNIQUES 8 (2011).

8 *See* MATTHEW RIMMER, INTELLECTUAL PROPERTY AND CLIMATE CHANGE: INVENTING CLEAN TECHNOLOGIES 39–82 (2011); Ahmed Abdel-Latif, *Intellectual Property Rights and the Transfer of Climate Change Technologies: Issues, Challenges, and Way Forward*, 15 CLIMATE POL'Y 103, 103–126 (2015).

9 Neither the original UNFCCC treaty nor the Kyoto protocol expressly mentions intellectual property in any of their provisions. However, the role of intellectual property rights has acquired interest in the past few years. At COP 18 in Doha, the UNFCCC body charged with climate change technology policy decided to include intellectual property rights as an area for which clarity would be needed on its role in the development and transfer of climate technologies.

10 *See* WIPO Informal Consultation, Climate Change and the Intellectual Property System: What Challenges, What Options, What Solutions? (Nov. 14, 2008).

states, business actors, and individual researchers have acknowledged the necessity of a technological collaborative mechanism in the field of clean technology to stimulate and encourage the transfer of existing and emerging green technologies among academia, public institutions and the private sector. At the fifteenth session of Copenhagen climate change Conference of the Parties (COP) in 2009, representatives of developing countries called for the adoption of international rules and mechanisms to increase collaboration in international research and dissemination of clean technologies through methods that are open source rather than proprietary.[11] More recently, the Paris Agreement adopted at the twenty-first session of the COP in 2015 invited the parties to support collaborative approaches to research and development, and facilitate access to technology (art. 10).[12] One promising and prominent knowledge-sharing mechanism for sharing knowledge that can be adopted is the patent pledge, whereby a patent holder makes a voluntary public commitment to make the patent available for use by any other person.

This chapter, organized in three sections, analyses the various forms of patent pledges related to green technologies and highlights the legal components required for the green technology sector. The first section presents the emergence of collaborative models for green technology innovation and their rationales. The second part examines the key forms of patent pledges related to environmentally-sound technologies including Eco-Patent Commons, GreenXchange and COSIA for the oil sands industry. The third part discusses the legal framework and governance rules for green patent pledges. The chapter concludes with observations on the viability of patent pledges for addressing broader dissemination of green technology in furtherance of UNFCCC goals.

---

[11] *See* Robert Collier & Josephine Mutugu, *Who Owns the Clean Tech Revolution? Intellectual Property Rights and International Cooperation*, IN THE UN CLIMATE NEGOTIATIONS, CTR. FOR ENVTL. PUB. POL'Y, GOLDMAN SCHOOL OF PUB. POL'Y, U. OF CAL., BERKELEY 21 (2009); Matthew Rimmer, *supra* note 8 at 311.

[12] United Nations Framework Convention on Climate Change, Adoption of the Paris Agreement, Paris, FR., Nov. 30–Dec. 11, 2015, UN Doc. FCCC/CP/2015/L.9 (Dec. 12, 2015).

I. THE EMERGENCE OF COLLABORATIVE MODELS FOR GREEN TECHNOLOGY INNOVATION AND THEIR RATIONALE

According to the Directorate for Science, Technology and Industry of the Organisation for Economic Co-operation and Development (OECD), the environment for innovation has totally changed in the past few years. Competition is increasing globally; knowledge has become more multidisciplinary and more diverse, making innovation riskier and more expensive. The development of an effective innovation strategy requires new mechanisms that facilitate the circulation of knowledge between independent parties. Private sector actors investing heavily in green technologies recognized the need to find a new solution to an old challenge by seeking new approaches to get rapid access to clean technologies.[13]

For decades, private sector firms negotiated different types of partnerships, joint ventures, and licensing agreements to obtain technologies held by others to bring new products to the market.[14] However, the urgent need for green technology diffusion and the complexity of some technologies that are critical to addressing climate change has led to new collaborative structures and sharing of technologies that benefit both innovators and society at large. The "own and protect" model for intellectual property rights that dominated global markets evolved, in this area, gradually towards a "sharing and collaboration" model. These collaborative models of green technology innovation have been inspired by their successful implementation in other sectors, such as information and communication technology (ICT) and telecommunication.[15] They

---

[13] *See* Koen De Backer, Vladimir Lopez-Bassols & Catalina Martinez, *Open Innovation in a Global Perspective: What Do Existing Data Tell Us?* 7 (Org. for Econ. Coop. & Dev., STI Working Paper 2008/4, 2008); *The OECD Innovation Strategy: Getting a Head Start on Tomorrow*, ORG. FOR ECON. COOP. & DEV. 1 (2010).

[14] *See* Keith E. Maskus & Ruth L. Okediji, *Intellectual Property Rights and International Technology Transfer to Address Climate Change: Risks, Opportunities and Policy Options*, Issue Paper No. 32, INT'L CTR. FOR TRADE AND SUSTAINABLE DEV. 3 (2010).

[15] *See* Collier & Mutugu, *supra* note 11; Brad Biddle, Frank X. Curci, Timothy F. Haslach, Gary E. Marchant, Andrew Askland & Lyn Gaudet, *The Expanding Role and Importance of Standards in the Information and Communications Technology Industry*, 52 JURIMETRICS J. 177, 177 (2012); Dieter Ernst, *American's Voluntary Standards System: A "Best Practice" Model for Innovation*

have also emerged on a voluntary basis, by technology holders who believe in the benefits of sharing technologies from several sources. Nevertheless, patent pledges raise the question of what can motivate patent holders to limit the enforcement of their patents and to widely disseminate their technological inventions.

Patent pledges provide several significant advantages not only for private firms but also for government, research centres and society in general. First, sharing patents promotes the advancement of research and development by allowing firms full access to and use of previous knowledge. Little progress would be made if firms were required to reproduce all the experiments of their predecessors.[16] Moreover, some innovations become more valuable when they are shared. Patents pledged in a pool became available to other innovators and can resolve disputes over blocking patents.[17] Sharing innovation facilitates access by overcoming intellectual property obstacles and accelerating scientific progress. Second, sharing patents may also enable firms to verify the findings of their competitors before spending their resources and efforts on flawed research. One of the problems currently challenging scientific research is the unreliability of research results. Many results disclosed in the past few years could not be replicated.[18] Third, the disclosure of patent information among competitors can serve to reduce research and development costs. The presence of numerous patents owned by different right-holders may no longer be an obstacle for firms when obtaining

---

Policy? (East-West Center Working Papers, Economics Series, No. 128, 2012); Jorge L. Contreras, *A Brief History of FRAND: Analyzing Current Debates in Standard Setting and Antitrust Through a Historical Lens*, 80 ANTITRUST L. J. 39, 39 (2015).

[16] *See* Anatole Krattiger & Stanley P. Kowalski, *Facilitating Assembly of and Access to Intellectual Property: Focus on Patent Pools and a Review of Other Mechanisms*, in INTELLECTUAL PROPERTY MANAGEMENT IN HEALTH AND AGRICULTURAL INNOVATION: A HANDBOOK OF BEST PRACTICES 138 (Anatole Krattiger et al. eds., 2007); Geertrui Van Overwalle, Esther Van Zimmeren, Birgit Verbeure & Gert Matthijs, *Models for Facilitating Access to Patents on Genetic Inventions*, 7 NATURE REVIEWS GENETICS 143, 144 (2006).

[17] Blocking patents are patents that block further development and commercialization of a product because of potential infringement when the product is used, manufactured or sold. *See* Steven C. Carlson, *Patent Pools and the Antitrust Dilemma*, 16 YALE J. ON REG. 359, 362 (1999).

[18] *See* The Economist, *Problems with Scientific Research: How Science Goes Wrong*, ECONOMIST (Oct. 19, 2013).

access to patented technologies.[19] A simple contribution can permit researchers to acquire the technology needed to efficiently pursue their activities. Firms usually prefer to avoid developing research streams that are the subject of numerous patents.[20] Finally, a fourth benefit resides in the fact that green patent pledges may help private sector firms to develop their negative public image gained over the past years as venture capitalists protecting their investments.

Despite the potential advantages of patent pledges, a number of significant criticisms can be associated with the use of collaborative mechanisms. The first concern is that private firms might lose their competitive advantage by allowing their competitors, or any third party, to make use of their patents while covering the costs of maintaining intellectual property (IP) rights. The concept of social-entrepreneurial enterprise can be advanced in this case to justify the emergence of patent pledges for clean technology innovation. It allows entrepreneurship to focus on social, cultural and environmental goals that benefit society rather than merely maximizing individual profits. Socially responsible enterprises can contribute part of their technology to promote transfer of clean innovation and to increase sustainable development. An additional concern is that patent pledges may shield trivial or invalid patents. Some partners may seek to obtain access to the pool of patents by offering negligible patents or ones that are likely to be invalidated in court.[21] Green patent pledges can avoid this situation by evaluating and selecting the patents pledged by each contributor.

II. MODALITIES OF PATENT PLEDGES IN GREEN TECHNOLOGY

In the context of environmental innovation, patent pledges are designed as cooperative ventures that allow green technology holders to pledge

---

19 *See* Yann Joly, *Open Source Approaches in Biotechnology: Utopia Revisited*, 59 ME. L. REV. 385, 400 (2007); Heller & Eisenberg, *supra* note 7 at 698; David E. Adelman & Kathryn L. DeAngelis, *Patent Metrics: The Mismeasure of Innovation in the Biotech Patent Debate*, 85 TEX. L. REV. 1677, 1699 (2007).

20 *See* Josh Lerner, *Patenting in the Shadow of Competitors*, 38 J. LAW & ECON. 463, 464 (1995).

21 Krattiger & Kowalski, *supra* note 16 at 147.

their patented technologies for widespread free use.[22] They simplify the access procedures and facilitate the non-exclusive use of materials for non-commercial purposes. Participation in and adhesion to such a collaborative model requires ownership of an intellectual property right and the pledge is usually subject to certain conditions. Green patent pledges usually take the form of community pledges, not unilateral pledges.[23] However, they do not yet address issues of product standardization or standards-development organizations (SDOs) due to the diversity of green technology innovation.[24]

Sharing or cooperative pools of pledged patents usually take the form of either a repository of donated patents relating to a specific field of research, or a system to facilitate the licensing process or other exploitation of the patent. Unlike contributing a patent to the public domain, patent pledges provide control to its members over the shared knowledge. Members of the pool share their innovation, which is covered by an intellectual property right, and allow others to use the protected work. Any improvement based on the pledged invention should be provided back to the rest of the members, with the same condition applied to access the pool. Nevertheless, the patent pledge is not a pure licensing agreement. Members do not have the right to negotiate the licensing condition of the new innovation, since it is pre-negotiated in the terms of accession.

While several green technology-sharing projects exist, three models are the most significant, by virtue of their participants and the value of the patents shared. The first is the "Eco-Patent Commons", a green technology patent-sharing of donated patents; the second is the "GreenXchange", a web-based marketplace that facilitates negotiating

---

[22] *See* Cynthia Cannady, *Access to Climate Change Technology by Developing Countries: A Practical Strategy*, INT'L CTR. FOR TRADE AND SUSTAINABLE DEV. (2009).

[23] As described by Contreras in Chapter 1, patent pledges are usually divided into two principal categories: community pledges and unilateral pledges. Community pledges are made by members of a specific group, according to some predetermined form or formula, with respect to a defined technology or set of patents. Unlike community patent pledges, unilateral pledges are made by firms independently and do not follow a pre-determined format. *See* Contreras, Chapter 1.

[24] Technical standards are used in the Information and Communication Technologies (ICTs) industry to ensure that products manufactured by different vendors can communicate and interoperate with one another seamlessly and invisibly to the consumer. Wi-Fi, USB and HTTP are examples of technical standards used in the technology marketplace. *See* Contreras, Chapter 1.

and licensing agreements between patent holders and potential licensees; and the third is Canada's Oil Sands Innovation Alliance (COSIA) model, a semi-open mechanism of sharing green knowledge.

A. Eco-Patent Commons

The Eco-Patent Commons (EPC)[25] is the first technology-sharing initiative that was established to foster access to green technology innovation. It was launched in January 2008 by the World Business Council for Sustainable Development (WBCSD), a Geneva based group, in collaboration with a number of large multinational companies, including IBM, Nokia, Pitney Bowes and Sony. The main objective of the Eco-Patent Commons was to promote and encourage cooperation and collaboration between green patent holders and potential users, to accelerate the innovation process and facilitate a sustainable development.[26]

The Eco-Patent Commons found its origins in the success of the Open Source model in the computing and software industries. It created a pool of knowledge by encouraging intellectual property rights holders to share patents for inventions that directly or indirectly provide environmental benefits. The main characteristic of this model was that patents pledged are made available to anyone for free use. No royalty is required from members to make use of the patent pledged, provided it is used in a product or process that produces some environmental benefit.[27] Individuals, public and/or private research and development centres, universities and companies could join the pool by simply pledging at least one patent. The ownership right remained with the pledging party.

The pledgers signed a non-assert pledge promising not to enforce the donated patent rights against those who use the patented technology to achieve an environmentally beneficial result including machines, manufactures, processes and part of a product or service. According to the ground rules of the EPC:

---

25 *See also* Contreras, Chapter 1.

26 *See* The Eco-Patent Commons, ECO-PATENT COMMONS, http://ecopatentcommons.org/.

27 *See* Mark Van Hoorebeek & William Onzivu, *The Eco-Patent Commons and Environmental Technology Transfer: Implications for Efforts to Tackle Climate Change* 4 CARBON & CLIMATE L. REV. 13, 18 (2010); Estelle Derclaye, *Not Only Innovation but also Collaboration, Funding, Goodwill and Commitment: Which Role for Patent Laws in Post-Copenhagen Climate Change Action*, 9 J. MARSHALL REV. INTELL. PROP. L. 657, 663 (2010).

> Implementers can make, use, sell, and import infringing machines, manufactures, processes, or compositions of matter under patents on the patent list without payment of any royalty or similar payments to patent pledgers if such infringing items alone or when included in a product or service, achieve an environmentally beneficial result.

The donated patents are not in the public domain, since the pledgers retained a defensive termination option.[28] The ground rules of the EPC revealed that the non-assert obligation survives and remains in force even when members withdraw from the commons. Hitachi, for example, withdrew from the Eco-Patent Commons in 2012. However, its patent relating to parts recycling, pledged in 2011, is still used by members of the Eco-Commons.

Since the launch of the Eco-Patent Commons, 105 eco-friendly patents have been contributed by 11 companies representing a variety of industries worldwide including Bosch, Dow, Fuji Xerox, Hewlett-Packard, IBM, Nokia, Pitney Bowes, Ricoh, Sony, Taisei and Xerox, in addition to the hosting organization, the Environmental Law Institute in Washington, DC.[29] More recently, the Executive Board of the Eco-Patent Commons decided on May 18, 2016 to cease operations with no further patents being processed or added, and no new members being accepted. However, the existing pledges will remain intact and irrevocable.

The key strength of the EPC was the diversity of patents pledged across different industries, which facilitate the transfer of knowledge

---

[28] According to the EPC Ground Rules: "A Patent Pledger may, at its option, terminate and render void *ab initio* its non-assert with respect to a party if: (a) That party is a member of the Commons and such party (or someone acting in concert with that party) asserts an unpledged patent, with a primary IPC [International Patent Classification] class on the Classification List, against that Patent Pledger's infringing machines, manufactures, processes, or compositions of matter (including products, services, and components thereof) where such infringing items alone (or when included in a product or service) reduce/eliminate natural consumption, reduce/eliminate waste generation or pollution, or otherwise provide environmental benefit, or (b) The party is not a Member of the Commons and asserts any patent infringement claim against that Patent Pledger or our infringing machines, manufactures, processes, or compositions of matter (including products, services, and components thereof). In the non-assert, the 'party' and the 'Pledger' includes their respective affiliates". *See Eco-Patent Commons Ground Rules*, WORLD BUS. COUNCIL FOR SUSTAINABLE DEV., http://ecopatentcommons.org/about/rules.

[29] *See A Leadership Opportunity for Global Business to Protect the Planet*, THE ECO-PATENT COMMONS (July 2012), http://ecopatentcommons.org/sites/default/files/docs/ecopatentbrochure.pdf.

among green technology innovators. Nonetheless, several concerns have been raised regarding the absence of major energy players in developing and deploying green technologies. Recent analysis also shows that most of the patents pledged are neither used nor represent an essential source of business advantage to their owners. Bronwyn Hall and Christian Helmers, in their study "Can Patent Commons Help?" argue that these donated patents can be used as informational tools to drive green innovation towards the interest of pledging firms. Literature on patent pledges in the context of software showed that pledging non-essential patents would enable firms to mold the wider approvability regime that governs their activity.[30] In fact, the climate change technology industry is relatively new despite the ICT's sector. Firms are still looking for the appropriate format of sharing their essential green patents with other partners.

B. GreenXchange

The GreenXchange (GX) initiative is a web-based marketplace where companies can collaborate and share their intellectual property rights, which can lead to new sustainable innovation. The GreenXchange was born during conversations leading up to the World Economic Forum in Davos in 2009 and was launched in 2010 by Nike, Best Buy, Yahoo! and Creative Commons, along with six other organizations[31] with the underlying belief that the best way to stimulate sustainable innovation is through open innovation.[32] The GreenXchange philosophy is based on

---

[30] Bronwyn H. Hall & Christian Helmers, *Innovation and Diffusion of Clean/Green Technology: Can Patent Commons Help?*, 66 J. ENVTL ECON & MGMT 33, 37 (2013).

[31] The six member organizations are IDEO, Mountain Equipment Co-op, nGenera, Outdoor Industry Association, salesforce.com and 2degrees.

[32] The open innovation concept asserts that a company or organization should make greater use of external ideas in its business and allow its own ideas to go out beyond its own boundaries to others to use in their businesses. It is the use of purposive inflows and outflows of knowledge to accelerate internal innovation, and expand the markets for external use of innovation. Companies can commercialize internal ideas through channels outside of their current businesses in order to generate value for the organization. In addition, ideas can also originate outside the firm's own laboratories and be brought inside for commercialization. The open innovation model is typically described in contrast to the traditional closed innovation model, in which companies tended to innovate internally relying primarily on their own research and development departments to develop new products and process. *See* HENRY CHESBROUGH,

sharing existing patents held by corporations and universities using the open source community model for licensing pioneered by Creative Commons.

The mechanism adopted for sharing intellectual property rights is the GX semi-structured public license, which reserves some rights to the IP rights-holder while allowing others who are interested to acquire the right to use the patent in their own research. The licensing structure is available for use by any interested party, regardless of whether they are a member of the GX. Interested parties need to accept those license terms before accessing and using the technology.

GreenXchange's model provided three types of licensing structures: a standard option, a standard Plus option, and a research non-exempt option. The standard option offers GX users the right to utilize the patented technology for commercial or non-commercial use. The standard Plus option gives GX users a license that requires a payment and/or sets out restrictions, for example, the use of technology in a certain field or geographic area. The research non-exempt option promises that the IP rights-holder will not enforce its rights against those who use the technology for academic research, or improve and adapt the patented technology for non-commercial use.[33]

The main difference between the GX initiative and the Eco-Patent Commons model is the right of patentees to reserve their ownership and control of their patent rights. In addition, the pledgers can choose whether or not to charge a fee for the use of their pledged patent.[34] This ability to reserve should, in theory, encourage the contribution of more valuable patents. In the first two years GreenXchange received 463 patents; the majority were posted by Nike and the rest were provided respectively by Best Buy and the University of California at Berkeley.

Despite the interest it generated, the GX initiative has not been able to satisfy its original objectives. Most of its members did not pledge any patents to the GX, and according to Roya Ghafele and Robert O'Brien, the vast majority of the posted IP cannot be used in the creation of

---

OPEN INNOVATION: THE NEW IMPERATIVE FOR CREATING AND PROFITING FROM TECHNOLOGY 1 (2003).

[33] *See* Roya Ghafele & Robert D. O'Brien, *Open Innovation for Sustainability: Lessons from the GreenXchange Experience*, INT'L CTR. FOR TRADE AND SUSTAINABLE DEV. (June 2002); Lane, *supra* note 5.

[34] *See* Hall & Helmers, *supra* note 30 at 36; Ghafele & O'Brien, *supra* note 33; Krishna Ravi Srinivas, *Sink or Swim: Eco-Patent Commons and the Transfer of Environmentally Sustainable Technologies*, 2 BRIDGES TRADE BIORES TRADE & ENV'T REV. 16, 16 (2008).

commercial products. The challenge to develop the GX model resides in the lack of serious intention to collaborate and share innovation with other partners. Retrospective analysis suggests that the primary objective for GX members was to obtain access to knowledge in the pool and to build relationships rather than developing green technology innovation.[35]

C. Canada's Oil Sands Innovation Alliance (COSIA)

Canada's Oil Sands Innovation Alliance (COSIA) is a recent model of green technology collaboration. It was established in March 2012 between 12 leading oil sands producers to accelerate the pace of improvement in environmental performance in Canada's oil sands through collaborative action and innovation.[36] Members are invited to share their green technology along with relevant IP rights to accelerate innovation efforts while reducing the impact of oil sands on the environment. Each member provides other COSIA partners with access to research results and royalty-free patent use rights; however, members are bound by non-assertion clauses not to enforce patent or other IP rights against another party.

The COSIA model can be classified as a semi-open mechanism for collaboration. Green patents are shared among members of the alliance to resolve patent gridlocks in the oil sand industry. A third party has to join the alliance or to negotiate and acquire licenses to use patent pledges by COSIA members. The exclusivity of patent pledges among the alliance members distinguishes the COSIA model from the Eco-Patent Commons or the GreenXchange models where, in contrast, access is open to anyone interested in the technology. In addition, COSIA members retain the right not to license the shared technology to any other parties. COSIA has not yet filed any patents in Canada or in the United States. However, its members may be active in filing under their respective company names. Since its founding in 2012, COSIA has become one of the most active

---

[35] *See* Roya Ghafele & Robert D. O'Brien, *Open Innovation for Sustainability: Lessons from the GreenXchange Experience, An ICTSD Policy Brief*, 2013 INT'L J. OF ECON. BEHAV. AND ORG., 13, 16 (2013).

[36] COSIA currently includes 13 companies controlling about 90 percent of the total production in the oil sands: BP Canada, Canadian Natural Resources Limited, Cenovus Energy Incorporation, ConocoPhillips Canada Resources Corporation, Devon Canada Corporation, Imperial Oil, Nexen, Shell Canada Energy, Statoil Canada Limited, Suncor Energy Incorporation, Syncrude Canada Limited, Total E&P Canada Limited and Teck Resources Limited. *See Members*, CANADA'S OIL SANDS INNOVATION ALLIANCE, http://www.cosia.ca/about-cosia/members.

collaborative innovation hubs in Canada, with members sharing 936 green technologies and innovations that cost over CDN$1.3 billion.[37]

In summary, the three sharing arrangements of green patents described above demonstrate that pledged patents are not fully in the public domain to be used by anyone interested. They offer a primary access commitment based on broad provisions indicating the access condition for both members and the public over the patent pledged. Secondary or non-royalty commitments have not occurred yet in the green patent pledges.[38] In most cases, patent holders in these models have only an obligation to offer their patents on a royalty-free basis.

III. TOWARDS A LEGAL FRAMEWORK FOR GREEN PATENT PLEDGES

The concept of collaborative innovation that facilitates the circulation of knowledge is not new. It has been adopted over the past few years in various sectors and among different industries. The form and structure of collaborative mechanisms depend on the nature and characteristics of the knowledge in need.

International treaties and national intellectual property laws do not have specific provisions for protecting or sharing green patents. The intellectual property system is closely interrelated with many technologies that help in mitigating and limiting the impact of climate change, whereas IP systems make no substantial distinction between green or environmentally friendly and other technologies. At the same time, the global system of IP rights does not include provisions that would create legal barriers to the creation of a green patent pledges mechanism. Patent pledge mechanisms can be established for all types of innovation, but their establishment and organization is a challenging

---

37 See *2016 COSIA Project Portfolio*, CANADA'S OIL SANDS INNOVATION ALLIANCE, http://www.cosia.ca/uploads/files/performance-goals/COSIA-2016-Project-Portfolio.pdf.

38 Pledge commitments fall, according to Contreras, into three general categories: (1) the primary commitment to license patents, either on royalty-free or FRAND terms, or not to assert patents at all (primary access commitments), (2) more detailed commitments relating to the royalty rates or other amounts that will be charged (secondary royalty commitments), and (3) non-royalty commitments. Some patent pledges may contain one, two or all three types of commitments. *See* Contreras, Chapter 1.

matter. It requires an interdisciplinary coordination of scientists, legal professionals, business professionals and support from the industry.

The first challenge is related to the governance of green patent pledges and the entity that should ideally manage the pledge system. No standard criteria exist for green technology. It could be an international agency, a government sponsored agency, or a new private independent entity established to receive and exploit patents pledged to the pool. Eco-Patent Commons, for example, was hosted by the Environmental Law Institute in Washington, DC; GreenXchange was managed by private sector firms; and COSIA created an alliance with a separate administration body.

The best practice in other industries (such as the optical disc industry) is to let an independent license administrator manage the pool.[39] However, that might not be the appropriate solution for green technology innovation due to its characteristics and rapid impacts on health and environment. An international body similar to the WIPO GREEN initiative administrated by the World Intellectual Property Organization or the Green Climate Fund (GCF) under the United Nations Framework Convention on Climate Change (UNFCCC) could be the suitable entity to manage the green patent pledges around the globe,[40] where the credibility and legitimacy of an international organization will dismiss concerns of different stakeholders on several levels: developed versus developing countries; government versus private sector firms; individual innovators versus multinational entities.

The proposed global pool of green pledged patents aims to cover the current gap in the UNFCCC process by providing a secure channel for green technology deployment and transfer among various players, in both developed and developing countries, to share green innovation. The

---

[39] *See* Simon den Uijl, Rudi Bekkers & Henk J. de Vries, *Managing Intellectual Property Using Patent Pools: Lessons from Three Generations of Pools in the Optical Disc Industry*, 55 CALIF. MGMT. REV. 31, 34 (2013).

[40] The current mandates of WIPO GREEN and the GCF do not, however, include the possibility of creating a global collaborative mechanism for patent pledges. The GCF was established in 2009 within the framework of the UNFCCC to assist developing countries with climate change mitigation and adaptation practices. It supports projects, programs, policies and other activities only in UNFCCC developing country parties. The fund's business model framework has not yet developed approaches for involving the private sector. As for the WIPO GREEN initiative, it consists of a freely accessible online database and a broad network that brings together technology providers with those seeking green, innovative solutions. Its mandate does not include the licensing, commercialization or collaborative development of green technology innovation.

structure may benefit from the database collected under the WIPO GREEN initiative and the fund available at the GCF to facilitate the transfer and diffusion of green technologies.

The second challenge relates to the rules and regulations of such green mechanisms. In addition to the basic provisions dealing with the scope of the license and the rights over improvements, two main categories need special attention: the accession rules and the validity of patents pledged. Accession rules should be based on fair, reasonable and non-discriminatory terms. Hence, access should be granted automatically to all who meet eligibility criteria and are engaged in making technology improvements available on similar terms with a voluntary exception for firms based in developing countries. A third party should be able to have access to the shared technology under FRAND terms. This approach has the potential to prevent abusive practices by patent holders and eliminates a major barrier in accessing to green technology. Government may also play a vital role with respect to pledging patents derived from fully or partially publicly funded research related to green technology at no cost.

Finally, the validity of the patents pledged remains one of the unresolved concerns in managing a green patent pledge. The pledger is usually required to provide a valid patent in order to join the network. None of the three discussed models indicates whether the pledgers should keep the patent pledged in force by paying the cost of maintaining their patents and what the sanction in the case of expiration or invalidity may be.[41] The proposed structure of green pledges includes a provision to provide a valid patent to avoid pledging negligible or non-essential green patents. Pledger benefits are liable to be suspended in cases where IP rights over a pledged patent are lost due to negligence. Although it may be unreasonable to request the pledgers to disseminate and share their patents with others while continuing to pay the patent renewal fees to the national patent office, the social responsibility of pledgers in combating the harmful effects of climate change arguably could justify the obligation to maintain the validity of the patent pledged.

---

[41] According to the Eco-Patent Commons Ground Rules "Any company or other patent holder can participate as a Member in the Commons, whether or not a member of the Environmental Law Institute. Membership in the Commons is contingent on a party having one or more approved pledged patent(s) in force ... Payments of maintenance fees on pledged patents are in the sole discretion of the patent holder. When a pledged patent lapses or otherwise becomes unenforceable, the patent holder shall provide written notice to the Commons and the patent list will be updated." *See Eco-Patent Commons Ground Rules 3*, WORLD BUS. COUNCIL FOR SUSTAINABLE DEV., http://ecopatentcommons.org/about/rules.

CONCLUSION

According to UN Secretary-General Ban Ki-moon:

> [c]limate change is one of the most complex, multifaceted and serious threats the world faces. The response to this threat is fundamentally linked to pressing concerns of sustainable development and global fairness; of vulnerability and resilience; of economy, poverty reduction and society; and of the world we want to hand down to our children … We cannot go on this way for long … We cannot continue with business as usual. The time has come for decisive action on a global scale.[42]

Global climate change mitigation and adaptation require new solutions to an old challenge by seeking new approaches to get rapid access to clean technologies. In the most recent climate change conference held in December 2015 in Paris, Parties unanimously recognized the central role of technology development and transfer in achieving climate change goals. The Paris Agreement calls for an effective technology mechanism to facilitate the technology development and transfer in support of climate change mitigation and adaptation.

Green patent pledges are a new mechanism of collaboration and knowledge sharing that may work within the existing intellectual property legal regime in supporting the implementation of the Paris Agreement. They aim to simplify the process of finding accurate clean technologies and facilitate access to such technology. The governance of green patent pledges should be provided by an international entity sponsored and affiliated with an international organization where credibility and legitimacy can serve to resolve any concerns. The legal character of the arrangement should grant access to third parties interested in advancing the cause of climate change adaptation and mitigation. The structure of the model should be based on fair, reasonable and non-discriminatory terms to encourage the participation of innovators from around the globe. Social entrepreneurship considerations and the urgency of climate change risk provide incentives for various stakeholders to contribute with their technological innovations. Green patent pledge mechanisms may provide policy makers with a new answer to the old concern on how to accelerate the transfer and dissemination of affordable climate friendly technologies among developed and developing countries.

---

42 Ban Ki-moon, Secretary General of the United Nations, Address to the High-Level Event on Climate Change (Sept. 24, 2007).

PART II

Litigation involving patent pledges

5. Patent pledge enforcement theories[1]

Jorge L. Contreras

If patent pledges are to be meaningful from a legal standpoint, and not merely gratuitous statements, they must to some degree be legally enforceable. A variety of legal theories have emerged over the years regarding the enforceability of patent pledges. These theories are based in contract law, antitrust and competition law, property law and other legal areas. This chapter reviews and critiques existing theories surrounding patent pledge enforcement, and concludes with the author's own "market reliance" theory.

I. THE CONTRACTUAL PARADIGM

The patent pledges that have attracted the most attention in recent years have been FRAND commitments, which litigants and courts have increasingly described as "contractual."[2] As every first year law student learns, a contract under the common law is an enforceable promise that meets certain requirements such as consideration, offer, acceptance, and mutual assent.[3] At first blush, the interpretive and normative principles of contract law seem well suited to addressing the enforceability of patent pledges. But despite its initial appeal, contract doctrine fails in several fundamental regards to address the broad spectrum of patent pledges. This failure stems, at its root, from a fundamental mismatch between the

---

[1] This chapter is based on Jorge L. Contreras, *A Market Reliance Theory for FRAND Commitments and Other Patent Pledges*, 2015 UTAH L. REV. 479 (2015), with permission of the author.

[2] *See e.g.*, Microsoft Corp. v. Motorola, Inc., 854 F. Supp. 2d 993, 999 (W.D. Wash. 2012) ("The court agrees with Microsoft that … Motorola has entered into binding contractual commitments to license its essential patents on RAND terms").

[3] *See* RESTATEMENT (SECOND) OF CONTRACTS § 17(1) (1981).

paradigmatic contractual transaction (a direct bargain between two parties) and the more fluid and multilateral set of relationships that characterize patent pledges.

A. Third-Party Beneficiaries

Under a contract theory for enforcing patent pledges, the "contract" is theoretically formed between the patent holder and the relevant standards-development organization (SDO), either through the patent holder's membership in the SDO and accession to the SDO's policies, its execution of a formal membership agreement, or its submission of a letter of assurance (LOA) to the SDO. But in disputes over standards-essential patents, it is seldom the SDO that wishes to enforce the patent holder's pledge. SDOs are generally small, not-for-profit organizations that rarely have the resources or inclination to engage in patent litigation. Instead, the party wishing to enforce the FRAND commitment is usually a third party who wishes to implement a standard in a product using technology that infringes one or more patents. To do so under a common law contract theory, the manufacturer must invoke the third-party beneficiary doctrine. Thus, as described in the Restatement (Second) of Contracts, a third party that is an intended beneficiary of a contract between two contracting parties may sue to enforce that contract.[4] If the contracting parties did not intend that a third party benefit from the contract, then the third party is unable to enforce the contract.[5]

In most cases involving third-party beneficiaries, the intended beneficiary is known to the contracting parties and is either a named individual or a defined group of persons (such as an individual's heirs or legatees). The failure to identify a specific beneficiary, however, is not fatal.[6] Thus, if B promises to pay anyone from whom A purchases an automobile, and A purchases an automobile from C, then C may bring an action against B as the intended beneficiary of the contract, even though C's identity was not known to A or B at the time the contract was made.[7] At least two federal district courts have expressed some level of acceptance of this

---

4 Id. at § 302(1).

5 Id. § 315.

6 Id. at § 308 (1981) ("It is not essential to the creation of a right in an intended beneficiary that he be identified when a contract containing the promise is made").

7 Id. at § 308 cmt. a, illus. 2.

third-party beneficiary theory regarding the enforcement of FRAND commitments.[8]

However, application of the third-party beneficiary doctrine to FRAND commitments and other patent pledges presents serious doctrinal challenges. To apply the doctrine, one must first determine whether the contracting parties intended to confer on one or more third parties the direct benefit of their contract. The strongest indicator of such intent is an express statement in the contract itself. A few SDOs include statements concerning third-party beneficiaries in their membership agreements, bylaws, or intellectual property policies.[9] Most, however, have not done so (yet). For the majority of SDOs, the intent to confer third-party beneficiary status must be inferred from other facts.

In order to claim third-party beneficiary status, the putative third-party beneficiary must be identified or discernible with sufficient specificity. Depending on their construction, FRAND commitments can be made for the benefit only of members of the SDO, or members as well as nonmembers (i.e., all manufacturers of products implementing a standard).[10] SDO members can make a stronger case for third-party beneficiary status than nonmembers can. Because most SDOs are membership-based associations, it is not hard to envision an SDO wishing to confer a benefit on all of its members through a network of FRAND commitments, just as it does through other activities such as meetings, professional networking, and publications. The question becomes somewhat more complex when considering members who join the SDO after the FRAND commitment is made and members who exit the SDO. As discussed above, it is not necessary that beneficiaries be specifically identifiable at the time a pledge is made, but at some point, either in terms of number of beneficiaries or time elapsed since the promise was made, the parties' intention with respect to beneficiaries becomes attenuated.

---

[8] Microsoft Corp. v. Motorola, Inc., 854 F. Supp. 2d 993, 1002–03 (W.D. Wash. 2012); Apple, Inc. v. Motorola Mobility, Inc., 886 F. Supp. 2d 1061, 1085 (W.D. Wis. 2012). *See also* ESS Tech., Inc. v. PC-Tel., Inc., No. C-99-20292 RMW, 1999 WL 33520483, at *3 (N.D. Cal. Nov. 4, 1999) (declining to dismiss claim for breach of a FRAND commitment brought by nonmember of SDO against patent holder).

[9] *See*, e.g., Wireless Innovation Forum, Intellectual Property Policy § 1.3 (2012), http://www.wirelessinnovation.org/assets/documents/policy_on_intellectual_property_rights.pdf ("Each … [implementer] shall be a third party beneficiary of all such obligations").

[10] *See* id. at 27 (indicating eight of ten SDOs studied had FRAND commitments that applied to all implementers, rather than only members of the SDO).

A more challenging case for third-party beneficiary status arises with respect to nonmembers of the SDO. Many of the justifications that exist for an SDO to benefit its own members do not exist with respect to nonmembers. And it can be argued that extending the benefits of FRAND licensing to nonmembers reduces both nonmembers' incentives to join the SDO and a competitive advantage that SDO members might have over nonmembers. Moreover, nonmembers are not themselves bound by the policies and agreements of the SDO and are thus not required to grant licenses to SDO members. For all of these reasons, an SDO's intent to benefit nonmembers, absent an express indication of this intent, is questionable.

B. Indefiniteness

The common law has traditionally treated contracts whose material terms are not specified with sufficient certainty as lacking both mutual assent and evidence of the parties' intent to be bound.[11] When parties reach a preliminary agreement but contemplate further negotiation or the execution of a formal contract, this preliminary expression of intent (an "agreement to agree") typically does not create a binding contract.[12]

Patent pledges are, by their very nature, indefinite. FRAND commitments, for example, specify only that a license must be granted on terms that are "fair, reasonable and non-discriminatory." Key terms such as price, duration, and scope are left open to future negotiation. Of course, such omissions are not always fatal to contract enforceability, and both the Uniform Commercial Code[13] and courts interpreting common law contracts[14] have permitted parties to leave certain key terms open for future determination. Nevertheless, FRAND and other commitments embodied in SDO policies could suffer from too much indeterminacy to be found enforceable. Several recent judicial decisions critical of the vagueness and indeterminacy of SDO policy language underscore this point.[15]

---

[11] RESTATEMENT (SECOND) OF CONTRACTS § 33(3).

[12] JOHN P. DAWSON, WILLIAM HARVEY, STANLEY HENDERSON, DOUGLAS BAIRD, CONTRACTS: CASES AND COMMENTS 383 (9th ed. 2008).

[13] U.C.C. § 2-305(1) (2008).

[14] *See* 1 ARTHUR LINTON CORBIN, CORBIN ON CONTRACTS § 4.3, at 575–76 (Joseph M. Perillo ed., rev. ed. 1993).

[15] *See* TruePosition, Inc. v. LM Ericsson Tel. Co., 977 F. Supp. 2d 462, 470 (E.D. Pa. 2013) (finding that the Working Procedures of the 3GPP standards group were "too indefinite to support the formation of a contract"); Rambus, Inc.

II. PROMISSORY ESTOPPEL

A patent pledge is a *promise*. It may not be a promise that meets the strict requirements for the formation of a common law contract, but it is a promise nonetheless, and should, under most circumstances, be enforced. The doctrine of promissory estoppel prevents a party from shirking a promise that should be enforced though it lacks consideration, mutual assent, or other formal requirements of contract law.[16] The Restatement (Second) of Contracts summarizes the basic elements of promissory estoppel, as observed in the United States today, as "[a] promise which the promisor should reasonably expect to induce action or forbearance on the part of the promisee or a third person and which does induce such action or forbearance is binding if injustice can be avoided only by enforcement of the promise."[17] A finding of promissory estoppel turns on the existence of a promise and the promisee's subsequent detrimental reliance.[18] In assessing reliance, "[t]he law may not question the adequacy of consideration but it *must* (by definition) question the adequacy of reliance."[19] To this end, the doctrine of promissory estoppel only requires promisors to honor promises that others have actually and justifiably relied upon.[20]

The doctrine of promissory estoppel offers an implementer a more attractive vehicle than common law contract to enforce FRAND commitments and other patent pledges. Estoppel avoids many of the technical hurdles imposed by common law contract doctrine and does not depend on the conceit of bilateral bargaining to be enforced. To enforce a FRAND commitment under an estoppel theory, an implementer need only show the patent holder made a promise, the patent holder intended it to be relied upon, and the implementer did, in fact, justifiably and detrimentally rely on that promise.

---

v. Infineon Technologies AG, 318 F.3d 1081 (Fed. Cir. 2003), *cert. denied*, 540 U.S. 874 (2003) (finding a "staggering lack of defining details" in the relevant SDO patent policy).

16 3 Eric Mills Holmes, Corbin on Contracts § 8.3, at 9 (Joseph M. Perillo ed., rev. ed. 1996).

17 Restatement (Second) of Contracts § 90(1) (1981).

18 Brian A. Blum, Contracts: Examples and Explanations § 8.6.1, at 198 (3d ed. 2004).

19 Daniel J. Bussel & Arthur I. Rosett, Contract Law and Its Application 543 (8th ed. 2011).

20 E. Allan Farnsworth, Contracts § 2.19, at 95 (4th ed. 2004).

Nevertheless, in complex markets characterized by thousands of patents and dozens of patent holders, demonstrating specific reliance can be challenging. Moreover, only the promisee may seek to enforce a promise under a promissory estoppel theory. In the case of FRAND commitments, the direct promisee is typically the SDO. Although it has been postulated, the third-party beneficiary doctrine has not been widely recognized in the context of promissory estoppel.[21] Thus, if a manufacturer is not the direct recipient of the patent holder's promise (as is typically the case), it may face further difficulty in enforcing that promise.

Some SDOs, recognizing the value of promissory estoppel to potential implementers of their standards, have attempted to fashion policy workarounds to overcome obstacles to estoppel claims. For example, IEEE includes the following text in its standard letter of assurance: "By signing this Letter of Assurance, you … acknowledge that users and implementers of the [Proposed] IEEE Standard identified … above are relying or will rely upon and may seek enforcement of the terms of this LOA."[22] Such statements are intended to establish that the promisor (the patent holder) is aware that others are likely to rely on its FRAND commitment—a useful showing when making a case for detrimental reliance.[23] But such statements do little to establish that the implementer did, in fact, rely on the patent holder's specific promise. Thus, despite this well-intentioned policy language, the doctrine of promissory estoppel currently remains an imperfect solution for the general enforcement of FRAND commitments and other patent pledges.

III. ANTITRUST

Antitrust law has also been proposed as a means for enforcing patent pledges. Enforcement agencies in both the United States and European Union have recently indicated a willingness to prosecute potential breaches of patent pledges using the tools of antitrust and competition law.[24] Commentators have also advocated the use of antitrust remedies

---

21 RESTATEMENT (SECOND) OF CONTRACTS § 90 cmt. c (1981).

22 IEEE-SA STANDARDS BOARD BYLAWS § 6.2 (2015), *Letter of Assurance for Essential Patent Claims*, IEEE, § G.

23 RESTATEMENT (SECOND) OF CONTRACTS § 90 cmt. b (1981) ("The promisor is affected only by reliance which he does or should foresee ….").

24 Statement of the Federal Trade Commission, Google Inc., F.T.C. File No. 121-0120, at 3 (F.T.C. Jan. 3, 2013).

and enforcement as a means for policing compliance with standards-related commitments.[25]

A. Monopolization and Deception

Section 2 of the Sherman Antitrust Act of 1890 makes it unlawful to "monopolize, or attempt to monopolize … any part of the trade or commerce among the several States."[26] To prevail on a claim for monopolization or attempted monopolization, a plaintiff must prove that the defendant had power in the relevant market and willfully sought, acquired, or maintained that power in an unlawful manner.[27] The FTC may also bring claims for monopolization and attempted monopolization under Section 5 of the Federal Trade Commission Act (FTC Act).[28]

The theory underlying monopolization claims in the context of patent pledges holds that standards, once adopted broadly in the marketplace, can confer market power on the holders of patents covering those standards.[29] Abuse of such market power could constitute unlawful monopolization or attempted monopolization.[30] Accordingly, some have argued that claims of monopolization may serve as effective means of ensuring that parties comply with their FRAND commitments.[31]

Most actions for monopolization in the standards context have involved claims that the patent holder deceived either an SDO or other SDO participants regarding its patents. This theory received at least some support from the U.S. Court of Appeals for the Third Circuit in *Broadcom Corp. v. Qualcomm, Inc.*, which reasoned that a patent holder's intentionally false promise to license standards-essential patents

---

[25] *See*, e.g., George S. Cary, Mark W. Nelson, Steven J. Kaiser, Alex R. Sistla, *The Case for Antitrust Law to Police the Patent Holdup Problem in Standard Setting*, 77 ANTITRUST L.J. 913, 921 (2011).

[26] 15 U.S.C. § 2 (2012).

[27] *See*, e.g., Verizon Commc'ns Inc. v. Law Offices of Curtis V. Trinko, LLP, 540 U.S. 398, 407 (2004).

[28] 15 U.S.C. § 45.

[29] *See generally* AM. BAR ASS'N, ABA SECTION OF ANTITRUST LAW, HANDBOOK ON ANTITRUST ASPECTS OF STANDARD SETTING 115–17 (2d ed. 2011) [hereinafter ABA ANTITRUST HANDBOOK] (discussing cases in which federal courts have addressed "whether a monopolist's refusal to license intellectual property may provide a basis for a monopolization claim").

[30] Id.

[31] *See*, e.g., Renata B. Hesse, Deputy Assistant Attorney Gen., U.S. Dep't of Justice, Address at the 2nd Annual Antitrust Law Leaders Forum: IP, Antitrust and Looking Back on the Last Four Years 19 (Feb. 8, 2013).

on FRAND terms *could* violate Section 2.[32] Such deception, the court noted, "harms the competitive process by obscuring the costs of including proprietary technology in a standard and increasing the likelihood that patent rights will confer monopoly power on the patent holder."[33]

The FTC has also brought monopolization claims based on deceptive conduct within an SDO. In *Rambus, Inc.*,[34] the FTC found Rambus liable for violation of Section 5 of the FTC Act, based on an underlying violation of Section 2 of the Sherman Act.[35] In analysing the element of deception constituting Rambus's exclusionary conduct, the FTC relied on its 1983 policy statement on deception, which requires a "misrepresentation, omission, or other practice" that was likely to mislead others acting reasonably under the circumstances.[36] The FTC concluded that Rambus engaged in such deception, and when combined with the resulting harm to competition, found Rambus liable for monopolization.[37]

While monopolization and attempted monopolization are powerful legal claims, they do not seem well suited as general means for policing FRAND commitments and other patent pledges. First, under the formulation stated by the Third Circuit, a deception of some kind must be shown to make a claim of monopolization.[38] Second, as the D.C. Circuit held in *Rambus, Inc. v. FTC*,[39] even when deceptive conduct is present, it "must have an anticompetitive effect in order to form the basis of a monopolization claim."[40] In overturning the FTC's holding, the court explained that deception "simply to obtain higher prices normally has no particular tendency to exclude rivals and thus to diminish competition."[41] Accordingly, the court held the FTC failed to establish that Rambus unlawfully monopolized the relevant markets.[42]

---

32 501 F.3d 297, 314 (3d Cir. 2007).

33 Id.

34 Rambus, Inc., No. 9302, 2006 WL 2330117 (F.T.C. Aug. 2, 2006), *rev'd sub nom.* Rambus Inc. v. FTC, 522 F.3d 456 (D.C. Cir. 2008).

35 Id. at *2.

36 *FTC Policy Statement on Deception*, FED. TRADE COMM'N (Oct. 14, 1983).

37 *Rambus*, 2006 WL 2330117, at *2.

38 *But see* Hesse, *supra* note 31, at 21 (noting that some commentators have suggested that a monopolization claim under Section 2 may not in fact require deception during the standardization process).

39 522 F.3d 456 (D.C. Cir. 2008).

40 Id. at 464.

41 Id.

42 Id. at *467*.

Given the difficulty of establishing a claim for monopolization and the potential lack of deception in many cases, it seems unlikely that an antitrust monopolization theory will prove to be useful as a general legal theory for enforcing parties' patent pledges.[43]

B. Exclusion and Essential Facilities

Another approach that has been suggested to enforce patent pledges under Section 2 of the Sherman Act is to characterize a patent holder's failure to grant (or offer) an appropriate license, or its attempt to enjoin a manufacturer from using a standardized technology, as a unilateral refusal to deal. Such refusals can give rise to liability under Section 2 if they are intended to create or maintain a monopoly or withhold access to an "essential facility."[44]

But as Professor Tom Cotter observes, refusal to deal claims, both generally and relating to essential facilities, have become increasingly difficult given courts' generally expansive view of patent holders' right to exploit their assets in the manner they select.[45] Thus, in addition to demonstrating that a patent holder seeks to exclude a competitor through its conduct, it must show that "the defendant intended to engage in predatory—and not merely competitive—behavior."[46] In the context of patent pledges, this is a high burden of proof. In fact, even in *Broadcom*, in which the court found that Qualcomm had engaged in exclusionary conduct in violation of Section 2, the court refrained from applying the refusal to deal doctrine.[47] Accordingly, monopolization claims based on refusals to deal in the context of patent pledges, while possibly effective in a limited number of cases, are unlikely to form a consistent and reliable basis for the enforcement of patent pledges.

---

43 *See* Robert A. Skitol & *Kenneth* M. Vorrasi, *Patent Holdup in Standards Development: Life After* Rambus v. F.T.C., ANTITRUST, Summer 2009, at 31.

44 *See* 3 PHILLIP E. AREEDA & HERBERT HOVENKAMP, ANTITRUST LAW: AN ANALYSIS OF ANTITRUST PRINCIPLES AND THEIR APPLICATION ¶ 709 (3d ed. 2008); 2 JULIAN O. VON KALINOWSKI, PETER SULLIVAN, MAUREEN MCGUIRL, ANTITRUST LAWS & TRADE REGULATION § 25.04(3)(a) (2d ed. 2014).

45 Thomas F. Cotter, *Comparative Law and Economics of Standard-Essential Patents and FRAND Royalties*, 22 TEX. INTELL. PROP. L.J. 311, 332–34 (2014).

46 MiniFrame Ltd. v. Microsoft Corp., No. 11 Civ. 7419 (RJS), 2013 WL 1385704, at *4 (S.D.N.Y. Mar. 28, 2013), *aff'd*, 551 F. App'x 1 (2d Cir. 2013), *cert. denied*, 135 S. Ct. 223 (2014).

47 Broadcom Corp. v. Qualcomm, Inc. 501 F.3d 297, 316–17 (3rd Cir. 2007).

C. Unfair Methods of Competition

The FTC has authority under Section 5 of the FTC Act to prosecute "unfair methods of competition" and "unfair or deceptive acts or practices."[48] While monopolization and attempted monopolization are both actionable under Section 5, Section 5 also encompasses conduct beyond monopolization.[49] In the standards context, it is possible that breaches of a patent holder's FRAND commitments may themselves constitute unfair methods of competition or unfair acts and practices under Section 5, even absent deception.

In 2008, the FTC brought a Section 5 action against Negotiated Data Solutions (N-Data) in connection with a patent reading on IEEE's 802.3 Fast Ethernet standard.[50] In 1994, the patent's original owner, National Semiconductor, pledged to IEEE that it would license the patent for a flat fee of $1,000 to any party implementing the standard.[51] National Semiconductor eventually transferred the patents to Vertical Networks, which then transferred the patents to N-Data, which allegedly indicated that it did not intend to honor National's original $1,000 licensing offer.[52] The FTC, in bringing an action under Section 5, argued that N-Data's disavowal of National's earlier patent pledge constituted an unfair method of competition, as well as an unfair act or practice.[53] The case was resolved through a consent order in which N-Data agreed to honor National's original patent pledge.[54]

The FTC renewed its use of Section 5 to address suspected violations of FRAND commitments in 2012, when it initiated investigations of

---

48 15 U.S.C. § 45(a)(1) (2012).

49 *See*, e.g., William E. Kovacic & Marc Winerman, *Competition Policy and the Application of Section 5 of the Federal Trade Commission Act*, 76 ANTITRUST L.J. 929, 930–32, 934–37 (2010) ("Congress intended Section 5 to be a mechanism for upgrading the U.S. system of competition law by permitting the FTC to reach behavior not necessarily proscribed by the other U.S. competition statutes, including the 1890 Sherman Act and the Clayton Act").

50 Negotiated Data Solutions LLC, No. C-4234, 2008 WL 4407246, at *1–5 (F.T.C. Sept. 22, 2008).

51 *See* id. at *2.

52 *See* id. at *4–5.

53 *See* id. at *1.

54 *See* id. at *6, *9.

Robert Bosch GmbH and Motorola Mobility/Google.[55] The Bosch case involved allegations that patent holders improperly used FRAND-committed patents to seek injunctive relief against potential vendors of standardized products. According to the FTC's complaint,[56] SPX, a firm that Bosch sought to acquire, had participated in an SDO developing standards for automotive cooling systems.[57] Despite having made a FRAND commitment to the SDO, SPX asserted two patents covering the SDO's standards against alleged infringers and then sought injunctive relief to prevent future sales of infringing products.[58] The FTC argued that SPX's attempt to obtain injunctive relief in the face of its FRAND commitment was inherently coercive and oppressive, and thereby constituted an unfair method of competition in violation of Section 5.[59] The FTC offered the caveat that "[w]hile not every breach of a FRAND licensing obligation will give rise to Section 5 concerns," enforcement may be required "when such a breach tends to undermine the standard-setting process and risks harming American consumers ..."[60]

Despite the FTC's invocation of Section 5 to condemn non-deceptive breaches of FRAND commitments in *Bosch*, it is not clear that Section 5 offers an optimal general theory for enforcing patent pledges. First, the boundaries of Section 5 in actions that do not involve monopolization and deception are relatively unclear, and there is still significant disagreement both among commentators and FTC commissioners themselves regarding the appropriate extent of Section 5 liability.[61] Relying on such an uncertain and judicially untested standard as the principal mechanism for enforcing patent pledges could make the enforcement of such pledges less predictable and thus diminish their value as market-wide assurances. Second, even if the parameters of Section 5 were clarified to cover breaches of patent pledges with greater reliability, an action under

---

[55] *See* Statement of the Federal Trade Commission, Robert Bosch GmbH, F.T.C. File No. 121-0081, at 1–3 (F.T.C. Nov. 26, 2012); Decision and Order, In re. Motorola Mobility LLC & Google Inc, FTC Docket No. C-4410 (June 23, 2013). For a more in-depth analysis of these cases and their antitrust implications, *see* Cotter, *supra* note 45, at 327–29.

[56] Robert Bosch GmbH, 155 F.T.C. 713 (2013).

[57] *See* id. at 715–19 (2013).

[58] *See* id. at 718–19.

[59] However, the FTC also acknowledged that SPX's conduct likely did not violate Section 2 of the Sherman Act. Id. at 833 n.7.

[60] Robert Bosch GmbH, 155 F.T.C. at 835.

[61] *FTC Statement of Enforcement Principles Regarding "Unfair Methods of Competition" Under Section 5 of the FTC Act*, FED. TRADE COMM'N (Aug. 13, 2015).

Section 5 can be brought by only the FTC in its enforcement capacity, and not by private litigants. Thus, such actions depend on the enforcement priorities and resources of the FTC and as such cannot provide a reliable means for enforcing patent pledges across the board.

IV. PATENT MISUSE

Some commentators have suggested that violations of FRAND commitments and other misconduct in the standard-setting context should be addressed under a patent misuse theory.[62] Patent misuse is an equitable defense to a claim for patent infringement that excuses infringement upon a showing that the patent holder sought to exceed the scope of the patent grant.[63] Patent misuse doctrine finds roots in both antitrust and patent law and has been used to address conduct including the tying of a patent license to the purchase of unpatented articles, the collection of royalties following the expiration of a patent's term, and the collection of royalties on sales of unpatented articles. The consequences of a finding of misuse are severe and often result in a patent becoming unenforceable until the effects of the misuse have been sufficiently dissipated or "purged."[64]

Under current judicial interpretations, a finding of patent misuse requires that the patent holder attempted to exceed the bounds of the patent grant. Yet charging a royalty to license a valid, unexpired patent, even an unreasonably high one, is squarely within a patent holder's rights. In fact, the U.S. Patent Act goes even further and expressly provides that a patent holder's complete refusal to license a patent will *not* constitute an act of patent misuse.[65] Thus, at least under current U.S. law, patent misuse would be a challenging theory to use for the general enforcement of patent pledges.

---

[62] *See* Daryl Lim, *Misconduct in Standard Setting: The Case for Patent Misuse*, 51 IDEA 559, 559–60 (2011); Daryl Lim, *Standard Essential Patents, Trolls and the Smartphone Wars: Triangulating the End Game*, 119 PENN. ST. L. REV. 1, 86–90 (2014).

[63] *See* Scott Paper Co. v. Marcalus Co., 326 U.S. 249, 256 (1945) (stating that "any attempted reservation or continuation in the patentee or those claiming under him of the patent monopoly, after the patent expires, whatever the legal device employed, runs counter to the policy and purpose of the patent laws").

[64] U.S. Gypsum Co. v. Nat'l Gypsum Co., 352 U.S. 457, 465 (1957).

[65] 35 U.S.C. § 271(d)(4) (2012) ("No patent owner … shall be … deemed guilty of misuse or illegal extension of the patent right by reason of his having … refused to license … any rights to the patent …").

V. EQUITABLE SERVITUDE

Some commentators have recently analogized patent pledges to encumbrances "running with the land" under real property law.[66] They identify several areas in which this property-based characterization would yield benefits: FRAND commitments would more readily bind subsequent owners of pledged patents, FRAND commitments would be harder to avoid and negate in bankruptcy proceedings, and specific performance might be more readily available to enforce such commitments.[67]

A property-based theory for enforcing patent pledges is attractive, as it could bind the affected patents themselves, in an *in rem* manner, rather than patent holders, which may be transient and subject to change. But while a property-based characterization of FRAND commitments could have benefits, it is not clear that such an approach is viable on a theoretical or practical level. At a theoretical level, one of the primary difficulties in analogizing patent-related encumbrances to real property servitudes is that patents are not real property; they are, at most, treated in some respects as personal property,[68] and servitudes on personal property are generally disfavored in the law.[69]

At a practical level, the equitable servitude approach might prove useful in describing patent pledges that are clearly delineated and attached to one or more identified patents, like easements recorded in the deeds of parcels of realty. But most FRAND commitments are not so well specified. And a real property analogy is less likely to hold as to FRAND commitments that are made with respect to a patent holder's portfolio in general, without reference to particular patents, or by means of implied commitments to abide by an SDO's bylaws. Thus, the equitable servitude theory, even if theoretically appealing, might only have applicability to a subset of patent pledges.

---

66 Jay P. Kesan & Carol M. Hayes, *FRAND's Forever: Standards, Patent Transfers, and Licensing Commitments*, 89 IND. L.J. 231, 294–304 (2014).

67 Id. at 296–300.

68 35 U.S.C. § 261 (2012) (deeming patents to "have the attributes of personal property").

69 *See*, e.g., Thomas W. Merrill & Henry E. Smith, *Optimal Standardization in the Law of Property: The* Numerus Clausus *Principle*, 110 YALE L.J. 1, 18 & n.68 (2000) ("American precedent is largely, if not quite exclusively, in accord" with the principle that "one cannot create servitudes in personal property").

VI. MARKET RELIANCE

In addition to the above theories, the author has proposed a hybrid "market reliance" theory that modifies the doctrine of promissory estoppel for the enforcement of patent pledges through the application of a market-based test derived from the "fraud on the market" test under the U.S. federal securities laws.[70]

Under the market reliance theory, it is unnecessary for a manufacturer who seeks to enforce a patent pledge to prove that it specifically relied on the pledge made by an identified patent holder. It is enough that the patent holder made such a commitment to the market at large, and that the manufacturer is or becomes a participant in that market by manufacturing or selling a product that uses a standard or other common technology that is subject to patent pledges. Thus, like the rebuttable presumption of reliance in securities fraud cases, the law should recognize a rebuttable presumption of reliance in the enforcement of patent pledges based on market reliance.

The presumption that a manufacturer relied on a patent holder's pledge may be rebutted. Evidence supporting rebuttal of the presumption might include (1) the implementer's knowledge that the patent holder's patents are not valid or not essential to a standard, (2) the patent holder's abandonment of the patents, (3) the implementer's entering into a license with the patent holder, (4) the implementer's purchase of all necessary components implementing the standard from the patent holder's existing licensees, or (5) the implementer's unequivocal refusal to enter into good faith negotiations to obtain a FRAND license from the patent holder. Each of these cases would potentially "sever the link" between the patent holder's breach of its FRAND commitment and the implementer's failure to obtain a license under the patent holder's standards-essential patents, thus justifying rebuttal of the presumption of reliance and, most likely, eliminating the implementer's market reliance claim against the patent holder.

Like both contract and promissory estoppel theories, market reliance depends on the making of a promise by a patent holder. Thus, if an SDO's policies are so ambiguous, indefinite, or incomplete that they do not reasonably convey a promise to the other participants or to the market in general, then an action for market reliance should not succeed. This is not to say, however, that in most cases it will not be possible to determine

---

70 Jorge L. Contreras, *A Market Reliance Theory for FRAND Commitments and Other Patent Pledges*, 2015 Utah L. Rev. 479, 479 (2015).

whether a public statement made by a patent holder is of sufficient gravity, formality, and specificity to qualify as an enforceable pledge. In fact, it is likely that most such pledges will be easily identifiable as such.

The market reliance theory also offers a different and more comprehensive approach to making patent pledges binding and enforceable on subsequent purchasers of committed patents. If a manufacturer is sued for patent infringement, it need not determine whether a patent pledge has been made and carried forward with respect to each patent being asserted. Rather, it need only determine whether the technology is part of a market characterized by patent pledges and whether the patents being asserted were once owned by a party making a patent pledge. If so, then the patents in the hands of the new owner (the party asserting them) should remain subject to the original owner's patent pledge.

While it is still incumbent on the manufacturer to discover, based on transfer and assignment records, some historical information regarding ownership of the patents being asserted, it is generally easier to discover whether a patent was once owned by a particular party than whether that patent is subject to a continuing patent pledge. Therefore, market reliance represents a more robust and reliable means of ensuring that patent pledges are enforced against subsequent holders of pledged patents.

One major benefit of the market reliance theory in the standard-setting context is that it eliminates the need to distinguish between SDO members and nonmembers. Under contract theory, SDO members are more clearly intended third-party beneficiaries than nonmembers, at least from the SDO's standpoint. Under a market reliance theory, however, all implementers of a standard, whether or not members of the SDO, are market participants and hence entitled to enforce the public promises made by patent holders.

While the market reliance theory is still relatively undeveloped, there are signs that some courts may be moving in this direction. For example, the Court of Justice of the European Union recently explained in *Huawei v. ZTE* that "an undertaking to grant licenses on FRAND terms creates legitimate expectations on the part of third parties that the proprietor of the SEP [standard essential patent] will in fact grant licenses on such terms."[71] The Court went on to find that, given these legitimate expectations, a refusal by a patent holder to grant a license on FRAND terms could constitute an abuse under European competition law (Article 102 of the Treaty on the Functioning of the European Union (TFEU)).

---

71 Case C-170/13, Huawei Technologies Co. Ltd. v. ZTE Corp. (Nov. 20, 2014).

CONCLUSION

Patent pledges have the potential to enable efficient and socially beneficial arrangements among patent holders and manufacturers of standardized or compliant products. However, in order for patent pledges to achieve their desired goals, they must be legally enforceable. Currently prevailing contractual understandings of patent pledges are both inaccurate and incomplete. While the equitable doctrine of promissory estoppel more closely hews to the nature of such pledges, its requirement of actual detrimental reliance is problematic. Similarly, the application of antitrust and property law principles are limited in the patent pledge context. It is thus possible that a market reliance theory may provide the most robust enforcement theory for patent pledges by introducing a rebuttable presumption of reliance when pledges are made broadly to a market.

6. Patent pledges at the U.S. International Trade Commission

Elizabeth I. Winston

The United States economy is dependent on regulating and protecting American industry and trade. Over the centuries, the United States government has regulated domestic industry through a variety of means, including tariffs and import restrictions. Tariffs were the primary means of regulation initially, and were administered by the United States Tariff Commission.[1] Over time, tariffs declined in importance and import restrictions increased in importance in regulations of domestic industry.[2] Reflecting this shift, in 1974, the Tariff Commission was renamed the United States International Trade Commission ("ITC").

Central to the mission of the ITC is its ability to protect domestic industry and promote trade by regulating "imports claimed to injure a domestic industry or violate U.S. intellectual property rights."[3] The ITC is entrusted with the task of determining whether a complainant has established: (1) unfair competition or an unfair act, for example, patent or trademark infringement; (2) importation, sale for importation, or sale after importation into the United States of the accused products; and (3) the existence of a domestic industry relating to the product in question. In investigations that are not based upon alleged infringement of federal statutory intellectual property rights, a complainant also must prove (4) that the alleged unfair act has caused or threatens to cause injury.[4]

If unlawful activities are found, then the ITC may issue a general exclusion order (GEO) directed to all articles that violate the U.S.

---

[1] William A. Perry, *Administration of the Import Trade Laws by the United States International Trade Commission*, 3 B.U. INT'L L.J. 345 (1985).

[2] Id.

[3] U.S. INT'L TRADE COMM'N, MISSION STATEMENT, http://www.usitc.gov/press_room/mission_statement.htm.

[4] 19 U.S.C. § 1337 (2015).

intellectual property rights and injure a domestic industry; the ITC can issue a limited exclusion order (LEO) directed to only the specific articles that are named in the complaint and violate the U.S. intellectual property rights; and/or the ITC can issue a cease and desist order directed to the persons engaging in the violations of the U.S. intellectual property rights.[5] Each of these allows the ITC to protect domestic industry in a different and powerful fashion.[6] The Trade Act of 1974 specifically gave the ITC the power to issue cease and desist orders, for instance, because:

> the existing statute, which provides no remedy other than exclusion of articles from entry, is so extreme or inappropriate in some cases that it is often likely to result in the Commission not finding a violation of this section, thus reducing the effectiveness of section 337 for the purposes intended.[7]

Cease and desist orders expanded the ITC's power, giving it the ability to regulate infringing methods for the first time, an important part of the imposition of import restrictions.

The ITC is not an agency established to protect intellectual property rights holders, but rather to protect the domestic industry using intellectual property rights and both its scope of interest and the scope of available remedies is limited by such. This chapter will focus on the ITC's investigations of violations based on patent infringement, but it is important to note that the ITC has the ability to regulate other forms of unfair competition and other unfair acts. By establishing and empowering the ITC, Congress has made it clear that it is a violation of United States law to import an article that infringes a patent and harms domestic industry.

---

5 Id.

6 Certain Welded Stainless Steel Pipe and Tube, Inv. No. 337-TA-29, USITC Pub. 863 (Feb. 22, 1978) (Final) ("Prior to 1974 the sole power of the Commission in section 337 cases was to recommend to the President an exclusion order").

7 Report of the Committee on Finance to Accompany H.R. 10710, Trade Act of 1974, S. Rep. No. 93-1298, at 198 (1974).

I. STATUTORY RELIEF IS NOT JUDICIAL DECISION MAKING

A. Injunctive Relief

The Constitution of the United States gives Congress the power to "promote the progress of science and useful arts, by securing for limited times to authors and inventors the exclusive right to their respective writings and discoveries."[8] The Patent Act, based in the United States Constitution, grants patentees the right "to exclude others from making, using, offering for sale, or selling the invention throughout the United States."[9] One way to enforce this right to exclude is through injunctive relief.[10] Injunctive relief is deeply rooted in United States patent law, going back almost 200 years. In 1790, Congress passed the first Patent Act, establishing that a patent was an exclusive right and providing for monetary damages if the patent right was infringed. Within 20 years, Congress authorized injunctive relief as a remedy for patent infringement. Today, in language virtually unchanged since that first authorization, the current statute reads:

> The several courts having jurisdiction of cases under this title may grant injunctions in accordance with the principles of equity to prevent the violation of any right secured by patent, on such terms as the court deems reasonable.[11]

Injunctive relief in patent infringement suits upholds the very purpose of the grant of a patent – the right to exclude others from practicing the patented art.[12] Prior to 2006, it was "the general rule that an injunction will issue when infringement has been adjudged, absent a sound reason for denying it."[13] Injunctive relief is a powerful tool, and when wrongfully applied, the results can be crippling to an innocent party.

Outside of patent law, permanent injunctions were never a default remedy, and were issued only after the courts determined that the party seeking the permanent injunction passed that rigorous test, and that the

---

8 U.S. CONST., art. 1, § 8, cl. 8.

9 35 U.S.C. § 154 (2015).

10 35 U.S.C. § 283.

11 Id.

12 *See*, e.g., Richardson v. Suzuki Motor Co., 868 F.2d 1226, 1246–47 (Fed. Cir. 1989) ("Infringement having been established, it is contrary to the laws of property, of which the patent law partakes, to deny the patentee's right to exclude others from use of his property").

13 Id.

equities dictated issuance of the injunction. In 2006, the Supreme Court, in *eBay v. MercExchange*,[14] held that this test applies equally to patent holders seeking injunctive relief, overturning a decision by the Federal Circuit holding "that courts will issue permanent injunctions against patent infringement absent exceptional circumstances."[15] Therefore, today, a patent owner seeking a permanent injunction against an infringer must prove the following four elements:

> (1) that it has suffered an irreparable injury; (2) that remedies available at law, such as monetary damages, are inadequate to compensate for that injury; (3) that, considering the balance of hardships between the plaintiff and defendant, a remedy in equity is warranted; and (4) that the public interest would not be disserved by a permanent injunction.[16]

Patent owners who have made patent pledges may have a difficult time satisfying the first two factors set forth by the Supreme Court. To further understand the issues inherent in this, we can look to one recent example. Agere is a patent owner, a member of IEEE, and the owner of two patents that it designated as essential to the 802.11 standard. Per IEEE's terms, Agere "submitted Letters of Assurance, as required by the IEEE Standards Board Bylaws, stating that it 'is prepared to grant a license to an unrestricted number of applicants on a worldwide, non-discriminatory basis and on reasonable terms and conditions.'"[17] Agere's agreement to license its patent to all applicants renders moot any argument that monetary damages are inadequate to compensate for any injury. By definition, Agere is stating that it will license the essential patents, and that a monetary figure can be assigned to the license agreement. If a party is later found to infringe, the court can determine what a reasonable royalty should be, and assess damages that are at least that amount.

This does not mean that Agere should never be able to enjoin another party from infringing a patent essential to an IEEE standard.[18] Injunctions are on-going remedies, and in some instances have been shaped by courts as an award of on-going royalties rather than an order enjoining infringement altogether. Damages are mainly a salve for past injuries. If

---

14 547 U.S. 388 (2006).

15 MercExchange, L.L.C. v. eBay, Inc., 401 F.3d 1323, 1339 (Fed. Cir. 2005), *vacated*, 547 U.S. 388 (2006).

16 *eBay*, 547 U.S. at 391.

17 Realtek Semiconductor Corp. v. LSI Corp., 946 F. Supp. 2d 998, 1001 (N.D. Cal. 2013).

18 Id. ("[A]n injunction may be warranted where an accused infringer of a standard-essential patent outright *refuses* to accept a RAND license").

Agere can show that another party outright refuses to take a license, that infringement will continue, despite a payment of damages, or that injunctive relief is the only equitable remedy, then we have a patent hold-out as opposed to patent hold-up. A patent hold-up occurs when a patentee asserts a:

> patent to exclude a competitor from a market or obtain a higher price for its use than would have been possible before the standard was set, when alternative technologies could have been chosen. This type of patent hold-up ... may induce prospective implementers to postpone or avoid making commitments to a standardized technology or to make inefficient investments in developing and implementing a standard in an effort to protect themselves. Consumers of products implementing the standard could also be harmed to the extent that the hold-up generates unwarranted higher royalties and those royalties are passed on to consumers in the form of higher prices.[19]

A patent hold-out, on the other hand, arises when a party outright refuses to negotiate a license with the patentee in the hopes of escaping a reasonable royalty rate altogether. However, both patent hold-ups and patent hold-outs are the exception to the normal practice.[20] It is more difficult, post *eBay*, to receive injunctive relief, and if a party has agreed to a patent pledge, then the tightened requirements of *eBay* and the normal course of fair dealing between parties, rather than patent hold-outs and hold-ups, renders injunctive relief more of a theoretical possibility than a realistic threat, as it should be.[21] Fewer injunctions have been

---

[19] U.S. DEP'T OF JUSTICE & U.S. PATENT & TRADEMARK OFFICE, *Policy Statement on Remedies for Standards-Essential Patents Subject to Voluntary F/RAND Commitments* (Jan. 8, 2013) [hereinafter DOJ & PTO].

[20] *See*, e.g., TELECOMM. INDUS. ASS'N., *Re: Federal Trade Commission Request for Comments and Announcement of Workshop on Standard-Setting Issues (Patent Standards Workshop, Project No. P11-1204)* FED. TRADE COMM'N, at 4 (June 14, 2011) ("TIA has never received any complaints regarding ... 'patent hold-up' and does not agree that 'patent holdup' is plaguing the information and telecommunications technology ... standard development processes").

[21] James Ratliff & Daniel L. Rubinfeld, *The Use and Threat of Injunctions in the RAND Context*, 1 J. COMPETITION L. & ECON. 1, 9 (2013) ("[T]he existence of that threat does not lead to holdup as feared by those who propose that a RAND pledge implies (or should embody) a waiver of seeking injunctive relief. If RAND terms are reached by negotiation, the negotiation is not conducted in the shadow of an injunctive threat but rather in the shadow of knowledge that the court will impose a set of terms if the parties do not reach agreement themselves").

granted by district courts post *eBay*,[22] and, patent pledges interpreted properly should limit injunctions further when irreparable harm cannot be proven. As can be seen from the Agere example, if Agere has agreed to license its patent to everyone, then one measure of its harm could be the amount of licensing fees that the infringer refused to pay.

B. ITC Exclusion Orders

That being said, an ITC exclusion order is not an injunction – it is directed at the products, not the parties. Even if a patent pledge renders injunctive relief at best a theoretical possibility, a different analysis must take place for exclusion orders – a statutorily mandated remedy to protect trade rather than an equitable remedy designed to protect the parties. The difference between exclusion orders granted under Section 337 and injunctions granted under the Patent Act, 35 U.S.C. § 283 follows "the long-standing principle that importation is treated differently than domestic activity."[23] Again, by statute, the ITC is required to issue an exclusion order upon the finding of a Section 337 violation absent a finding that the effects of one of the statutorily enumerated public interest factors counsel otherwise.

> As contrasted with the remedial scheme established by Congress for proceedings before the Commission, the statutory remedies available in proceedings before the district courts are quite different. In addition to the remedy of damages under 35 U.S.C. § 284, Congress gave district courts the discretion to grant injunctive relief and in doing so made explicit that such discretion is to be exercised "in accordance with the principles of equity … on such terms as the court deems reasonable."[24]

The traditional principles of equity do not apply to the ITC, which grants relief through a different statutory underpinning that requires an evaluation of set public interest factors rather than the "equitable concerns at issue in *eBay*."[25] As the Federal Circuit said so deftly, "[t]he scope of the public interest factors recited in Section 337 is a matter of statutory interpretation not necessarily informed by the same principles of equity relevant to the grant of permanent injunctive relief under 35 U.S.C.

---

22 *See* Colleen Chien & Mark Lemley, *Patent Holdup, the ITC, and the Public Interest*, 98 CORNELL L. REV. 1, 9–10 (2012).

23 Spansion, Inc. v. Int'l. Trade Comm'n., 629 F.3d 1331, 1359 (Fed. Cir. 2010).

24 Id.

25 Id.

§ 283."[26] An exclusion order does not prohibit a foreign manufacturer from attempting to import articles into this country; rather it orders the United States Customs and Border Protection ("Customs") to block the importation of illegal articles. The ITC does not issue injunctions, and does not need to change its standards to "better align it with the traditional four-factor test in *eBay Inc. v. MercExchange*, to enhance consistency in the standards applied at the ITC and district courts."[27] *eBay* does not apply to the ITC, because, again, an exclusion order is not an injunction, and because of the difference between the fundamental purpose of the ITC and the Patent Act.

This distinction can, perhaps, be best understood with respect to non-practicing entities. A non-practicing entity filing a complaint at the ITC, and bringing a lawsuit in federal district court with respect to a patent could find different outcomes in each action. A non-practicing entity has a very difficult burden in meeting the first two *eBay* factors. If a company is focused solely on monetizing its patents through licensing, a non-practicing entity in other words, then the patents are nothing more than economic vehicles to that entity, rendering any harm reparable through monetary damages. Therefore, a non-practicing entity is extremely unlikely to obtain an injunction in federal district court.

On the other hand, that same non-practicing entity has a different burden when filing a complaint in the ITC. The public interest factors, discussed in more detail below, require no showing of irreparable harm – focusing instead on the competitive conditions in the United States economy and the impact on the public health and welfare of consumers. A non-practicing entity must show the existence of a domestic industry in order to file a complaint in the ITC, but that domestic industry requirement can be met by demonstrating an investment in domestic patent licensing. In other words, a non-practicing entity licensing its patents in the United States has an explicit statutory right to file a complaint seeking an exclusion order in the ITC. If infringement is found, the public interest factors do not inhibit the issuance of an exclusion order based solely on the economic behavior of the complainant. The non-practicing entity unable to obtain an injunction in federal court, because of its licensing practice, is able to obtain an exclusion order from the ITC, if the non-practicing entity prevails. The statutory relief available to the ITC is not the same as the judicial decision making rendered under

---

[26] Id.

[27] Press Release, The White House, *Fact Sheet: White House Task Force on High-Tech Patent Issues* (Jun. 4, 2013).

eBay. This scenario highlights the essential difference between an injunction and an exclusion order.

The Patent Act exists to promote the progress of science and the useful arts, the ITC exists to protect the United States domestic industry and trade. Protecting trade and promoting science and the useful arts requires different focuses. The ITC regulates trade, and can regulate trade by issuing an exclusion order without a finding of irreparable harm. In a recent case, it was argued that "the public interest inquiry in [the ITC] is similar to the traditional test for injunctive relief" applied under *eBay.*[28] The ITC correctly responded to the argument by pointing out "that *eBay* does not apply to Commission remedy determinations."[29] The Federal Circuit held that "Congress intended injunctive relief to be the normal remedy for a Section 337 violation and that a showing of irreparable harm is not required to receive such injunctive relief."[30] The Federal Circuit pointed to Congressional history to support this holding. "[I]n passing the Tariff Act of 1930 … Congress eliminated the monetary remedy for intellectual property import violations, representing a legislative determination that an injunction is the only available remedy for violations of Section 337."[31] The Federal Circuit then looked to the 1988 amendments to Section 337, which removed "the requirement of proof of injury to the domestic industry and making it unnecessary to show irreparable harm to the patentee in the case of infringement by importation."[32] The Congressional Committee that drafted the amendments expressly stated that it did "not intend that the ITC, in considering the public health and welfare, or the President, in reviewing the ITC's determination on policy grounds, will reintroduce these requirements."[33]

> Given the different statutory underpinnings for relief before the Commission in Section 337 actions and before the district courts in suits for patent infringement … *eBay* does not apply to Commission remedy determinations under Section 337 … . The difference between exclusion orders granted under Section 337 and injunctions granted under the Patent Act, 35 U.S.C. § 283, follows "the long-standing principle that importation is treated differently than domestic activity."[34]

---

28 *Spansion*, 629 F.3d at 1358.
29 Id.
30 Id.
31 Id.
32 Id.
33 Id.
34 Id.

Exclusion orders are a valuable remedy that, as a matter of policy, not just reality, must remain available to parties to patent pledges.[35] Even a cursory examination of procedures at the ITC will illustrate the importance of the public interest in every facet of an ITC determination, fundamental to the very nature of an exclusion order. Exclusion orders are not injunctions. In one patent pledge, Google asserted that, with respect to the covered patents, Google "shall neither (i) initiate legal proceedings against the other party's standard essential patents nor (ii) seek injunctive relief in litigation commenced after the date of this letter for their respective standard essential patents." Google goes on to define "injunctive relief" as used in this agreement to include "exclusion orders issued by the U.S. International Trade Commission pursuant to 19 U.S.C. § 1337."[36] Along these lines, the FTC, the United States Patent and Trademark Office ("USPTO") and the Department of Justice ("DOJ") have argued before the ITC that exclusion orders should not be issued with respect to standards-essential patents, because of the risk of patent hold-up.[37] Again, this does not reflect the fundamental difference between exclusion orders and injunctions.

Section 337 actions give the ITC the power to investigate complaints brought by owners of United States intellectual property who allege that they are being subjected to unfair competition due to the importation of

---

[35] DOJ & PTO, *supra* note 19 ("An exclusion order may still be an appropriate remedy in some circumstances, such as where the putative licensee is unable or refuses to take a F/RAND license and is acting outside the scope of the patent holder's commitment to license on F/RAND. For example, if a putative licensee refuses to pay what has been determined to be a F/RAND royalty, or refuses to engage in a negotiation to determine F/RAND terms, an exclusion order could be appropriate. Such a refusal could take the form of a constructive refusal to negotiate, such as by insisting on terms clearly outside the bounds of what could reasonably be considered to be F/RAND terms in an attempt to evade the putative licensee's obligation to fairly compensate the patent. An exclusion order also could be appropriate if a putative license is not subject to the jurisdiction of a court that could award damages. This list is not an exhaustive one").

[36] Letter from Allen Lo, Deputy Gen. Counsel, Google, to Gordon Day, President, IEEE (Feb. 8, 2012).

[37] Certain Wireless Devices with 3G and/or 4G Capabilities and Components Thereof, Inv. No. 337-TA-868, 2014 WL 2965327 (USITC June 13, 2014) (Preliminary) ("The essence of the arguments made by the FTC and PTO/DOJ against the availability of exclusion orders is that by having an exclusion order hanging over the negotiations, there is a risk of 'Patent holdup': that is the owner of the IPR may obtain remuneration beyond the value of the IP, because it is a standard").

infringing products into the United States. The patentee is not using the patent against another company, the patentee is not initiating a patent lawsuit – there is no lawsuit, only an investigation. One argument that patent pledges should not apply to the ITC is that the patentee is not bringing suit over patent infringement, but rather is alleging that the domestic industry is being injured due to the importation of infringing articles, and is asking the United States government to investigate that allegation. If the ITC decides to institute an investigation, then the ITC is protecting U.S. domestic industry, not the patentee's rights. ITC jurisdiction is limited to imported products, and cannot extend to domestic production. The ITC can only protect industry through the issuance of an exclusion order or a cease and desist order – there are no other remedies, and the patentee cannot be awarded damages by the ITC.

However, the ITC has enforced covenants not to sue with respect to ITC investigations, despite the fact that it is the executive branch of the government investigating and enforcing laws as required by the Constitution of the United States.[38] Why? Because a covenant not to sue renders irrelevant any question of patent infringement, meaning there is no violation under which to bring an ITC action. Infringement is the use of the patent without permission of a patent holder. A covenant not to sue is permission of a patent holder to use the patent in appropriate circumstances.[39] That permission renders void any potential infringement, removing any basis for the filing of a complaint at the ITC. This logic should extend to the enforcement of patent pledges as well.

Tesla's broad patent pledge (see Chapter 1 and Appendix) limits its scope to "good faith" users, allowing "other manufacturers to use its patents in 'good faith' – essentially barring those users from filing patent-infringement lawsuits against [Tesla] or trying to produce knock-offs of Tesla's cars."[40] Under the above analysis, if a party is using a patent in good faith, then Tesla has no basis to file a complaint in the ITC, since the party is not infringing, but is using the patent in good faith with the permission of the patent pledge. On the other hand, if a party is not operating within the scope of the patent pledge, then Tesla is entitled to protection of its patents and its domestic industry, regardless of its patent pledge to allow others to use its patents in good faith. Tesla may

---

[38] Texas Instruments Inc. v. Tessera, Inc., 231 F.3d 1325, 1331 (Fed. Cir. 2000) ("[S]ection 337 proceedings at the ITC are recognized as litigation").

[39] Gen. Protecht Grp., Inc. v. Leviton Mfg. Co., 651 F.3d 1355, 1363–64 (Fed. Cir. 2011).

[40] Jerry Hirsch & Tiffany Hsu, *Elon Musk Opens up Tesla Patents; It "Isn't Entirely Altruistic,"* L.A. TIMES (Jun. 12, 2014).

file a complaint in the ITC, and bring suit in the federal court system, and will face different standards in each.

II. PUBLIC INTEREST FACTORS

The statutory language giving the ITC its powers sets forth a demanding four-prong test for determining whether an exclusion order is in the public's interest. These public interest factors are critical to understanding the difference between injunctions and exclusion orders.[41] Since 1974, Congress has required the ITC to consider the impact on the public interest before ordering a remedy for a violation. In order to issue a remedy, the ITC must find the lack of a detrimental effect of the remedy order on the following four elements: "(1) the public health and welfare; (2) competitive conditions in the United States economy; (3) the production of like or directly competitive articles in the United States; and (4) United States consumers."[42] This inquiry is the fundamental difference between actions in the district courts and actions in the ITC, and renders the traditional test for injunctive relief that district courts apply under *eBay* superfluous. "The legislative history of the amendments to Section 337 indicates that Congress intended injunctive relief to be the normal remedy for a Section 337 violation and that a showing of irreparable harm is not required to receive such injunctive relief."[43] As discussed above, when Congress passed the Tariff Act of 1930,[44] Congress "eliminated the monetary remedy for intellectual property import violations, representing a legislative determination that an injunction is the only available remedy for violations of Section 337."[45] Furthermore, in easing the requirements to bring suit in the ITC under the Omnibus Trade and Competitiveness Act of 1988,[46] Congress rendered unnecessary any showing of "irreparable harm to the patentee in the case

---

41 S. Rep. 100-71, at 128 (1987) ("The importation of any infringing merchandise derogates from the statutory right, diminishes the value of the intellectual property, and thus indirectly harms the public interest").

42 19 U.S.C. § 1337(d)(1) (2015).

43 Spansion, Inc. v. Int'l. Trade Comm'n., 629 F.3d 1331, 1358 (Fed. Cir. 2010).

44 Smoot-Hawley Act, Pub. L. No. 71–361, 46 Stat. 590 (codified as 19 U.S.C. § 1304–683).

45 *Spansion*, 629 F.3d at 1358.

46 Pub. L. No. 100–418, 102 Stat. 1107 (codified in scattered sections of 19 U.S.C.).

of infringement by importation."[47] This is one of the most important differences between the *eBay* factors required for injunctive relief, and the findings required for a determination of a violation of Section 337 by the ITC. To suggest that the ITC can be aligned with *eBay* is to ignore Congressional intent.[48]

Since 1974, when Congress amended Section 337 to require the ITC to consider public interest factors in determining whether a remedy should be issued for a violation, there have been only three investigations in which the ITC has found that a patent owner's rights are infringed, but that public interest dictated no remedy be issued.[49] In 1978, the ITC determined that the importation of automatic crankpin grinders violated Section 337, however "the public interest factors enumerated in subsections (d) and (f) of the statute preclude the imposition of a remedy."[50] The ITC concluded:

> [T]he public interest considerations, namely the domestic industry's inability to supply crankpin grinders which can be used to produce on a timely basis more energy efficient automobiles, and the engine producer's need for additional automatic crankpin grinders prior to the expiration of the patent are stronger than complainant's rights to enforcement of its patent monopoly through a remedy pursuant to section 337.[51]

Shortly thereafter, in 1980, the ITC investigated inclined-field acceleration tubes and components thereof that were used for scientific research. Finding that the "investigation raises significant public interest issues – pure scientific research and the advancement of knowledge" the ITC concluded that there was a violation, but that there should be no

---

47 *Spansion*, 629 F.3d at 1358.

48 White House Press Release, *supra* note 27 ("Change the ITC standard for obtaining an injunction to better align it with the traditional four-factor test in *eBay Inc. v. MercExchange*, to enhance consistency in the standards applied at the ITC and district courts").

49 Certain Automatic Crankpin Grinders, Inv. No. 337-TA-60, USITC Pub. 1022, at 17 (Dec. 1979) (Final) (citing S. Rep. No. 93-1298, 197 (1974)) [hereinafter *Crankpin Grinders*]; *see* Certain Devices for Connecting Computers via Telephone Lines, Inv. No. 337-TA-360, USITC Pub. 2843, at 10 (Dec. 1994) (Final); Certain Fluidized Supporting Apparatus & Components Thereof, Inv. Nos. 337-TA-182/188, USITC Pub. 1667, at 5 (Oct. 1984) [hereinafter *Fluidized Supporting Apparatus*]; Certain Inclined-Field Acceleration Tubes & Components Thereof, Inv. No. 337-TA-67, USITC Pub. 1119, at 21–22 (Dec. 1980) [hereinafter *Acceleration Tubes*].

50 *Crankpin Grinders*, *supra* note 49, at 1.

51 *Crankpin Grinders*, *supra* note 49, at 20.

remedy.[52] The ITC found that "basic scientific research … is precisely the kind of activity intended by Congress to be included when it required the Commission to consider the effect of a remedy on the public health and welfare."[53] There were alternatives available, but the cost and performance of those alternatives rendered the alternatives unacceptable to the public. The most recent decision in which the ITC found the public interest to outweigh the protection of domestic industry was issued in 1984 in an investigation into hospital beds particularly adapted for burn victims.[54] A violation was found, but the ITC held that public health considerations overrode the interests of the exclusive patent licensee seeking the exclusion order.[55] The Commission took note of the findings of the Administrative Law Judge ("ALJ") that "if a temporary exclusion order were issued some patients might not have access to burn beds at all in the interim period" and that "the patented burn beds 'provide benefits unavailable from any other device or method of treatment.'"[56]

In each of these cases the ITC found violations of Section 337, but issued no remedy since the public interest factors outweighed protecting our domestic industry. The patents at issue affected traditional public interest concerns: health, transportation, and scientific research. The statute mandates that every ITC investigation evaluate the public interest factors, and these considerations are not meant to be given mere lip service. On the contrary "public health and welfare and the assurance of competitive conditions in the United States economy must be the overriding considerations in the administration of this statute."[57]

Emphasizing the importance of the public interest factors, the United States Trade Representative stated that:

> [I]n any future cases involving SEPs that are subject to voluntary FRAND commitments, the Commission should be certain to (1) to examine thoroughly and carefully on its own initiative the public interest issues presented both at the outset of its proceeding and when determining whether a particular remedy is in the public interest and (2) seek proactively to have the parties develop a comprehensive factual record related to these issues in the proceedings before the Administrative Law Judge and during the formal remedy phase of the investigation before the Commission … . In addition the

52 *Acceleration Tubes*, *supra* note 49, at 21.

53 *Acceleration Tubes*, *supra* note 49, at 22.

54 *Fluidized Supporting Apparatus*, *supra* note 49, at 5.

55 Id. at 25.

56 Id. at 23.

57 *Acceleration Tubes*, *supra* note 49, at 22 (quoting S. Rep. 93-1298, 197 (1974)).

> Commission should make explicit findings on these issues to the maximum extent possible … . The Commission is well-positioned to consider these issues in its public interest determinations.[58]

This weighing of the public interest is one of the fundamental differences between ITC investigations and litigation through the federal court system. A brief overview of ITC procedure will illustrate both the importance of the public interest factors at the ITC and some of the differences between ITC proceedings and federal litigation. ITC actions begin with the filing of a complaint. In that complaint, the complainant must submit a statement on the public interest that addresses "how issuance of the requested relief … in this investigation could affect the public health and welfare in the United States, competitive conditions in the United States economy, the production of like or directly competitive articles in the United States, or United States consumers."[59] The complainant's statement must also address the statutorily set forth public interest factors.[60] Nearly all complaints result in investigations.[61] The filing of a complaint initiates a 30-day time period in which the Commission determines whether to institute an investigation. During that time period, the public and proposed respondents are asked to comment on "whether the requested investigation raises public interest concerns,"[62] and parties and the public have an opportunity to submit comments and respond to any issues set forth in the complaint or the complainant's statement on public interest.[63] Public interest submissions by the public are a relatively new feature of ITC investigations. Prior to 2011, such focus on the public interest occurred only after an ALJ recommended the issuance of an exclusion order, but under a rule change adopted by the Commission in 2011, parties and the public can submit briefs (an apt

---

58 Letter from Michael B.G. Froman, U.S. Trade Rep., to Irving A. Williamson, Chairman, USITC (Aug. 3, 2013).

59 Commencement of Preinstitution Proceedings, 19 C.F.R. § 210.8(b)(2013).

60 As set forth in section 337, the complainant must address what the impact of a potential exclusion order would be on "the public health and welfare, competitive conditions in the United States economy, the production of like or directly competitive articles in the United States, and United States consumers." 19 U.S.C. § 1337 (2015).

61 INT'L TRADE COMM'N TRIAL LAWYERS ASS'N, *Frequently Asked Questions* (Jun. 1, 2015) ("[O]nly in extremely rare circumstances does the ITC decide not to institute an investigation").

62 Paul C. Goulet & P. Andrew Riley, *An Option for Public Interest Factfinding at the Commission*, 337 REPORTER (Sept. 2010).

63 19 C.F.R. § 210.8(c).

term when the filing must be no longer than five pages) on the public interest factors after the complaint is filed and before the investigation is instituted.

Upon institution of an investigation, the Chief ALJ at the ITC assigns an ALJ to the investigation and may further assign an investigative attorney from the Commission's Office of Unfair Import Investigations ("OUII"), to function as an independent litigant representing the public interest in the investigation. The Commission can go a step further, and specifically delegate fact-finding on the public interest to the ALJ assigned to the case as part of the investigation.[64] Since the rule change in 2010, the Commission has delegated public-interest fact-finding in 39 investigations, almost 25% of all investigations filed.[65] As the investigation proceeds, the ALJ issues an initial determination, which the Commission may review at its discretion.

If the Commission does not review the initial determination, the ALJ's decision becomes the ITC's final determination. If at least one Commissioner votes to review the initial determination, then the Commission reviews the initial determination before issuing the ITC's final determination. After the ITC determines that a violation of Section 337 has occurred, then the Office of the United States Trade Representative ("USTR") reviews the final determination.[66] The USTR receives the decision of the ITC, and can review and disallow the ITC's proposed order within 60 days.[67] The district courts do not face this additional step, nor should they. There is a judicial process that promotes the science and useful arts and an executive process that provides support for the domestic industry and trade. If the USTR does not specifically disapprove the ITC's determination within a 60-day period, then the determination stands as the final determination and judgment can be effectuated.[68] During each of these stages, public interest factors may be evaluated.

The presence of the public interest factors in every stage of the ITC's considerations, and the absence of a requirement of irreparable harm, reflect the fundamental differences between injunctions and exclusion orders. Patent pledges may make proving irreparable harm vastly more

---

[64] 19 C.F.R. § 210.8(b).

[65] Shara Aranoff, *Lessons from 5 Years of Public Interest Delegation at the ITC*, LAW360 (Aug. 5, 2015, 10:10 AM).

[66] *See* 19 U.S.C. § 1337(j)(2) (2015); Assignment of Certain Functions under Section 337 of the Tariff Act of 1930, 70 Fed. Reg. 43,251 (July 26, 2005).

[67] 19 U.S.C. § 1337(j)(2).

[68] Id.

difficult, but they may also tilt the finding of public interest factors so that an exclusion order is not an automatic result of the filing of a complaint before the ITC. The vast majority of patent pledges that have been litigated in the ITC are those involving standard setting organizations. In fact, no non-SEP patent pledges have been raised in actions at the ITC. However, the numerous complaints filed regarding infringement of standard essential patents provide a basis for understanding the broader issue, and are part of the important conversation in deciding why a statutorily required protection of domestic industry is not satisfactorily circumvented by a patent pledge. Again, the pledges may circumvent injunctive relief, and take it out of the picture for patent hold-ups at a minimum, but Section 337 actions do not exist to protect the patentee, but rather the industry. The *in rem* nature of 337 jurisdiction means that the *in personam* jurisdiction over contractual issues will never be a good fit at the ITC.

The year 2013 marked the first time the ITC issued exclusionary relief on a FRAND encumbered SEP. It also brought a rare disapproval of the ITC's order. There have only been six investigations in which the United States Trade Representative of the Executive Office of the President ("USTR") has disallowed the remedy issued by the ITC.[69] The most recent disapproval came after a complaint was filed by Samsung seeking exclusion of certain Apple smartphones and tablets, most notably early generation iPhones, which infringed a patent owned by Samsung and were subject to a voluntary FRAND commitment. The ITC found a violation of Section 337, and issued an exclusion order as well as a cease and desist order. The President, through USTR Michael Froman, disapproved of the Commission's exclusion order for policy reasons, stating that "[l]icensing SEPs on FRAND terms is an important element of the Administration's policy of promoting innovation and economic progress and reflects the positive linkages between patent rights and standards

[69] Certain Welded Stainless Steel Pipe and Tube, Inv. No. 337-TA-29 (Feb. 22, 1978) (Final); Certain Headboxes and Papermaking Machine Forming Sections for the Continuous Production of Paper, and Components Thereof, Inv. No. 337-TA-82, USITC Pub. No. 1197 (Nov. 1981) (Final); Certain Molded-In Sandwich Panel Inserts and Methods for their Installation, Inv. No. 337-TA-99, USITC Pub. No. 1246 (May 1982) (Final); Certain Alkaline Batteries, Inv. No. 337-TA-165, USITC Pub. No. 1616 (Nov. 1984) (Final), *aff'd*, Duracell Inc. v. U.S. Int'l Trade Comm'n, 778 F.2d 1578 (Fed. Cir. 1985); Certain Dynamic Random Access Memories, Inv. No. 337-TA-242, USITC Pub. No. 2034 (Nov. 1987) (Final); Certain Electronic Devices, Including Wireless Communication Devices, Portable Music and Data Processing Devices, and Tablet Computers, Inv. No. 337-TA-794 (May 31, 2013).

setting."[70] USTR Froman went on to state that "in any future cases involving SEPs that are subject to voluntary FRAND commitments" the Commission should evaluate whether a hold-up is occurring as well as the question of what the impact of such is on the public interest factors.[71] The USTR was concerned with "the various policy considerations … . [a]s they relate to the effect on competitive conditions in the U.S. economy and the effect on U.S. consumers."[72] This decision has echoes of the only antitrust action that resulted in a remedy issued by the ITC. In 1978, the ITC ordered 11 Japanese firms to cease and desist engaging in unfair competitive practices in the manufacturing and importing of certain welded stainless steel pipe and tube, and to not price the product below the average variable cost of production without commercial justification.[73] This predatory pricing scheme was found to restrain trade in the United States.[74] That decision, too, was disapproved of by the President, despite the detrimental effect on competition, due to other policy reasons.[75]

In evaluating the public interest factors, it has become routine for the ALJ to hear from expert witnesses on behalf of both the complainant and the respondent, as well as multiple fact witnesses. Third parties often submit comments on the public interest factors, and find themselves faced with requests for documents and testimony. Discovery during the investigations focuses not only on the validity of the patents at issue, and the infringement claims, but also on the impact on the public interest factors. All of these allows the ALJ to build a detailed record on the public interest factors, and gives the ALJ the unique opportunity to fully evaluate the impact of a potential exclusion order per the ITC's statutory mandate.

It is clear that an exclusion order may be detrimental to the public interest factors.[76] This is true of all exclusion orders, and the detrimental effect on the public interest must be weighed against the benefit of an exclusion order by the ITC. In the 860 investigation, for instance, the

---

70 Letter from Michael B.G. Froman, U.S. Trade Rep., to Irving A. Williamson, Chairman, USITC (Aug. 3, 2013).

71 Id.

72 Id.

73 *In re* Certain Welded Stainless Steel Pipe and Tube, USITC Inv. No. 337-TA-29 (1978), 43 Fed. Reg. 17,789–90 (Apr. 22, 1978).

74 Id.

75 Id. (specifically enumerated among these reasons was "[t]he detrimental effect of the imposition of the remedy on the national economic interest").

76 19 U.S.C. § 1337 (2015).

Commission evaluated the argument that an exclusion would create a shortage of semiconductor lasers, which would harm competitive conditions in the United States economy. The Commission ultimately found that there were numerous non-infringing alternatives to the accused products that would fill the demand that could result from the exclusion of the accused products. The respondents in that case were arguing for a modification of the exclusion order based on the public interest factors, arguing that it was in the public's interest to delay the implementation of the exclusion order.

In the 543 investigation, the ITC did modify its exclusion order, based on the public interest factors, allowing infringing products already being imported to remain in the United States, while excluding future imports of infringing products. The balancing of the public interest factors allows the ITC to modify and limit its exclusion orders, but still enforce its statutory mandate. The development of a detailed public interest record, and the ability to tailor exclusion orders are a fundamental difference between an injunction and the statutorily mandated remedy of an exclusion order.

Section 337 does not ask whether the patent that forms the basis of a complaint is subject to a patent pledge, nor should it. A patent holder should not be denied the opportunity to file a complaint at the ITC because the patent is subject to a patent pledge. The Department of Justice has speculated that the threat of seeking an exclusion order could be used as improper leverage by the holder of a FRAND-encumbered, standards-essential patent to "pressure an implementer of a standard to accept more onerous licensing terms than the patent holder would be entitled to receive" otherwise.[77] This is mere speculation, and the ITC is statutorily mandated to evaluate the public interest factors, and determine the competitive conditions of the United States economy. If the benefit of an exclusion order affecting an SEP would be outweighed by the detrimental impact of such an order on the public interest, then such a remedy is not appropriate.[78] This is a determination for the ITC to make, and not a remedy to be proactively removed by a patent pledge. As Judge Essex stated in an investigation of a complaint concerning an SEP:

---

[77] DOJ & PTO, *supra* note 19, at 6.

[78] The ITC has relied on public interest factors to delay the start of an exclusion order and to adjust the scope of an exclusion order recognizing the fact that even though an exclusion order may be the appropriate remedy, the public may benefit from an amelioration of the exclusion order. *See* Colleen Chien & Mark Lemley, *Patent Holdup, the ITC, and the Public Interest*, 98 CORNELL L. REV. 1, 28, 33 (2012).

> [T]here is no evidence that the [ITC] ought to go beyond the statute, and assume that the remedy of an exclusion order should be removed from the case. Neither the agreements imposed by the [SSO], nor the law nor public policy require us to offer [the alleged offenders] a safe haven, where they are free to avoid their own obligations under the agreements, can manufacture potentially infringing goods without license or consequence, can seek to invalidate the IPR in question, and yet are free from the risk of a remedy under 19 USC 1337. This one sided administration of the law is against both the Administrative Procedure Act 5 USC § 554 and Commission regulation 19 CFR § 200.735-101.[79]

An exclusion order is an appropriate remedy for infringement of a patent subject to a patent pledge, if the public interest factors do not dictate otherwise. Section 337 makes no distinction between patents that are subject to a patent pledge, or that are essential to a standard. If there is a violation of Section 337 based on infringement of patents subject to such, the ITC will evaluate public interest factors during its remedy determination. The Commission "is a creature of statute, and must find authority for its actions in its enabling statute."[80] The issuance of an exclusion order is a statutory mandate that can be overcome only by evidence that the enumerated public interest factors are frustrated. The mere possibility that a threat of patent hold-up or hold-out harms competitive conditions in the United States and United States consumers does not rise to the level of requiring a finding of irreparable harm to the patentee before the issuance of an exclusion order. The availability of an exclusion order – in situations where a patent pledge is in play – remains critical to a continuing balance of encouraging contribution and participation while still allowing access to patents subject to such pledges.

CONCLUSION

When a patent pledge sets forth such vague terms as "in good faith" or "fair and reasonable", litigation will be, at times, inevitable. Stipulations such as these have been the source of interminable litigation, but can hardly be said to replace the role of the ITC. It is well within the jurisdiction of the ITC to determine the impact of patent pledges on domestic industry, and to evaluate the public interest in participation in

---

[79] Certain Wireless Devices with 3G and/or 4G Capabilities and Components Thereof, Inv. No. 337-TA-868, 2014 WL 2965327 (USITC June 13, 2014) (Preliminary).

[80] Kyocera v. Int'l Trade Comm'n, 545 F.3d 1340, 1355 (Fed. Cir. 2008).

patent pledges, as well as enforcement of the same. Congress determined that it should be illegal to import articles that infringe patents and impact domestic industry. The policy considerations are very different than the policy considerations in the federal court system. There is no requirement that domestic industry be harmed, or that the patentee suffer an irreparable injury in order to file a complaint at the ITC. Exclusion orders are not injunctions, and the public interest factors statutorily mandated at the ITC are not the same as the equitable factors used to determine whether injunctive relief is appropriate.

Voluntary public commitments made by patentees, in the form of patent pledges, limit the enforcement and exploitation of their patents, but do not limit the role of the ITC in protecting domestic industry. The ITC exists to protect domestic industry, and not the patent. If the patent is being used within the context of the patent pledge, then no violation has occurred, since it is not infringement to use a patent as allowed by the patentee. If infringement occurs by use of the patent outside the scope of the pledge, then the patent pledge may still preclude the seeking of injunctive relief, but not exclusion orders. Exclusion orders are an appropriate remedy for infringement of a patent subject to a patent pledge, unless the exclusion order is contrary to the public interest. An exclusion order is not an injunction, and can be not conclusively precluded by a patent pledge. The exclusion order is a statutory mandate that can be overcome only by evidence that the statutorily enumerated public interest factors are frustrated, and requires no showing of irreparable harm, as required to obtain injunctive relief. The availability of an exclusion order remains critical to a continuing balance of encouraging participation in patent pledges, while still preventing unfair competition and protecting our domestic industry.

7. Voluntary patent pledges: enforcement in Germany

Catharina Maracke and Axel Metzger

I. INTRODUCTION

Germany has been a forerunner for Free and Open Source software (FOSS) license enforcement.[1] Consequently, it is likely that voluntary patent pledges announced in the context of Free and Open Source software will eventually be tested in German courts. Another aspect that makes a comparative analysis of German law with regards to patent pledges relevant is the difference between U.S. and German contract law.[2] In particular, the requirements to form a binding contract under German law are less restrictive compared to contract law in U.S. and other common law jurisdictions. For example, German law does not require the exchange of "consideration" in order to create a binding contractual commitment. In practice, this means that patent pledges, which do not qualify as binding contracts under U.S. law, can still be considered binding contracts under German law.

These different legal consequences may lead to unexpected results, which cannot always be avoided by adding a choice-of-law clause.[3] Under German law, a party may only choose the applicable law with regard to those questions which may be characterized as contractual according to German and European principles of conflict of laws. The same principles apply to unilateral commitments. A choice-of-law provision may thus be used to determine the applicable law for questions such

---

[1] *Judgements*, INSTITUTE FOR LEGAL QUESTIONS ON FREE AND OPEN SOURCE SOFTWARE, http://www.ifross.org/en/v-judgements, accessed Dec 21, 2016.

[2] *See* Contreras, Chapter 7 (discussing the application of U.S. contract law theories to the enforcement of patent pledges).

[3] *See* Council Regulation 593/2008, The Law Applicable to Contractual Obligations (Rome I), 2008 O.J. (L 177) art. 3.

as offer, acceptance and consideration, interpretation of contracts, warranty and liability, and so on. However, the proprietary aspects of license contracts or unilateral dispositions of intellectual property rights are subject to the principle of territoriality and covered by the law of the country for which protection is sought. Typical proprietary aspects are questions like ownership and transferability of intellectual property rights and licenses, requirements and consequences for exhaustion, *in rem* effects of licenses against third parties, and so on.[4] As a consequence, patent holders using patent pledges should not be surprised if the enforcement of promises made in patent pledges will take place in German courts and will be governed by German law.

II. VPPS AS (PATENT LICENSE) CONTRACTS UNDER GERMAN LAW

Voluntary patent pledges (VPPs) are not addressed to any particular individual or company. Instead, they are aimed at a specific market and intended to encourage market participants to invest in the covered technology.[5] However, depending on the exact language and interpretation of the respective wording, voluntary patent pledges could be described as contractual under German law.

Freedom of contract (*Vertragsfreiheit*) is one of the fundamental rights under German law. As a general principle and apart from a few exceptions stated in the German Civil Code,[6] contracts can contain whatever the parties agree upon.[7] Unlike the common law contract doctrine, German contract law does not require consideration. However, offer and acceptance are required to form a binding contract.

---

[4] *See* EUROPEAN MAX PLANCK GROUP ON CONFLICT OF LAWS IN INTELLECTUAL PROPERTY (CLIP), CONFLICT OF LAWS IN INTELLECTUAL PROPERTY: THE CLIP PRINCIPLES AND COMMENTARY (2013).

[5] *See* Contreras, Chapter 1.

[6] *See*, e.g., Bürgerliches Gesetzbuch [BGB] [Civil Code], § 138 (allowing legal transactions contrary to moral principles or exploiting the other person due to undue advantages) (English translation available at http://www.gesetze-im-internet.de/englisch_bgb/index.html, accessed Dec. 21, 2016.

[7] *See* id. Furthermore, they do not have to be in any particular form (e.g. in writing or by registration), unless specifically required by law.

A. Contract Law

The offer to form a binding contract requires a declaration of intent (*Willenserklaerung*) including the intention to be bound (*Geschaefts-wille*). Interpretation of both must reflect the perspective of the offeree, so that the offer has to be interpreted based on "what the [offeree] must have understood if observed objectively".[8] Looking at the experience learned from FOSS licenses, which are commonly seen as license agreements between licensor and licensee and therefore as contracts under German law, patent pledges can be qualified as an offer to form a binding contract under German law, if the respective language shows a clear intention to be legally bound.[9] Consequently, when a patent pledge explicitly states that it is not to be legally binding, for example Paul Graham's "The Patent Pledge",[10] a binding contract must be denied. But any patent pledge drafted to be legally binding may be seen as a valid offer according to German contract law and any use of the pledged patents may be seen as an acceptance. Acceptance does not necessarily have to reach the offeror. Instead, a contract is considered to have come into effect without communication of acceptance to the offeror if such communication is not expected according to ordinary usage or if the offeror has waived such communication.[11] Similar to the legal analysis of FOSS licenses under German law, both alternatives may apply to patent pledges: The patent owner waives the communication requirement by relying on the public pledge and it is also common practice not to notify the patent owner if the patent pledge is drafted as a public promise to assure the market rather than one individual or one particular company.[12]

However, the fact that patent pledges are addressed to any one particular party poses another question of German private law: Since patent pledges are formulated for an indefinite number of users and therefore form an indefinite number of potential contracts, they may be

---

8 Id. at §157.

9 An intention to be legally bound is missing if the offeror only provides basic information about a specific product and thereby encourages other interested parties to make an offer, so-called "*invitatio ad offerendum*" (*Schaufenster-beispiele*).

10 *The Patent Pledge*, PAUL GRAHAM (Aug. 2011) http://paulgraham.com/patentpledge.html, accessed Dec. 21, 2016. *See also* Contreras, Chapter 1.

11 Bürgerliches Gesetzbuch [BGB] § 151.

12 *See* TIM ENGELHARDT & TILL JAEGER, THE INTERNATIONAL FREE AND OPEN SOURCE SOFTWARE LAW BOOK 107 (2011).

regarded as standard business terms, which are subject to additional restrictions stated in sections 305–310 of the German Civil Code. These restrictions are supposed to protect parties and especially consumers when entering contracts that contain standard business terms. As a general rule, standard business terms can only be legally binding components of contracts if 1) the user of such terms either explicitly or in other reasonably noticeable manner refers to the standard terms, and thereby gives the other party the opportunity to take notice of all details of those terms, and if 2) the other party agrees with those standard terms.[13] In theory, these detailed requirements may pose a problem for the standard language of patent pledges to become part of a legally binding contract; however, in practice, it can be assumed that the user of pledged patents has taken note of and agreed with all details of the respective pledge.[14] Moreover, most patent pledges are used between two companies, while most German rules on standard business terms only apply in transactions with consumers.

In summary, voluntary patent pledges could be constructed as legally binding contracts under German law, if the respective language shows clear intention to be legally bound.

B. Interpretation of Contracts

To understand the legal consequences of interpreting patent pledges as contracts, the character of the contract must be determined since special contracts are governed by different principles under German law.[15]

1. Patent license contract

One possible interpretation may result in a patent license contract: The promise not to enforce patents may be seen as the patent owner's consent to use the patents. Looking at the exact wording of most of the prominent patent pledges, the declaration of intent constitutes the "promise not to enforce the respective patent." Taken literally, this does not show any will to sell or license the respective patent. The promise not to enforce patents (even if under certain conditions) does not mention any intended transfer of exclusive or non-exclusive rights, which would be required for a patent license. From the perspective of customary practice or "what the offeree

---

[13] *See* Bürgerliches Gesetzbuch [BGB] § 305.

[14] *See* Till Jaeger & Axel Metzger, Open Source Software 201 (4th ed. 2016).

[15] *See* Bürgerliches Gesetzbuch [BGB] § 157 (taking into account good faith and customary practice).

must have understood if observed objectively" it is also clear that neither a transfer of the patent nor a license can be expected. Only a specific performance can be anticipated, namely the performance not to enforce the pledged patents.

Assuming that a patent pledge is still drafted in a way that suggests interpretation as a patent license contract, any infringement claim by the patent holder will be denied. Since a pledge can only be interpreted as a non-exclusive license, the license grant itself (disposition) will be considered non-transferable under German law if the licensor has not explicitly agreed to the transfer.[16] Such a consent can also be given in advance if clearly stated in the pledge, for example as shown in Google's Open Patent Non-Assertion Pledge.[17] Also, the exhaustion principle will apply to products using the respective (pledged) patents when these products have been put on the market within the EU or any European Economic Area (EEA) member state.[18]

2. Covenant not to sue

Additional arguments for the analysis of a patent pledge in the context of German contract law may be drawn from interpreting a covenant-not-to-sue under German law.[19] An agreement stating that the patent holder will not assert a patent claim against the other party may either be qualified as a mere procedural contract (a so-called *pactum de non petendo*) or as a substantive contract which excludes the patent claim and can in turn be treated as a license grant. The District Court of Mannheim interpreted a covenant not to sue in a recent case as a mere *pactum de non petendo*.[20] The controversial settlement agreement combined an explicit non-exclusive license for one party with a mere covenant not to sue for the other side. The court inferred from this difference in wording that the parties would have stipulated an explicit license for the other side as well if they had wanted to. As a consequence, the covenant not to sue did only bind the parties to the settlement agreement and not, after the patent was transferred, the transferee who successfully enforced the patent in

---

16 Georg Benkard, Patentgesetz 705, § 103 (11th ed.2015).

17 See Google, *Open Patent Non-Assertion Pledge*, Appendix.

18 Maximilian Haedicke & Henrik Timmann, Patent Law Handbook 804 (2014).

19 Under German law, a covenant not to sue must meet the requirements of a contract to be binding. Ronny Hauck, *Rechtsnatur und-wirkungen eines covenant-not-to-sue*, 5 ZGE/IPJ 206, 223 (2013).

20 LG Mannheim [District Court Mannheim], Apr. 23, 2010, 7 O 145/09, GRUR-RR 2011, 49 (Ger.).

court. Since it was not qualified as a license contract, any *in rem* effect was negated.

3. How German courts may interpret patent pledges as contracts

Following the analysis offered by the District Court of Mannheim, it is likely that German courts would qualify patent pledges as mere procedural contracts in cases where they can find clear indications that the parties explicitly did not want to enter a license agreement. However, German courts may also interpret patent pledges as implied patent license contracts if the wording shows clear characteristics comparable to a patent license, though avoiding the term "patent license". In the case of Google's Open Patent Non-Assertion Pledge[21] the promise not to assert patent claims is embedded into a broader set of promises and duties which are typical for license contracts: It shall not only bind Google and controlled entities but also their successors and persons or entities to whom Google might transfer the pledged patents. The IBM Statement of Non-Assertion of Named Patents Against OSS[22] explicitly states: "We are pledging the free use of 500 of our U.S. patents as well as all counterparts of these patents issued in other countries, in the development, distribution, and use of open source software." This specific language indicates that the pledge should also imply the (substantive) right of the recipient to use the patented inventions and not just prevent claims on a procedural level.

III. PATENT PLEDGES AND NON-CONTRACT LEGAL THEORIES UNDER GERMAN LAW

Although it may be easier to qualify a patent pledge as a contractual arrangement under German than U.S. contract law, not all patent pledges discussed fulfill all the necessary criteria for a binding contract under sections 145–157 of the German Civil Code.[23] However, this does not imply that those non-contractual pledges are without legal effect for other actors in the relevant technology market. German law provides legal principles for the construction of non-contractual unilateral declarations on the use of intellectual property that may help to clarify the possible legal consequences for technology users relying on those pledges.

---

21 Google, *Open Patent Non-Assertion Pledge*, *supra* note 17.

22 *See IBM Statement of Non-Assertion of Named Patents Against OSS*, Appendix.

23 *See* Bürgerliches Gesetzbuch [BGB] § 147–57.

A. Unilateral Waiver

One possible strategy to give legal effect to a patent pledge, which does not qualify as a bilateral contract, could be to interpret the statement as a waiver of the covered patents. A waiver is typically seen as a unilateral declaration, which relinquishes the covered right with *in rem* effect.[24] This strategy has been suggested in Germany for the interpretation of unilateral statements with regards to the copyright in a work, for example if the statement "reproduction permitted" is printed on sheet music. In the context of copyright, the German Federal Court has stated that copyright may not be waived entirely, because it may also not be transferred according to section 29 German Copyright Act (1965), but that a unilateral waiver is possible for single economic rights (e.g. the right of distribution).[25] However, such a waiver of economic rights in favor of the general public is not undisputed in copyright law literature, and a number of authors regard it as invalid.[26]

Moreover, this waiver theory has not yet been tested in court under German patent law. Admittedly, patents may be transferred under German and European patent law.[27] The patent (or single patent claims[28]) may also be subject of a waiver.[29] But such a waiver must be submitted "by written declaration to the Patent Office".[30] The requirements for a written declaration follow the general principle in section 126 of the German Civil Code, which states that the waiver document must be signed by the issuer with his name in his own hand, or by his notarized initials. This

---

[24] Bundesgerichtshof [BGH] [Federal Court of Justice] Feb. 23, 1995, I ZR 68/93, GRUR 1995, 673, 675 Mauer-Bilder (Ger.).

[25] Id. In this case artists, who had painted pictures on the Berlin wall, claimed for a share of the revenues from the later commercialization of the pieces of the wall. The court denied a waiver of the right of distribution in the case.

[26] *See*, e.g., HAIMO SCHACK, URHEBER- UND URHEBERVERTRAGSRECHT 181 (6th ed. 2015); THOMAS DREIER & GERNOT SCHULZE, URHEBERRECHTSGESETZ 334 (4th ed. 2013). *But see* AXEL NORDEMANN & JAN BERND NORDEMANN, URHEBERRECHT 555–56 (11th ed. 2014); ULRICH LOEWENHEIM, URHEBERRECHT 625, (4th ed. 2010).

[27] *See* Patentgesetz [PatG] §15(1) (1981); Convention on the Grant of European Patents, art. 71, Oct. 5, 1973, 1065 U.N.T.S. 276.

[28] GEORG BENKARD, PATENTGESETZ 770 (11th ed. 2015).

[29] *See* PatG § 20, European Patent Convention, art. 99, Rule 75 of the Implementing Regulations to the Convention on the Grant of European Patents of 5 October, 1973, as last amended by decision of the Administrative Council of the European Patent Organization of 9 December, 2004.

[30] Id.

requirement is not met by a simple public announcement. Moreover, the German Federal Court has been strict with its interpretation of the requirement that a waiver be submitted "to the Patent Office." The court refused to give any legal effect to a declaration of waiver expressed in a court settlement.[31] Thus, a mere public statement in electronic form cannot be constructed as a valid patent waiver.

B. Simple Consent

A voluntary patent pledge in a public announcement, which does not constitute an offer for the conclusion of a contract, may still be characterized as a simple consent to the use of the covered technology.[32] The German Federal Court has lately applied this approach in a prominent copyright case *Vorschaubilder*[33] dealing with Google's image search. According to the Federal Court, Google's use of copyright protected material as thumbnails in its image search function is justified by the implied consent of the concerned rights holders. The court inferred this implied consent from the fact that the rights holders made images available on the Internet without technological measures to block the image search function. Such a consent permits the use of the copyrighted material but does not give any enforceable right to the user.[34] Also, the consent may be revoked with effect for the future at any time but not with retroactive effect.[35] Since the simple consent does not provide the user with any enforceable rights, it is not required that the rights holder declares its intention to be bound.[36]

---

31 Bundesgerichtshof [BGH] [Federal Supreme Court] Dec. 1, 1961, I ZR 131/56, GRUR 1962, 294 – Hafendrehkran (Ger.).

32 On consent in German civil and intellectual property law. *See* ANSGAR OHLY, "VOLENTI NON FIT INIURIA": DIE EINWILLIGUNG IM PRIVATRECHT 346 (2002).

33 Bundesgerichtshof, [BGH] [Federal Supreme Court] Apr. 29, 2010, I ZR 69/08, GRUR 2010, 628 – Vorschaubilder (Ger.). *See* on the case Leistner, The German Federal Supreme Court's Judgment on Google's Image Search: A Topical Example of the "Limitations" of the European Approach to Exceptions and Limitations, IIC 2011, 417.

34 Bundesgerichtshof, [BGH] [Federal Supreme Court] Apr. 29, 2010, I ZR 69/08, GRUR 2010, 628 – Vorschaubilder (Ger.).

35 Id.

36 Id.

The *Vorschaubilder* decision has been harshly criticized by commentators, who argue that it disregards fundamental principles of civil law.[37] One should therefore be careful to avoid generalization on the basis of this case. Nonetheless, the case shows the potential of the doctrine of consent for the "accepted use" of intellectual property. Such a characterization could even be allowed if the pledge is explicitly drafted as "not legally binding"[38] because it possesses the nature of a simple consent that is without binding effect for the future and revocable at any time.

Patent holders using these simple pledges should, however, be barred from claiming damages for the use of their patented technology in the past. As long as a simple consent has not been revoked, it precludes any claim for patent infringement that has been committed in the past.[39] As a consequence, the principles of exhaustion should be applicable to products manufactured by users relying on the patent pledge. But the preclusion of claims comes to an end whenever the pledge is revoked. Users should also be careful if the patent has been transferred and the transferee has not announced whether the pledge will be upheld or revoked. The simple consent has no *in rem* effect and does not bind the transferee. Companies using technology on the basis of a simple patent pledge therefore bear considerable economic risk. Any investment in products or services depending on the protected technology may be jeopardized by the patent holder after a revocation of the patent pledge.

C. Good Faith as Defense

Finally, if a public pledge may neither be qualified as a contract offer nor as simple consent, the defendant in a patent case may still raise the general defense of "good faith" stated in section 242 of the German Civil Code. A patent holder declaring in public that its patents will not be enforced but suing users of the patented technology may be said to be behaving inconsistently with that public declaration. The defendant could therefore argue on the basis of the "*venire contra factum proprium*" doctrine, a subcategory of the broader principle of good faith. The doctrine of "*venire contra factum proprium*" has been applied by German courts in many different areas. However, the court practice in patent cases

---

37 *See*, e.g., *Spindler, Bildersuchmaschinen, Schranken und konkludente Einwilligung im Urheberrecht: Besprechung der BGH-Entscheidung "Vorschaubilder,"* GRUR 2010, 785, 789–92 (2010).

38 *See supra* note 10.

39 Ansgar Ohly, "Volenti Non Fit Iniuria": Die Einwilligung im Privatrecht 346 (2002).

is meager.[40] The few reported cases concern situations in which the patent holder declared during examination or opposition proceedings that it would not claim certain varieties of a technology, but later brought claims for exactly those varieties against a defendant who relied on his declaration. The application of the "*venire contra factum proprium*" doctrine in case of a broken patent pledge has not yet been tested in German courts. The chance of success with this defense is therefore hard to predict.

CONCLUSION

Voluntary patent pledges have become increasingly popular over the past years. Even though these patent pledges are made by different means and with different strategic goals, they share several characteristics. As described in Chapter 1, such pledges are often drafted to encourage other companies and competitors to make investments and to further innovate based upon the covered technology. In that respect, patent pledges show great potential to provide a new basis for innovation. However, companies and individuals who take advantage of these pledges to facilitate innovation do so in reliance on their enforceability. Thus, it is critical that patent pledges are legally binding and enforceable.

The analysis of German law provided above has shown that, depending on the language, patent pledges may be interpreted as patent license contracts, procedural contracts, or simple consents, each with differing legal consequences. In addition, the defendant may use arguments based on good faith. Since the legal effects given to pledges depend primarily on their legal characterization, future research in the field should not only reflect commonly known legal instruments but look carefully at the parties' intent and the motivation behind the patent pledge. While the patent holder may not be willing to enter a legally binding contract or license because of known legal consequences, such as patent exhaustion or the first sale doctrine, it may still want competitors to use the technology and make investments. Pledge recipients may want to enjoy the benefits of immediate access to technology without lengthy and often costly license negotiations. Both parties have legitimate interests and must be brought into a fair balance. But maximum flexibility for the pledgor will not always meet the requirements and prospects of the

40 GEORG BENKARD, PATENTGESETZ 770 (11th ed. 2015).

pledge recipient. Without a clear legal answer to these questions, it is even more important to further discuss and engage in the use of patent pledges.

PART III

Competition law and patent pledges around the world

8. Is patent reform via private ordering anticompetitive? An analysis of open patent agreements

Matthew W. Callahan and Jason M. Schultz

I. INTRODUCTION

In the five years from 2010 through 2015, there have been numerous attempts to create new forms of private "collective action" to address a range of perceived problems in the patent ecosystem, from "abusive" litigation to patent quality to general concerns about scope and claim over-breadth as well as licensing transaction costs. Drawing from the success of patent pools and cross-licenses as well as open source and open content copyright licenses, a group of Open Patent Agreements (OPAs) have emerged, from the Open Invention Network (OIN) license[1] to the Eco-Patent Commons[2] to License On Transfer (LOT)[3] to the Defensive Patent License (DPL),[4] each of which makes various patent pledges[5] to mitigate current patent problems. Each OPA is a singular document or legal instrument; however, each is also designed to create a powerful "network effect" where the impact of the agreement increases

---

1 *About OIN*, OPEN INVENTION NETWORK, http://www.openinvention network.com/about-us/.

2 *About the Eco-Patent Commons*, ECO-PATENT COMMONS, https://ecopatent commons.org/about-eco-patent-commons.

3 LOT Network, *The LOT Network Solution*, LOTNET, http://www.lotnet.com/lotnet-solution/index.cfm [hereinafter LOT, home].

4 DEFENSIVE PATENT LICENSE, http://www.defensivepatentlicense.org/; Jason Schultz & Jennifer M. Urban, *Protecting Open Innovation: The Defensive Patent License as a New Approach to Patent Threats, Transaction Costs, and Tactical Disarmament*, 26 HARV. J.L. & TECH. 1 (2012). One of the authors of this chapter also helped draft the DPL.

5 This terminology refers to the patent pledges taxonomy developed by Contreras, Chapter 1.

with every additional party. Yet whenever networks of actors agree on specific obligations or actions, especially ones that hold interests in relevant intellectual property, such an agreement also implicates competition policy – and liability. This chapter contemplates this topic in the context of United States federal antitrust law. Specifically, it looks at how antitrust regulators and doctrines will likely react to OPAs, both in their nascent forms and over time if they are successful at attracting large networks of users. OPAs, as we define them, involve efforts to license patents broadly to all-comers for royalty-free use, usually on certain conditions that aspire to promote widespread innovation and reduce patent litigation.[6]

No court or regulator has directly confronted the issue of whether these OPAs would violate antitrust laws. By looking at the related court decisions and regulatory guidance on patent pools and open source copyright licenses, Section II of this chapter attempts to build a framework for evaluating patent pledges generally. Section III of this chapter applies this framework to OPAs, concluding that OPAs should survive most antitrust challenges under existing U.S. law.

II. BACKGROUND: OPAS AND ANTITRUST LAW

A. Patent Pools and OPAs

Collective action via patent agreements is nothing new. Patent pools have been around in the United States since at least the mid-1800s, starting

---

[6] *See* Eric Adler, *The Basics of Open Patent Licensing*, TECHCRUNCH (Apr. 23, 2015). While exact statistics are not available, the OPA governing the largest number of patent grants is probably that contained in software licensed under free and open source software licenses. Someone who contributes code under the terms of the GNU General Public License (GPL) pledges not to enforce any patent rights covering that code against subsequent licensees (implicitly in older versions of the license, and explicitly in later ones). *See* GNU General Public License version 2.0 § 6 (1991), https://www.gnu.org/licenses/gpl-2.0.html#SEC1 (containing the implicit patent grant); BRADLEY M. KUHN & ANTHONY K. SEBRO, JR., COPYLEFT AND THE GNU GENERAL PUBLIC LICENSE: A TUTORIAL 28–29 (2014) (explaining the implicit patent grant in GPLv2); GNU General Public License version 3.0 § 11 (2007), https://www.gnu.org/licenses/gpl-3.0.en.html (containing the explicit patent grant). However, because the GPL is primarily a copyright license with so-called "patent peace" provisions in it, it is beyond the scope of this chapter to consider.

with the Sewing Machine Combination (1856–77).[7] More recent examples include patent pools for video formats, mobile network technology, and even diagnostic genetic testing.[8] Pools allow multiple parties to combine their patents for a variety of pro-innovation purposes, such as an efficient means to resolve ongoing patent disputes and to lower transaction costs for cross-licensing blocking patents among repeat-player competitors.[9] Applicable patents are usually defined by their economic and technological roles, that is, as substitutes or complements within a particular technological domain. However, as with many collective action arrangements, competition concerns inevitably emerge. Still, regulators and courts have allowed such pools to exist when, "in a case involving blocking patents, such an arrangement is the only reasonable method for making the invention available to the public[.]"[10] Pools may also encourage firms to enter the innovation race on a particular technology so they can be the first to patent key aspects and maximize their individual returns from the pool's profits.[11]

On the other hand, this incentive to "race" may be misplaced or even socially wasteful if it "encourages duplicative research and strategic patenting."[12] Moreover, once a pool is formed, it can lessen the economic and cultural incentives among participants to invest in research and development of new technologies. After all, if everyone in the pool gets a share of the pie, why spend the money to develop new recipes and bake new pies?[13] Conversely, for competitors outside the pool, there can be greater incentives to "invent around" pool-covered technologies in order to avoid higher licensing fees which make it more difficult to offer technologies covered by the pool at a price competitive with pool members.

---

[7] *See generally* Petra Moser, *Patents and Innovation: Evidence from Economic History*, 27 J. OF ECON. PERSPECTIVES 23 (2013); Carl Shapiro, *Navigating the Patent Thicket: Cross Licenses, Patent Pools, and Standard Setting*, in 1 INNOVATION POLICY AND THE ECONOMY 119 (Adam B. Jaffe, et al. eds., 2001).

[8] Moser, *supra* note 7.

[9] Id.

[10] Id. (quoting *International Mfg. Co. v. Landon*, 336 F.2d 723, 729 (9th Cir. 1964)).

[11] Id.

[12] Id.

[13] Id. (noting that incentives to free-ride are particularly strong for pools that include "grantback provisions," which require members to offer all new patents to the pool, and innovative members may abandon the pool to protect their patents) (citing Reiko Aoki & Sadao Kagaoka, *The Consortium Standard and Patent Pools*, 55 ECON. REV. 345 (2004).

Open patent agreements exhibit many of the same characteristics as patent pools, but not all. They are often focused on a particular technology or technological standard with the same intent to reduce litigation costs/risks and to lower cross-licensing transaction costs. However, unlike traditional patent pools, they typically offer licenses to patents on the basis of pledges or conditions related to "openness" – generally understood as encouraging inclusiveness in the development of technologies instead of intellectual property's traditional exclusive emphasis. For example, the Open Invention Network (OIN) offers royalty-free licenses to its entire patent portfolio on the Linux operating system as long as each licensee agrees to grant a similar license for its patents on Linux to every other licensee in the network. As such, it holds itself out as "a shared defensive patent pool with the mission to protect Linux"[14] that was created to "ensure a level playing field for Linux, safeguarding developers, distributors and users from organizations that would leverage intellectual property to hinder its growth and innovation."[15] Most importantly, it is free to join the network as long as one commits to the cross-licensing model.

The License On Transfer (LOT) network also focuses on safeguarding its members from patent litigation through an "open" approach to licensing. To join LOT, members agree that, if they ever transfer ownership of any of their patents in the future, every member of the network at that time will receive a royalty-free license to every transferred patent. In theory, this discourages so-called "patent trolls" from acquiring any LOT patents, as the act of acquisition will immunize network members from any future threats from those patents. The cost of joining LOT varies, but the costs are largely administrative and proportional to the size and revenue of the joining entity.[16]

The Defensive Patent License (DPL), co-authored by one of the authors of this chapter, also focuses on leveraging licensing rights in favor of openness and litigation reduction.[17] Modeled on the General Public License (GPL), the DPL tracks many of the mechanisms of the OIN, but without any centralized organizational entity or any specific

---

[14] *About OIN*, *supra* note 1.

[15] *FAQ*, Open Invention Network, https://www.openinventionnetwork.com/press-room/faqs/ [hereinafter OIN, *FAQ*].

[16] LOT Network, *FAQs*, LOTNET, http://www.lotnet.com/learn-more/faqs.cfm [hereinafter LOT, *FAQs*].

[17] The full text of the DPL version 1.1 is available at http://defensivepatentlicense.org/content/defensive-patent-license. *See also* Schultz & Urban, *supra* note 4 (introducing the DPL).

technological focus. DPL licensors agree to offer royalty-free licenses to their entire patent portfolios, and licensees, in turn, agree never to assert any of their patents offensively against any member of the DPL network. If a licensee breaches, each licensor has the option of terminating the license. If a particular licensor wishes to cease offering DPLs to new network members, they must give the network six months' notice. Upon leaving, the former Licensor's DPLs can be converted into fair, reasonable, and non-discriminatory (FRAND) royalty-bearing licenses.

In looking at these OPAs, certain commonalities emerge related to competition and innovation analysis. First, they place no restrictions on additional licensing activity either inside or outside of their networks; any network member can strike customized deals with any other network or non-network member. If two members of the OIN network wish to enter into a joint distribution deal involving certain patented products, the OIN license would not preclude a separate side license as part of that transaction as long as it did not breach the OIN prohibition on infringement actions against developers, distributors, or users of the Linux system. Second, OPAs do not place any restrictions on licensing or litigation behavior outside of the network. Third, because the cost of joining most OPAs is free or, at most, administrative, the barriers to any new entrant are extremely low.

B. Antitrust Law and Legal Frameworks

Antitrust law is, famously, divided into business practices which are per se illegal and those which are evaluated under the "rule of reason."[18] Courts have found per se antitrust violations in cases where, after long experience, the practice restrains trade in almost all of its occurrences.[19] Without such a history, the Supreme Court has expressed reluctance to find a per se antitrust violation "where the economic impact of certain practices is not immediately obvious."[20] Business practices that are not per se violations are evaluated instead under the rule of reason. When courts look at an activity under the rule of reason, they take into account "a wide variety of factors, including specific information about the relevant business, its condition before and after the practice was imposed,

---

18 *See* Leegin Creative Leather Prods., Inc. v. PSKS, Inc., 551 U.S. 877, 887–89 (2007).

19 *See* id. at 887–88.

20 State Oil Co. v. Khan, 522 U.S. 3, 10 (1997) (internal quotation marks omitted) (quoting Fed. Trade Comm'n v. Ind. Fed'n of Dentists, 476 U.S. 447, 458–59 (1986)).

and the practice's history, nature, and effect."[21] The rule of reason thus provides a more forgiving, case-by-case analysis than the per se violations.

Given that OPAs are a relatively new phenomena and one where the economic impact is far from certain, OPAs will likely be evaluated under the rule of reason. This is reinforced by the fact that the United States Department of Justice (DOJ) and the Federal Trade Commission (FTC) have both stated that they generally evaluate patent pools under the rule of reason,[22] and the United States Court of Appeals for the Federal Circuit has likewise stated that the rule of reason is appropriate when licensing agreements are related to a larger collaborative effort.[23] Moreover, in evaluating an antitrust challenge to the open source licensing of the Linux operating system, the Seventh Circuit applied the rule of reason, finding that the General Public License (GPL) used was reasonable under that test.[24]

Under the rule of reason, a court or regulator must still confront the question of what factors to consider. The rule of reason is difficult to apply in practice and the Supreme Court has provided little guidance on the issue.[25] Partly as a result of the underdeveloped jurisprudence, the cutting edge of antitrust law in recent years has been developed by the

---

21 Kimble v. Marvel Entm't., LLC, 135 S. Ct. 2401, 2408 (2015) (internal punctuation and quotation marks omitted) (quoting *State Oil Co.*, 522 U.S. at 10).

22 *See* U.S. DEP'T OF JUSTICE & FED. TRADE COMM'N, ANTITRUST GUIDELINES FOR THE LICENSING OF INTELLECTUAL PROPERTY § 3.4 (1995) [hereinafter DOJ & FTC, GUIDELINES]. In August 2016, the DOJ and FTC proposed an update to these guidelines; while not yet formally adopted, the current proposed guidelines are functionally the same in all respects relevant to this chapter. *See* U.S. DEP'T OF JUSTICE & FED. TRADE COMM'N, ANTITRUST GUIDELINES FOR THE LICENSING OF INTELLECTUAL PROPERTY PROPOSED UPDATE – REDLINE (Aug. 12, 2016); *see also* id. at n.84 (collecting instances where the FTC and DOJ have found individual patent pools to be pro-competitive).

23 Princo Corp. v. Int'l Trade Comm'n, 616 F.3d 1318, 1336 (Fed. Cir. 2010) (en banc) (quoting Polk Bros. v. Forest City Enters., Inc., 776 F.2d 185, 189 (7th Cir. 1985)).

24 *See* Wallace v. IBM Corp., 467 F.3d 1104, 1107 (7th Cir. 2006); cf. Heidi S. Bond, *What's So Great About Nothing? The GNU General Public License and the Zero-Price-Fixing Problem*, 104 MICH. L. REV. 547, 556–60 (2005) (arguing that price-fixing under the GPL should be evaluated under the rule of reason).

25 This is a common refrain in the antitrust literature. *See*, e.g., Thomas A. Piraino, Jr., *Making Sense of the Rule of Reason: A New Standard for Section 1 of the Sherman Act*, 47 VAND. L. REV. 1753, 1760–67 (1994).

administrative agencies charged with enforcing antitrust law, most notably the DOJ and the FTC.[26] As a result, guidance from the DOJ and the FTC provides the best starting point for which factors to evaluate under the rule of reason in determining whether OPAs violate antitrust law. In particular, while OPAs are not the same as patent pools, they do involve the collective action of multiple patent holders and share many of the attributes of OPAs that would interest regulators. Because of this close relationship, and because the antitrust considerations about patent pools are relatively well developed, we look to the DOJ and FTC guidance on patent pools to provide some basis for OPA antitrust analysis.

The DOJ/FTC guidance identifies two main concerns regarding patent pools: (1) that "horizontal coordination among the pool's licensors could lead to a reduction in price competition among downstream products"; and (2) that "combining patent rights in a pool could discourage R&D, new product development, and cost-reducing process innovations."[27] In evaluating specific patent pools, the agencies have looked at factors such as whether, in these pools, "licensors would retain the right to license their patents individually, the scope of grant-back clauses would be limited, the license agreement would be available to all interested licensees, and the pool would provide a clear understanding of the contents of the license."[28]

The main judicial opinion to evaluate open source copyright licenses under the rule of reason also considered such concerns, largely finding them absent in the open source software context. In an opinion by Judge Frank Easterbrook, the Seventh Circuit held, "[t]he GPL and open-source software have nothing to fear from the antitrust laws"[29] and that "the GPL does not restrain trade. It is a cooperative agreement that facilitates production of new derivative works, and agreements that yield new products that would not arise through unilateral action are lawful."[30]

---

26 *See* William Blumenthal, *Models for Merging the U.S. Antitrust Agencies*, 1 J. ANTITRUST ENFORCEMENT 24, 27–29 (2013).

27 U.S. DEP'T OF JUSTICE & FED. TRADE COMM'N, ANTITRUST ENFORCEMENT AND INTELLECTUAL PROPERTY RIGHTS: PROMOTING INNOVATION AND COMPETITION 67 (2007) [hereinafter DOJ & FTC, INNOVATION AND COMPETITION].

28 Id. at 71–72 (footnotes omitted).

29 *Wallace*, 467 F.3d at 1108.

30 Id. at 1107; *accord* Wallace v. Free Software Found., Inc., No. 1:05-CV-0618-JDT-TAB, 2006 WL 2038644, at *3 (S.D. Ind. Mar. 20, 2006) ("[T]he GPL in no way forecloses other operating systems from entering the market. Instead, it merely acts as a means by which certain software may be copied, modified and redistributed without violating the software's copyright protection. As such, the

German courts have agreed.[31] While some scholars have asserted viral components of the GPL and other viral copyleft licenses have been called anticompetitive, even the scholars making this claim doubt that current antitrust law would find them illegal without legislative reform.[32]

With these frameworks in mind, we now turn to the question of OPAs, competition, innovation, and antitrust liability.

III. OPAS AS REASONABLE RULES FOR PATENT INNOVATION AND COMPETITION

A. Horizontal Coordination and Price Competition

1. Horizontal coordination

The DOJ and FTC guidance expresses concern that "horizontal coordination among the [patent] pool's licensors could lead to a reduction in price competition among downstream products[.]"[33] The main threat of "horizontal coordination" is that it requires patent holders, many of whom may be competitors in the same market, to come to agreements about pricing, at least at the early stages of development and distribution. Preventing horizontal competitors from colluding to extract rent at the expense of consumers is one of the core concerns of antitrust law.[34]

In looking at horizontal coordination, it is instructive to contrast OPAs with another kind of patent pledge: Defensive Patent Aggregators (DPAs). DPAs are non-practicing entities that license and acquire patents on behalf of member companies in order to reduce the future uncertainty of litigation and reduce the cost of any potential liability. For instance, DPA Allied Security Trust (AST) implements what is called a "catch-and-release" defensive acquisition approach. It requires that companies

---

GPL encourages, rather than discourages, free competition and the distribution of computer operating systems, the benefits of which directly pass to consumers. … [Plaintiff] does not adequately set forth an injury to competition as a whole").

31 LG Frankfurt, Sept. 6, 2006, No. 2-6 O224/06 (13) (Ger.) (holding GPL was enforceable, even though it set the price for alterations of software at zero, not an antitrust violation) (discussed in Jennifer Buchanan O'Neill & Christopher J. Gaspar, *What Can Decisions by European Courts Teach Us About the Future of Open-Source Litigation in the United States*, 38 AIPLA Q.J. 437, 448 (2010)).

32 *See* Stephen M. Maurer, *The Penguin and the Cartel: Rethinking Antitrust and Innovation Policy for the Age of Commercial Open Source*, 2012 UTAH L. REV. 269 (2012).

33 DOJ & FTC, GUIDELINES, *supra* note 22, at 67.

34 *See* Texaco Inc. v. Dagher, 547 U.S. 1, 5 (2006).

pay it a subscription fee.[35] In exchange, it coordinates anonymous negotiations among its member companies about how much they are willing to contribute to the acquisition of certain patents and, based on these negotiations, it purchases a patent.[36] All parties to the bid are given licenses; then the patent is resold on the open market, and the profits are divided among the bidding companies.[37] RPX Corporation, another DPA, provides licenses to subscribing companies for as long as they are members.[38] RPX seeks to purchase either patents or licenses for its members, including patents that are involved in active litigation.[39] RPX is very large, claiming to represent 10% of patent transactions on the open market.[40]

These two DPAs have faced antitrust litigation. Allied Security Trust was sued on claims that it conspired with its members to fix prices for a set of patents; however, the court did not reach the merits of the claims, instead dismissing the case due to lack of antitrust standing.[41] RPX Corporation was sued in federal court on similar claims that it was part of a "hub-and-spoke conspiracy" to monopsonize a patent market by convincing all RPX subscribers to agree not to pay above a certain price for patents owned by the plaintiff.[42] The case was later dismissed by the court after a jury found the defendants did not infringe on the plaintiff's patent.[43] While neither case reached the merits of the antitrust claim, it is

---

35 MARTA BELCHER & JOHN CASEY, HACKING THE PATENT SYSTEM: A GUIDE TO ALTERNATIVE PATENT LICENSING FOR INNOVATORS 5–6 (2014).

36 Id.

37 Id.

38 Id. at 7–9.

39 Id.

40 Id. at 8.

41 Siti-Sites.com, Inc. v. Verizon Comm., Inc., No. 10 CIV 3751 DLC, 2010 WL 5392927, at *2 (S.D.N.Y. Dec. 29, 2010) (finding that plaintiff was not owner of the patents affected by the alleged conduct and thus lacked antitrust standing) *aff'd,* 428 F. App'x 100 (2d Cir. 2011).

42 *See* Cascades Computer Innovation LLC v. RPX Corp., No. 12-CV-1143 YGR, 2013 WL 6247594, at *1 (N.D. Cal. Dec. 3, 2013) (denying motion to dismiss).

43 *See* Cascades Computer Innovation LLC v. RPX Corp., No. 12-CV-01143-YGR, 2016 WL 705982, at *5 (N.D. Cal. Feb. 23, 2016); Cascades Computer Innovation LLC v. RPX Corp., No. 12-CV-01143-YGR, 2016 WL 2993094, at *2 (N.D. Cal. Mar. 25, 2016).

clear that some risk exists in coordinating networks to agree on paying or bidding a particular price for a particular patent.[44]

OPAs, however, lack any specific means or mechanism for horizontal coordination of purchases or bidding on patents. In fact, the standard language of all OPA agreements suggests no real benefit to coordination, as the terms of any OPA-related transaction will be identical regardless of the party, patent, or technology involved. Communication between parties, other than through the mechanism of the license, is neither required nor provided for. This does not mean it is impossible that two users of an OPA would conspire to fix prices horizontally, but only that being users of the OPA does not make it any more or less likely to happen. The users of the OPA will be just as guilty, and just as susceptible to proof of guilt, as two conspirators who are not part of the OPA. The kind of coordination that gives RPX, AST, or other actors the potential to set prices, either as purchasers or sellers, never occurs with OPAs.

2. Price competition

Even assuming horizontal coordination among OPA patent holders were possible, a subsequent decrease in price competition is also unlikely.[45] This is for two reasons. First, because barriers to joining OPA networks are extremely low or nonexistent, OPA network members cannot rely on OPAs to maintain monopoly pricing; if they did, outside competitors would simply enter the market and take whatever OPA patents were required to compete. Second, any attempt to reduce competition through "predatory pricing" of OPA patents would fail, as predatory pricing only occurs when there is the possibility of a subsequent rise in prices.[46] The Seventh Circuit, in an opinion by Frank Easterbrook dismissing a predatory pricing claim against IBM for distributing software under the GPL, stated "[w]hen [competitor] exit does not occur, or recoupment is improbable even if some producers give up the market, there is no antitrust problem."[47] Thus, the requirement of royalty-free licensing in

---

44 *See also* Samsung Elecs. Co. v. Panasonic Corp., No. C 10-03098 JSW, 2015 WL 10890655, at *5 (N.D. Cal. Sept. 30, 2015) ("Anticompetitive effects may arise from patent pooling arrangements that require payment for a pool of rights without a realistic opportunity as a practical matter to obtain individual licenses from individual owners as opposed to a single license from the pool"); Weyerhaeuser Co. v. Ross-Simmons Hardwood Lumber Co., 549 U.S. 312, 315 (2007) (holding that predatory pricing theory applies to predatory bidding).

45 DOJ & FTC, Guidelines, *supra* note 22, at 67.

46 Wallace v. IBM Corp., 467 F.3d 1104, 1106 (7th Cir. 2006).

47 Id.

OPAs should not raise price competition problems since there is no strategy for recoupment in the form of future profits.

If anything, parties breaching OPAs could open themselves up to antitrust liability. Prof. Jorge Contreras has suggested that patent pledgers inducing other parties to rely on a pledge and then abandon it may violate antitrust law under a "market reliance" theory.[48] The FTC in recent years has shown an interest in bringing suit against deceptive practices in the patent space. For instance, in 2013, the FTC accepted a consent decree over a proposed merger which involved a company that had promised certain standard-essential air conditioning patents on FRAND terms and allegedly breached that promise.[49]

B. Discouraging Innovation

The other major concern of the DOJ and FTC in evaluating patent pools is that they "could discourage R&D, new product development, and cost-reducing process innovations."[50] This invites the consideration of the effects of the OPA licensing models on innovation generally.

Open patent agreements operate very differently from traditional patent pools in that their members do not receive any direct revenue from the agreements but do benefit in the reduction of litigation uncertainty and expense as well as reduction in the payment of potential licensing fees. The lack of direct revenue could, in theory, discourage research and development (R&D), new product development, and other cost-reducing process innovations. However, as we discuss below, the benefits of OPAs directly encourage all three of these activities thus outweighing any concerns that might exist regarding these factors. All OPAs provide royalty-free licensing opportunities but only when all their other conditions are met. Rather than discouraging R&D among licensees, such opportunities encourage it. By removing the fear, uncertainty, and doubt of litigation among network members, each entity has the incentive to develop complementary and follow-on technologies to any patented product or service they have licensed. Moreover, because they know that any of their competitors will be able to enter the network and license any of their patents for free at any time, network members will have incentives to be constantly innovating ahead of their patent portfolio, so as to keep first-mover advantage on any new innovations. Investments in

---

[48] Contreras, Chapter 5.

[49] Decision and Order, In the Matter of Robert Bosch GmbH, No. C-4377, 2013 WL 1911293 (FTC April 23, 2013).

[50] Id. at 67.

R&D will be further protected through the use of non-disclosure agreements (NDAs) on unpatented trade secrets and "know-how" techniques, especially those that involve cost-reducing processes. Moreover, OPA network members continue to have the concurrent opportunity to generate revenue through licenses outside the networks.

1. OPAs encourage R&D through traditional licensing outside of their networks

Firstly, OPAs are not designed to compete with or replace traditional revenue-generating licensing markets. Rather, they are meant as complements to those licenses and to facilitate competition at the products and services layer. For instance, the GNU/Linux operating system licensed under the GPL competes in the computer operating system market with closed source, proprietary operating systems produced by companies like Microsoft and Apple.[51] Developers of products and services often acquire licenses for each operating system in order to maximize adoption across systems. The balance between open and closed models has proven so beneficial for consumers that when a Microsoft-led consortium sought to acquire patents essential for the operation of the GNU/Linux operating system, the DOJ wrote a letter to the consortium insisting that the acquired patents be licensed under the GPL to maintain the competition.[52] In fact, open intellectual property can actually spur higher rates of innovation among non-open intellectual property holders through competition. A study tracing the history of the open source typesetting program TeX found that the simultaneous existence of commercial, closed source projects and open source projects benefited consumers because when one set of projects failed to meet a need in the market, the competing set of projects stepped in to meet the need.[53] Moreover, as OPAs remain open over time to all-comers and gain strength as they gain more network members, this is also likely to be considered procompetitive.[54]

---

51 *See* NETMARKETSHARE, *Realtime Web Analytics with No Sampling*, http://www.netmarketshare.com/ (click on Operating Systems, then Desktop Share).

52 Press Release, U.S. Dept. of Justice, CPTN Holdings LLC and Novell Inc. Change Deal in Order to Address Department of Justice's Open Source Concerns (Apr. 20, 2011).

53 *See* ALEXANDRE GAUDEUL, DO OPEN SOURCE DEVELOPERS RESPOND TO COMPETITION?: THE LATEX CASE STUDY 5 (2006).

54 *See* Leegin Creative Leather Prods., Inc. v. PSKS, Inc., 551 U.S. 877, 891 (2007) ("New products and new brands are essential to a dynamic economy, and if markets can be penetrated by using resale price maintenance there is a

2. OPAs in the absence of traditional patent licensing markets: benefits in the traditional market

All of the previous hypotheticals assume a world in which a traditional patent licensing model remains viable, or in which the possibility of such a market remains viable. What about a market in which the OPA completely displaces traditional patent licensing? If the OPA achieves this position through conspiracy, that might still be punishable under traditional antitrust law. However, even without a traditional conspiracy, a market could develop in which the competitive benefits of joining an OPA are so strong that no rational market entrant would ever choose to employ a traditional patent licensing strategy. Such a market would lead to two questions: (1) would companies continue to innovate in the absence of a traditional licensing market? and (2) if the companies do decrease or stop producing new products, will this decrease innovation in the market?

Turning to the first question: would companies still patent technology? Because OPAs draw their strength from the size of their networks, having patents is a key ingredient to OPA success. In addition, because OPAs also desire to protect their members from frivolous lawsuits by non-members, there is a strong incentive to file patents in order to block non-member attempts to claim patents for OPA innovations. In terms of the second question: assuming the OPA removes all incentive to patent, will companies continue to innovate? As open source software and now hardware companies have demonstrated, strong incentives exist to innovate using open licensing models; in fact, many companies that contribute to the GNU/Linux codebase are not remunerated directly for their expenditures, but recoup those costs through providing support to enterprises using the software.[55] Moreover, as Justice Stevens has noted in concurrence, "firms that innovate often capture long-term benefits from doing so, thanks to various first-mover advantages, including lock-ins, branding, and networking effects."[56] Various empirical studies have

procompetitive effect"); Securities & Exchange Commission, *Self-Regulatory Organizations; C2 Options Exchange, Incorporated; Notice of Filing & Immediate Effectiveness of a Proposed Rule Change to Amend the Fees Schedule*, 78 Fed. Reg. 8,621, 8,626 (Jan. 31, 2013) ("[N]ew market entrants and new business models have procompetitive effects").

[55] *See* Robert McMillan, *Red Hat Becomes Open Source's First $1 Billion Baby*, WIRED (Mar. 28, 2012).

[56] Bilski v. Kappos, 561 U.S. 593, 651 (2010) (Stevens, J., concurring).

supported these theories.[57] In addition, other intellectual property law, such as trade secrets or trademark, may still protect innovations that are not protected by patent law. Thus, innovation is likely to continue even in the unlikely event that patenting rates decrease or slow down.

Another benefit of providing free patents is that, by increasing the number of entrants into a market, the number of people and institutions dedicated to improving the technology in that market increases. The DOJ and the FTC have stated that "[r]estraints that encourage licensees to develop and market the licensed technology or that reduce the transaction costs of licensing the technology are more likely to be found reasonable."[58] In open source contexts, this benefit has long been considered an important part of the reason to open source a project. As early open source pioneer Eric S. Raymond put it, "[g]iven a large enough beta-tester and co-developer base, almost every problem will be characterized quickly and the fix obvious to someone" (or, in its most famous formulation, "given enough eyes, all bugs are shallow").[59] The benefit of these improvements will then be available to OPA users for free, speeding the dissemination of new technology and benefiting consumers.

Attracting new entrants may also steal mindshare away from rival enterprises. For instance, Google's smartphone operating system, Android, was able to quickly expand its market share in part because it was released under an open license and smartphone manufacturers and developers were able to access it for free.[60] By freely licensing its intellectual property, Google ensured that no other company (such as Apple or Nokia, the two dominant smartphone manufacturers of the time) would gain enough market power to hurt Google's core business of online advertising. Android is presently the dominant mobile phone operating system in the world, with over 80% of the market.[61]

---

57 *See*, e.g., ADAM B. JAFFE & JOSH LERNER, INNOVATION AND ITS DISCONTENTS: HOW OUR BROKEN PATENT SYSTEM IS ENDANGERING INNOVATION AND PROGRESS, AND WHAT TO DO ABOUT IT (2004).

58 DOJ & FTC, INNOVATION AND COMPETITION, *supra* note 27, at 10.

59 Eric S. Raymond, *Release Early, Release Often*, in THE CATHEDRAL AND THE BAZAAR (2000).

60 Bill Gurley, *The Freight Train That Is Android*, ABOVE THE CROWD (Mar. 24, 2011).

61 *See* IDC, Smartphone OS Marketshare, 2016 Q2, http://www.idc.com/prodserv/smartphone-os-market-share.jsp. While Google has faced antitrust scrutiny over its actions promoting Android, the allegations all involve Google's refusal to license its closed-source programs without bundling of other Google services, not over its open source codebase. *See* Mark Scott, *Russian Authorities Rule Google Broke Antitrust Regulations*, N.Y. TIMES (Sept. 14, 2015), http://

3. OPAs in the absence of traditional licensing markets: benefits outside of the traditional market

Traditional market benefits like those mentioned in the last section do not capture the full range of effects created by private ordering systems. Many actors create value, both benefits to social welfare and concrete monetary value, in response to non-monetary incentives. OPAs are well positioned to harness some of these motivations, with procompetitive effects.

Because courts have long made clear that any social welfare created other than economic efficiency is irrelevant for the purposes of antitrust liability,[62] this discussion will focus on the economic benefits of ideologically motivated actors.

As Judge Easterbrook wrote about software licensed under the GPL, "[t]he lack of money changing hands in open source licensing should not be presumed to mean that there is no economic consideration … . There are substantial benefits, including economic benefits[.]"[63] Wikipedia, for instance, was constructed out of volunteer labor and is largely given away for free; while difficult to value, estimates of its free market commercial value place it in the tens of billions of dollars.[64] The incentives to contribute such volunteer labor may be ideological ("I am benefitting my beliefs"), social ("I gain recognition from my peers"), or something else. However, the effect of harnessing these motivations may be to open up markets that did not exist and could not exist without an OPA.

In fact, OPAs arguably solve or mitigate certain anticompetitive effects of traditional patent markets. Innovation does not require a patent system, and it especially does not require a patent system structured the way that the United States currently structures its patent system. Scholars have long recognized that the traditional patent licensing market suffers from market inefficiencies, and many have questioned if the money spent on

---

www.nytimes.com/2015/09/15/technology/russian-authorities-rule-google-broke-antitrust-rules.html?_r=0; Natasha Lomas, *Europe's Antitrust Chief Confirms Android Objections*, TECHCRUNCH (Apr. 20, 2016), https://techcrunch.com/2016/04/20/europes-antitrust-chief-confirms-android-objections/.

[62] *See* Nat'l Soc'y of Prof'l Eng'rs v. United States, 435 U.S. 679, 689–90 (1978); United States v. Socony-Vacuum Oil Co., Inc., 310 U.S. 150, 220–22 (1940).

[63] Jacobsen v. Katzer, 535 F.3d 1373, 1379 (Fed. Cir. 2008); *see also* id. at 1378 ("Open source licensing has become a widely used method of creative collaboration that serves to advance the arts and sciences in a manner and at a pace that few could have imagined just a few decades ago").

[64] *See* Jonathan Band & Jonathan Gerafi, *Wikipedia's Economic Value* 1 (2013), https://papers.ssrn.com/sol3/papers.cfm?abstract_id=2338563.

patent licensing, litigation, and enforcement comes at the expense of other, more procompetitive business activities. As an alternative, some economists believe that "the most robust markets for ideas are those where ideas are free."[65] Prices of IP at any price above zero can have a radically chilling effect on potential entrants into the market for that IP.[66]

Patent licensing markets are famously opaque. It is difficult for potential licensees to get information about whether patents will survive a challenge, whether other patents read onto their invention, and how much other licensees are paying for the same patent.[67] Patent holders have incentives to obfuscate, both by exaggerating the worth of their patents and by hiding the patents until it is too late for a potential licensee to redesign a product to avoid infringement. By offering everything for free, OPAs solve this problem. In addition, OPAs provide a way for patent holders to get some value in exchange for their patents (in the form of licenses and non-assertion guarantees from other DPL users) with transaction costs that are almost nonexistent. The U.S. Supreme Court has recognized that high transaction costs are a valid business justification for coordination of licensing when it found that music publishing license company BMI was not liable for antitrust violations for coordinating licenses across the entire music industry.[68]

Economists have called the sensibility that drives certain people to exit markets on ideological grounds "repugnance."[69] Thus, for instance, people are resistant to using a traditional money-for-goods market to allocate human organs, so a well-designed market for human organs will not place a monetary value on the organs themselves.[70] Similarly, the appropriate scope of intellectual property rights, and in particular the potential for expansive intellectual property regimes to restrict freedom, is a moral issue to many people. Organized opposition to the patent right on moral grounds has a long history; it extends at least as far back as the anti-patent movement in 19th-century Germany, which opposed patents not merely on economic grounds but because awarding patents unfairly

---

65 *See* Joshua S. Gans & Scott Stern, *Is There a Market for Ideas?*, 19 INDUS. & CORP. CHANGE 805, 808 (2010).

66 *See* id. at 828 ("[N]ot only is the cost of information replication low, but the demand curve for information goods becomes highly elastic at a zero price (and relatively inelastic at any positive price)").

67 Mark A. Lemley & Nathan Myhrvold, *How to Make a Patent Market*, 36 HOFSTRA L. REV. 257 (2008).

68 BMI v. CBS, 441 U.S. 1 (1979).

69 *See* Gans & Stern, *supra* note 65, at 828.

70 *See* id.

benefitted inventors at the expense of the scientists whose work provided the basis for the inventions.[71] Today, many activists favor categorically ceasing patent protection for software patents.[72] Even those not morally opposed to the entire IP market structure may object to aggressive enforcement of IP rights. For instance, the record companies that sued end user copyright pirates suffered large amounts of bad press,[73] and a patent troll that sued podcasters for royalties wound up in a highly publicized clash with comic Adam Carolla.[74] If potential innovators who refuse to participate in a traditional patent licensing market can be enticed into innovating to join an OPA, the entire economy may realize large benefits—benefits that could outweigh those that the market would have generated under the traditional patent licensing model.

Given the range of procompetitive benefits available to a user of an OPA, it is difficult to imagine that a court would find the implementation of an OPA violates antitrust law, even if the OPA operates to the exclusion of traditional patent licensing.

CONCLUSION

Private-ordering patent strategies, at least those implementing an open patent agreement, should prove robust in the face of antitrust challenges. While some embrace the patent licensing market as it is and attempt to work within it, open patent agreements offer an alternative vision of incentives for innovation. Fortunately, antitrust law is flexible enough to incorporate both perspectives, which gives patent holders and licensees the freedom to innovate not just in their products, but in how they structure their businesses. As the United States looks to reform its patent system, open patent agreements may prove to be important models for the legal system of the future.

---

[71] *See* Markus Lang, *The Anti-Patent Movement Revisited: Institutional Change and Cognitive Frames*, in NINETEENTH-CENTURY GERMANY 10 (2010).

[72] *See* Matt Lee, *End Software Patents (ESP) Project Formed to Eliminate Software Patents*, FREE SOFTWARE FOUNDATION (Feb. 28, 2008, 12:55 p.m.).

[73] *See*, e.g., Mitchell Martin, *Backlash Awaits Napster-Bashing Record Industry*, N.Y. TIMES (Mar. 26, 2001).

[74] *See* Daniel Nazer, *The Good, the Bad, and the Ugly of Adam Carolla's Settlement with the Podcasting Troll*, ELECTRONIC FRONTIER FOUNDATION (Aug. 18, 2014).

9. Enforcing patent pledges under EU law

Rafal Sikorski

I. INTRODUCTION

There are various means of assuring access to pledged patents, including SEPs subject to FRAND commitments. These include contract law, promissory estoppel, antitrust law and finally a recourse to a novel approach, namely the market reliance theory, which is a variation on the promissory estoppel doctrine.[1] In the EU the implementers of pledged patents may try to protect their interests in the use of such patents on fair and reasonable terms by resorting to similar or equivalent doctrines as those referred to above. In the case of contract law, implementers of technologies protected by such patents would have to refer to the national laws of the EU member states or the laws of non-member states, if they are applicable. Contract law is not regulated at the EU level, EU law would only be of assistance for the purpose of finding the law applicable to eventual contractual obligations arising as a result of patent pledges.[2] Similarly, it is the member states' laws that would provide answers as to whether various equitable remedies were available. For that purpose, the relevant law of the country for which protection is sought would be applicable. This would also be the case with defenses based on abuse of right or breach of rules of good faith doctrines.

In the EU, however, the implementers of pledged patents could also resort to EU law in order to protect their interests. This is especially the case with EU competition law and article 102 of the Treaty on the

---

[1] *See* Contreras, Chapter 5.

[2] Regulation (EC) No. 593/2008 of the European Parliament and of the Council of 17 June 2008 on the law applicable to contractual obligations, 2008 O.J. (L 117), art 4(1), 6(1) (Rome I).

Functioning of the European Union (TFEU),[3] which deals with abuses of dominant position. In fact the users of FRAND pledged patents have frequently invoked competition law defenses in order to protect themselves against patent holders who allegedly acted contrary to their FRAND commitments by seeking permanent injunctions in patent infringement proceedings before national courts.[4] The EU competition law proved to be an effective tool, not only in the hands of the Commission enforcing EU competition laws in the public interest, but also in the hands of private parties who implement standard technologies in their products. The Court of Justice of the European Union (CJEU) ruling in *Huawei v. ZTE* also clarified the conditions for applying competition law defenses in patent infringement disputes before the national courts of the member states.

EU law could also be of assistance to implementers of pledged patents when they are faced with injunctions in patent infringement proceedings in other respects. The EU directive on the enforcement of intellectual property rights[5] harmonizes member states' laws with respect to remedies available to intellectual property holders, including both interlocutory and permanent injunctions. The provisions of the preamble to the directive as well as the directive itself support the idea that remedies, including injunctions, should be applied in a balanced manner, so that interests of both IP holders and IP users are considered and the remedies are not a means of abuse. Although the provisions of the directives may not be directly applied in proceedings between two private parties,[6] as it is in the member states' laws that implement directives which are applicable to disputes between private parties, EU directives might be applied when national courts interpret national laws implementing them. The IP enforcement directive could thus be used to deny injunctive relief, while leaving the holder with claims for monetary compensation for the use of patents. This view is supported by scholars in Europe, who inspired by

---

3 Consolidated Version of the Treaty on the Functioning of the European Union, art. 276, Mar. 30, 2010, 2010 O.J. (C 83) 47 [hereinafter TFEU].

4 Miguel Rato & Nicolas Petit, *Abuse of Market Dominance in Technology-Enabled Markets: Established Standards Reconsidered?*, 9 EUR. COMPETITION J. 1, 24 (2013).

5 Corrigendum to Directive 2004/48/EC of the European Parliament and of the Council of 29 April 2004 on the enforcement of intellectual property rights (O.J. L 157, 30.4.2004), 2004 O.J. (L 195) 16 [hereinafter Directive 2004/48].

6 For the CJEU case law on lack of horizontal direct effect of the directives see: Case 152/84 Marshall v. Southampton and South-West Hampshire Area Health Auth., 1986 E.C.R. 723, ¶ 48; Case C-91/92 Faccini Dori v. Recreb, 1994 E.C.R. I-3325, ¶ 20.

the US Supreme Court's *eBay* ruling,[7] claim that certain provisions of the directive could be used to justify a more flexible approach to the application of injunctive relief in patent infringement cases.[8]

Finally, provisions of Europe's unitary patent package that deal with patent remedies also seem to be capable of providing assistance to users of pledged patents.[9] The Agreement on the Unified Patent Court[10] as well as the draft Rules of Procedure[11] provide room for more flexible application of injunctive relief. It seems that the drafters were to some extent influenced by the *eBay* ruling. This flexibility could be particularly applied in a manner favorable to those that use technologies protected by pledged patents, including but not limited to SEPs subjected to FRAND commitments made within the standard-setting context.

The purpose of this chapter is to look at legal means available under EU law which could be used by implementers of pledged patents in order to protect themselves against patent holders who act contrary to their public commitments to license their patents. The chapter will be particularly focused on providing access to SEPs that are subject to FRAND commitments made in the standard-setting context. It seems that in the European Union it is the EU law and not the law of the member states that has played the major role in providing relief to implementers of pledged patents so far. In this chapter references will also be made to the relevant provisions of the Agreement on the Unified Patent Court, which forms part of the EU unitary patent package, but which legally is an

---

[7] eBay Inc. v. MercExchange, L.L.C., 547 U.S. 388 (2006).

[8] Ansgar Ohly, *"Patenttrolle": oder: Der Patentrechtliche Unterlassungsanspruch unter Verhatnismasigkeitvorbehalt? Aktuelle Entwiclungen im US-Patentrecht und ihre Bedeutung fur das deutsche und europaische Patentsystem*, 2008 GEWERBLICHER RECHTSSCHUTZ UND URHEBERRECHT, INTERNATIONALER TEIL (GRUR INT.) 787, 798 (2008).

[9] I refer here to the legal instruments establishing the European Unitary Patent, namely: Regulation (EU) No. 1257/2012 of the European Parliament and of the Council of 17 December 2012 implementing enhanced cooperation in the area of the creation of unitary patent protection, 2012 O.J. (L 361) 1; Council Regulation (EU) No. 1260/2012 of 17 December 2012 implementing enhanced cooperation in the area of the creation of unitary patent protection with regard to the applicable translation arrangements, 2012 O.J. (L 361) 89; Agreement on a Unified Patent Court, 2013 O.J. (C 175) 1.

[10] Agreement on a Unified Patent Court, Feb. 19, 2013, https://www.unified-patent-court.org/sites/default/files/upc-agreement.pdf.

[11] Preliminary provisions for the Rules of Procedure (Rules) of the Unified Patent Court, the latest draft version is available at: http://www.unified-patent-court.org/images/documents/UPC-Rules-of-Procedure.pdf.

international agreement between the member states and as such does not form part of the EU legal system.[12]

II. EU COMPETITION LAW DEFENSE

A. Introduction

Implementers of technologies protected by pledged patents invoke EU competition laws primarily in cases where holders of patents encumbered with FRAND commitments, made in the context of standard-setting carried out by SDOs, seek injunctive relief in patent infringement proceedings in national courts.[13] Thus, the EU competition law defense is primarily raised against SEP holders. In July 2015, the CJEU, in reply to a request for a preliminary ruling from the Dusseldorf Landgericht in a patent infringement dispute between ZTE and Huawei, issued a judgment in which it clarified the circumstances under which seeking injunctive relief could constitute abuse of dominant position held by the SEP holder within the meaning of article 102 TFEU.

Implementers of FRAND encumbered patents, in addition to invoking competition law defenses in courts of the member states in patent infringement proceedings, seek assistance from the EU Commission. They notify the Commission of refusals to grant patent licenses relating to SEPs so that the Commission may initiate proceedings relating to such anticompetitive practices.[14] In fact in a number of cases the EU Commission found that patent holders, who made FRAND commitments within the standard-setting context and who later – contrary to those commitments – sought injunctive relief in patent infringement proceedings against SEP implementers, abused their dominant position within the meaning of article 102 TFEU. As the Commission decisions are binding for the national courts,[15] they may later be used in patent infringement

[12] For critical assessment of the unitary patent package in Europe see: Reto Hilty, Thomas Jaeger, Mathias Lamping, Hans Ullrich, *The Unitary Patent Package: Twelve Reasons for Concern* (Max Planck Inst. for Intell. Prop. & Competition L., Research Paper No. 12-12, 2012).

[13] Rato & Petit, *supra* note 4, at 24.

[14] In both *Motorola* and *Samsung* cases the injunction proceedings before the national courts were already under way. In both cases, Apple filed complaints relating to enforcement of SEPs by the SEPs holders.

[15] Council Regulation (EC) No. 1/2003 of 16 December 2002 on the implementation of the rules on competition laid down in Articles 81 and 82 of the Treaty, art. 16(1), 2003 O.J. (L 1) 1, 13 [hereinafter Regulation 1/2003].

proceedings before those courts. A decision establishing abuse of dominance would automatically lead to the defense based on EU competition law being successfully raised. Additionally, filing a complaint and subsequent commencement of competition proceedings by the EU Commission might also result in a national court staying the civil proceedings in a patent infringement dispute before it.[16]

Factual patterns leading to disputes over access to FRAND encumbered SEPs are similar, irrespective of the jurisdiction. Patent holders who, during the standard-setting process, promised to license their patents on FRAND terms, propose licensing terms that, in the opinion of the potential licensees, are neither fair nor reasonable or are discriminatory. The implementers, who already apply the technologies protected by such patents, do not agree to such terms. As a result, the patent holders initiate patent infringement proceedings before national courts of a member state and seek injunctive relief. The implementers in turn invoke a competition law defense, based on the EU or national competition laws, or both.

Potential licensees claim that they are willing to conclude the licensing agreement but that the terms offered by the licensors were not FRAND terms and that they should not be forced to accept them. The licensees further claim that the licensors, by refusing to offer licenses on FRAND terms and by seeking injunctions in patent infringement proceedings, abuse their dominant position within the meaning of article 102 TFEU. It is also worth noting that SEP holders practically never blatantly refuse to conclude licensing agreements relating to their standard essential patents.

In *Samsung* there was a dispute over access to Universal Mobile Telecommunications System (UMTS) SEPs owned by Samsung.[17] Samsung pledged to license those patents on FRAND terms to European Telecommunications Standards Institute (ETSI), the SDO that developed the UMTS standard. Apple argued that it was willing to take a FRAND license but Samsung refused to license these SEPs on FRAND terms and sought injunctions, both preliminary and permanent, in various EU member state courts. In *Motorola* there was a dispute over access to General Packet Radio Service (GPRS) SEPs owned by Motorola. Motorola pledged to ETSI to license GPRS SEPs on FRAND terms. Apple claimed that it was willing to conclude a license agreement with Motorola. However, Motorola decided to seek injunctions from a court in

---

16 Id.

17 Case AT.39939, Samsung – Enforcement of UMTS Standard Essential Patents, Comm'n Decision (Apr. 29, 2014) (summary at 2014 O.J. (C 350/8)) [hereinafter *Samsung*].

Germany.[18] In both cases Apple claimed that the SEP holders infringed article 102 TFEU.

In its most recent decision in *Huawei v. ZTE*,[19] the CJEU was asked to deliver a judgment in a similar factual setting. Huawei is the holder of a standard essential patent relating to the 4G LTE telecommunications standard. During the standard-setting process carried out by the European Telecommunication Standards Institute, Huawei undertook to grant licenses on FRAND terms. ZTE implemented the LTE standard, which resulted in the infringement of Huawei's SEP. ZTE subsequently engaged in negotiations with Huawei. Since the negotiations did not lead to the conclusion of a licensing agreement Huawei initiated patent infringement proceedings against ZTE in the Dusseldorf court.

ZTE claimed that Huawei's refusal to license was contrary to its FRAND licensing commitment made to ETSI and that it amounted to an abuse of the dominant position within the meaning of both EU and German competition laws. The CJEU was asked to give a preliminary ruling in order to clarify the circumstances in which the actions of a SEP holder amount to an abuse of dominant position within the meaning of article 102 TFEU. In other words the CJEU was asked by the German court to draw a fine line between those cases where seeking injunctive relief by a SEP holder amounts to an abuse and cases in which such a SEP holder would be entitled to demand an injunction against a party using the protected invention but not genuinely willing to conclude an agreement.

B. Conditions for the Availability of the EU Competition Law Defense

SEP implementers who intend to rely on a competition law defense in patent infringement proceedings initiated by SEP holders acting contrary to their FRAND commitments must show that conditions for establishing abuse of dominant position are satisfied. If it is established that the SEP holder abuses its dominant position by exercising its patent against the SEP user, such use will not constitute patent infringement. Exercise of a patent in circumstances that constitute an abuse of the dominant position within the meaning of article 102 TFEU does not deserve protection in

---

18 Case AT.39985, Motorola – Enforcement of GPRS Standard Essential Patents, Comm'n Decision (Apr. 29, 2014) (summary at 2014 O.J. (C 344/6)) [hereinafter *Motorola*].

19 Case C-170/13, Huawei Technologies Co. Ltd. v. ZTE Corp. (Nov. 20, 2014).

national courts of the member states. Granting protection to a SEP holder in such circumstances would undermine the effectiveness of EU law.

Firstly, as the competition law defense is based on the alleged abuse of dominant position, the patent holder must hold such a position.[20] Secondly, the patent holder must abuse its dominant position. Thirdly, it must be remembered that the patent holder is generally entitled to obtain an injunction against the unauthorized user of the patent. This is also the case with patent holders who hold a dominant position in the relevant market. Therefore, if the licensee is not a genuinely willing licensee, injunctive relief should be available to the patent holder.[21] Otherwise the users would be encouraged not to enter into licensing agreements and the patent owners consequently would be deprived of the compensation for the use of their inventions. This could diminish the patentee's incentive to invest in innovation. Thus, a licensee's unwillingness to conclude a licensing agreement constitutes an objective justification for the SEP holder to seek injunctive relief.

1. Dominant position

In cases dealing with abuse of dominant position by SEP holders, SEP holders' dominant position in the relevant technology markets is hardly ever questioned.[22] In fact most, if not all, of the disputes in the EU relate to SEPs in ITC markets. These are characterized by strong network effects. Thus, once the markets tip to a given technological standard, there is no room for competing standards. Generally, the holders of potentially competing technologies do not exert competitive pressure on the owners of SEPs. At least in the short or mid term it is very unlikely. Market participants are consequently locked in to a given standard.

2. Abuse of the dominant position

For a competition law defense to be available, the patent holder must abuse its dominant position. Mere holding of a dominant position does not suffice. The circumstances in which the exercise of IP rights, including patents, could constitute abuse of dominant position have been

---

20 Case 85/76, Hoffmann-La Roche & Co. v. Comm'n, 1979 E.C.R. 461, ¶ 38.

21 Damien Geradin, *The European Commission Policy Towards the Licensing of Standard-Essential Patents: Where Do We Stand?*, 9 J. OF COMPETITION L. & ECON. 1125, 1129 (2013).

22 Case COMP/38.636 – Rambus, Comm'n Decision (Dec. 9, 2009) [hereinafter *Rambus*]; *Motorola*, *supra* note 17, ¶¶ 221–70; *Samsung*, *supra* note 16, ¶¶ 45–51.

the topic of debate in the EU for many years. The EU competition law generally recognizes the freedom of the patent holder to decide whether to license its patent at all, as well as to decide with whom and on what terms licenses should be granted. The CJEU admits, however, that there are exceptional circumstances in which the patent holder is under an obligation resulting from competition law to grant a license[23] The question is whether such an obligation exists with respect to standard essential patents. Does the fact that during the standard-setting process a FRAND commitment was made constitute such exceptional circumstances?[24]

a) Exceptional circumstances In order for the exercise of IP rights, including patents, to be treated as an abuse of dominant position within the meaning of article 102 TFEU, the CJEU has always required the existence of exceptional circumstances. In *Magill*[25] and *IMS Health*[26] the CJEU stated that these exceptional circumstances consisted of hindering the appearance of a new product for which there was consumer demand.[27] The "new product" requirement was strongly debated in the EU legal literature.[28] This is not surprising because the new product concept is rather vague. What constitutes a new product has never been entirely clear. Additionally, the "new product" requirement might be problematic in the context of standardized technologies. Declining access to IP rights protecting such technologies, at least in some cases, will not inhibit the appearance of a new product, though it is likely to affect competition in downstream product markets.

It seems that the CJEU, by requiring that the refusal to license an IP right inhibit the appearance of a new product, was primarily concerned

---

[23] Case 238/87, Volvo v. Veng, 1988 E.C.R. 6211, ¶ 9; Joined Cases C-241/91 P and C-242/91 P, Radio Telefis Eireann (RTE) and Indep. Television Publ'ns Ltd. (ITP) v. Comm'n, 1995 E.C.R. I-743, ¶ 50 [hereinafter *Magill*]; Case C-418/01, IMS Health GmbH & Co. v. NDC Health GmbH & Co., 2004 E.C.R. I-5039, ¶ 52 (referred to as: *IMS Health*); Case T-201/04, Microsoft Corp. v. Commission, [2007] E.C.R., p. II-3620.

[24] *Samsung*, *supra* note 16, ¶ 56.

[25] *Magill*, 1995 E.C.R. I-743.

[26] *IMS Health*, 2004 E.C.R. I-5039.

[27] *Magill*, 1995 E.C.R. I-743, ¶ 50; *IMS Health*, 2004 E.C.R. I-5039, ¶ 52.

[28] Nicolas Petit, *Injunctions for FRAND-Pledged SEPs: The Quest for an Appropriate Test of Abuse under Art. 102 TFEU*, 9 EUR. COMPETITION J. 677, 683–84 (2013).

with dynamic efficiency and innovation. Indeed, both intellectual property and competition laws are primarily concerned with dynamic competition, that is, competition through innovation and substitution. To require by means of competition law a license for the purposes of strengthening competition by imitation could undermine the foundations of intellectual property, including patent law. Certainly the incentive function of IP rights would be negatively affected.

It is important to recognize, however, that both *Magill* and *IMS Health* were decided in particular circumstances and the standard for assessment of abusive behavior applied in those cases does not necessarily properly address the competition consequences of denying access to SEPs encumbered with FRAND commitments, or more generally denying access to technological standards. The "new product" requirement results in a very formalistic approach towards the assessment of the exercise of IP rights in competition law. What should be crucial for the proper competition law analysis is to properly grasp the nature of competitive harm in cases where access to SEPs is denied.

Firstly, in the markets where standards are a necessity, such as the markets in the ITC sector, there is tremendous follow-on innovation that builds on top of the standard technologies. Access to standards therefore is likely to boost dynamic competition, rather than hamper it. The telecommunications and consumer electronics markets provide ample evidence of the vibrant dynamic competition built upon technological standards. Therefore, denying access to standards protected by IP rights, including patents, could have negative chilling effects on follow-on innovation. It could also additionally have negative effects on static competition in product markets where the IP rights such as SEPs are an indispensable input.

Secondly, in some markets and in the case of some standards, there is in fact very little room for follow-on innovation. It could be either the result of the nature of standard or the nature of customer and consumer expectations. The two cases decided by the German Supreme Court, namely the *Orange Book Standard*[29] and *Standard-Spundfass*[30] are both very illustrative in this respect. In the first case – where the standard concerned the CD technology – at least with respect to the market for discs – there was probably not much room for further substantial

---

[29] Bundesgerichtshof [BGH] [Federal Court of Justice] June 13, 2004, KZR 39/06 (Ger.).

[30] Bundesgerichtshof [BGH] [Federal Court of Justice] May 6, 2009, KZR 40/02 (Ger.).

innovation. It was thus rather unlikely that extensive follow-on innovation could be built on top of the CD standard. In the second case, the chemical industry demanded from its suppliers that the products – containers for chemicals – comply with an established standard. Follow-on innovation was neither expected nor demanded by the industry.

Since in both of these cases there was little room for competition by substitution and follow-on innovation, dynamic competition should not be the primary concern from the perspective of competition law. In both cases, however, what was possible was static competition on price. Such static competition would, however, only be possible if there was access to standardized technologies enabling mere imitation. In such cases access to standardized technologies was the only means of assuring that competition is not restricted.

The Commission's *Motorola* and *Samsung* decisions discussed above as well as the CJEU's *Huawei v. ZTE* ruling suggest that both the CJEU and the Commission properly assume that denying access to standard essential patents poses a serious threat to competition. The Commission points out that injunctive relief sought by SEP holders could harm both dynamic competition – by foreclosing access of innovative standard-compliant products, as the SEPs could not be worked around. The Commission points out that exclusion of market participants could also reduce downstream competition relating to price for the standard-compliant products. Additionally, the Commission observes that consumer choice might be restricted as a result of foreclosure of access to downstream product markets. The CJEU in *Huawei v. ZTE* also points out that access to SEPs is essential for the maintenance of competition in downstream product markets. By denying access to SEPs the SEP holder could restrict access to downstream markets to other competitors.

Both the Commission in its *Samsung* and *Motorola* decisions as well as the CJEU in *Huawei v. ZTE* seem to have abandoned the "new product" requirement. Both also assume that exceptional circumstances exist in the standard-setting context in which access to a SEP is necessary to participate in the downstream market, and where the SEP holder has made a FRAND commitment.[31] Looking at the argumentation of both the Commission and the CJEU from a competition law perspective, the importance attached to the FRAND commitment and the fact that it creates legitimate expectations for third parties that the SEP proprietor

---

[31] *Motorola*, *supra* note 17, ¶ 281; Case C-170/13 Huawei Techs. Co. v. ZTE Corp., 2013 EUR-Lex CELEX LEXIS 0170, at ¶ 53 (Nov. 20, 2014).

will grant licenses on FRAND terms is rather unusual. The concept of abuse of dominant position in article 102 TFEU is an objective one.[32] From the competition law perspective, what matters is the potential harm to competition. That results from denying access to an asset that is essential for the operation in downstream product markets as well as for the follow-on innovation that builds upon the standard technology. The fact that FRAND commitments induce reliance by third parties and that these commitments are later disregarded is not crucial to competition law analysis. However, reasoning that refers to legitimate expectations is certainly important when considering the availability of equitable defenses against the SEP holders who deny granting licenses and seek injunctive relief in patent infringement proceedings.

b) Examples of abuses of dominant position by SEP holders The SEP holder's dominant position can be abused in a number of ways. The SEP holder may simply refuse to license its patent no matter what licensing terms are offered by the licensee. This appears to occur rarely in cases when FRAND commitments are made in standard-setting contexts. Alternatively, the patent holder may either demand excessively high royalties[33] or impose unfair licensing terms other than those relating to royalties.[34] The SEP holder may for example offer to conclude a licensing agreement on terms that are considered to be anticompetitive within the meaning of articles 101 or 102 TFEU.

Article 102 TFEU provides examples of terms that might constitute abuse. The list of abuses in article 102 TFEU is, however, by no means exhaustive. Article 102(a) specifies that abuse might consist of imposing unfair purchase prices. In fact a competition law defense is frequently raised when the royalties demanded by the patent holders are excessively high. So when courts decide upon the availability of a competition law defense in a given case they consider the fairness and reasonableness of the royalties but in light of the requirements of the competition law and not the "fair and reasonable" component of the FRAND commitment. The court would similarly assess the "fairness" of royalties with respect to technology protected by patents subject to a FRAND pledge – as is predominantly the case with standards adopted by SDOs – as well as those that protect a technology that became a de facto standard due to its market success.

32 Case C-170/13, ¶ 45.
33 TFEU, *supra* note 3, art. 102(a).
34 Id.

Paradoxically then it is the exploitative nature of the abuse of dominant position that is the most frequently raised ground for the competition law defense. This is somewhat problematic. The EU Commission has after all clearly prescribed its competition law enforcement objectives under article 102 TFEU.[35] They are centered around exclusionary rather than exploitative practices. This is also the case because the Commission is unwilling to become a price setting institution. The Commission recognizes that it is very difficult to assess when the price is abusive. That is especially the case with patents protecting standardized technologies. In the case of SEPs it is extremely difficult if not impossible to find other IP rights that could be used as material for price comparison.

The availability of a competition law defense may also result from discriminatory treatment of the licensees by the patentee. Article 102(c) TFEU provides that the abuse may constitute of applying dissimilar conditions to equivalent transactions with other trading partners, therefore placing them at a competitive disadvantage. The non-discrimination requirement should not be underestimated. It applies to all licensing conditions, not only royalties. In fact, the non-discrimination component might be of greater importance than the requirement of reasonableness and fairness, as the technology implementers operating in the product markets are more likely to accept unfair terms as long as they are equal for all market participants. Again, this particular non-discrimination requirement is derived from article 102(c) TFEU directly and not via the FRAND commitment made by the patent holder during the standard-setting process.[36] Thus again the non-discrimination requirement could be interpreted in the same way with respect to patentees holding SEPs encumbered with FRAND commitments and SEPs not the subject of any pledge, as is the case with patents protecting de facto standards.

Abuse of dominance might also consist in the patent holders demanding potential licensees to enter into agreements on disadvantageous

---

[35] Communication from the Commission: Guidance on its enforcement priorities in applying Article 82 of the EC Treaty to abusive exclusionary conduct by dominant undertakings, 2009 O.J. (C 45) 7.

[36] It is clear from the EU Commission Horizontal Guidelines as well as the Technology Transfer Guidelines that in the case of standard technologies the duty to license on FRAND terms is derived from the provisions of EU competition law. See to that effect: Communication from the Commission: Guidelines on the applicability of Article 101 of the Treaty on the Functioning of the European Union to horizontal co-operation agreements, 2011 O.J. (C 11) 1, and Communication from the Commission: Guidelines on the application of Article 101 of the Treaty on the Functioning of the European Union to technology transfer agreements, 2014 O.J. (C 89) 3 [hereinafter *TTG*].

terms. Article 102(a) TFEU explicitly mentions abuses consisting in imposing unfair trading terms. These disadvantageous terms may consist of terms that have the potential to restrict competition themselves. As the Commission rightly stated in its *Motorola* decision these might include non-challenge or termination clauses allowing for termination of the license once validity of the licensed patent is challenged[37] or extensive grant-back obligations.[38] Non-challenge and termination clauses help patentees keep their invalid patents and collect royalties for their use. This stifles rather than promotes innovation and thus is contrary to the principles upon which the patent system is founded. Extensive grant-back obligations, particularly resulting in transfer of rights or exclusive licenses to improvements, may have a chilling effect on follow-on innovation. One may be less interested in improving the licensed technology if one cannot benefit from such improvements. Competition concerns also arise when licensees are obliged not to challenge the essentiality of the licensed patents. Licensees should not, as a matter of competition law, be required to pay for patents that are not necessary to implement a technical standard.

3. Objective justification

The last of the requirements that must be met in order to establish abuse of dominant position within the meaning of article 102 TFEU is the lack of objective justification for the patent holder to seek an injunction. Certainly, the patent holder should be entitled to an injunction to protect its interests, particularly its interest in obtaining compensation for the use of the invention. That objective justification will certainly be present where the licensee is unwilling to conclude a licensing agreement and either rejects it outright – which is likely uncommon – or where the licensee obstructs the negotiation process and negotiates in bad faith.[39]

The CJEU addressed directly the issue of assessing the licensee's willingness to conclude a licensing agreement in *Huawei v. ZTE*. Placing excessively harsh requirements on licensees might severely hamper their ability to raise successful defenses based on EU competition law. Such harsh requirements could also undermine the effectiveness of EU competition law. It is important to note that the questions referred to the CJEU in *ZTE v. Huawei* came from the German court. In fact the Dusseldorf Landgericht decided to examine the compatibility of the

---

37 *Motorola*, *supra* note 17, ¶¶ 329–36.
38 *TTG*, *supra* note 35, ¶¶ 133–40.
39 Id. at ¶¶ 128–32.

requirements placed on the potential licensees by the German Supreme Court in the *Orange Book Standard* case with EU competition law, particularly with article 102 TFEU. Thus to fully understand the decision of the CJEU in *Huawei v. ZTE*, it is first necessary to review the German law background to the CJEU's ruling.

In the *Orange Book Standard*, the German Supreme Court set out the conditions that a potential licensee must meet in order to be considered a willing licensee of a SEP. It is only when these conditions are met that the licensee might successfully invoke a competition law defense in patent infringement proceedings. Firstly, the defendant must show that it made an unconditional offer to conclude a licensing agreement to the patent proprietor. The offer must be made on terms which the patent owner cannot reject without violating the prohibition of discriminatory or anticompetitive behavior. Secondly, the defendant, who at the time of making its offer already uses the patent, must show that it complies with the terms of the licensing offer made. In particular with respect to the royalty obligations, the defendant must show that the royalties are already being transferred to an escrow account. Thirdly, when the terms of the licensing agreement are made by the patent owner, and the patent owner either makes an offer on terms that are excessive or declines to set the royalty level, it is sufficient that the potential licensee makes an unconditional offer according to which the patent owner should determine the amount of the royalties according to its reasonable discretion.

The conditions set by the German Supreme Court are quite a burden to potential licensees. It is the potential licensees who must first come up with an unconditional offer. The problem is that the licensee might not simply be able to come up with a FRAND offer. Article 102(c) TFEU demands that there be no discrimination. The licensee is, however, unlikely to know the terms of the agreements already concluded by the patentee with other licensees. It seems unjust to demand from him an unconditional offer which when accepted could put him at a disadvantage against other parties operating in the product market where the essential patent is required. What is even more striking is that the German Supreme Court requires that the potential licensee come up with terms that the licensor could not reject without violating competition laws. This means that the licensee must act to its own detriment and must offer terms that are the most beneficial terms that the SEP holder could demand from the licensee without violating competition laws. Generally speaking, the conditions developed by the German courts were very favorable to patent holders. They also made it difficult for willing licensees to raise a competition law defense in order to safeguard access to SEPs.

In *Huawei v. ZTE* the CJEU was asked to clarify the conditions that a potential licensee must meet in order to be considered a "willing" licensee and consequently a beneficiary of the competition law defense in patent infringement proceedings. The Dusseldorf court asked the CJEU to decide whether it was sufficient for the licensee to establish itself as a willing licensee if the licensee declared itself only generally as a willing licensee to the holder of the SEP patent, or whether the potential licensee was required to come up with an unconditional offer. In essence the Dusseldorf court asked the CJEU to decide who should come up with the initial offer. Subsequent questions were conditional upon the answer to the first question and related to the required content of the binding offer and the behavior of the licensee with respect to past infringements and the need to fulfill the obligations as proposed in the offer. It is worth noting that the requirement that the patent user be a willing licensee is also essential from the perspective of a more flexible approach towards granting injunctions under patent law itself. The standard formulated by CJEU in *Huawei v. ZTE* may thus have consequences reaching beyond disputes in which a competition law defense was raised.

Prior to the CJEU decision, an interesting opinion came from Advocate General Wathelet.[40] Wathelet suggested that it was sufficient for the licensee to establish itself as a willing licensee against the patent holder, when the licensee only generally expressed its willingness to conclude the licensing agreement. It is not the licensee who must first come up with the terms of the license and make an unconditional offer. It is up to the licensor, before it seeks an injunction from the court, to alert the infringer in writing – unless it is established that the licensee is fully aware of the infringement[41] – and provide it, in any event, with a written offer that includes all the terms normally included in the licensing agreement for the particular sector.[42] The offer, the Advocate General proposed, must particularly contain the royalty levels and provide explanation as to how they are calculated.[43] Thus, the Advocate General proposed a significant change to the practice of the courts in Germany.

In *Huawei v. ZTE* the CJEU largely followed the opinion of the Advocate General. The CJEU ruling is certainly in favor of standard technology users that are willing to be granted a SEP license. The CJEU concentrated on two important issues. Firstly, it clearly stated that the

---

[40] Case C-170/13 Huawei Techs. Co. v. ZTE Corp., 2013 EUR-Lex CELEX LEXIS 0170 (Nov. 20, 2014).

[41] Id. at ¶ 84.

[42] Id. at ¶ 85.

[43] Id. at ¶ 85.

potential licensee is not required to come up with an unconditional offer in the first place. The burden is on the SEP holder, who must first alert the user of the possible infringement and then present to the potential licensee a written offer that specifies the licensing terms, including the royalties. Secondly, the CJEU demands from the patent user that the negotiations of the licensing contract are conducted in good faith. That means that the potential licensee should reply promptly to the offer of the licensor, especially when it disagrees with the terms offered by the SEP holder. The court thus takes into account the interests of the patentee in obtaining compensation for the use of its patent.

The Dusseldorf Landgericht in *Huawei* was successful in using the CJEU to amend the standards for assessment of licensees' willingness formulated by the German Supreme Court in the *Orange Book Standard*. It seems that the standard adopted by the CJEU provides for a better balance between the interests of patent holders and the interests of the licensees as well as the interest of the public in maintaining access to SEPs which are vital for the vibrant dynamic and static competition in downstream markets where inventions protected by standard essential patents are incorporated. The CJEU does not foreclose the licensor from demanding an injunction from the court, but the threat of an injunction from the perspective of the patent user is certainly less imminent. The decision in *Huawei v. ZTE* also reflects the requirement to safeguard the effective application of EU law. It strengthens private enforcement of EU competition law by means of a competition law defense. The *Huawei v. ZTE* judgment can thus be used more effectively in order to protect users of standard technologies from abusive conduct of SEP holders.

III. INTRODUCING FLEXIBILITY TO INJUNCTIVE RELIEF IN EU LAW

A. Introduction

The competition law defense has proved to be a relatively efficient tool to protect market participants against injunctions sought by holders of SEP patents. However, for a competition law defense to succeed, the willing licensee needs to prove the conditions required for establishing abuse of the dominant position within the meaning of article 102 TFEU or the relevant provisions of national competition laws. These conditions, as the case law relating to injunctions of SEPs in the ICT sector shows, are not very difficult to prove. Disputes rather center on the question of willingness of the licensee as well as fairness and reasonableness of the licensing terms proposed by the parties during negotiations. On the whole licensees often prevail in such disputes and successfully persuade the courts to decline injunctive relief.

The question, however, remains as to the enforceability of patent pledges in contexts other than standard-setting. Such pledges might also induce reliance on the part of the technology user, which might in turn result in investments and eventually when the patent holder changes its mind may lead to substantial sunk costs. The conditions allowing a potential beneficiary of a pledge to raise a competition law defense might not always be met. Therefore, recourse to competition law in such cases would be of little help to the patent user. A question arises whether there are other ways to assist the willing licensees in such cases. As has already been observed in the introductory section of this chapter member state laws might provide relief in such cases via various equitable doctrines such as abuse of rights or patent abuse doctrines. The remaining section of the chapter will look at the EU regulation of injunctions – a typical IP remedy against IP infringements.

In most EU member states, injunctions in IP infringement cases have traditionally been nearly automatic. Injunctions have traditionally been perceived as a remedy that is best suited to protect the interests of a holder of any type of exclusive right. Recently, however, the automatic granting of patent injunctions began to be questioned in the EU. This was to a large extent in the aftermath of the US Supreme Court's *eBay* ruling. The *eBay* decision, which paved the way for a more flexible approach towards injunctive relief, also attracted significant attention in the EU legal literature.[44] The question that needs to be answered is whether there is room for greater flexibility towards granting injunctions in IP infringement cases under EU law. If indeed there is room for flexibility in granting injunctive relief, such flexibility could be used to protect the interests of parties that acted in good faith in relying on pledges made by patent holders.

The question is whether such flexibility is mandated by EU law and particularly by the provisions of directive 2004/48 on the enforcement of intellectual property rights which also deals with injunctions.

---

[44] Ohly, *supra* note 8, at 787–98.

B. Proportionality as the Source of Flexibility in Directive 2004/48 (IP Enforcement Directive)

The purpose of directive 2004/48 was to harmonize measures, procedures and remedies essential for the enforcement of intellectual property rights in the European Union. The directive harmonizes remedies with respect to all types of intellectual property rights, including patents. The central question to be considered in this chapter is whether the provisions of the directive allow for a flexible application of injunctive relief when patent pledges are made. Particularly, the question is whether the directive allows the member states courts, when deciding upon injunctive relief, to take into consideration the fact that patent holders have encumbered their patents with a pledge to make their patent protected inventions available for use by third parties.

Section 5 of Directive 2004/48 deals with a number of measures. Firstly, article 10 provides for corrective measures, such as recall or definitive removal of goods infringing intellectual property rights from the channels of commerce. Secondly, article 11 requires that the member states ensure the availability of injunctions prohibiting further continuation of infringements of intellectual property rights once such infringements were found by the court. Finally, article 12 provides that member states may ensure that in certain cases the courts are entitled to grant monetary compensation instead of granting injunctive relief or applying one of the corrective measures.

Article 3 of directive 2004/48 contains general rules governing the application of specific measures envisaged by the directive. Firstly, article 3(1) states that measures, procedures and remedies shall be fair and equitable. Secondly, article 3(2) states that the measures, procedures and remedies shall be effective and dissuasive – which seems to favor the right holders' interests – but also at the same time requires that they are proportional – which also seems to suggest that the interests of the users of IP rights should be taken into consideration. Finally, article 3(2) provides that the measures should be applied so as to avoid creation of barriers to legitimate trade as well as to provide safeguards against their abuse.

There are two major sources of flexibility with respect to the application of injunctive relief. Firstly, some degree of flexibility could result from the application of alternative measures envisaged in article 12 directive 2004/48. Article 12, however, is only optional. The member states are not obliged to implement it into their domestic laws. Secondly, that flexibility could also be derived from requirements of fairness and equitable character as prescribed by article 3(1) or proportionality resulting from article 3(2).

The first source of flexibility, found in article 12, seems to be rather narrowly defined. It allows the courts, instead of granting injunctions or ordering the corrective measures envisaged by the provisions of article 10, to grant monetary compensation to the right holder. However, this is possible only when the following conditions are met: (1) the infringer acted unintentionally, and without negligence; (2) the execution of injunctions or the corrective measures would lead to disproportionate harm; and (3) pecuniary compensation appears reasonably satisfactory. Article 12, however, will probably not be of significant help to implementers of pledged patents. The pledge itself is unlikely to be the source of the right to use the invention. It is after all unlikely that it could be a source of a contractual licensing relationship. The implementer will thus be in the position of a conscious and willful infringer.

The general principles governing the application of procedures, measures and remedies, found in article 3 directive 2004/48, seem to be more promising. In EU legal literature Ansgar Ohly for example has advocated the proportionality principle that allows under certain circumstances the substitution of the injunctive relief with payment of compensation. The instances where injunctive relief could be denied would certainly be familiar to US lawyers. The author suggests that injunctive relief could be denied when the invention is of relatively minor importance when compared to the whole product, or when the patent holder does not itself practice the patent but only benefits from granting licenses.[45] The author admits, however, that the injunction could be denied only for certain periods of time, namely to allow the implementer to work around the protected invention.[46]

Article 3 requires a balanced system of remedies in EU intellectual property law. Such a balanced approach is also justified in light of the provisions of the preamble to the directive. The recitals in the preamble to the directive provide an important context for the interpretation of the directive's provisions. In recital number 17 it is expressly stated that remedies should be applied in a manner that would take into consideration specific characteristics of each case. Recital number 24 also provides that measures aimed at preventing future infringements should

45 Id. at 798.

46 Id.

be justified by the circumstances of a given case. The fact that a pledge was made could be treated as a circumstance that justifies compensation rather than an injunction. A pledge could thus be an argument against rigorous protection of exclusivity of a patent holder. There seems to be no reason not to take advantage of the flexibility that results from the proportionality principle in cases where the patent holder by pledging its patent publicly states that it is interested in obtaining monetary compensation rather than in protecting its exclusivity.

C. Flexibility in Applying Injunctive Relief in the EU Unitary Patent Package

Unitary IP titles in the EU have been available for many years in the areas of trademarks and industrial designs. The unitary patent package, comprising two EU regulations – namely regulation 1257/2012 and regulation 1260/2012 – as well as the international agreement concluded by the Member States – namely the Agreement on the Unified Patent Court – aims at creating a single EU-wide patent right. Whether the unitary patent package enters into effect remains to be seen, as the ratification process is under way. The controversies surrounding the EU unitary patent package are beyond the scope of this chapter.

It is interesting, however, to look at the way in which the patent remedies were drafted in the package. The provisions relating to remedies are located in the Agreement on the Unified Patent Court (UPCA). Article 62 UPCA deals with interlocutory injunctions, and article 63 UPCA deals with permanent injunctions. It is particularly the second provision that requires attention. Article 63 states that where the court finds that there is an infringement of the patent the court may grant an injunction against an infringer prohibiting the continuation of that infringement. Again the wording of article 63 is likely to be familiar to American lawyers. Section 283 of the US Patent Act (35 U.S.C.) is drafted in a similar manner.

It is obvious that the intention of the drafters was to allow the unified patent court room for discretion in order to balance the interests of users and the patent holders. The need for flexibility is additionally strengthened by the fact the unified patent court would also be required to consider the general provisions relating to the application of remedies found in directive 2004/48 and particularly articles 3(1) and 3(2) discussed above. Commentators in the EU already advocate that the approach to injunctions resembles the one already applied by the courts in the US following the *eBay* decision.[47] This means that the court before granting an injunction should also consider that a patent holder, when pledging a patent, publicly states its intention of not being interested in enforcing the exclusivity but rather in obtaining compensation for its use.

CONCLUSION

EU law might be of assistance to market actors in enforcing patent pledges made by patent holders. With respect to standards-essential patents the case law of the national courts as well as decisions of the EU Commission and particularly the CJEU in *ZTE v. Huawei* show that the EU competition law defense has been both a useful and a successful tool in enforcing FRAND commitments made in the context of standardization. In such cases the conditions for establishing abuses within the meaning of article 102 TFEU are usually met. Interestingly though it needs to be stressed that, when the competition law defense is considered, it is competitive harm that is required, and not the fact that a pledge is not respected by the maker. In the case of denying access to standard essential patents, the existence of competitive harm is hardly questionable – both as far as dynamic competition and static competition are concerned. EU competition law may not be an efficient tool to enforce patent pledges in the case of many other patent pledges, however. This is because, in many other instances when pledges are made, patent holders lack a dominant position.

Developments in the US, particularly in the aftermath of the *eBay* decision, have also influenced the way in which European lawyers approach patent remedies, including injunctive relief. The search for flexibility in directive 2004/84 as well as the wording of the Agreement on the Unified Patent Court show that there is growing understanding that injunctive relief should not be granted automatically. There seems to be increasing acceptance of the view that the balancing of interests in certain circumstances requires that injunctive relief be replaced by monetary compensation. This opens up room for those who wish to enforce patent pledges via a more flexible approach to injunctions.

---

[47] Reto Hilty, Thomas Jaeger, Matthias Lamping, Roberto Romandini, Hanns Ullrich, *Comments on the Preliminary Set of Provisions for the Rules of Procedure of the Unified Patent Court* 8 (Max Planck Inst. for Intell. Prop. & Competition L., Research Paper No. 13-16, 2013).

10. Patent pledges and antitrust law in Brazil

Ricardo Sichel

I. INTRODUCTION

Antitrust regulation is intended to promote free competition. As observed in Chapter 1, "antitrust and competition enforcement agencies in both the U.S. and Europe have found [fair, reasonable, and non-discriminatory] FRAND commitments to be one of the principal means by which firms can mitigate antitrust risk arising from collaborative standards development."[1] Brazilian antitrust law has largely accepted this conclusion, but the Brazilian prohibition on domination of a market, even if that domination is purely the result of a competitor's efficiency, must also be considered.

When analysing this issue, consideration should be given to whether collaborative standards development has an impact on efficiency as it is understood under Brazilian antitrust law. The law also provides that limiting market access to new competitors can also be considered a form of domination and therefore a violation of the antitrust law. This position is consistent with that taken by the European Commission in its actions against Microsoft. In its 2004 decision, the Commission found that "Microsoft violated European law by failing to disclose certain interoperability information to vendors of work group server operating system products."[2] As a result, the Commission ordered Microsoft to make this interoperability information available on a FRAND basis. Microsoft's compliance with the Commission's decision became the subject of subsequent litigation, leading, among other things, to the Commission's imposition of fines on Microsoft in 2008 totaling nearly one billion

[1] Contreras, Chapter 1 at p. 33.
[2] Case COMP/C-3/37.792 Microsoft, Comm'n Decision of 24 Mar. 2004.

Euros.[3] In Brazil, Microsoft was also fined for the misuse of its dominant position in 2004.

The way that technology is licensed must also be considered, as certain forms of technology licensing may hinder innovation. In addition, a balance between the monopolistic implications of patents against the benefit to society as a whole should be analysed.

This chapter will address antitrust considerations related to patent pledges in view of Brazilian antitrust law and related regulations of the Brazilian Patent Office.

II. BRAZILIAN PATENT LAW

The patent system authorized by the Brazilian Constitution is explicitly related to social and technological development.[4] In the Brazilian context, the temporally limited monopoly of a granted patent should spur the economic development of the country. According to the Brazilian Constitution, the law shall assure the authors of industrial inventions a temporary privilege for their use, as well as protection of industrial creations, in view of the social interest and the technological and economic development of the country.[5]

There are certain parameters for granting a patent, according to the Brazilian Constitution and laws. A patent is granted for a limited period of 20 years. The patented invention must protect an object or a procedure that is new and solve a technical problem in a novel way. It must also be a way to ensure social and economic development. These rules are based on the idea that a granted monopoly is an exception to free competition that must otherwise be preserved.[6]

As a consequence of the constitutional limitations on the rights inherent in a patent, patents may be regulated with antitrust measures. This sentiment is reflected in patent law in that the misuse of a granted patent—including how it is licensed—may cause damage to free competition by distorting the market. Patent misuse is not a question of gained efficiency, but whether the patent owner imposes upon the market

[3] Case T-201/04, Microsoft Corp. v. Commission, 2007 E.C.R. II-3601.

[4] Constituição Federal [C.F.] [Constitution] art. 5, XXIX (Braz.).

[5] Id.

[6] Denis Borges Barbosa, *Licenças Compulsórias por Abuso de Patentes*, Santos & Borges Barbosa, at *13 (2002), http://www.nbb.com.br/pub/propriedade15.pdf [hereinafter Borges Barbosa, *Compulsórias*].

certain trade conditions that are unacceptable. The House of Representatives (Câmara dos Deputados) has suggested that antitrust authorities should pay attention to anticompetitive actions regarding the misuse of patents.[7]

The protection of intellectual property has the potential to promote innovation and economic benefit, as seen in developed countries, but the role of intellectual property protection has also been controversial in many developing countries in Latin America. In some situations, it is argued that the protection of intellectual property may hinder economic development. Importing technology does not confer on the importer the capacity to develop it, a capacity that has to be facilitated by establishing adequate policies in order to compete internationally. This question becomes politicized, for example, when considering the case of pharmaceutical products, in which patent protection has the objective of market domination, while public health concerns focus on price and broad availability of patented drugs.

Though the new Patent Law came into effect in 1996, the number of Brazilian patent filings did not markedly increase. Today, a majority of patent holders in Brazil are foreign companies. The highly concentrated technological knowledge and the insufficient investment in research and development have lowered the rate of development, especially considering the lack of interchange between university and companies.

Conducting technological research by using and copying products commercialized in the international market was one of the strategies used by Japan in the second half of the 20th century in order to achieve rapid growth and development.[8] The Japanese example shows how a lower level of intellectual property protection can have a direct impact on growth and development in an emerging technological sector. On the other hand, it must be remembered that countries that simply import technology do not improve their internal capabilities for research. Finally, it is important to note that technology holding countries are more inclined to transfer technology to countries with a high level of intellectual property protection. Consequently, patent systems may be considered efficient promoters of technology development in countries where there is an adequate research and science policy. Brazil, it should be remembered, has developed technology in the offshore prospection of oil and

[7] Newton Lima, A Revisão da Lei de Patentes: Inovaç ão em Prol da Competitividade Nacional 290 (2013).

[8] Kenichi Ohno, *Economic Development of Japan*, 2006 Grips Development Forum 65 (2006).

gas and also in the pharmaceutical industry, including through domestic companies such as Butantã and Farmanguinhos.

III. ADMINISTRATIVE BODIES UNDER BRAZILIAN ANTITRUST LAW

The Brazilian Antitrust Law (12529/2011)[9] establishes the Brazilian System for Protection of Competition (SBDC) and sets forth preventive measures and sanctions for violations of the economic order, guided by the constitutional principles of free competition, freedom of initiative, the social role of property, consumer protection and prevention of the abuse of economic power.[10] By establishing the possibility of compulsory licenses of patents, the new law has introduced a way to prevent the misuse of economic power. The SBDC has established two bodies to administer its enforcement: the Administrative Council for Economic Defence (CADE) and the Secretary for Economic Monitoring of the Ministry of Finance.[11]

The Secretary for Economic Monitoring of the Ministry of Finance must, according to the law, opine on aspects relating to the promotion of competition; the proposed changes in acts establishing norms or standards of general interest of economic agents, consumers, or users of services subject to public consultation by the regulatory agencies; and, when deemed appropriate, applications for review of rates and drafts.[12]

The CADE is comprised of the following bodies: (i) the General-Superintendent, which will analyse and issue decisions on antitrust investigations and review proceedings; (ii) the Administrative Tribunal of Economic Defence (Tribunal); and (iii) the Department of Economic Studies (DEE), responsible for issuing economic studies to assist the General-Superintendent and the Tribunal.[13] The Tribunal is comprised of a president and six commissioners each holding a term of four years, with consecutive terms of reappointment prohibited.[14] This Tribunal has

---

[9] 12,529/2011, de 30 Novembro, 2011, Diário Oficial de 30.11.11 (Braz.) [hereinafter Law no. 12,529/2011].

[10] Id. at art. 1.

[11] Id. at art. 2.

[12] Id. at art. 19.

[13] Id. at art. 5; *see also* Mayer Brown & Tauil & Chequer, *The New Brazilian Antitrust Law*, MAYER BROWN (2011), https://www.mayerbrown.com/public_docs/The_New_Antitrust_Law-English.pdf.

[14] Law no. 12,529/2011, *supra* note 9, at art. 6.

the authority to enforce Law no. 12529/2011, its rules and internal regulations, to decide on violations of the economic order and apply the penalties set forth by law. There have been 16 patent-related decisions made by CADE thus far; all of them are associated with concentration acts and the way they may hinder free competition.

IV. ANTITRUST ANALYSIS OF PATENTS, PATENT LICENSES AND PATENT PLEDGES

Given the tension between intellectual property protection and the promotion of innovation and development, patent pledges offer a different route for innovation that avoids many of the conflicts that might otherwise arise. The concepts involved in patent pledges assure that all players in a market will be able to access a certain technology, not just a few selected firms. The idea involved is to grant access to the market for all other participants in order to enable continuous technological development. As described in Chapter 1, patent pledges take many forms, one of the most common being FRAND commitments. These commitments encourage the establishment of a standardized technology through the promotion of patent licenses with defined conditions. For example, these commitments have enabled the widespread adoption of standards such as Wi-Fi and USB in products that are universally enjoyed.

A principal function of antitrust authorities is to promote free competition. Actors in the market act distinctly, as they have different sources of information and different business mechanisms. The ideal functioning of every market cannot easily be defined because the players are different, especially when it comes to the negotiation of patent licenses. The main objective of the patent holder, in general, is to get the best fiscal return while also ensuring that its monopoly remains in force.

While the government should not regulate all market functions, it has an obligation to prevent misuse of economic power at the expense of the public interest. Under Brazilian law, the misuse of economic power when involving immaterial goods requires two factors: the intentional non-exploration of a determinate immaterial good and a determination that immaterial goods are being licensed, but with anticompetitive agreements.[15]

---

[15] Borges Barbosa, *Compulsórias*, *supra* note 6.

The economic power of patents can also be abused through licensing structures such as "cross licensing" and "patent pooling" if they undermine competition. For example, abuses can be found based on the imposition of royalties for goods that are not patented or the prohibition of alternate products that could be more competitive. According to TRIPS the way "to correct anti-competitive practices may be taken into account in determining the amount of remuneration in such cases."[16] The burden of proving that an anticompetitive practice is being practiced falls on the licensee.

Article 36 of the antitrust law also contains prohibitions on actions that seek to: limit, restrain, or injure free competition or free initiative, control the relevant market for goods or services, arbitrarily increase profits, or exercise a dominant position abusively by controlling 20% or more of the relevant market. This percentage level may be modified by the antitrust agencies for specific sectors of the economy.

These rules are generally applicable and are not directed specifically toward the misuse of patent rights. However, the law considers monopolizing or preventing the exploitation of industrial or intellectual property rights or technology a possible violation.[17]

As a consequence, arrangements that restrict free trade and competition, in order to avoid violation of the antitrust laws, must have social and technological benefits. Like a patent pool, a patent pledge may have the consequence of blocking access of certain technologies for those who do not wish to agree to the license. There might be an advantage to society in the reduction of the costs involved in obtaining a certain technology. On the other hand, the existence of such an agreement could inhibit competition by restraining the number of potential competitors in a market.

V. COMPULSORY LICENSES UNDER BRAZILIAN LAW

One solution to this problem can be the imposition of compulsory patent licenses when patent pledges or patent pools are found to reduce competition. This possibility is foreseen in article 31 of the TRIPS agreement and in article 68 of the Brazilian patent law. The grant of

---

16 *See* Final Act Embodying the Results of the Uruguay Round of Multilateral Trade Negotiations, Apr. 15, 1994, 1867 U.N.T.S. 14 [hereinafter TRIPS Agreement], at art. 31(k).

17 Id. at art. 36, XIV.

compulsory licenses is also regulated by the Paris Convention in article 5 (Stockholm Version).[18] The Patent Office has granted compulsory licenses of pharmaceutical patents in order to enable the promotion of health policy. The conflict between consumers and the pharmaceutical industry centers largely around this issue.[19] As a consequence of compulsory licensing measures, the Brazilian Health Ministry saved R$ 200 million (US$ 60 million) in 2007.[20]

As a remedy, the Administrative Court may also impose compulsory licenses of intellectual property rights for violations of Brazilian antitrust law.[21] Though these compulsory licenses are distinct from those issued by the Patent Office, their economic and market effects may be similar. However, compulsory licenses in cases of anticompetitive practices are subject to special treatment with regard to the remuneration to be paid to the patent holder.[22]

CONCLUSION

Technological policies are one of the most relevant bases for economic development. Due to technological development's effect on an economy, countries—such as Germany—have established short-term innovation goals until 2020, when certain fields—such as transport, security, and environment—will be stimulated.[23] In the Brazilian context, patent pledges must be analysed under both competition and patent law to see whether they support innovation and free competition or hinder it. Specifically in the development context, the analysis must take into account whether the pledge or patent pool works to facilitate innovation

---

18 Paris Convention for the Protection of Industrial Property, March 20, 1888, as revised at the Stockholm Revision Conference, July 14, 1967, 21 U.S.T. 1538, T.I.A.S. No. 6903, 828 U.N.T.S. 305.

19 Ricardo Luiz Sichel, Das Gemeinschaftspatentü bereinkommen und TRIPS 99 (2003).

20 Ministério da Saúde, *Ministry of Health's Spending on Drugs: Program Trends from 2002 to 2007*, 43 Rev Saude Publica. 674, 674–78 (2009).

21 TRIPS Agreement, *supra* note 16, at art. 38, IV(a) and art. 61, V.

22 Carlos M. Correa, Intellectual Property Rights, the WTO and Developing Countries: The TRIPS Agreement and Policy Options 90 (2000).

23 *Technology, Productivity and Job Creation: Best Policy Practices*, Org. for Econ. Co-operation and Dev. (1998), https://books.google.com/books/about/OECD_jobs_strategy_technology_productivi.html?id=Dvy8kCQWo30C.

both internationally *and* domestically in Brazil, rather than whether it merely facilitates efficiency and innovation between established international corporations.

11. Patent pledge enforcement in China

Elizabeth Xiao-Ru Wang

Patents are a relatively new phenomenon in China. China's modern patent law became effective on April 1, 1985, and in the early years of the law patent applications and grants were few. In 1999, China's patent office—the Chinese State Intellectual Property Office (SIPO)—granted over 100,000 patents during the course of the year for the first time.[1] However, Chinese patents have experienced explosive growth in the 21st century. According to data from the World Intellectual Property Office (WIPO), patent applications to SIPO increased almost fourteen-fold between 1998 and 2012, while the number of patents granted grew almost forty-five-fold over the same period. In 2013, China ranked first in the number of patent applications submitted, and ranked second in the number of patents granted.[2] In 2014, SIPO granted over 1.3 million patents in China.[3]

Although China is becoming a major player in the patent space and some Chinese companies, such as ZTE and Huawei, are among the world's most active patent applicants, patent pledges that limit the enforcement of a patent in China are generally unknown to date. Elon Musk's blog post in June 2014 which pledges that Tesla Motors will provide open access to its electric vehicle technology patents,[4] has

---

1 *Three Kinds of Patent Granted for Home and Abroad, 1997–2003*, ST. INTELL. PROP. OFF. (Oct. 20, 2004), http://english.sipo.gov.cn/statistics/200804/t20080416_380878.html.

2 WORLD INTELLECTUAL PROP. ORG., *Statistical Country Profiles: China* (2015), http://www.wipo.int/ipstats/en/statistics/country_profile/profile.jsp?code=CN.

3 STATE INTELLECTUAL PROP. OFFICE OF THE PEOPLE'S REPUBLIC OF CHINA, *Comparative Table 2 Contemporary Quantity Comparison of Three Kinds of Patents Grants from Home and Domestic between 2013 and 2014,* SIPO.GOV (2015), http://english.sipo.gov.cn/statistics/2014/12/201502/t20150204_1071534.html.

4 *See* Appendix.

inspired lively discussions among Chinese academics and companies.[5] However, there is no indication that Chinese companies have made patent pledges outside the commitment to license on fair, reasonable, and non-discriminatory (FRAND) terms under the context of standard setting.

The most notable feature about patent pledge enforcement in China is the active enforcement of the FRAND commitment, the most well-known type of patent pledge. The Chinese courts and China's three antitrust enforcement agencies have all undertaken activities with regard to FRAND issues. These activities reveal that China's approach to analysing and enforcing FRAND terms has been under the framework of the abuse of dominance provisions of the anti-monopoly law (AML).

The organization of the rest of this chapter is as follows: Section I provides an overview of patent pledges in China. It discusses the lack of patent pledges outside the framework of a standards development organization (SDO) and FRAND commitments. Section II summarizes the key enforcement activities related to FRAND issues in China. Section III concludes.

I. PATENT PLEDGES IN CHINA

The "patent pledge loans" that are popular in China should not be confused with the concept of patent pledges as discussed in this chapter. Around 2008, banks in China developed lending practices that allowed companies to use intellectual property, such as patents, as security against loans.[6] In 2013, patent pledge loans made by Chinese banks were secured by a large quantity of patents belonging to tens of thousands of companies. In these lending practices, patents are used as collateral for loans and do not face any of the commitments to limit their enforceability, which is the focus of this chapter.

In Chapter 1 of this volume, Contreras identifies four industry categories in which companies often make patent pledges. This chapter provides an overview of patent pledges in China in each of these four categories.

---

[5] *See*, e.g., Xiaran Zhang, *Tesla Give up its Patents: New Rules in Business World*, CHINA INDUS. & ECON. NEWS (June 23, 2014).

[6] Watson & Band Law Offices, *Chinese Patent Pledges Exceed CNY25 Billion in 2013*, LEXOLOGY (Mar. 18 2014).

A. Information and Communication Technology (ICT) Industries

China is the world's largest exporter of ICT products, such as smartphones, computers, and home appliances. Many Chinese companies are members of SDOs in the ICT sector. For example:

- The European Telecommunications Standards Institute (ETSI) has seven members from China.[7]
- The IEEE Standards Association has 31 corporate members from China.[8]
- The World Wide Web Consortium (W3C) has 19 members from China.[9]

The patent pledges made by the entities participating in SDOs apply to patents licensed to users in China as they are specified in each respective SDO's intellectual property rights (IPR) policy. Members of SDOs, foreign or Chinese, are subject to the patent pledges that they are required to make to the relevant SDO. Patent pledges, such as FRAND commitments, have been actively enforced through private litigation as well as government intervention in China.

B. Open Source Software

One industry insider noted that "China's open source communities are relatively small and don't have much influence."[10] However, large Chinese companies have contributed to international open source software and have developed their own open source software. For example, Alibaba, the Chinese e-commerce giant that set the record for the largest US-listed initial public offering, has developed four open source software platforms, including Tao code, which is one of the most actively used open source software applications in China.[11] Huawei, the world's third-largest smartphone maker and one of the world's largest telecom

---

[7] *Current Membership List*, ETSI, http://www.etsi.org/membership/current-members, accessed Dec. 30, 2016.

[8] *IEEE Corporate Member Index*, IEEE, http://standards.ieee.org/develop/corpchan/mbrs1.html.

[9] *Current Members*, W3C, http://www.w3.org/Consortium/Member/List, accessed Dec. 30, 2016.

[10] Matt Asay, *China Will Change the Way All Software is Bought and Sold*, READWRITE (Aug. 11, 2014).

[11] *The Alibaba Group Open Source Software List*, ALIBABA GROUP, http://alibaba.github.io/, accessed Dec. 30, 2016.

equipment vendors, also contributed to Open SAF and Apache Hadoop software. In addition, Red Flag Linux software was a series of projects partially backed by the Chinese government to develop an operating system for use across multiple platforms for Chinese developers.[12] Although a fair amount of open source software activity exists in China, my research in mainstream Chinese and English literature has not revealed any specific instances of patent pledges relating to these open source software developments.

C. Green Technology

Green technologies, including biofuels, solar thermal, solar photovoltaics, and wind energy, have been the subject of increased patent activity around the world. A study by WIPO reveals that more green technology patents were filed between 2006 and 2011 than in the previous 30 years combined, led by patents filed in China.[13] However, based on the Patent Pledge Database[14] Chinese companies to date have made patent pledges related to green technology. This is consistent with my own research in Chinese literature.

D. Life Sciences

A majority of Chinese patents on pharmaceuticals are related to natural medicines and traditional Chinese remedies. No evidence, either in the Patent Pledge Database (Appendix A) or in my research, indicates any relevant patent pledges in the life sciences industries in China.

In summary, despite rapid growth in Chinese patents in almost all areas, there is no indication that Chinese companies have made patent pledges outside the SDO setting. To date, the only form of patent pledges made by Chinese companies are those FRAND commitments that Chinese firms assume within SDOs when they become members.

---

[12] *About Red Flag*, LINUX, http://www.redflag-linux.com/about/summary.html, accessed Dec. 30, 2016.

[13] Sarah Helm, Quentin Tannock & Ilian Iliev, *Global Challenge Report, Renewable Energy Technology: Evolution and Policy Implications—Evidence from Patent Literature*, WORLD INTELL. PROP. ORG. (2014).

[14] Program on Info. Justice & Intell. Prop.—Am. Univ. Wash. Coll. L., Non-SDO Patent Statements and Commitments, http://www.pijip.org/non-sdo-patent-commitments/.

II. FRAND-RELATED ENFORCEMENT IN CHINA

Consistent with global trends, the active enforcement of FRAND commitments has generated considerable interest in China. As a country with a major manufacturing base and the world's largest consumer market, China has inevitably confronted issues surrounding FRAND terms, especially in the ICT sector.

China's AML prohibits a firm with a dominant market position from abusing its market power by charging an "unfairly high price," imposing unreasonable terms, and applying differential pricing and trade terms, among other types of objectionable conduct. China's approach to analysing and enforcing FRAND commitments has been under the framework of the abuse of dominance provisions of the AML. Concerns have centered on whether certain holders of FRAND-encumbered patents have demanded excessively high licensing rates and have imposed unreasonable licensing terms, or whether they might choose to do so in the future.

This section starts with an overview of the merger remedies imposed by the Anti-Monopoly Bureau of the Ministry of Commerce (MOFCOM), China's merger review agency, on companies holding FRAND-encumbered patents. It then summarizes the high profile litigation in which the Chinese courts set FRAND rates for the first time in China, *Huawei v. InterDigital* (IDC), followed by a discussion of administrative enforcement. It introduces the relevant provisions in China's State Administration for Industry and Commerce (SAIC) regulations on abuse of dominance in the IPR field, and finishes with a summary of the investigations conducted by the National Development and Reform Commission (NDRC) concerning potential antitrust issues surrounding FRAND terms.

A. FRAND-Related Conditions Imposed in MOFCOM's Merger Review Cases

Google's acquisition of Motorola Mobility in 2012

In May 2012, MOFCOM granted conditional approval for Google's acquisition of Motorola Mobility, a manufacturer of electronic communications devices. Google had developed many technologies crucial to the Android operating system for mobile devices, and Motorola had a considerable patent portfolio that contained many declared standard essential patents (SEPs) for communication technologies for which Motorola had made FRAND commitments.

One of the key concerns MOFCOM expressed in its review of the transaction centered on Google's incentive to license the patents it was acquiring from Motorola. MOFCOM was concerned that Google might attempt to abuse its dominant position in mobile operating systems to demand more favorable terms for licenses to the SEPs it was acquiring from Motorola. MOFCOM conditioned its approval of the deal on several commitments by Google, including a key commitment by Google to continue to license its Android operating system at no cost on an open source basis, and to treat all mobile device manufacturers in a non-discriminatory manner with respect to Android. Second, Google was required to maintain Motorola's commitments to license its SEPs on FRAND terms.[15]

Microsoft's purchase of Nokia's handset business in 2014

On April 8, 2014, MOFCOM granted conditional approval for Microsoft's acquisition of Nokia's handset business. Unlike most acquisition transactions in which the acquiring firm obtains the acquired firm's patent portfolio as well as its manufacturing functions, this proposed deal allowed Nokia to retain control of its patent portfolio relating to wireless communications while selling off its handset manufacturing business.

Recognizing that the combined firm may have lacked market power in any relevant product market, MOFCOM's review focused on the firms' likely post-acquisition IP licensing practices and their potential for abuse of dominance as owners of IPRs. In particular, MOFCOM emphasized its concern about the market power Microsoft might exercise from its ownership of commercially essential patents on Android phones, because for at least some of these commercially essential patents, Microsoft had previously made unilateral commitments to license on "reasonable and non-discriminatory terms," and at "low royalty rates."[16] In addition, MOFCOM was concerned that Nokia was stripped of its manufacturing functions and—thus without the need for cross-licensing—would be more likely to violate its FRAND commitments and seek excessive royalty rates for its thousands of communications-related declared SEPs.

To mitigate the concerns, MOFCOM imposed several conditions on both Microsoft and Nokia. Microsoft is required, among other terms, to continue to license its SEPs on FRAND terms, to continue to grant non-exclusive licenses of its non-SEPs to Chinese manufacturers under

---

[15] *Decision Clearing the Google/Motorola Mobility Acquisition with Conditions, Ministry of Commerce,* MOFCOM (May 19, 2012).

[16] *Open Specifications Dev Center*, MICROSOFT, https://msdn.microsoft.com/en-us/openspecifications/default, accessed Dec. 30, 2016.

the same terms it had previously been offering them, not to seek injunctions or exclusion orders against Chinese-produced smartphones that ride on Microsoft's SEPs, or to seek injunctions against potential non-SEP licensees unless they failed to negotiate in good faith.[17] Nokia, in turn, must continue to honor its FRAND commitments with respect to its SEPs.[18]

B. Private Litigation—*Huawei v. IDC*

Private litigation involving FRAND commitments has started to emerge in China over the last few years. The most significant case in which the Chinese courts have directly set FRAND rates for SEPs was *Huawei v. IDC*. The case arose out of a licensing dispute between Huawei, one of the world's largest manufacturers of telecommunications equipment, and the US technology company IDC, a key contributor to global wireless standards, which owns a large portfolio of patents in mobile technologies. Among IDC's patent portfolios, a number of them are declared as standard essential patents for an SDO—ETSI—with FRAND commitments.

In December 2011, in the Shenzhen Intermediate People's Court in Guangdong province, Huawei claimed that IDC had abused its dominant position in licensing wireless communication technology by seeking to impose unreasonable licensing conditions and by charging excessive licensing rates. It also claimed that IDC had violated its FRAND commitments. Huawei asked the court to determine the FRAND rate for the relevant SEPs owned by IDC.

On February 4, 2013, the Shenzhen Court issued its decision, which was subsequently upheld on appeal by the Guangdong People's Court. The Shenzhen Court found that IDC had violated the AML by abusing its dominant position through various licensing practices.[19] The Court also

---

17 Microsoft's commitments with respect to SEPs are indefinite in term, while its commitments with respect to non-SEPs are set to last for five or eight years. Id.

18 *Ministry of Commerce of the People's Republic of China, Anti-Monopoly Bureau, Decision Clearing Microsoft's Acquisition of Nokia Devices and Services Business with Conditions* (Apr. 8, 2014).

19 INTERDIGITAL, INC., ANNUAL REPORT TO THE UNITED STATES SECURITIES AND EXCHANGE COMMISSION, at *22 (Feb. 26, 2013). *See also* Ruosi Ye, Jianjun Zhu & Wenquan Chen, *Determining whether Standard-SEP Holder Abused its Dominant Position*, 3 J. ELECTRONIC INTELL. PROP. RTS. 46 (2013) [hereinafter Ye, *SEP Holder*] (China); Ruosi Ye, Ruosi Ye, Jianjun Zhu & Wenquan Chen, *Judicial Application of FRAND Rules in Disputes Involving Royalties for*

concluded that IDC had failed to offer to license the technologies to Huawei on FRAND terms. In particular, the court found that IDC had demanded an excessive royalty rate from Huawei that was many times higher than the rates entered into with other licensees, including Apple and Samsung. For Huawei's use of IDC's Chinese SEPs relevant to the 2G, 3G, and 4G wireless communications standards, the court set a maximum rate of 0.019% of the sales price of each Huawei product.[20] The parties subsequently reached a confidential settlement of their worldwide patent litigation and agreed to resolve their disputes through arbitration.[21]

C. SAIC's Regulation on Abuse of Dominance in the IPR Field

In April 2015, China's State Administration for Industry and Commerce launched the regulation titled "Regulation on the Prohibition of Conduct Eliminating or Restricting Competition by Abusing Intellectual Property Rights (the Regulation)." The Regulation identifies a number of potentially abusive practices related to licensing conduct, some of which explicitly reference standards and FRAND.[22]

- Article 7 prohibits firms from refusing to license IPR under reasonable terms without justification when the IPR "constitutes an essential facility for business operation."
- Article 10 prohibits firms from imposing unreasonable restrictions (e.g., exclusive grant-backs, prohibitions on challenging the validity of IPR, etc.).
- Article 11 prohibits firms from discriminatory licensing without justification.

Standard Essential Patents, 4 J. ELECTRONIC INTELL. PROP. RTS 54 (2013) [hereinafter Ye, *FRAND*] (China).

[20] *See* Huawei Tech. Ltd. v. InterDigital Tech. Corp., Yue Gao Fa Min San Zhong Zi 306, (Guangdong Higher People's Ct., 2013); *see also FRAND Royalty Rate Should be Limited to Patent Value, Judge in Huawei-InterDigital Case Says*, MLEX MARKET INSIGHT (Nov. 28, 2013); and *Huawei/InterDigital Appeal Affirms Shenzhen Lower Court on Standards Essential Patent*, CHINA IPR (Oct. 29, 2013).

[21] *See InterDigital Settles with Huawei*, WORLD INTELL. PROP. REV. (Jan. 7, 2014) http://www.worldipreview.com/news/interdigital-settles-with-huawei.

[22] *See* State Admin. for Indus. & Commerce, Regulation 74 (April 7, 2015).

- Article 13 provides guidance on standard setting activities. It states that "undertakings shall not use the standard setting and implementation of standards ... to eliminate or restrict competition during the exercise of IPR."

Anticompetitive conduct includes:

(1) when participating in the standard setting process, deliberately failing to disclose information on its right to the standard setting organization or to clearly give up its right, but asserting its patent right against implementers of such standard after its patent is involved in a standard;
(2) after its patent has become a standard essential patent, implementing conduct eliminating or restricting competition such as refusing to license, tying products or attaching other unreasonable trading conditions when transacting, in violation of the fair, reasonable and non-discriminatory principle.

At the time of this writing, SAIC has not concluded any investigations applying this newly issued regulation.

D. NDRC Investigations

NDRC's investigation of IDC

In June 2013, following the Shenzhen Court's decision in *Huawei v. IDC* and after receiving complaints, the NDRC launched a separate antitrust investigation of IDC. IDC was suspected of violating China's AML through "abusing its dominant market position and charging discriminatory prices of royalty fees for Chinese telecom manufacturers."[23] In addition, IDC was suspected of violating FRAND commitments in licensing its SEPs to Chinese telecom companies such as Huawei and ZTE.[24]

As the AML enforcement agency responsible for investigating price-related conduct, the NDRC developed a line of evidence demonstrating that the license fees offered by IDC to Chinese manufacturers were several times—and in some cases as much as ten times—higher than those offered to Samsung, Apple, and Nokia. After several rounds of negotiation in an effort to address the regulator's concerns, NDRC

---

[23] Press Release, NAT'L DEV. & REFORM COMM'N, *NDRC Press Release on the Status of its Antimonopoly Enforcement Activities* (Feb. 19, 2014).
[24] Id.

suspended its investigation on May 22, 2014, approving the following commitments from IDC:

(1) Whenever InterDigital engages with a Chinese Manufacturer to license InterDigital's patent portfolio for 2G, 3G and 4G wireless mobile standards, InterDigital will offer such Chinese Manufacturer the option of taking a worldwide portfolio license of only its standards-essential wireless patents, and comply with FRAND principles when negotiating and entering into such licensing agreements with Chinese Manufacturers.
(2) As part of its licensing offer, InterDigital will not require that a Chinese Manufacturer agree to a royalty-free, reciprocal cross-license of such Chinese Manufacturer's similarly categorized standards-essential wireless patents.
(3) Prior to commencing any action against a Chinese Manufacturer in which InterDigital may seek exclusionary or injunctive relief for the infringement of any of its wireless standards-essential patents, InterDigital will offer such Chinese Manufacturer the option to enter into expedited binding arbitration under fair and reasonable procedures to resolve the royalty rate and other terms of a worldwide license under InterDigital's wireless standards-essential patents. If the Chinese Manufacturer accepts InterDigital's binding arbitration offer or otherwise enters into an agreement with InterDigital on a binding arbitration mechanism, InterDigital will, in accordance with the terms of the arbitration agreement and patent license agreement, refrain from seeking exclusionary or injunctive relief against such company.[25]

NDRC's investigation of Qualcomm

Qualcomm Incorporated (Qualcomm) is a world leader in wireless technologies and is one of the world's biggest mobile chipmakers. It owns many SEPs encumbered with FRAND commitments. China is Qualcomm's largest market, accounting for nearly half of its global sales.

In November 2013, NDRC conducted dawn raids of Qualcomm's Beijing and Shanghai offices for potential AML violations. This investigation was triggered by company and trade association complaints lodged with the NDRC asserting that Qualcomm had "abused its market dominant position and charged discriminatory prices" in China. In

---

[25] *See* Patrick Van de Wille, *China's NDRC Accepts InterDigital's Commitments and Suspends Its Investigation*, INTERDIGITAL (May 22, 2014).

February 2015, the NDRC concluded its investigation and found that Qualcomm has a dominant position in the licensing of SEPs in various telecommunication technologies and the sales of baseband chips. Although not making explicit reference to the violation of FRAND commitments, NDRC identified three types of abusive conduct engaged by Qualcomm that are essentially consistent with a claim that Qualcomm violated its FRAND commitments:

(1) Charging excessive licensing rates. Specifically, NDRC found that Qualcomm failed to provide a list of patents during negotiations and charged royalties for portfolios including expired patents, that Qualcomm required free cross-licensing, and that Qualcomm used the entire device price as the royalty base;
(2) Bundling the licensing of SEPs with non-SEPs without justification; and
(3) Imposing unreasonable terms (i.e., conditioning the sales of baseband chips on a non-challenging clause in a license agreement) without justification.[26]

NDRC imposed a $975 million fine and ordered Qualcomm to stop its abusive conduct. In particular, Qualcomm agreed to implement a number of rectification measures including, for cellphones sold and used in China, Qualcomm will apply a royalty base of 65% of the price for the entire device, for example, smartphones, with royalties of 5% for 3G devices and 3.5% for 4G devices that do not implement CDMA or WCDMA, according to Qualcomm's news release. It also will provide a list of patents when negotiating licenses, and will not charge for expired patents. Furthermore, Qualcomm agreed not to request free cross-licenses and it will unbundle telecom licenses from other patents. In addition, Qualcomm will not condition sales of baseband chips on unreasonable terms, including not requesting non-challenge clauses.[27]

---

[26] *See* NAT'L DEV. & REFORM COMM'N, *Decision Against Qualcomm* (Mar. 2, 2015).

[27] Id; *see also* Press Release, QUALCOMM, *Qualcomm and China's National Development and Reform Commission Reach Resolution* (Feb. 9, 2015).

CONCLUSION

Over the last decade or so, China has become a major player in patent applications and patent grants. Some Chinese companies and organizations are among the world's most active patent applicants, and this new generation of patent owners is just beginning to be exposed to the complex issues of licensing and enforcing their patents. The concept that patent owners might willingly diminish their rights is still a new and unfamiliar idea at this stage in China. To date, no Chinese company, to the best of my knowledge, has made any patent pledge apart from commitments made as participants in SDOs.

A number of Chinese companies in the ICT sector have joined various SDOs, and as participants in the standards setting process, they are committed to uphold patent pledges made to those individual SDOs.[28] Like many other countries around the world, China is active in enforcing the FRAND commitments commonly requested by SDOs in the telecommunication industries. China's approach to analysing and enforcing FRAND commitments has relied upon the AML's framework for analysing complaints of abuse of dominance. In particular, complaints asserting excessively high licensing rates and unreasonable licensing terms, such as bundling and exclusive grant-backs, are a common thread in FRAND matters observed in China. While much attention has focused on FRAND commitments requested by SDOs in FRAND-related litigation outside China, Chinese authorities appear to place an emphasis on preserving FRAND commitments—as seen, for example, in MOFCOM's decision on the Microsoft/Nokia transaction—even when the FRAND commitments have been made unilaterally by individual companies outside the context of an SDO.

---

[28] *See* D. Breznitz & M. Murphree, *The Rise of China in Technology Standards: New Norms in Old Institutions*, RESEARCH REPORT PREPARED ON BEHALF OF THE U.S.-CHINA ECONOMIC AND SECURITY REVIEW COMMISSION (Jan. 13, 2013), http://www.uscc.gov/Research/rise-china-technology-standards-new-norms-old-institutions. *See also* Jorge L. Contreras, *Divergent Patterns of Engagement in Internet Standardization: Japan, Korea and China*, 30 TELECOMMUNICATIONS POLICY 916–34 (2014).

12. Patent pledges: Korean perspectives

Sang-Seung Yi and Yoonhee Kim

I. INTRODUCTION

The Korea Fair Trade Commission (KFTC) in 2014 amended its IPR Guidelines with a view to "curbing patent abuse" by owners of patents essential to the practice of technical standards ("standard-essential patents" or SEPs). Preceding this movement was the KFTC's investigation into Qualcomm's patent licensing practices, which concluded that Qualcomm violated Korean competition law by abusing its dominant position in the CDMA market, saying "the conduct of SEP owners reneging on FRAND commitments may *per se* raise competitive concerns."[1] On the flip side, other authorities in Korea (for example, the Seoul district court in *Samsung v. Apple*) gave weight to the unintended consequence of enforcing FRAND commitments that may allow a potential licensee to practice patented inventions embodied in the standard without adequate compensation to the SEP owner.

This chapter addresses the potential enforceability and effect of FRAND patent pledges in Korea and examines the circumstances under which Korean authorities may enforce such pledges. Section II reviews how a Korean district court in *Samsung v. Apple* interpreted patent pledges to a standard setting organization (Samsung's FRAND commitments to ETSI) and walks through the court's reasoning that Samsung was not liable for seeking injunctive relief against Apple for SEP infringement. Subsequently, the KFTC in early 2014 exonerated Samsung for similar reasons. While these decisions seem to conflict with the European Commission's (EC) enforcement action on the same matter, the discrepancy stems from different factual findings. Unlike the EC, the Korean authorities found Apple an *unwilling* licensee in Korea, partly

[1] [KFTC], 2009JiSik0329, Dec. 30, 2009, *aff'd in part*, [Seoul High Ct.], 2010Nu3932, June 19, 2013 (S. Kor.).

because Apple did not deposit in escrow a putative FRAND royalty, as it did in other jurisdictions.

Any seeming difference in the fundamental approach to FRAND commitments, however, was cleared when the KFTC issued revised IPR Guidelines in late 2014. In particular, the Guidelines proclaimed that seeking an injunction by a FRAND-encumbered SEP holder against a *willing* licensee could constitute a competition law violation—a stance similar to that taken by the EC and the U.S. Federal Trade Commission. Section III explores the KFTC's new IPR Guidelines.

In 2015, the KFTC took an aggressive stance on so-called "de facto" SEPs by reaching a consent decree with Microsoft on its acquisition of Nokia's mobile handset business. On the theory that post-merger Microsoft would have incentives to raise royalties on its de facto SEPs from handset makers that employ a competing operating system (OS) such as Android, the KFTC obtained a pledge from Microsoft that it would not raise royalties on its non-SEPs for the next seven years. According to Contreras' taxonomy,[2] Microsoft's commitments would be an example of a legally enforceable "unilateral patent pledge" made by a patent holder to government officials. Section IV examines this case more closely.

II. *SAMSUNG v. APPLE*: FRAND PLEDGES IN THE EYES OF A KOREAN COURT

In 2012, the Seoul district court in *Samsung v. Apple* examined under both contract law and competition law the potential enforceability and effect of FRAND commitments vis-à-vis third parties.[3] Having wrestled with defining the boundaries of the right and obligation of the parties in negotiating a FRAND royalty rate, the Korean court concluded that Samsung's patent pledge to the standard setting body (ETSI) was not enforceable by Apple. Similarly answered in the negative by the Seoul district court, and later joined by the KFTC in 2014, was whether Samsung's bid for injunctive relief based on FRAND-encumbered patents violated Korean competition law.

---

[2] *See* Contreras, Chapter 1. Some of Microsoft's patents are also subject to what Contreras calls "Platform Leadership pledges, as they are made to induce the market to adopt the patent holder's proprietary technology platform." Id. at p. 29.

[3] Seoul South Central District Court [Dist. Ct.], 2011GaHap39552, Aug. 24, 2012 (S. Kor.).

A. Contract Law May Not Be a Good Fit for Enforcing FRAND Pledges in Korea

It should first be noted that *Samsung v. Apple* may not offer a complete picture of how patent pledges would be analysed under Korean contract law, because, by operation of the choice-of-law provisions included in ETSI's IPR Policy, the Seoul district court was interpreting and applying *French* law. Nor did this case lead to binding precedent because the parties settled before a final decision on appeal. Nevertheless, given that *Samsung v. Apple* is the only court case to date in Korea addressing patent pledges from a contract law perspective, it is worth a closer look for guidance as to the circumstances under which patent pledges may be legally enforceable by third parties in Korea.

Less than a week after being sued in a U.S. district court, Samsung initiated a patent infringement action in Korea, seeking injunctive relief against Apple's smartphones and tablet PCs. The Seoul district court found claims of the asserted SEPs valid and infringed. Samsung had pledged to license its SEPs on FRAND terms and declared them essential to ETSI's 3G UMTS mobile wireless standard. Apple countered that Samsung breached its FRAND commitments by seeking an injunction. This "FRAND" defense relied on the argument that an enforceable contract was formed under ETSI's IPR Policy because Apple "accepted" Samsung's "offer" to license by implementing ETSI's wireless standard.

Applying French contract law to the case, the court was not persuaded that Samsung's FRAND pledges submitted to ETSI constituted an "offer" to license.[4] The court first noted that the pledges were lacking in the "material" terms of a license. According to the court, under French law, an offer to license must clearly set forth the material terms of the agreement. That is because the offer is the offeror's manifestation of willingness to be bound by those terms, and an agreement to royalty rates is material to formation of a contract.[5] ETSI's IPR Policy was not helpful in filling this gap because it did not specify criteria to determine FRAND rates. Hence, the court concluded that Samsung's FRAND pledges did not constitute an "offer" to license.

The court next addressed whether Apple "accepted" Samsung's offer by implementing the ETSI standard.[6] Rejecting Apple's position that the offer was accepted, the court held that Apple's unilateral implementation of the standard alone did not constitute acceptance. It reasoned that

---

[4] Id. at 173–74.

[5] *See* Contreras, Chapter 5 (analysing U.S. contract law).

[6] 2011GaHap39552, at 174–75.

acceptance must be communicated to the offeror. However, the record showed that Apple had not formally asked Samsung for a license, nor did it deposit appropriate FRAND royalties into an escrow account.

The court also rejected Apple's argument that it was entitled to enforce the pledges as a "third party beneficiary" to Samsung's agreements with ETSI.[7] It is noteworthy that the Korean court came to a different conclusion than U.S. courts that have considered the issue and recognized third party beneficiary status for standard implementers like Apple.[8] Interpreting French law as allowing a third party beneficiary claim only in exceptional circumstances such as where a promisor made a "stipulated condition for itself,"[9] the Korean court ruled that no contractual relationship would likely exist between ETSI and a SEP owner like Samsung. It reasoned that ETSI was not a market participant but rather a private organization in charge of administering the collective standard setting process.

With regard to the meaning of "FRAND," the court construed Samsung's FRAND pledges as imposing no more than a "duty to negotiate in good faith."[10] It reasoned that neither the language of the FRAND declaration nor ETSI's IPR Policy supported Apple's proposition that Samsung's submission of FRAND pledges should create for third parties an irrevocable and actionable right to be licensed. According to the court, such proposition would run counter not only to the goals of standardization by sanctioning de facto "compulsory" licenses, but also to the goals of the patent system by overprotecting "unwilling" licensees who would unilaterally practice SEPs by contesting patent validity or infringement.[11]

For the same reasons, the court held that Samsung was not estopped from seeking an injunction.[12] Having found unclear under French law

---

7 Id. at 175.

8 *See* Apple, Inc. v. Samsung Elecs. Co., Ltd., No. 11-CV-01846, 2012 WL 1672493, at *9-15 (N.D. Cal. May 14, 2012); Microsoft Corp. v. Motorola, Inc., 864 F. Supp. 2d 1023, 1032–33 (W.D. Wash. 2013), *aff'd*, 795 F.3d 1024 (9th Cir. 2015); *accord* In re Innovatio IP Ventures, LLC Patent Litig., No. 11C 9308, 2013 WL 5593609, at *17 (N.D. Ill. Oct. 3, 2013); Apple, Inc. v. Motorola Mobility, Inc., 886 F. Supp. 2d 1061, 1083-84 (W.D. Wis. 2012). This remains somewhat of an open question in the U.S. because no appellate court has directly addressed the third-party-beneficiary issue.

9 2011GaHap39552, at 175 (interpreting Article 1121 of the French Civil Code).

10 Id. at 177–80.

11 Id. at 179.

12 Id. at 180–82.

whether estoppel could be generally applicable to substantive legal issues like contract interpretation, the court held that Samsung had not given up its right to injunctive relief against unwilling licensees.

Apple countered that Samsung should not be awarded injunctive relief because it abused patent rights by seeking an injunction in breach of its FRAND commitments. The court was convinced, however, that neither party had participated in FRAND license negotiations *in good faith*.[13] The court first ruled that the duty of SEP owners to "negotiate in good faith" includes refraining from pursuing injunctive relief until an alleged infringer has expressed a refusal to negotiate. But the court went on to add that the SEP owner owes such duty only to "willing" licensees, for example, those who step forward to make a formal request to license or who agree to pay royalties without contesting patent validity and infringement.

Applying this rule, the court found both Samsung and Apple in breach of their duty to negotiate in good faith because the record showed that neither of them genuinely endeavored to close the "significant" gap in royalty rates they each claimed to be FRAND.[14] Here, Apple first asked that Samsung quote FRAND terms and disclose its terms with pre-existing SEP licensees. Samsung responded with an initial offer based on the sales price of the accused product, to which Apple counter-offered for Samsung's SEP portfolio license. No compromise was reached through the end of the trial. The court found that Samsung and Apple insisted on their respective initial proposals to the end of negotiation, as if they were more interested in the outcome of litigation than in actually reaching agreement on FRAND terms.[15] But at the same time, the court found that the record did not conclusively show that Samsung's initial offer was an excessive demand in conflict with the FRAND commitment.[16] Taking these findings into account, the court held that Samsung's conduct in seeking an injunction did not amount to an abuse of patent rights.

B. Competition Law Lends No Hand When a Party Did Not Negotiate in Good Faith

Turning next to the allegations under Korean competition law, the Seoul district court held that Samsung did not abuse its dominant position in the 3G mobile consumer electronics market in violation of Article

[13] Id. at 183–86.
[14] Id. at 184–86.
[15] Id. at 189.
[16] Id. at 186–90.

3-2(1)(iii) of the Monopoly Regulation and Fair Trade Act (MRFTA), which prohibits "unjustly hindering the business undertakings of others." It further held that Samsung did not violate Article 23(1) of the MRFTA, which prohibits unfair trade practices, for example, "unjustly refusing to deal or treating a trading party in a discriminatory manner." In so holding, the court made findings with respect to the negotiations between Samsung and Apple, including:[17]

1. In this action, Apple had not made a *formal* request to license Samsung's SEPs and did not concede that the SEPs were valid and infringed.
2. In foreign jurisdictions (e.g., the Netherlands and Japan), Apple moved to escrow royalty amounts in anticipation that Samsung's patents might be found valid and infringed, but Apple did not do the same in the Korea action.
3. Under ETSI's IPR Policy, the task of determining FRAND conditions was explicitly left to negotiations between a SEP owner and a standard implementer.
4. It was uncertain that Samsung's initial offer was excessive compared to the disclosed rates (0.8 to 3.25 percent[18]) that other SEP owners had proposed to potential licensees. Samsung also alternatively proposed cross-licensing during the negotiations with Apple.
5. A noticeable difference existed between Apple's counteroffer and what was customary for other firms in the telecommunications sector.
6. Although it could be inferred that this action was initiated in response to Apple's lawsuit against Samsung in the United States, the negotiations following this action still failed to reach any agreement on FRAND conditions.

Here, the court seems more attentive to evidence tending to show that Apple did not negotiate in good faith. Although it found that Samsung had market power[19] and left open the possibility that seeking an injunction based on SEPs could be an unfair trade practice or anticompetitive conduct that "unjustly" hinders the business of others, the court was not persuaded that Apple's business was "unjustly" hindered. It appears that Apple was viewed as an *unwilling* licensee having engaged

---

17 Id. at 204–08.
18 Id. at 188.
19 Id. at 201–02.

in "reverse hold-up." In contrast, the court does not appear to have found "patent hold-up" by Samsung.

Later, the KFTC expressed a similar view when it determined in 2014 that Samsung did not violate Korean competition law.[20] While the trial in *Samsung v. Apple* was underway, Apple petitioned the KFTC in 2012 to investigate whether Samsung's seeking of an injunction in the Seoul district court was unlawful as anticompetitive. With the acknowledgement that it was a matter of first impression to the Korean antitrust authority, the KFTC found no violation on Samsung's part, citing similar evidence presented in *Samsung v. Apple*. Notably, the KFTC reached the conclusion that, while it was not clearly shown that Samsung did not negotiate in good faith, Apple's conduct amounted to "reverse hold-up."

These decisions appear to be in conflict with the EC's enforcement action on the same matter. Samsung and Apple engaged in *global* licensing negotiations and when they could not settle their differences, they sued each other in many jurisdictions across the globe. In order to resolve the EC's concerns that Samsung's seeking of injunctions against Apple in several European countries could amount to an abuse of a dominant position prohibited by EU antitrust rules, Samsung offered to abstain from seeking an injunction in Europe for mobile SEPs for a period of five years against any company agreeing to: (i) a negotiation period of up to 12 months; and (ii) if no agreement is reached, a third party determination of FRAND terms by a court if either party chooses, or by an arbitrator if both parties agree.[21]

The discrepancy between the EC's and the Korean authorities' decisions, however, stems from different factual findings on the key question of the *willingness* of Apple to take a license on FRAND terms. The Korean authorities found Apple an *unwilling* licensee in Korea. In particular, the Korean court found that Apple did not deposit a putative FRAND royalty into escrow, as it did in other jurisdictions. In contrast, the EC "reached the preliminary conclusion that, at the time of Samsung's conduct, Apple could not be said to be unwilling to enter into a

20 Press Release, KFTC, Determination That Samsung Does Not Violate the Monopoly Regulation & Fair Trade Act by Seeking Injunctive Relief against Apple for SEP Infringement in Korea (Feb. 25, 2014).

21 Press Release, European Commission, Antitrust: Commission Accepts Legally Binding Commitments by Samsung Electronics on Standard Essential Patent Injunctions (Apr. 29, 2014), http://europa.eu/rapid/press-release_IP-14-490_en.htm?locale=en. For a full text of Samsung's final commitments, consult Case AT.39939, Samsung—Enforcement of UMTS Standard Essential Patents, Comm'n Decision (Apr. 29, 2014).

license agreement for Samsung's UMTS SEPs on FRAND terms and conditions."[22]

Moreover, the KFTC confirmed that its fundamental approach to FRAND commitments is not different from, but in line with, the EC's and the U.S. FTC's when it issued revised IPR Guidelines in late 2014.[23] We turn to the revised Guidelines in the next section.

III. THE 2014 IPR GUIDELINES: PATENT PLEDGES IN THE KFTC'S PERSPECTIVES

The 2014 IPR Guidelines stated, inter alia, that "an act of filing an injunction against willing licensees by a SEP holder who promised to license its SEP on FRAND terms can be determined as a behavior that restricts competition in the relevant market as it exceeds the reasonable extent of exercise of patent right."[24] At the same time, the Guidelines recognized the risk of reverse hold-up when a patentee cannot seek injunctive relief against an *unwilling* licensee, i.e., a standard implementer who is not willing to pay FRAND royalties.[25]

The Guidelines illustrated two circumstances in which an implementer can be viewed as an *unwilling* licensee: (i) a potential licensee refuses to "follow the decision made by a court or an arbitral institution" or

---

22 Case AT.39939, Samsung—Enforcement of UMTS Standard Essential Patents, Comm'n Decision (Apr. 29, 2014), http://ec.europa.eu/competition/antitrust/cases/dec_docs/39939/39939_1501_5.pdf. The EC did not explain why it found Apple a "not unwilling" licensee. In a related decision on Motorola Mobility Inc. (MMI), the EC found Apple a willing licensee, as "Apple had agreed to take a licence and be bound by a determination of the FRAND royalties by the relevant German court." Press Release, European Commission, Antitrust: Commission Finds That Motorola Mobility Infringed EU Competition Rules by Misusing Standard Essential Patents (Apr. 29, 2014), http://europa.eu/rapid/press-release_IP-14-489_en.htm?locale=en. The EC's full analysis on its rejection of MMI's claim that Apple was an unwilling licensee can be found at recitals (430)–(464) of its decision against MMI. *See* Case AT.39985, Motorola—Enforcement of GPRS Standard Essential Patents, Comm'n Decision, 76–81 (Apr. 29, 2014).

23 KOREA FAIR TRADE COMM'N, REVIEW GUIDELINES ON UNFAIR EXERCISE OF INTELLECTUAL PROPERTY RIGHTS (Dec. 2014) [hereinafter 2014 IPR Guidelines]. In late 2015, the KFTC solicited comments on the 2014 version for further revision. In March 2016, the KFTC issued a revised version, which we discuss in Section IV.B.

24 2014 IPR Guidelines, *supra* note 23, at § III.5.B.

25 2014 IPR Guidelines, *supra* note 23, at n.2—§ III.5.B.

otherwise refuses to "sign a licensing agreement on FRAND terms" or (ii) a potential licensee is not likely to pay FRAND royalties as, for example, when it "is near bankruptcy."[26] The revised Guidelines thus took a similar stance to the U.S. FTC and the EC in endorsing the principle that FRAND-encumbered SEP owners should not seek injunctive relief against willing licensees and in offering guidance for SEP owners to identify unwilling licensees against which they may seek injunctive relief.

The 2014 IPR Guidelines also made clear that FRAND commitments travel with SEPs. In a new provision addressing non-practicing entities, the revised Guidelines stated that "[w]hen licensing patent rights acquired from a third party, an act of imposing a royalty which is unreasonable given the usual trade practices, while at the same time refusing to apply FRAND terms which has applied to the previous patentee" can be viewed as "behaviors that could restrict competition in the relevant market as they exceed the rightful extent of patent rights."[27]

Also, the Guidelines took an aggressive approach to interpreting FRAND commitments. Examples of "demanding unfair conditions after being designated as technical standard [that] can be determined to be outside of the bounds of just exercise of patent rights" include:

1. Acts of avoiding or circumventing licensing on FRAND terms to strengthen market dominance or to exclude competitors (Section III.5.A(3)).
2. Acts of unfairly rejecting the licensing of a standard essential patent (Section III.5.A(4)).
3. Acts of unfairly imposing discriminatory conditions when licensing standard essential patents or of imposing an unreasonable level of royalty (Section III.5.A(5)).
4. An act of imposing conditions unfairly restricting the exercise of patent rights held by licensees or act of unfairly imposing conditions of cross-licensing of non-standard essential patents held by licensees (Section III.5.A(6)).

---

[26] Id. The English version incorrectly translated a "potential licensee" in the official Korean version as a "willing licensee." The Korean version is available at http://ftc.go.kr/laws/laws/popRegulation.jsp?lawDivCd=01&firstFtcRelLawNo=50.

[27] 2014 IPR Guidelines, *supra* note 23, at § III.7.B. The Guidelines added that they apply to "other patentees which are not NPEs." Id. at § III.7.

The Guidelines further explained that in determining whether particular conduct is "unfair," the KFTC will follow a rule of reason approach. Section II.2.D provides:

> When an exercise of IPRs increases both anti-competitiveness and [efficiency-enhancing effects], whether the exercise violates the Act or not in principle is determined after comparing the two effects through the fair comparison of the interests. When the [efficiency-enhancing effects] of the exercise concerned outweighs the anti-competitiveness, the exercise does not violate the Act. The term "unfairly" stated in Provision III of the Guideline means that the anti-competitiveness of an activity exceeds [efficiency-enhancing effects].[28]

Perhaps most controversial was the inclusion of de facto SEPs as FRAND-encumbered SEPs. With respect to Sections III.5.A(4)–(6) identified above, the Guidelines stated that "[t]his applies not only to standard technologies set by standards organizations, but also to technologies widely used as de facto standard technologies in related areas, such as technology selected as must-use technology when bidding for public organization projects."[29] In the next section, one of us offers a critical analysis of the KFTC's approach to patent pledges, beginning with a general discussion of FRAND commitments and then moving on to the KFTC's dealing with de facto SEPs.

---

[28] 2014 IPR Guidelines, *supra* note 23, at § II.2.D. The English translation uses the term "effectiveness" for "efficiency-enhancing effects." It seems that these translations played a part in leading some foreign commentators to believe that the 2014 IPR Guidelines did not adopt a rule of reason approach. For example, Kobayashi et al. say, "For these reasons, we strongly recommend that the KFTC adopt an effects-based approach to matters involving IPRs. Similarly, we strongly recommend that the KFTC avoid using any truncated effects-based analyses that rely upon presumptions rather than rigorous economic and empirical analysis to satisfy the burden of proof required to conclude that any particular conduct involving IPRs is likely anticompetitive." Bruce H. Kobayashi, Douglas H. Ginsburg, Koren W. Wong-Ervin & Joshua D. Wright, *Comment of the Global Antitrust Institute, George Mason University School of Law, on the Korea Fair Trade Commission's Revised Review Guidelines on Unfair Exercise of Intellectual Property Rights*, 3 (Oct. 5, 2015) (George Mason Legal Studies Research Paper No. LS 15-35).

[29] 2014 IPR Guidelines, *supra* note 23, at § III.5.A(4). This clause was deleted in the March 2016 revision. *See supra* Section IV.B.

IV. ANALYSIS OF THE KFTC'S APPROACH TO PATENT PLEDGES[30]

A. General Discussion of FRAND Pledges from a Competition Law Perspective

Whether particular conduct by a FRAND-encumbered SEP owner would constitute a competition law violation rather than mere contractual opportunism requires careful analysis. One of us has advanced the view that a pure "exploitative abuse" by a SEP owner, without some "bad" acts, is better addressed by contract law.[31] That is, as long as negotiations take place in an "open" environment free from the threat of injunctions (against willing licensees), the level of royalties itself should not be a competition law concern. However, if a breach of FRAND commitments threatens the integrity of the SEP selection process within a standard setting organization (SSO) that functions as a competitive process that replaces competition in the marketplace, it is not simply a matter of contract law. Rather, such a FRAND violation falls squarely within the essential prerogatives of competition law that protects the competitive process.

After obtaining an *ex post* monopoly position over implementers on the promise that it would grant a license on FRAND terms, a SEP owner's reneging on the very promise and seeking injunctive relief against a willing licensee is an example of harming the integrity of the standard setting process. Similarly, if the SEP holder is vertically integrated into the business of designing/making/selling a key component that practices the standard and achieves dominance in that market (as a whole or some product/geographic segments which constitute a relevant market), it should not condition the supply and the subsequent use of such a component on the end-product maker accepting the license. The reason is that refusal to supply its monopoly component to the end-product maker unless the latter signs the license contract is tantamount to the SEP holder seeking an injunction against the latter.[32]

Hence, a problem with the KFTC's stance on FRAND pledges may not arise as long as the KFTC adheres to its proclaimed rule of reason

---

30 The views expressed in this section are those of Sang-Seung Yi and do not necessarily represent the views of Yoonhee Kim.

31 Sang-Seung Yi, *Responsibilities of FRAND-Encumbered SEP Owners under Competition Law* (2015) (unpublished manuscript, on file with author).

32 Id.

framework and leaves pure contractual disputes over (open-ended) FRAND terms and conditions to a contract law court or arbitrator.

B. De Facto Standard Essential Patents: The 2016 Revision of the IPR Guidelines and Microsoft's Pledges to the KFTC in Its Acquisition of Nokia's Handset Business

In contrast, the 2014 Guidelines' inclusion of de facto SEPs in the section on FRAND-encumbered SEPs is problematic.[33] If a patent is not encumbered with FRAND commitments undertaken during formal standard setting processes or other pledges,[34] its owner should enjoy the normal prerogatives of a patent holder, including the right to exclude. Otherwise, the incentives to engage in innovative activities would be chilled.

Fortunately, in March 2016 the KFTC announced that de facto SEPs would be removed from the section on FRAND-encumbered SEPs. According to the accompanying press release:

> The amendment clarified the distinction between SEPs which are set by standard setting organizations (hereinafter SSOs) and de facto SEPs which have become widely used as a standard through a fierce market competition, thereby encouraging a just exercise of intellectual property rights.[35]

Even before the formal revision of the Guidelines, the KFTC had not engaged in undisciplined application of competition law to de facto SEPs. A prominent case that featured de facto SEPs is Microsoft's acquisition of Nokia's handset business.

Microsoft's proposed acquisition of Nokia's handset business and related patents in 2013 underwent an intensive investigation by the KFTC. De facto SEPs owned by Microsoft were the focus of the KFTC's

---

33 *See supra* note 29 and text accompanying.

34 *See* Contreras, Chapter 1 (providing a taxonomy of patent pledges and the conditions under which a particular pledge is actionable).

35 Press Release, KFTC, The KFTC Rationalizes Its Regulations on SEPs to Promote Technology Innovation (Mar. 30, 2016) (press release number 271). The 2016 Guidelines are attached to the press release. The official Korean version is available at http://www.ftc.go.kr/laws/laws/popRegulation.jsp?lawDivCd=01&firstFtcRelLawNo=768. For the revised portion of the Guidelines, see the official Korean press release (Mar. 30, 2016), http://www.ftc.go.kr/news/ftc/reportboView.jsp?report_data_no=6646. The press release states that it received public comments from December 16, 2015 to January 13, 2016 and finalized the amendment through a resolution of the full committee on March 23, 2016.

scrutiny. The KFTC's theory of harm is a form of the input foreclosure theory. According to the KFTC, after vertically integrating into the manufacture of smartphones, Microsoft has incentives to "unilaterally raise" royalties on its de facto SEPs (such as ActiveSync that synchronizes data with smartphones and computers) to handset makers that employ a *competing* OS, in particular Android.[36]

Thus the KFTC did not rely on the concept of the "essential facility" in order to regulate the pricing of the de facto SEPs—which might have chilling effects on incentives to develop widely used patents. Rather, the theory of harm that the KFTC advanced is *merger specific*. Because Microsoft's patents are widely used by Android handset makers, if an individual Android handset maker attempts not to use Microsoft's de facto SEPs, it will lose beneficial network effects arising from seamless interoperability with other Android devices. Hence, an individual handset maker has little recourse if Microsoft raises royalty rates. As such, the KFTC's theory of harm is more respectable than one might initially think.

The problem is that the KFTC's theory of harm does not fit with the factual circumstances in the Microsoft-Nokia merger. A significant weakness of the KFTC's theory is that post-merger Microsoft would have little *ability* to raise its royalty rates, because major Android handset makers are said to have long-term license contracts with Microsoft. Another weakness is that Microsoft has weak *incentives* to raise its royalty rates. Given the weak popularity of Nokia's (Lumia) smartphones, it is doubtful that Microsoft would benefit from raising royalties to Android handset makers. First, not many Android buyers would switch to Lumia smartphones in response to an increase in price induced by higher royalty rates. Second, Lumia smartphones have very low market shares.[37] Third, they are likely to have low margins.[38]

---

[36] Press Release, KFTC, The KFTC Roots Out the Possibility of MS's Abuse of Patent Rights, 1 (Aug. 24, 2015) (press release number 245) [hereinafter Microsoft Pledges to KFTC]. This press release included a summary of the consent decree and Microsoft's pledges to the KFTC. Id. at 2–5.

[37] According to Strategy Analytics, Microsoft's Windows Phones accounted for a 3.6% unit share in 2013 and 3.0% share in 2014. Surur, *Strategy Analytics Award Windows Phone 3% Market Share in Q4 2014*, WMPOWERUSER (Jan. 29, 2015).

[38] According to Canaccord's estimates, Microsoft (formally Nokia) had operating losses since 2012. Shira Ovide & Daisuke Wakabayashi, *Apple's Share of Smartphone Industry's Profits Soars to 92%*, WALL ST. J. (July 12, 2015).

Despite these weaknesses in the KFTC's liability theory, Microsoft offered commitments on its non-SEPs to allay the KFTC's concerns. Specifically, it "pledged to maintain royalties for non-SEPs at or below the current level, to ban the transfer of its non-SEPs, and not to bring lawsuits for injunctions or import bans against Korean smartphone and tablet manufacturers both at home and abroad."[39]

For the purpose of this discussion, it is important to note that some of Microsoft's key non-SEPs such as those on the ActiveSync suite of protocols are subject to Microsoft's earlier pledge to license them on FRAND terms at "low" royalty rates.[40] John Harkrider has argued that the emergence of ActiveSync as a de facto standard can be attributed, at least in part, to Microsoft's patent pledge. He explains, "Unlike many other *de facto* standards, which emerged solely from technical superiority or unfettered marketplace competition, Microsoft encouraged the industry to standardize on ActiveSync by promising to license its ActiveSync-essential patents on FRAND terms, at 'low royalty rates.'"[41] If so, Microsoft's key pledges on non-SEPs to the KFTC have merely reaffirmed its earlier patent pledge made to secure its "Platform Leadership."

Microsoft also offered to the KFTC a number of pledges on its SEPs, some of which go beyond the usual scope of FRAND commitments. First, Microsoft reaffirmed its adherence to FRAND commitments made to SSOs. Second, Microsoft promised not to seek an injunction or import ban for infringing those SEPs against smartphones or tablets "made by Korean domiciled smartphone or tablet manufacturers" on a *global* basis and not just in Korea. Third, Microsoft pledged that it would make those SEPs available for license without requiring that those licensees license their patents back to Microsoft (except for any patents they have that are essential to the same industry standard). Fourth, Microsoft committed not to transfer SEPs to any third party unless that transferee (i) agrees to adhere to the principles outlined above, and (ii) such transferee agrees that if it again transfers the acquired SEPs, it would require any subsequent transferee to adhere to the principles outlined above.[42]

---

[39] Microsoft Pledges to KFTC, *supra* note 36, at 3–4.

[40] *See* Contreras, Chapter 1.

[41] John D. Harkrider, *REPs Not SEPs: A Reasonable and Non-Discriminatory Approach to Licensing Commitments*, COMPETITION POL'Y INT'L ANTITRUST CHRON. (Oct. 2013), at 8.

[42] Microsoft Pledges to KFTC, *supra* note 36, at 4–5.

CONCLUSION

Being home to world-class handset makers such as Samsung Electronics and LG Electronics, Korea has been at the forefront of disputes and competition law issues concerning patent pledges, both formal FRAND commitments made during standard setting processes and unilateral pledges made to a government agency in order to resolve antitrust concerns.

The KFTC has converged with the U.S. FTC and the EC on the heatedly disputed issue of the availability of injunctive relief: a FRAND-encumbered SEP owner risks competition law liability if it seeks an injunction against implementers who are *willing* to take a license on FRAND terms and conditions. These competition authorities also clarified the circumstances under which an implementer can be deemed as *unwilling* (or unable) to pay FRAND royalties.

The KFTC drew criticism by not distinguishing in its IPR Guidelines between FRAND-encumbered SEPs and de facto SEPs without any enforceable pledges. In this area too, the KFTC has converged with other major competition authorities by cancelling the clauses that equated de facto SEPs to FRAND-encumbered SEPs.

PART IV

Patent pledges and innovation

13. The informational effects of patent pledges

Clark D. Asay

Patent pledges, as the existence of this volume suggests, are of growing interest to both scholars and practitioners. But why? They may be of interest to practitioners because patent pledges are, or may become, relevant in the specific industries in which the practitioners operate. For scholars, they are of interest at least in part because their proliferation seems to defy traditional theoretical premises underlying the patent system. In other words, if the economic benefits of a patent's exclusive rights are crucial to incentivizing innovators to invent, publicly disclose, and commercialize socially beneficial inventions, as traditional patent law theories teach, then why are increasingly more patent owners voluntarily limiting such rights through patent pledges?

This chapter attempts to help answer this question. It argues that the patent pledging phenomenon can be explained in part by more fully appreciating the informational effects of patents in patent pledging contexts. In other words, a key value of patents in such scenarios is as an informational tool; patent pledgers use patents to efficiently and credibly convey information to the relevant public about their innovation preferences and activities. Transmission of this information may then facilitate a variety of economic objectives, depending on the nature of the pledge.

None of this is to say that patents have ceased to play the more traditional roles that conventional patent law theories assign to them. Indeed, patents may play these traditional roles, as well as the informational ones described in this chapter, simultaneously. For instance, many patent pledgers specifically limit their pledges by retaining the ability to use the pledged patents defensively in response to patent assertions by others. Hence, such patents retain value as "sticks," even if they simultaneously have informational value. Furthermore, parties may limit their pledges to specific groups, such as when Microsoft pledged not to assert patents against non-commercial developers of open source software.[1] So while Microsoft abandoned certain economic opportunities associated with its patent rights vis-à-vis the pledged-to group, it retained those same opportunities vis-à-vis those left outside the pledge. Patent rights can thus represent a variety of different types of value to the patent holder simultaneously, depending on how the patent holder uses its patents. And, as this chapter will argue, the patent pledging phenomenon shows that one of the significant values that patents can provide patent holders is informational in nature.

I. PATENT LAW THEORY

Traditional patent law theories explaining the purposes of patents are well known in the literature. This section does not attempt to comprehensively survey each of them. Instead, it provides a brief overview of the predominant theories in order to set the backdrop for assessing the phenomenon of patent pledges. It should also be noted that some accounts of the patent system can fit within several of the below categories simultaneously, depending on how the account is framed. Hence, while the classifications below provide a useful shorthand for understanding traditional patent law theories, they should not be viewed too rigidly.

A. The Right to Exclude: A Patentee's Key Gain

Traditional patent law theories view the right to exclude as a patent's key benefit to the patent holder. While the various theories articulate differing reasons for granting this right to inventors, they all argue in one form or another that granting inventors rights of exclusion is vital to making the patent system work.

For instance, the predominant theory behind patent law justifies a patent's rights of exclusion as a necessary incentive to inventive behavior.[2] According to this theoretical school, these incentives are necessary because inventive ideas are intangible goods, and intangible goods have the characteristics of a public good: they are both non-rivalrous and non-excludable, meaning one party's use of the inventive idea does not

---

1 *See* Contreras, Chapter 1.

2 *See*, e.g., Mark A. Lemley, *The Myth of the Sole Inventor*, 110 MICH. L. REV. 709, 736–38 (2012) (reviewing this theory and the literature about it generally).

diminish others' ability to do the same and, without legal intervention, it is difficult to prevent others from doing exactly that. As a result, "utilitarian" or "economic incentives" theories postulate that parties will not engage in socially optimal levels of inventive activity for fear that others will simply appropriate the value of the invention without incurring the same costs. Patent law purportedly solves this riddle by granting inventors rights of exclusion in their inventions.

A related school of thought—what some call "disclosure" theory—views patents as necessary to ensure that inventors share their inventions with the public.[3] In other words, because intangible goods have the characteristics of a public good, inventors will keep their inventions secret, rather than share them with the public, absent legal intervention (even if they will still develop them). Patents provide the necessary legal intervention by granting inventors the right to exclude others from practicing their inventions. But in exchange, inventors are required to publicly disclose their inventions as part of the patenting process.[4]

"Prospect" theorists also view a patent's right to exclude as vital, but for different reasons. According to certain strands of this theory, granting an inventor broad rights of exclusion early on facilitates post-invention development and commercialization later.[5] As with granting mining rights in land, granting inventors with rights of exclusion provides them with the necessary incentives to further develop, license, and commercialize the invention. Patent law thus provides inventors the incentives necessary—in the form of rights of exclusion—to develop their patented inventions for the benefit of society.

Some scholars advocate a related theory based more directly on the "commercialization" of patented inventions. These scholars generally argue that the patent system fails to provide inventors with sufficient

---

3 Id. at 745–46.

4 What some call "coordination theories" are similar to disclosure theory in how they view rights of exclusion as crucial to making the patent system work for the public good. For instance, without rights of exclusion, parties may be loathe to share information with each other for fear that the other party will appropriate the value of it, or that the disclosing party will otherwise fail to capture the information's full value. Patents purportedly address this problem by allowing patent holders to exclude other parties from using the information, even absent a contractual relationship or evidence of copying. Patents may thus help facilitate transactions between parties, and disclosure in general, by providing a form of insurance against the possibility that a patent holder will lose out on realizing their technology's full worth.

5 *See*, e.g., Edmund W. Kitch, *The Nature and Function of the Patent System*, 20 J.L. & ECON. 265, 265 (1977).

rights of exclusion to further develop and commercialize their inventions.[6] Such scholars thus propose a number of reforms to the patent system that would provide inventors with greater incentives in the form of expanded rights of exclusion.[7]

A remaining theoretical camp focuses on the inherent rights that inventors may have in their inventions.[8] In other words, rather than viewing patent rights as strictly instrumental in bringing about broader societal benefits, natural rights theories view patents as justified on the basis of the effort and/or personal investment that inventors may have put into their inventions. Nonetheless, even within this camp, a patent's right of exclusion remains vital in order to safeguard these natural rights.

B. The Right to Exclude and Patent Pledges

Each of these schools of thought faces difficulty when taking into account patent pledges. Indeed, if the right of exclusion is vital to the patent system, as all of these theories argue for a variety of reasons, why do so many parties pursue patents, only to pledge those rights away? The centrality and role of the right to exclude thus needs rethinking in light of the phenomenon of patent pledging. Traditional theories, at least, offer no clear explanation for it.

For instance, utilitarian theory's prediction that parties will not engage in inventive behavior without exclusive rights in hand seems to fundamentally conflict with many patent pledging scenarios, in which parties voluntarily sacrifice some or all of the economic leverage that comes with a patent's rights of exclusion. If those economic rights were so vital to the party, why did it voluntarily give them up, even if only in part? Parties almost certainly have other economic rationales for doing so. But as Section II will more fully explore, those rationales suggest a different utility of patent rights, rather than supporting traditional utilitarian accounts of the patent system.

---

[6] *See generally* Michael Abramowicz, *The Danger of Underdeveloped Patent Prospects*, 92 CORNELL L. REV. 1065, 1065 (2007).

[7] Ted Sichelman, *Commercializing Patents*, 62 STAN. L. REV. 341, 341 (2010) (proposing a "commercialization" patent, in addition to traditional patents, in order to better incentivize post-invention commercialization of patented technologies).

[8] *See generally* ROBERT P. MERGES, JUSTIFYING INTELLECTUAL PROPERTY 31–101 (2011).

Disclosure theories face obstacles for similar reasons. In the patent pledging scenario, patent owners appear willing to disclose their inventions to the public by filing for the patent, while simultaneously giving up some portion of the right that was purportedly necessary as an incentive to the disclosure. As such, the bargain may be entirely one-sided to the extent that society obtains both the disclosure and limitations on the patent holder's rights via the pledge. And this all suggests that patent pledging scenarios hint at a different value proposition for patent rights than the disclosure and related accounts propose.

Prospect and commercialization accounts of the patent system also seem to flounder, at least in part, when taking into account patent pledges, and do so for similar reasons. If parties need rights of exclusion as incentives to post-invention development and commercialization, as these theories teach, why do parties choose, in some cases, to curtail the rights that they do have? Again, simply because these parties may have other economic motives for doing so does not directly support traditional prospect and commercialization accounts. Instead, it suggests different economic uses of patent rights.

Natural rights theories may initially seem the most consonant with patent pledging, simply because these theories do not focus on the instrumental nature of patents. Instead, as mentioned, they generally argue that the right to exclude arises based on the effort the inventor invested in the invention; what a party does with that right afterwards may be viewed as irrelevant to these theories.

But even natural rights theories view patents as instrumental in some sense. The Lockean "reward-for-labor" notion, for instance, posits limitations on the rewarded rights to the extent they unduly interfere with the ability of others to engage in similar activities.[9] Even "personhood" theories typically distinguish between fungible and non-fungible inventions and tailor the rights granted accordingly.[10]

In other words, while patent rights may not be primarily instrumental under this school of thought, the downstream effects that patents have are still accorded weight under these theories. As such, even under these non-majoritarian views, the values that patents serve are still important to assess. And the phenomenon of patent pledges suggests a different value for patents than simply the right to exclude, which ultimately is one of

---

9 *See generally* Wendy J. Gordon, *A Property Right in Self-Expression: Equality and Individualism in the Natural Law of Intellectual Property*, 102 YALE L.J. 1533, 1533 (1993).

10 *See generally* Margaret Jane Radin, *Property and Personhood*, 34 STAN. L. REV. 957, 957 (1982).

the more important values of patents in the natural rights camp to the extent that this right safeguards the efforts and personhood of inventors.

II. THE GROWTH OF PATENT PLEDGES

The growing phenomenon of patent pledges thus appears to defy the most typical justifications for patents. These theories focus on the patent holder's right to exclude others from practicing the patented invention and, typically, the direct economic benefits that flow from that right. But in the patent pledging scenario, the pledger purposefully volunteers some or all of that economic leverage in pursuit of some other aim. What are those aims, and what do they tell us about patents in general?

This section argues that patent pledgers often seem to use patents as informational tools. In other words, parties make patent pledges in order to efficiently and credibly convey information to the relevant public about themselves and their innovation preferences and activities. Patents are thus valuable to pledgers and recipients of the pledges in part because of the signaling effects that they enable. This particular value of patents, in turn, provides some justification of patents in spurring innovative activity, while also providing guidance on how the patent system might be reformed in order to better adapt to this reality.

A. Patents as Informational Tools

Though the most typical patent law theories view patents primarily as exclusionary tools, some scholars have argued that patents are valuable to inventors based on the information they convey about the patent holder. For instance, Clarisa Long argues that patents are valuable to parties in part because they help convey credible information to capital markets about the inventor.[11] In other words, firms obtain patents, inter alia, because doing so effectively signals to investors that the firm is engaging in innovative behavior. These signals may then translate into greater market support for the inventor and their goods and services. Hence, for many inventors the value of a patent goes beyond simply whether the inventor, through exercising a patent's right of exclusion, will obtain economic rents that exceed the cost of obtaining the patent. Instead, patents are also valuable because of the information that they convey.

This chapter builds on Long's work in arguing that, in patent pledging scenarios, a significant value of patents is as an informational tool.

[11] *See* Clarisa Long, *Patent Signals*, 69 U. CHI. L. REV. 625, 625–28 (2002).

Pledgers use patents in these scenarios to efficiently and credibly signal to the relevant public the pledger's innovation activities and preferences.

But not all informational purposes are the same. For instance, in Long's account, she argues that patents are used to convey information primarily to capital markets, while also noting that they may be used to communicate information to the labor market as well.[12] In the pledging scenario, however, patents are often useful in conveying information to product markets. That is, as Section II.B will discuss, pledges are often primarily directed at competitors or other parties developing technology related to the patents, not just at or primarily to capital or labor markets.

Furthermore, while patent pledges may be intended to convey information to capital and labor markets in addition to product markets, Long's account still falls short in providing a persuasive explanation as it relates to typical patent pledging scenarios. For instance, in Long's account, patent holders obtain patents in order to provide proof to investors that they are engaged in serious innovation. While this type of information may still be gleaned from patents that ultimately become part of a pledge, the pledge itself conveys additional informational signals that Long's account does not address.

Last, Long's account does not appear to view rights of exclusion as integrally related to the informational value that inventors may derive from patents, at least explicitly.[13] In other words, patents may entail value on the basis of the right to exclude, and patents may entail value on the basis of their informational purposes, and these values can exist simultaneously. But in Long's narrative, these respective values of patents do not appear to depend on one another in any significant way.

In contrast, this chapter argues that, in many patent pledging contexts, a patent's rights of exclusion are often an important component of successfully utilizing patents as informational tools, as will be discussed further in Section III *infra*. In sum, patents are often valuable to parties because of their informational utility. And in many cases, that informational utility is enhanced through the rights of exclusion that come with a patent.

12 Id. at 641.

13 Id. at 627 (arguing that the exclusionary value of patents—what she calls the "simple view"—fails to capture other purposes and values that patents may serve).

B. A Taxonomy of Patent Pledges

This section builds on Contreras's taxonomy of patent pledges presented in Chapter 1 in order to better illustrate this chapter's arguments regarding the informational effects of patent pledges. Contreras breaks pledges down based on the subject and scope of the pledges, the forms they take, as well as the commercial motivations of the pledgers in making them. He concludes that some pledges should be more readily legally enforceable than others because such pledges are more likely to induce reliance by other market participants. In other words, if specific types of pledges have the effect of prompting third parties to alter their commercial behavior, then courts should more readily enforce these types of pledges.

But despite the differences that Contreras notes in terms of form, substance, and motivation, a unifying theme emerges: in each case, the pledge conveys information about the pledger and its research and development activities. Patents can thus act as an efficient and credible means by which to signal information about the pledgers to different markets.

For instance, parties that join Standards Development Organizations ("SDOs") and thereby agree to license their relevant patents to other participants on fair, reasonable, and non-discriminatory ("FRAND") terms may communicate several things about their innovation activities and preferences. First, their commitment may suggest that ensuring interoperability of their commercial products with those of others, or that being in a position to help determine the standards, is more valuable to them than preserving all possible economic leverage that their patents may otherwise provide.

On the other hand, the confined nature of the FRAND commitment may communicate that the SDO pledger still intends to extract some direct economic benefit from its patent rights, or at least it reserves the right to do so. Otherwise, the party may simply pledge royalty-free licenses to others within the organization, as some parties in fact do. Hence, FRAND committers appear to use patents for a variety of informational purposes, even in cases where they still may ultimately utilize their rights of exclusion in a more traditional fashion (i.e., to collect rents).

Other types of pledges are similar in their informational purposes, even if different in their informational content. For instance, companies that have established their products as a de facto standard in a given industry may make patent pledges to the relevant public in order to bolster the standard by encouraging others to develop ancillary products and services that utilize it. Again, the patent pledge in such a scenario can signify a number of things, depending on the precise scope and form of it. But it at least communicates that collaborative development on the basis of the de facto standard is more economically beneficial to the patent holder than simply seeking to extract patent royalties from third parties that practice its patented inventions. In such a case, inclusion is more economically valuable than exclusion. But the pledge also simultaneously communicates that deviating from the company's standard may extinguish any such patent goodwill, since such a deviation does not align with the pledger's economic purposes in making the pledge.

Patent pledges aimed at encouraging adoption of a still-emerging technology are also largely valuable, to both pledgers and the relevant public alike, on the basis of their signaling effects. For instance, when Elon Musk posted Tesla's patent pledge on the company's blog, it triggered a number of responses from commentators, ranging from claims of a publicity stunt to praise for the company because of its forward thinking.[14] But what seems near certain is that no other third party will simply rely on the blog post in undertaking significant development activities in the same area. Instead, Tesla's patent pledge seems primarily intended to invite the relevant public to join it in promoting the adoption of an emerging electronic car standard, while preserving the right to sort out the details of how such collaborations will look going forward.[15] Patents and the associated pledges in these cases thus also largely function as an informational tool. Of course, using patents in this manner certainly has economic logic behind it. But utilizing patents as informational tools suggests a different type of economic logic than what traditional accounts of patents posit.

In other cases, pledgers may obfuscate or severely limit their patent pledges. But these more limited types of pledges also serve informational purposes. For instance, the intent behind a limited pledge may be to communicate to the relevant public that the patent holder is not fully decided about their innovation preferences, or is not generally committed to an open, collaborative model of innovation. At the same time, the pledger may hope with the pledge to signal to the relevant public some goodwill and thereby engender support within that sector of the public.

---

14 *See*, e.g., Jerry Hirsch & Tiffany Hsu, *Elon Musk Opens up Tesla Patents: It "Isn't Entirely Altruistic,"* L.A. TIMES (June 12, 2014); Alexander C. Kaufman, *Tesla's Clever Patent Move Is Already Paying Off*, HUFFINGTON POST (June 18, 2014, 12:59 PM).

15 Eric Blattberg, *Here's What Tesla's "Good Faith" Patent Stance Actually Means*, VENTURE BEAT (June 14, 2014, 9:57 AM).

For instance, when Microsoft made its patent pledge to non-commercial open source software developers, it may have done so largely in order to help improve its public image in developer communities. Microsoft might also claim that the pledge contributes generally to social welfare by facilitating the activities of such non-commercial developers. But even if both of these things are true, arguably the more important message to the public was implicit in the limited scope of the pledge: everyone else remains fair game.

And by many accounts, that is precisely how Microsoft has subsequently acted in leveraging its vast patent portfolio against commercial developers and users of Android and Linux, two of the most important open source software projects in the world.[16] Hence, in this type of scenario as well, patent pledgers utilize their patents to convey important information to the relevant public about their innovation preferences and themselves in general, even if the message differs from what many would prefer.

In sum, patent pledgers use patents as tools in conveying information to the relevant public regarding their innovation activities and preferences. With some pledges, the message may be primarily one of continuing exclusion, while in other cases it may be more focused on inclusion. But in either case, the pledger, as well as the pledged-to parties, derives value from the patents because of their informational potencies.

This is not to suggest that this informational value is the only value of a patent in a pledging context. As discussed in Chapter 1, pledgers entertain a variety of economic rationales in making pledges. And some of those economic rationales may center on a patent holder ultimately exercising their rights of exclusion, such as in the FRAND and Microsoft examples above. But the types of economic benefits that motivate the pledges appear to be more diverse than what traditional patent law theories suggest, particularly in scenarios where the pledge's signal is primarily one of inclusion. Indeed, in such contexts the informational value of a patent may be the primary economic benefit that a patent holder derives from a patent.

But even if patents are useful as informational tools, what makes them so? The next section turns to this question and discusses different aspects

[16] Mary Jo Foley, *Samsung Paid Microsoft $1 Billion in Android Patent-Licensing Royalties in 2013*, ZDNet (Oct. 4, 2014, 1:04 PM).

of the patent regime that make patents efficient and credible as informational tools. Section IV then analyses certain features of the patent system that may make patents less effective in these regards.

III. PATENT LAW'S INFORMATIONAL FEATURES

A. How Exclusion (Sometimes) Bolsters Patents as Informational Tools

United States patent law generally allows a patent holder to exclude others from making, using, offering to sell, selling, or importing into the U.S. the patented invention.[17] As discussed, this right of exclusion is often viewed as the predominant value of a patent because it allows the patent holder to obtain direct economic remuneration from others that make use of the patented technology.

But a patent's rights of exclusion prove important in using patents as informational tools as well. First, the right to exclude, coupled with a patent pledge limiting that right, is itself a powerful message. For instance, a party committing to allow others to use its technology may not convey much of a message if it does not have some legal entitlement to forbid others from doing so. Purporting to sacrifice a government-granted property right, on the other hand, helps underscore the seriousness and credibility of the message, as well as the future intentions of the pledger. As signaling theory in other disciplines teaches, this is so because the behavior is costly, which costliness aids third parties in inferring information about the signaler.[18] The core rights of exclusion that come with a patent thus facilitate using patents to convey information to the market, even—and perhaps, particularly—when that message is largely about inclusion and collaboration.

Second and related, this right of exclusion helps establish a key baseline against which the pledge can be assessed in terms of informational content. For instance, if a party possesses a trove of key patented inventions in a particular technological area and pledges that the public may use them, the surrendered right of exclusion in such a case more ably conveys the magnitude of the commitment, as well as the intentions of the pledging party. Tesla's commitment to license its patents relating to electric vehicle technology may be one such example. If, on the other

---

[17] 35 U.S.C. § 271(a) (2012).

[18] *See* Michael Spence, *Job Market Signaling*, 87 QUART. J. ECON. 355, 358 (1973).

hand, a party commits to license to the public a few, relatively insubstantial patents covering non-essential technologies, the implicit message might be of enduring exclusion rather than clear inclusion. But in either case, a patent's initial endowment of exclusion is essential to effectively conveying the patent holder's intentions.

In sum, the rights of exclusion that come with a patent are certainly valuable to some parties because they allow them to procure direct economic benefits through their exercise. But the same rights can also be valuable in the patent pledging scenario as a key means by which to signal a party's intentions of inclusion, exclusion, or a mix of both.

B. Patent Law's Disclosure Requirements

Patent law includes additional doctrines that help make patents useful as informational tools. For instance, patent law includes a number of information "disclosure" requirements. First, patent law's "enablement" requirement stipulates that a patent applicant must disclose enough technical details in the application to enable someone of ordinary skill in the particular "art" to practice the invention "without undue experimentation."[19] Though this enablement standard does not require that patentees disclose every relevant detail of their invention, it does require that patent applicants disclose sufficient information such that some skilled person would be able to replicate the invention without significant obstacles.

Second, patent law requires that an applicant disclose enough technical details such that a person of ordinary skill in the relevant art would recognize that the applicant actually invented what he or she claims to have invented.[20] While this "written description" requirement often overlaps with the enablement requirement discussed above, there are cases in which this latter requirement forces the applicant to disclose more technical details than the enablement standard, alone, would require.[21]

Third, patent law requires patent applicants to disclose their "best mode" of practicing the invention.[22] Though recent patent law reforms

---

[19] 35 U.S.C. § 112(a) (2012). *See also* Sean B. Seymore, *Heightened Enablement in the Unpredictable Arts*, 56 UCLA L. REV. 127, 127 (2008).

[20] Dennis Crouch, *An Empirical Study of the Role of the Written Description Requirement in Patent Examination*, 104 NW. U. L. REV. 1665, 1669 (2010).

[21] *See*, e.g., Gentry Gallery, Inc. v. Berkline Corp., 134 F.3d 1473 (Fed. Cir. 1998).

[22] Crouch, *supra* note 20.

have significantly weakened this requirement, it technically remains on the books.[23] It thus may continue to prove important in ensuring that patent applicants disclose technical details that they otherwise would withhold.

Fourth, patent law requires applicants to state their inventions in definite and clear terms in the form of "claims" towards the end of the patent document.[24] Patent claims are often analogized to the "metes and bounds" of a land deed, whereby the applicant charts out the periphery or boundaries of that to which they purport to have exclusive rights.[25] The frequently cited rationale for requiring patent claims is that they help provide the public with clearer notice of what the patent holder alleges to own, and what, therefore, remains unencumbered.[26]

Last, typically all of these disclosures eventually become publicly available once a patent application is published and indexed, typically 18 months from the time the patent application was filed, or once the patent actually issues.[27] Hence, the disclosures required as part of the application process in most cases become accessible to the public.

Collectively, these disclosure requirements are important in facilitating the role and value of patents as informational tools, particularly in the patent pledging context. First, they provide pledgers with a ready means by which to convey information. That is, because patent applicants are required to make these disclosures as part of the application process, and those disclosures become publicly available in most cases, the patent document itself becomes a standardized means by which to relay information to the public.

For instance, when Tesla made its patent pledge, the public could readily determine what patented inventions relating to electric vehicles were implicated by accessing the publicly available patent documents relating to Tesla's technology. Of course, the precise meaning and scope of the patent document remains unclear until a court of law actually rules on these issues (and perhaps remains somewhat unclear even thereafter).

---

[23] *See*, e.g., Brian J. Love & Christopher B. Seaman, *Best Mode Trade Secrets*, 15 YALE J. L. & TECH. 1, 1 (2012–2013).

[24] Jeanne C. Fromer, *Claiming Intellectual Property*, 76 U. CHI. L. REV. 719, 732 (2009).

[25] Richard L. Wynne, Jr., *Patent Law*: Warner-Jenkinson Co. v. Hilton Davis Chemical Co.: *How Can the Federal Circuit Control the Doctrine of Equivalents Following the Supreme Court's Refusal to Set the Standard?*, 50 OKLA. L. REV. 425, 436 (1997).

[26] Id. at 444–45.

[27] 35 U.S.C. § 122 (2012).

But the basic parameters and scope of the pledged technologies would nonetheless be available through the patent document.

Thinking of the alternative helps illustrate the importance of the patent document in this regard. For instance, imagine that Tesla did not obtain patents on many of its innovations and instead, to the extent possible, kept its innovations secret. If it later decided to pledge these secrets to the public based on changing preferences, the lack of patents in facilitating that pledge could prove to be a significant obstacle. For instance, the company would be forced to spend significant time and resources collecting and documenting the information that it wished to share with the public. And even if it did so, the form and substance of the information may be such that the relevant public would have trouble navigating it. While such a homegrown system may have some informational advantages if done well, the cumulative advantages of patents are nonetheless manifest in at least four ways.

First, as mentioned, the patent document is a formalized, well-understood means by which to disclose technical information. Hence, even though ambiguities will remain in the document, its standardized nature will mean that third parties should have some familiarity in navigating it.

Second and related, patented information allows pledgers to be more precise in their messaging. For instance, because the patent includes formal patent claims that identify the boundaries of what the patent covers, the patent provides pledgers with a means by which to identify specifically what the pledge covers and what remains outside of it.

Third, as discussed in the preceding section, a patent's exclusive rights also aid the patent pledger in using patents as informational tools. Hence, combining the informational potencies of such rights with the informational advantages of patent law's disclosure requirements makes the patent system difficult to match in terms of informational advantages.

Last, a homegrown solution would fail to provide Tesla and others with non-informational value that patents may otherwise confer. For instance, Tesla intimated in its pledge that it retained the ability to use its patents defensively as a "stick." Hence, patents provided Tesla not only with informational value, but with defensive value as well. This final point again underscores the argument made throughout this chapter that patents may confer on their owners a variety of different types of value simultaneously. While the informational value of a patent may be significant to a patent holder, that value need not be the only value they derive from their patent and, in fact, often is not.

In sum, patent law's disclosure requirements can be valuable because they help make the patent valuable to the patent holder and the public as an informational tool. Rather than being a necessary sacrifice in order to obtain the patent, per what many traditional patent law theories teach, patent law's disclosure requirements thus may often prove to be a boon to patent pledgers when using patents as informational instruments.

IV. PATENT LAW'S NON-INFORMATIONAL DIMENSIONS

The last section reviewed several doctrines under patent law that aid patent holders in using patents as informational tools in the patent pledging context. But in certain other respects, patents fall short as informational tools. This may be unsurprising since the traditional theoretical underpinnings of patent law view the right to exclude as the main value proposition of a patent, and any disclosures as a tradeoff for, rather than a benefit to, the patent applicant. The next section explores several aspects of patent law that reflect these preoccupations of traditional law theory, and which, in consequence, may hamper patents as informational tools. Perhaps unsurprisingly, they prove to be some of the same doctrines that facilitate using patents as informational tools.

A. The (Too) Absolute Right to Exclude

As discussed above, traditional patent law theories assign great importance to a patent's rights of exclusion. And for many patentees, these rights may be the primary reason that they pursue patents.

It is thus unsurprising that the right to exclude is fairly robust as implemented in patent law. For instance, patent law includes no independent invention defense to patent infringement.[28] In other words, if two parties independent of one another develop the same invention, and one of those parties obtains a patent on the invention, that party, armed with the patent, can exclude the other party from practicing the invention. It is true that recent patent law reforms have expanded "prior user rights," which allow a party that previously invented and practiced an invention a limited right to continue to do so, even if another party subsequently obtains a patent that covers that invention.[29] But as others have chronicled, there are a number of significant limitations to this exception that

---

[28] Samson Vermont, *Independent Invention as a Defense to Patent Infringement*, 105 MICH. L. REV. 475, 476–81 (2006).

[29] Jacob Neu, *Patent Prior User Rights: What's the Fuss?*, 66 VAND. L. REV. EN BANC 1, 1 (2013).

make it an extremely narrow one.[30] In sum, the right to exclude that comes with a patent remains rather absolute in most cases.

This robust right to exclude can disserve the informational purposes of patents. And this is so despite the ways that this right may facilitate such purposes, as discussed above. The most obvious reason is that, in spite of the presence of a pledge, rights of exclusion may remain intact because the legal enforceability of the pledge remains uncertain. In other words, the threat of a pledger reversing course and asserting its patent rights in an exclusionary manner may, in some cases, introduce sufficient uncertainty into the marketplace that the informational takeaway is simply one of avoidance. Hence, while the right of exclusion may in some cases facilitate informational purposes, its rather absolute nature can also make informational content difficult to decipher. For such reasons, an analysis of which pledges should be enforceable is considered, inter alia, by Contreras in Chapter 5.

The value of patents as informational tools could thus be enhanced with some alterations to a patent's rights of exclusion. First, a patent pledge should count for something legally, even if not a full-blown license. For instance, a pledge might be found to be a legally enforceable commitment to enter such a license. In some respects, as discussed in Chapter 5, this is what already exists in the FRAND context. Of course, plenty of disputes arise in the FRAND context in terms of what the FRAND commitment actually means. But even given this reality, the FRAND commitment means that the parties are at least one step closer to accessing each other's technology, even if the next step can be somewhat messy.

Similarly, in patent pledging contexts outside the FRAND scenario, the pledge might function as a legally enforceable commitment to enter a license agreement with the other party, and that license must conform with whatever parameters the pledge includes. Put differently, the pledge might function as a de facto compulsory licensing scheme, at least in the sense that, once the pledge is issued, third parties are entitled to obtain some license to the pledged technology, even if the exact details must still be worked out. Such legal enforceability may, of course, dissuade some parties from making patent pledges. But presumably many pledgers have already taken into account such possibilities in deciding to make the pledge in the first place. And for those parties that are dissuaded by such legal enforceability, it may be better for the marketplace as an informational matter if their pledges are never made.

30 Id.

Second, as I have argued elsewhere, patent law may be well served with a conditional independent invention defense to patent infringement.[31] In other words, if parties are willing in general to give up their right to assert patents against others except in defensive scenarios, these parties should not be liable for patent infringement if they independently invented technology that another party patents. This is thus one way that patent law could be reformed in a way that moderates rights of exclusion and thereby formally institutionalizes a form of patent pledging. Granted, such a system defines the specific pledge and thus may be viewed as accommodating only a narrow range of pledging. But it nonetheless represents one way by which patent law's rights of exclusion could be modified in order to better support parties wishing to use patents—and their rights of exclusion—primarily as an informational tool in pursuit of greater inclusion.

B. Improving Disclosure

A perhaps obvious way to make patent law better at serving informational purposes is to improve disclosure requirements under patent law. Section III.A above laid out patent law's basic disclosure requirements. Yet despite these doctrines, a number of scholars argue that patents perform suboptimally in disclosing to the public useful information regarding the scope of the patents and the technical achievements of the inventors.[32]

This may be so for a number of reasons. For instance, patent drafters may generally have incentives to craft patent claims broadly while disclosing as little technical information as possible. That patentees seek the broadest claims possible is intuitive: the broader the claims, the more technical territory the inventor can claim vis-à-vis others.

Limiting technical disclosures, while still technically satisfying patent law's disclosure requirements, makes sense for related reasons. For instance, if an inventor discloses too much technical detail in its patent application, a court may read limitations into the patent claims from these technical disclosures. As a result, the inventor will own less technical territory. While courts are not supposed to read limitations from the rest of the patent document into the patent claims as a general matter,

---

[31] Clark D. Asay, *Enabling Patentless Innovation*, 74 MD. L. REV. 431, 431 (2015).

[32] *See*, e.g., Lisa Larrimore Ouellette, *Do Patents Disclose Useful Information*? 25 HARV. J.L. & TECH. 531, 548 (2012) (reviewing this literature).

they sometimes do based on a variety of patent law doctrines.[33] Indeed, core patent law requires courts to read patent claims "in light of the specification."[34] So the fewer disclosures a patent drafter can make while still satisfying patent law's disclosure requirements, generally the better.

Inventors may have other reasons for disclosing as little technical information as possible. For instance, inventors may hope to retain certain technical information as trade secrets, even if such technical information relates to the invention for which a patent is sought. Trade secret status is advantageous because it can last perpetually, whereas patent rights expire generally after about 20 years.[35] Hence, to the extent that a patent applicant can withhold technical details while still satisfying patent law's disclosure requirements, that party may be able to retain such information as trade secrets for a much longer time period than a patent would allow.

In some contexts such as software, some scholars argue that these and related incentives have led inventors to claim basic functions beyond their particular means for accomplishing the function.[36] And inventors have done so in many cases without disclosing many technical details regarding the means by which to perform the claimed function.[37] From the perspective of the public good, the worst of both worlds results: patents issue with overly broad claims, while falling short in disclosing useful technical information that may otherwise justify the claims' broad scope.

The informational value of patents highlighted in this chapter helps guide proposals relating to addressing concerns about patent law's disclosure requirements. First, recognizing the informational value of patents bolsters the case for more disclosure generally. This is so because more disclosure may actually enhance the value of patents. As discussed above, traditional patent law theories typically identify the inventor's disclosures as a heavy sacrifice, and robust rights of exclusion as the inventor's key benefit necessary to secure that sacrifice. But appreciating a patent's informational value suggests that disclosures can be a key benefit, too.

---

33 Phillips v. AWH Corp., 415 F.3d 1303, 1312–23 (Fed. Cir. 2005) (en banc).

34 Id.

35 Andrew A. Schwartz, *The Corporate Preference for Trade Secret*, 74 OHIO ST. L.J. 623, 630–33 (2013).

36 Mark A. Lemley, *Software Patents and the Return of Functional Claiming*, 2013 WIS. L. REV. 905 (2013).

37 Id.

Relatedly, if these disclosures do make patents more valuable in some respects, that should also make us less wary of weakening robust rights of exclusion. This is particularly so since rights of exclusion, when too robust, can hinder rather than facilitate the informational purposes of patents, as discussed above.

Second, the informational value of patents may also guide specific proposals on how best to improve disclosure. For instance, a long-standing debate in patent law focuses on how best to construe the scope of patent claims.[38] Historically, courts focused primarily on the technical merit of the invention in deciding a patent's breadth. For instance, if the patented invention was groundbreaking at the time, then a court was more likely to give the patent a broader scope than otherwise. More recently, the emphasis has shifted to limiting a patent based on the extent to which the patent document puts the public on notice of its scope. In other words, a patent's scope should not exceed what the relevant public, after having read the patent, would understand the patent to cover.

But viewing patents as informational tools suggests this is a false choice. Preserving and bolstering a patent's informational value requires both improving the notice function of patents and a focus on the invention's technical merits. After all, improving notice would presumably enhance the quality and accuracy of the information that a patent pledger conveys through the pledge. And focusing on the technical merits of the invention would improve a patent's informational value by effectively communicating to the relevant public the actual significance of the patent and any associated pledge.

This all suggests an alternative narrative of the patent application process. Indeed, rather than viewing this process as a tug-of-war between a grudging inventor and a demanding patent examiner, the informational value of patents suggests that the patent application process might be better viewed as an author-editor relationship in which the parties work together to produce a document that clearly reflects the inventor's technical contributions as well as giving as clear notice as possible of the patent's scope. The patent can then be used for both traditional, exclusionary purposes as well as informational ones. Of course, traditional approaches to patent drafting may continue to favor claiming broadly

---

[38] Dan L. Burk & Mark A. Lemley, *Fence Posts or Sign Posts? Rethinking Patent Claim Construction*, 157 U. PA. L. REV. 1743, 1744–47 (2009). *See also* J. Jonas Anderson & Peter S. Menell, *Informal Deference: A Historical, Empirical, and Normative Analysis of Patent Claim Construction*, 108 NW. U. L. REV. 1, 1 (2013) (presenting the results of a comprehensive empirical analysis of the Federal Circuit's claim construction jurisprudence from 2000 through 2011).

while disclosing minimally. But better recognizing the informational value of patents provides reasons to push back against the necessity of this approach.

V. IMPLICATIONS

The informational value of patents and patent pledges described herein has several other implications for patent law and policy generally. First, the informational value of patents in the patent pledging context suggests that parties are increasingly using patents as a means of inclusion rather than one of exclusion. Of course, patents have always been used as a means of inclusion in some sense; robust patent licensing has existed since patents have. But the type of inclusion that many patent pledgers are fostering has more to do with the informational value of patents than their legal enforceability and the direct economic benefits that may flow from that legal entitlement (as in the licensing context). In other words, while patent holders have long accepted economic remuneration in exchange for a patent license, in many patent pledging contexts patent holders utilize their patents as an informational tool aimed at including third parties within their research and development activities. And unlike the typical licensing scenario, the pledgers do so without exchanging their rights of exclusion for the amount of economic remuneration that the patent may otherwise demand.

Second and related, this inclusionary value of patents may suggest that patents are not as at odds with "open innovation" as is often believed. I have argued elsewhere that patents are inherently problematic for those that prefer open innovation.[39] And I have suggested reforms to patent law that would better accommodate such parties.[40] But in reality, very few innovators make an either/or choice. In other words, most innovators probably prefer open innovation in some cases, and closed innovation in others. Patents may thus be one of the more effective means for enabling parties to pursue both traditional closed models of innovation as well as more inclusionary ones.

This all suggests that patents are more multi-dimensional than traditional patent law theories teach. Rights of exclusion need not be exercised merely in order to exclude. Instead, parties can and do use patent rights in effectively and credibly conveying information about

39 Asay, *supra* note 31.
40 Id.

their development activities. And improving a patent's informational proclivities as discussed above would enhance this particular value of a patent.

Last, even in cases where a party uses a patent pledge primarily to signal to the market enduring exclusion, the informational value of the patent is still manifest in such a case. Third parties can then internalize that signal and plan their development activities accordingly. In such cases, the exclusionary and informational values of patents combine in fostering the patent holder's objectives. And while those objectives may not be in accordance with the preferences of outside observers, they nonetheless instill in the marketplace greater certainty that, in the end, may foster increased levels of innovation.

CONCLUSION

Patents have informational values that have previously received less attention than they deserve. Indeed, the growing phenomenon of patent pledges suggests that patent holders are utilizing patents for informational purposes in ways that defy traditional accounts of the patent system.

This phenomenon is an opportunity for, rather than a threat to, the patent system. Indeed, better appreciating the informational values of patents, and updating patent law to enhance these values, would serve both patent holders and the public. It would serve patent holders by making patents even more multi-dimensional than they already are, thereby enhancing their value. It would serve the public because the public would receive such multiple (and enhanced) benefits of patents.

Some will certainly worry that focusing less on the exclusionary value of patents in favor of these informational features will hamper the patent system. But the patent pledging phenomenon suggests that many parties have already made this choice. Better accommodating such parties by enhancing the informational value of patents is not, therefore, simply a good idea in theory. It is, instead, one that adapts patent law to the practices of many current patent holders.

14. Open innovation and patent pledges

Mariateresa Maggiolino and Maria Lillà Montagnani

I. INTRODUCTION

As noted in Chapter 1, over the years an increasing number of patent holders have been relaxing the grip on their own patents by making self-limiting commitments, even outside the framework of Standard Setting Organizations (SSOs). Restraining their traditional prerogatives via one or more covenants, among which non-assertion pledges are the most common, these patent holders have freely chosen to make the access, transfer, and use of their inventions easy, cheap, and safe for both research and commercial purposes. While adopting these many self-limiting commitments, some patent holders have also been experiencing diverse ways to uniformize these commitments by defining a new private order, made of standardized licensing terms and conditions – so called Open Patent (OP) licenses.

The patent pledges and covenants that have been used in the OP experience generate the same level of "openness". While certain patent pledges and covenants fit within the broader open innovation (OI) movement, others solely commit patentees to share their patents reciprocally and to prevent their patents from falling prey to patent trolls. While some pledges and covenants have set the grounds to make patents open toward whoever is interested in them, on the main condition that this unknown re-user will make her own follow-on innovation equally open, others have contributed to create large "clubs of patentees" that are inwardly open but are closed to non-members.

This chapter analyses how and when patent pledges and covenants, opening patented knowledge via standardized licenses, fit within the broader Open Innovation (OI) movement. To do this it traces the development of OI as a need for alternative models to manage innovation (Section II) from its first and most successful experience, that is, Open Source Software (OSS) (Section III), to the diverse experiences that nowadays fall within this label (Sections IV and V), showing that each case aims at opening "something" different. Then, it analyses a specific case of opening, that is, the opening of patented knowledge through standardized pledges and covenants – a case that falls within the OP phenomenon – to illustrate the diverse degrees of openness that these standardized pledges and covenants can achieve. It concludes by revealing that, because of the above diverse grades of openness, not all patent pledges and covenants fit the open innovation movement.

II. THE EMERGENCE OF ALTERNATIVE MODELS OF MANAGING INNOVATION

From a market-oriented point of view, strong and broad IPRs may jeopardize the pace and transfer of innovation. The ecosystem has responded to a scenario in which IPRs are ubiquitous, overlapping, and fragmented, by developing different off-line tools, such as Defensive Publishing,[1] Patent Portfolios,[2] and Patent Pools.[3] The advent of the Internet has been offering new opportunities to solve issues regarding both the theoretical model for explaining innovation and the problems related to its ownership and management. This is the case of the Open Source movement, as well as the other cases that can be grouped under the label of open science, not to mention the impact that Creative Commons licenses have generated on the circulation of copyrighted content online.[4] Open source software is the first and most successful example of an alternative licensing regime that fits a different model of innovation. This chapter examines the successful features of the OSS

---

[1] *See*, e.g., Ed Levy, Emily Marden, Ben Warren, David Hartell & Isaac Filate, *Patent Pools and Genomics: Navigating a Course to Open Science?*, 16 B.U. J. SCI. & TECH. L. 75, 98 (2010).

[2] As an example of patent portfolios in specific fields *see* Thomas M. Mackey, *Nanobiotechnology, Synthetic Biology, and RNAI: Patent Portfolios for Maximal Near-Term Commercialization and Commons for Maximal Long-Term Medical Gain*, 13 MARQ. INTELL. PROP. L. REV. 123 (2009).

[3] *See also* Robin C. Feldman, *The Open Source Biotechnology Movement: Is It Patent Misuse?*, 6 MINN. J. L. SCI. & TECH. 117, 124 (2004).

[4] *See* Creative Commons, *When We Share, Everyone Wins*, http:// creativecommons.org. *See*, e.g., Niva Elkin-Koren, *What Contracts Can't Do: The Limits of Private Ordering in Facilitating a Creative Commons*, 74 FORDHAM L. REV. 101 (2005); Michael W. Carroll, *Creative Commons and the New Intermediaries*, 45 MICH. ST. L. REV. 45 (2006).

model and then examines how and if open patent licenses can build on that success.

III. OPEN SOURCE SOFTWARE

The open source software (OSS) phenomenon emerged as an alternative to the traditional "all rights reserved" licensing models for computer programs. Instead, the originator discloses computer program source code and allows third parties to have access, use, and modify it, often for free. OSS implements a new model of innovation that blurs together the "collective action model" – which consists in not establishing a property right upon inventions and works of art, and unconditionally supplying them to a common pool – and the "private investment model" – where innovation follows from a plan of balanced incentives that flow from private parties' property rights.[5]

All the above is possible because of the way in which copyright is licensed in OSS projects. Computer programs produced and distributed with OSS do not belong to the public domain, instead they are copyright protected software. But OSS licenses enable any third party that complies with the open license to use, modify, and distribute the source code that is disclosed. This is necessary for two reasons: first, the need to prevent third parties from copyrighting OSS products in place of their first developers;[6] second, the need for a tool, such as copyright licensing agreements, whereby those who enjoy and modify OSS source code and computer programs are required to comply with rules that guarantee the survival and proliferation of the OSS phenomenon. For instance, pioneer OSS developers could impose a "no-challenge clause", which obliges later OSS developers not to question the validity of the original copyright on the OSS products,[7] or a "viral clause",[8] which requires later OSS

---

5 *See* Eric von Hippel & Georg von Krogh, *Open Source Software and the "Private-Collective" Innovation Model: Issues for Organization Science*, 14 ORG. SCI. 209 (2003).

6 *See* Sara Boettinger & Dan L. Burk, *Open Source Patenting*, 1 JIBL 221, 224 (2004).

7 This type of clause is also named "patent peace" or "retaliation" clause. It provides that the license will terminate if the licensee initiates litigation (including a cross-claim or counterclaim in a lawsuit) alleging that any patent claim is infringed by making, using, selling, offering for sale, or importing the programme or a part of it.

8 Boettinger & Burk, *supra* note 6, at 224; Donna M. Gitter, *Resolving the Open Source Paradox in Biotechnology: A Proposal for a Revised Open Source*

developers to make their improved source code and software available under the same contractual terms the original developers set. When a Berkeley Software Distribution (BSD) license was released without this viral clause, Microsoft used code distributed under the BSD license in Windows XP and other products that it then distributed through the traditional "all rights reserved" licensing model, the only condition being that it acknowledged that it had used software licensed under the BSD license.

Since OSS can be freely used by anyone, anywhere, for any purpose, some have questioned whether it is possible to profit from OSS and whether it is an economically sustainable model.[9] There are companies that make relevant profits, such as Red Hat, Caldera, and SUSE (Novel), through the "distribution" of the Linux operating system.[10] With OSS products, companies can provide services like installing; support and training; upgrading and customizing; and commit to shield the product against IP-related liability.[11] Using OSS, these companies have developed new business models whose added-value rests on the choice of selecting a specific version of the OSS product – since open source products compete on the technical merits, and on the provision of services, from maintenance, to customization, support, and training – that they can offer together with the OSS products.[12]

In this way, OSS uses private ordering, based upon contracts, in order to manage open innovation. After all, since IPR is intended to foster

---

Policy for Publicly Funded Genomic Databases, 43 HOUS. L. REV. 1475 (2007). *See also* Greg R. Vetter, *Commercial Free and Open Source Software: Knowledge Production, Hybrid Appropriability, and Patents*, 77 FORDHAM L. REV. 2087 (2009).

[9] *See*, e.g., François Lévêque & Yann Ménière, *Copyright versus Patents: The Open Source Software Legal Battle*, 4 REV. OF ECON. RES. ON COPYRIGHT ISSUES 27, 28 (2007).

[10] *See*, e.g., Ronald J. Mann, *The Commercialization of Open Source Software: Do Property Rights Still Matter?*, 20 HARVARD J. L. & TECH. 1 (2006); Sandeep Krishnamurthy, *An Analysis of Open Source Business Models*, in MAKING SENSE OF THE BAZAAR: PERSPECTIVES ON OPEN SOURCE AND FREE SOFTWARE (Joseph Feller, Brian Fitzgerald, Scott Hissam & Karim Lakhani eds., 2004); Vetter, *supra* note 8.

[11] This is, for example, the case of the Novell-Microsoft agreement that offers a shield to Novell's customers against the risk of violating Microsoft's IPRs.

[12] Sandeep Krishnamurthy, *An Analysis of Open Source Business Models*, in PERSPECTIVES ON FREE AND OPEN SOURCE SOFTWARE 279 (J. Feller ed., 2005); RON GOLDMAN & RICHARD P. GABRIEL, INNOVATION HAPPENS ELSEWHERE: OPEN SOURCE AS BUSINESS STRATEGY (2005).

innovation, OSS provides an alternative, flexible, and voluntary legal tool that can be used to overcome the difficulties inherent in current IP regimes,[13] without requiring universal reform of them.[14]

IV. THE OPEN INNOVATION MOVEMENT

Outside of the open source software movement, many open innovation enterprises significantly diverge in relation to what they aim to "open". Some projects – such as PLoS, ArXiv, SourgeForge, HapMap, and BLAST – "open" scientific journals, repositories, and databases storing and pulling together tools and data to guarantee free and easy access to basic knowledge.[15] In the domain of bioinformatics, genomics, and synthetic biology several projects open the source code of proprietary software developed to standardize and manage bio-data, whether protected by copyright or patent.[16] They also make it possible to access basic, upstream knowledge by "opening" databases that pull together software tools with genetic materials.[17]

Other OI initiatives deal with patentable innovation in different ways. For example, TDi, and DNDi are web-based, non-profit collaborative communities of scientists that host inventions, which are not patented and/or have fallen into the public domain, to foster drug research for

---

[13] *See* Katherine J. Strandburg, *Evolving Innovation Paradigms and the Global Intellectual Property Regime*, 41 CONN. L. REV. 861, 880–81 (2009).

[14] Estelle Derclaye, *Not only Innovation but also Collaboration, Funding, Goodwill and Commitment: Which Role for Patent Laws in Postcopenhagen Climate Change Action*, 9 THE JOHN MARSHALL REV. OF INTELL. PROP. L. 161, 167 (2010); Yann Joly, *Open Source Approaches in Biotechnology: Utopia Revised*, 59 MAINE LAW REVIEW, 386 (2007).

[15] *See* Stephen M. Maurer, *New Institutions for Doing Science: From Databases to Open Source Biology*, paper presented to the European Policy for Intellectual Property Conference on Copyright and database protection, patents and research tools, and other challenges to the intellectual property system (Maastricht, Nov. 24–25, 2003), http://www.merit.unimaas.nl/epip/papers/maurer_paper.pdf.

[16] *See* Robin Feldman & Kris Nelson, *Open Source, Open Access, and Open Transfer: Market Approaches to Research Bottlenecks*, 7 NORTHWESTERN JOURNAL OF TECHNOLOGY AND INTELLECTUAL PROPERTY 24 (2008); Stephen M. Maurer, *Open Source Drug Discovery: Finding a Niche (or Maybe Several)*, 75 UMKV L. REV. 1, 6 (2007).

[17] Consider, for instance, the NCBI Toolkit, which collects some utilities, like formatdb and blastall, developed for the production, use, and distribution of some gene-databases, such as GenBank, Entrez, and BLAST.

neglected diseases. On the other hand, there are initiatives that regard patented innovations such as PatentCommons[18] which, born with the intent of answering the software patent threat and supported by the Linux foundation,[19] now works as a "facilitator" of patent trades by offering an online library of 500 software patents that their 16 owners make available to third parties on individualized terms and conditions that are publicly available online.[20] But because each of the collected patents has different licensing terms and conditions, PatentCommons does not offer a comprehensive and easy-to-manage uniform contractual scheme pivoting around specific patent pledges that apply to all the patents belonging to the repository.

Within OI we can also encompass those patent pledges under which corporations publicly announce their intention of not asserting their patents against others acting in good faith or within a business characterized by some given features.[21] This opening does not take place via a license authorizing the use of the patent, but via pledges of questionable enforceability.[22] In addition, these examples of patents opened via pledges often do not tend to occur within structured systems that spell out the steps according to which someone becomes a user of those patents, thus revealing a lower degree of organization and awareness. For patent pledges to have the same industry-wide impact that OSS has achieved, patent pledges need to be made in a more coordinated and structured manner.[23] It is against this backdrop that the diverse phenomena that we identify as open patent licenses, that is, standardized pledges and covenants aimed at opening patented inventions – should be assessed so to verify whether they really fit the open innovation concept.

---

[18] *See The Commons*, THE PATENT COMMONS PROJECT, http://www.patentcommons.org/.

[19] *See* Oliver Alexy & Markus G. Reitzig, *Private-Collective Innovation, Competition, and Firms' Counterintuitive Appropriation Strategies* (Aug. 20, 2011), https://ssrn.com/abstract=1430328 or http://dx.doi.org/10.2139/ssrn.1430328.

[20] In practice, via the repository set up by PatentCommons, possible licensees may get to know what patents and what conditions are available, without incurring cumbersome one-to-one negotiations.

[21] *See* Contreras, Chapter 1 (categorizing such patent pledges).

[22] *See* Contreras, Chapter 5 (discussing enforceability of patent pledges).

[23] *See* Contreras, Chapter 1 (describing distinction between coordinated and uncoordinated pledges).

V. OPEN PATENT LICENSES THROUGH STANDARDIZED PATENT PLEDGES

Patent holders have become increasingly interested in private ordering structures whereby, through specific and standardized patent pledges and covenants, they seek to reduce the concerns and costs connected with the trading and use of patents and to the development of follow-on inventions.[24]

An initial example is provided by those patent repositories that, unlike PatentCommons, are equipped with standardized open patent licenses. To make it easier and faster to innovate and implement industrial processes that improve and protect the global environment, the Eco-Patent Commons (EPC) (see Chapter 4), launched in 2008 by IBM, Nokia, Sony, and Pitney Bowes, created a set of default rules that apply to all patents included in the repository.[25] These rules are available online[26] and establish the conditions under which patents can enter the "commons", and users (other patentees or final users) can employ them. In particular, EPC includes patents capable of achieving environmentally beneficial results. These patents come with a non-assertion pledge that, subject to a defensive termination provision, remains in force irrespective of the patentee's withdrawal.[27] Then, all those who are interested in using those patents will be capable of doing so free of charge. To be sure, Eco-Patent Commons ceased its operational activities on May 18, 2016.

A similar license, developed within the field of biology though, is the "BioBrick™ Public Agreement",[28] a free-to-use legal tool allowing individuals, companies, and institutions to make their standardized biological parts be free for third parties to use. In this case, however, the license – which is publicly available on a centralized website – is to be

---

[24] *See* Mariateresa Maggiolino, Intellectual Property and Antitrust: A Comparative Economic Analysis of US and EU Law 37 (2011).

[25] *See* discussion of EPC in Chapters 1 and 4.

[26] *Eco-Patent Commons: Joining or Submitting Additional Patents to the Commons*, Eco-Patent Commons, http://ecopatentcommons.org/sites/default/files/docs/ecopatentgroundrules.pdf.

[27] Indeed, EPC establishes that, though members are free to withdraw their patents from the "commons" at any time, the non-assertion pledge covering the withdrawn patents survives and remains in force for all patents granted to the commons.

[28] *See The BioBrick Public Agreement (BPA)*, BioBrick Found., https://biobricks.org/bpa/.

used together with a repository of the licensable materials (whether patented or not) which is equally publicly accessible.

Since 2005 another set of uniform pledges has been employed within the BiOS initiative,[29] launched by CAMBIA,[30] an Australian independent, non-profit research institute, with the intent of establishing a legal framework enabling common access to some biotechnological technologies and facilitating their development. BiOS makes available a worldwide, non-exclusive, royalty-free, non-assertion license both to make and use the granted technology and to license back improvements either for commercial or noncommercial uses. For instance, by subscribing the two BiOS-compatible agreements regarding "health technologies" and "plant molecular enabling technologies", patentees allow the use of their technology without requiring royalties or other conditions. Users agree to not appropriate the fundamental core of the technology and to license back their improvements to whomever contributed to their development. In other words, BiOS-compatible contracts establish a system of cross-licensing under which what is licensed is not only the base technology, but also its improvements which must be shared with whoever supports their development.

A similar, if not stronger, combination of patent sharing and pooling is seen in the Open Invention Network (OIN),[31] a defensive patent pool with the mission to protect Linux. Since its launch in 2005, OIN has gained strong industry support with backing from Google, IBM, NEC, Philips, Red Hat, Sony, and SUSE.[32] OIN invites any company, project, or developer that is working on Linux, GNU, Android, or any other Linux-related software to join and use, free of charge, the software patents licensed under its uniform terms and conditions. As a whole, OIN works as a central administrator by creating a patent pool where patents, gathered in a repository, are both less expensive and easier to manage than proprietary ones. In addition, by requiring licensees to license their patented technology under the same conditions they have received, OIN creates another mechanism capable of adding to the traditional defensive function that pools already have: that of spreading patented knowledge.

Recently two other standardized licenses have also appeared online: the Defensive Patent License (DPL) and the License on Transfer (LOT)

---

29 *See BiOS Initiative*, BIOS, http://www.bios.net/daisy/bios/home.html.

30 For the story of CAMBIA *see* Andrés Guadamuz-Gonzáles, *Open Science: Open Source Licences in Scientific Research*, 7 N.C. J.L. & TECH. 321 (2005–2006).

31 *See* OPEN INVENTION NETWORK, http://www.openinventionnetwork.com/.

32 *See* discussion at Chapter 8.

Network. Interestingly, they derive from the two theoretical models envisaged respectively by professors Schultz and Urban in 2012,[33] and by Hayes and Schulman in 2013.[34] Both theoretical models are online pools among all patentees who agree to cross-license their patents on the same terms and conditions, as long as these terms and conditions are mutually respected.[35] However, in the Hayes and Schulman version, originally named the Modified Defensive Patent License (MDPL), there is a substantial difference as to the revocation clause.[36] Unlike the DPL, which only concerns future patents (i.e., those patents filed or acquired after the "discontinuation date"), the MDPL is effective for all patents. Under the MDPL the patent holder releases the whole portfolio previously licensed, while under the DPL the irrevocable and perpetual license only affects the patent portfolio existing at the moment of entry and during the participation period. According to the scholars that conceived the schemes, the above differences find a justification in the types of entities that they want to involve in such "fenced environments." Whereas the DPL runs the risk of only appealing to small and medium companies with the promise of being part of a decentralized, large proprietary defensive portfolio whose costs and benefits are distributed across its users, the MDPL seeks to engage big stakeholders by modifying some of the DPL's clauses that would be too risky for them (such as the irrevocable and perpetual nature of the DPL grant). In particular, given the network effects that such environments are likely to generate, the MDPL aims at having large and established companies involved to achieve enough scale to "cover" the whole industry or economic sector.

---

33 Jason Schultz & Jennifer M. Urban, *Protecting Open Innovation: The Defensive Patent License as a New Approach to Patent Threats, Transaction Costs, and Tactical Disarmament*, 26 HARVARD J. L. & TECH. (2012).

34 David L. Hayes & C. Eric Schulman, *A Response to a Proposal for a Defensive Patent License (DPL)* (July 27, 2013), https://ssrn.com/abstract=2054314 or http://dx.doi.org/10.2139/ssrn.2054314.

35 Both licenses contain a non-assertion pledge, whereby a licensee must forgo any offensive patent claims against other license users or risk revocation of that license by the licensor, subject to a defensive termination provision, a free of charge pledge, and a discontinuation clause, which is where they differ mostly.

36 Revocation or discontinuation clauses govern the cases where patentees take a step back and set themselves free from their previous commitments. The main goal of these clauses is to guarantee that the "opened" patents remain available to those who were licensees at the time of the withdrawal. In other words, in the great majority of OP experiences the OP licenses will remain in force, but the withdrawn patentees will regain the power to exercise their traditional prerogatives concerning their own inventions.

The two schemes do not aim at fostering open innovation via the spreading of patented knowledge; rather, they support open innovation by assuming that the innovation-friendly environments that they create will grow thanks to their own economic profitability and the network effects that they will trigger.

The first model to be implemented has been the MDPL through the License on Transfer (LOT) Network, launched in July 2013. The platform already contains nearly 300,000 patent assets, including over 50,000 US issued patents.[37] Differently from other structures, the LOT agreement provides that the each of the licenses concluded within the Network becomes effective only when the related patents are transferred to third parties. The main reason for this mechanism is avoiding patent litigation that occurs after patent assertion entities acquire patents to seek financial gain by enforcing them against others.

In 2014, the DPL moved from the theoretical to the practical and became available for patentees with the launch of the DPL website.[38] The aim of the initiative is encouraging innovation by providing a legal tool that will guarantee freedom to operate, will limit the risk of third party patent assertions, will encourage participation in the patent process, and will reduce litigation costs. DPL 1.1 is already available for use and can be freely adopted by any patentee that joins the DPL community by declaring, on any publicly available website, her commitment to offer any patent she holds or obtains under the DPL to anyone who makes a similar commitment.[39] By opting into the DPL network and adopting the pledges and covenants included in the DPL 1.1, patentees are eligible to receive royalty-free licenses under the patent portfolios of every other DPL user. Anyone taking a license promises to put all of her patents under the DPL, and, in the event that the patents are sold, DPL users must legally obligate the new owner to abide by prior DPLs. If one ceases offering

---

[37] *LOT Overview Presentation*, LOT NET, http://www.lotnet.com/userfiles/files/LOT%20Overview%20Presentation%20(Specialists)%20-%20Mar%2020%202015.pdf.

[38] *Troll Proofed. Innovation Protected*, DEFENSIVE PATENT LICENSE, http://www.defensivepatentlicense.org/.

[39] In even more practical terms, the patentee is encouraged to email the "Offering Announcement URL" to the DPL Foundation at defensivepatent@gmail.com so that others can learn about it and contact her to accept her licenses. In addition to sending the link to her Offering Announcement, the patentee should also include her current contact information for licensing purposes and a list of her patents (including country of issue, patent no., and title). *See Frequently Asked Questions*, DEFENSIVE PATENT LICENSE, http://www.defensivepatentlicense.org/content/frequently-asked-questions#how-does-the-dpl-work.

one's patents under the DPL, previous licensees will keep their DPLs royalty-free, but the "leaving user" may have her licenses converted from royalty-free to FRAND at the discretion of the remaining licensors.[40]

CONCLUSIONS: OPEN PATENT PLEDGES ACCOMMODATING OPEN INNOVATION

Within a more general trend aiming at finding alternative ways of fostering and managing innovation that goes under the name of open innovation, patent holders have begun to open patents through pledges and open licenses. In this context, open patent licenses have flourished as a tool by ensuring sets of uniform terms and conditions for some classes of interests and needs that pivot around open patents. In this way, they function similarly to successful open source software projects.

However, if we compare the purpose of OI with the achievements of OP licenses we realize that they are not always aligned. Although all OP licenses rely on a non-assertion pledge coupled with a defensive termination clause, creating a reciprocity mechanism between the parties, these conditions may enable sharing the results of patented inventions but not opening the inventive process itself. Consider, for example, the case of DPL and LOT, which create organized structures that make it possible for patentees to open their patents within "safe environments" that can coexist with the outside world where patents are traditionally traded and licensed for fees. These OP licenses create online pools among patentees who agree to cross-license their patents on the same terms and conditions. Therefore, these licenses arguably raise a "fence" around the safe environments that they define. Within this fenced environment, different rules not only govern the parties' exploitation of patents, they also affect the process of innovation. In fact, these fenced environments are open only to patentees: they give rise to clubs of patentees that are open inward but still closed to the rest of the world.[41] After all, in the case of DPL and LOT, patentees – and, in particular, big firms holding valuable

---

[40] See *Defensive Patent License V1.1, Article 2(e)*, DEFENSIVE PATENT LICENSE, http://www.defensivepatentlicense.org/sites/g/files/g1216936/f/201412/DPL%201.1.pdf.

[41] *See also*, Contreras, Chapter 1 (distinguishing between unilateral and community patent pledges).

portfolios – as the ones primarily worried about patent trolls, are naturally interested in these defensive tools.[42]

In order to open up the *process of innovation* and create "safe environments" that work as springboards for future innovation, it is necessary to provide covenants that, like grant-back or viral clauses, cover technological improvements and follow-on innovation. Patent pledges and covenants fit within OI movement when, instead of being conceptualized primarily to deal with patentees' needs and wants, are meant to create "unfenced environments" accommodating first and foremost the interests of the users of the opened patents. These solutions will enable patent users to become part of the innovative processes and inventors on their own. By allowing users to enjoy open patents on uniform terms and conditions, these patent pledges create the conditions for the innovative process itself to become a real collective experience as advocated by the OI philosophy.

---

42 *See* Clark D. Asay, *Enabling Patentless Innovation*, 74 MD. L. REV. 431 (2015) (explaining that patent trolls can act against individuals patentees, foundations, and big corporations. Yet, the last are their only and actual target because they are the ones who hold the big money).

15. The role of patent pledges in the cloud

Liza Vertinsky

I. A BRIEF OVERVIEW OF THE CLOUD COMPUTING INDUSTRY

The U.S. National Institute of Standards and Technology (NIST) defines cloud computing as "a model for enabling convenient, on-demand network access to a shared pool of configurable computing resources (e.g., networks, servers, storage, applications, and services) that can be rapidly provisioned and released with minimal management effort or service provider interaction."[1] Put more simply, cloud computing is a form of computing that utilizes shared computer resources accessed over the internet or through mobile devices to deliver on-demand computing services. The cloud is a metaphor for the large data centers that perform the computing tasks desired by the end users.

This idea of concentrating computing resources at the center of a network rather than in user terminals is not new, but rather marks a return to the mainframe models of the 1950s, 1960s and 1970s. The use of the term "cloud computing" to refer to a distinct model of computing is new, however, and the rapid growth in cloud computing applications and services has produced what is now considered to be a distinct cloud computing industry.

While there are many firms offering different kinds of cloud computing applications and services, the industry is dominated by a small number of large firms. Amazon, Google, Microsoft and IBM are among the leaders in terms of market share and market influence, with Amazon by far in the lead in market share.[2] Other companies important in the

---

[1] *See* e.g., Peter Mell & Tim Grance, *NIST Definition of Cloud Computing*, Version 15, NAT'L INST. OF STANDARDS AND TECH. (Oct. 7, 2009).

[2] *See* e.g., Lydia Leong, Douglas Toombs & Bob Gill, *Magic Quadrant for Cloud Infrastructure as a Service Worldwide*, GARTNER (May 18, 2015); Charles

cloud computing space include Salesforce.com, which pioneered software as a service, VMware and its competitor Citrix, which offer software for clouds, and Rackspace, which is leading a large coalition for free cloud software and provides its own public cloud and related services.[3] On top of cloud computing platforms sit an increasing number of successful cloud computing companies such as LinkedIn (offers cloud based recruiting software), NetSuite (offers cloud based business software), WorkDay (offers cloud based HR and finance software) and AthenaHealth (offers cloud based services for electronic health records), to name a few, all of which offer software as a service in targeted areas.

While the market leaders operate in all major segments of cloud computing and provide platforms for both developers and consumers, their business models and the ways in which these companies compete and expect to make money vary. In its current form the cloud computing market has been roughly stratified into three different segments: infrastructure as a service (IaaS), platform as a service (PaaS), and software as a service (SaaS).[4] IaaS involves raw computing resources, analogous to virtualized hardware, providing customers with computing infrastructure for data storage, management and manipulation. It allows companies to outsource computing equipment and resources while giving them flexibility in how to deploy the infrastructure for their own purposes. Amazon has by far the lion's share of this market with its Amazon Web Services (AWS) platform. PaaS provides a platform and environment for building applications and services over the internet, operating essentially as a cloud based operating system. Microsoft and Google are among the market leaders in this segment, although Amazon's AWS is increasingly encompassing services that resemble those offered by a PaaS platform. PaaS examples include Google AppEngine, Microsoft Azure, and AWS Elastic Beanstalk. SaaS involves preconfigured software applications offered as a web based service to end users, like Google Docs and Gmail. These market categories increasingly overlap, however, as firms compete with alternative cloud platforms and accommodate new and disruptive technologies.

The cloud computing market is also differentiated into private, public and hybrid clouds. Private clouds are computing platforms that are under

---

Babcock, *Amazon, Microsoft, IBM, Google Capture Cloud Market*, INFO. WKLY. (July 28, 2015).

[3] *See* e.g., Julie Bort, *The 10 Most Important Companies in Cloud Computing*, BUS. INSIDER (Apr. 20, 2013).

[4] *See* e.g., *Demysitfying SaaS, PaaS and IaaS*, SKYTAP (Mar. 22, 2011) (discussing the different categories).

the control of a single customer, operated within the customer's firewall and under its own control. Public clouds can be used by anyone anywhere, based on a model of pooled, shared computing resources accessed over the internet. Hybrid clouds involve a combination of public and private cloud computing, allowing companies to keep certain computing functions or databases in house and have others externally provided via a public cloud. Amazon and Google focus primarily on public clouds, IBM began with a focus on private clouds but has subsequently found the need to embrace hybrid and public cloud strategies as well, and Microsoft has taken the lead in offering hybrid clouds.[5]

Differences in business models translate into differences in intellectual property strategies. Strategic choices include decisions about which parts of the cloud computing system to protect as proprietary and which parts to develop internally or bring in house, as well as decisions about interoperability, compatibility, portability and standardization. Amazon, the market leader, would probably like to keep its already large existing customer base locked into Amazon's public cloud through a proprietary intellectual property strategy with limited interoperability and data portability. Microsoft, with its focus on hybrid clouds and interest in selling complementary software, necessarily favors more interoperability.[6] Google and IBM have aligned themselves with proponents of an open source cloud, although with different views about what an open cloud should look like and with different business objectives in mind.[7] Companies like Rackspace that provide managed cloud services have less interest in proprietary cloud technology and stand to benefit from open source cloud platforms upon which to build their value adding services.[8] For the largest players, such as Amazon, Google and Microsoft, their roles as providers of cloud platforms and their interests in setting and controlling industry standards to support their platforms influence the ways in which they think about and plan to obtain and use intellectual property, as further discussed below.

---

5 *See* e.g., Matt Weinberger, *Google just Made a Move to Leapfrog Microsoft and Amazon in the Cloud Wars*, BUS. INSIDER (July 16, 2015).

6 *See* e.g., Rob Marvin, *The Cloud in 2014: An Open, Interoperable Ecosystem*, SOFTWARE DEV. TIMES (Dec. 26, 2014).

7 *See* e.g., David Mytton, *What's the Real Reason Microsoft and Google Are Releasing Open Source?*, INFOWORLD (Feb. 2, 2016); Antone Gonsalves, *IBM Makes OpenStack the Cloud Platform to Beat*, READWRITE (Mar. 5, 2013).

8 *See* e.g., Matt Weinberger, *Why Cloud Computing Leaders Must Hang Together or Hang Separately*, BUS. INSIDER (May 18, 2015).

II. PATENTS IN THE CLOUD

While the strategies of companies in the cloud computing industry may vary, they share in common the pursuit of expanding patent portfolios. The growth of cloud computing as a distinct industry has been accompanied by a ballooning of patent applications and patents directed at cloud computing technologies. Microsoft, IBM and Red Hat Inc. were among the first to start filing patent applications that included the term "cloud computing" in the description of their inventions, with applications filed in 2008 and 2009.[9] The number of patent applications that reference cloud computing and the cloud in the text of the patent document and the number of different companies and individuals seeking such patents has increased exponentially since then. A search of the U.S. Patent and Trademark Office database in May 2016 yields 836 U.S. patents and 1,697 patent applications with "cloud computing" in the title and/or abstract and 16,311 U.S. patents and 36,243 patent applications that include "cloud computing" somewhere in the description of the invention.[10] The relevant patent landscape also encompasses technologies that predate the use of the term "cloud computing" as well as many new technologies that are not labeled as cloud technologies per se but which are important to cloud computing.

The largest players in cloud computing have already obtained patents covering many of the methods and techniques used to run data centers,[11] as well as patents covering many other aspects of cloud computing.[12] IBM and Microsoft appear to have some of the largest U.S. patent portfolios relevant to cloud computing. IBM claims that it had more than 3,000 patents relating to cloud computing, data analytics and online security issued in 2014.[13] Microsoft has an estimated 1,020 issued U.S. patents relating to various aspects of cloud computing technology.[14] Amazon and Google may at least initially lag behind in terms of the

---

[9] *See* Nicholas Reeve, *Cloud Computing: Patents and the Art of Semantics*, republished from Society for Computers and the Law, REDDIE (Aug. 28, 2015).

[10] Search of U.S. Patent and Trademark Office patent database done on May 3, 2016.

[11] *See* e.g., Jack Clark, *Forget the Mobile Patent Wars: These Web Giants Have Patented Your Data Center*, THE REGISTER (July 11, 2014).

[12] *See* e.g., Steve Brachmann, *The Year of the Cloud: Cloud Computing Goes Mainstream*, IP WATCHDOG (Jan. 6, 2014).

[13] *See* e.g., George Leopold, *Patent Leader IBM Targets Cloud Tech*, ENTERPRISE TECH. (Jan. 12, 2015).

[14] *See* e.g., Maulin Shah, *Cloud Computing: Will Innovation Stem from Patent Licensing?*, PATENTVUE (Feb. 1, 2014).

number, but not necessarily the importance, of issued patents covering cloud-related technologies.[15] There are also many smaller players investing in patents on inventions relevant to cloud computing, some of which might acquire blocking intellectual property. Lawsuits from non-practicing entities targeting cloud computing have already started to emerge.[16]

The growing number of patents relevant to cloud computing, combined with differences in how patents are being used by companies with different business models, create the potential for new intellectual property battlegrounds. Differences between open source and proprietary cloud computing strategies and between competing open source strategies will shape these battlegrounds. There is already intense competition between primarily proprietary cloud strategies, such as that pursued by Amazon and Microsoft, and open-ish cloud computing strategies, such as those pursued by IBM and Google.[17]

Amazon pursues a primarily proprietary intellectual property strategy in conjunction with its proprietary cloud platforms. Amazon was the pioneer in providing cloud computing infrastructure as a service and continues to have the largest cloud infrastructure market share.[18] Amazon's revenue model is focused on retaining existing customers and growing the number of new customers that use its hosting and online retail sales services.[19] There are strong economies of scale and strong network effects for Amazon – the larger the number of customers, the lower its cost of providing public cloud services and the more valuable the cloud platform is to proprietary application developers and therefore also to customers.

Amazon's intellectual property strategies are designed to maintain its IaaS platform Amazon Web Services (AWS) as a tightly controlled proprietary platform and, not surprisingly, it has not opened up its patent portfolio through patent pledges. Indeed, it has also been reluctant to make its application programming interfaces (APIs) generally available

---

15 Id.

16 *See* e.g., Simon Phipps, *Patent Trolls Target Their Next Victim: Cloud Computing*, INFOWORLD (Jan. 13, 2014).

17 *See* e.g., Brandon Butler, *Sizzling Open vs Proprietary Debate Heats Up in the Cloud*, NETWORK WORLD (Apr. 18, 2012).

18 *See* e.g., Amrita Jayakumar, *The Rise of Amazon Web Services*, WASH. POST (Apr. 23, 2015).

19 *See* e.g., Greg McFarlane, *Amazon Never Makes Money but No One Cares*, INVESTOPEDIA (Sept. 2, 2014).

to allow interoperability with other cloud applications and cloud platforms. An API can be simply understood as "a set of requirements that govern how one application can talk to another." APIs make it possible to move information between programs, and allow applications to run on alternative operating systems.[20] The Federal Circuit decision in Oracle versus Google, which found that parts of Oracle's Java API set were entitled to copyright protection, suggests that Amazon can continue to control – and limit – interoperability through the legal shadows cast over unauthorized use of its APIs.[21] Amazon has only recently started to engage in limited efforts to support interoperability between its cloud computing platform and private cloud systems, seeking to retain customers who may want to move their workload back and forth from Amazon's public cloud to their own private computers. Amazon's limited effort to open up its APIs has taken the form of an agreement with Eucalyptus, a start-up cloud company that provides Linux based open source software for building private clouds.[22] The agreement allows Eucalyptus to use Amazon's APIs to create interoperability between private clouds and Amazon's cloud computing platform. Amazon has also been noticeably quiet while other projects, such as an open source cloud system called CloudStacks, use Amazon's APIs to make their systems interoperable with Amazon's platform.[23]

While Microsoft is also pursuing a largely proprietary cloud strategy, its strategy builds in some degree of openness and interoperability with other cloud platforms. Microsoft has made large investments in its hybrid cloud platform, Microsoft Windows Azure, and is now in fierce price competition with Amazon and Google to capture cloud computing customers.[24] Part of this competition involves promoting Azure as an

---

[20] *See* e.g., Brian Proffitt, *What APIs Are and Why They're Important*, READWRITE (Sept. 19, 2013).

[21] *See* Oracle America, Inc. v. Google Inc., Nos. 13-1021, 1022 (Fed. Cir. May 9, 2014).

[22] *See* e.g., Joe Brockmeier, *Amazon Taps Eucalyptus as Private Cloud Partner*, READWRITE (Mar. 22, 2012).

[23] *See* e.g., Ted Samson, *Amazon Deal Alone Can't Save Eucalyptus from OpenStack*, INFOWORLD, (Mar. 23, 2012).

[24] *See* e.g., Barb Darrow, *Microsoft Woos Startups with More Free Cloud Offers*, FORTUNE (July 3, 2015).

open cloud,[25] both to attract customers and to drive sales of its proprietary complementary software.[26] These interests may help to account for Microsoft's recent decision to allow Microsoft customers to move Windows applications to competitor Google's cloud through what it calls the Microsoft License Mobility Program.[27] Microsoft has also engaged in some open source licensing and some limited patent pledges directed mainly at, but not limited to, facilitating interoperability of its software products with different computing systems. Microsoft's interest in interoperability has not stopped it from bringing patent infringement suits against other cloud computing companies, however, such as one brought against Salesforce.com for Microsoft patents relating to cloud and web functionality.[28]

IBM, Rackspace and Google have all advocated for an open source approach to cloud computing, but with varying ideas about what the open platform should look like and about just what intellectual property should be provided in an open source way.[29] Rackspace was one of the earliest proponents of an open source cloud computing platform, positioning itself as the open source alternative to Amazon with its co-development of OpenStack.[30] OpenStack was started in 2010 as a joint project between Rackspace Hosting and NASA. It is an open source cloud operating system that provides a set of software tools for building and managing cloud computing platforms.[31] OpenStack Foundation was formed in 2012 to promote the development, distribution and adoption of OpenStack as an open source cloud computing software platform.[32] As

---

25 *See Open Cloud*, MICROSOFT, https://www.microsoft.com/en-us/Openness/OpenCloud.

26 *See* e.g., Ed Bott, *Apple, Google, Microsoft: Where Does the Money Come From?*, ZDNET (Feb. 6, 2014).

27 *See* e.g., Julie Bort, *Microsoft's Brilliant Move to Make Money from Archrival Google*, BUS. INSIDER (Dec. 8, 2014).

28 *See* e.g., Peter Bright, *Microsoft Files Rare Patent Lawsuit Against Salesforce.com*, ARSTECHNICA (May 19, 2010); Tony Bradley, *Salesforce Patent Settlement a Win for Microsoft Azure*, PCWORLD (Aug. 5, 2010).

29 *See* e.g., Paul Teich, *Google Teams with Rackspace, Has Cloud Growth Stalled?*, FORBES (Apr. 6, 2016).

30 *See* e.g., Brandon Butler, *Cloud Computing Showdown: Amazon vs Rackspace vs Microsoft vs Google*, COMPUTERWORLDUK (Dec. 4, 2012).

31 OpenStack is managed by OpenStack Foundation, an open source cloud computing community with over 189 organizations and over 9,100 individual participants. *See Software*, OPENSTACK, http://www.openstack.org/software/.

32 *See* e.g., Jodi Smith, *The OpenStack Foundation Lumbers toward a Stronger IP Policy*, MIRANTIS (Jan. 19, 2015).

was the case with the development of Linux, OpenStack has been heavily supported by large corporate players, such as IBM, with their own interests in the evolution of the open source platform.

IBM followed Rackspace with its announcement that all of its cloud offerings would be built around the open source operating system OpenStack.[33] IBM has supported OpenStack as an open source platform upon which to build IBM proprietary software and services in much the same way as it has used the Linux open source operating system. Google runs its own proprietary non-OpenStack public cloud. It nonetheless recently joined the OpenStack Foundation, perhaps driven in part by its interest in making its Google Cloud Platform a seamless complement to OpenStack and by its interest in integrating its software container technology into non-Google environments.[34] Google's competitive advantage stems in part from its unique cloud infrastructure and the bargaining power it has in the infrastructure market, advantages that depend upon maintaining a sufficiently large market share, making Google quick to respond to customer needs for this kind of interoperability.

Not surprisingly, it is these three companies, IBM, Google and Rackspace, that have been active in making patent pledges relevant to cloud computing platforms, including both pledges relevant to an open internet and pledges specific to newer cloud computing technologies. The competition over alternative visions of "open" is evident in the strategies that they have each pursued in their dealings with open source software enterprises.

III. PATENT PLEDGES IN THE CLOUD

IBM was one of the first companies to make unilateral patent pledges, pledging not to assert 500 of its patents against open source software in 2005.[35] Ironically, the pledge coincided with an announcement from the U.S. Patent and Trademark Office that IBM was at the top of the list of

---

33 *See* e.g., Eric Knorr, *What IBM's Embrace of OpenStack really Means*, INFOWORLD (Mar. 11, 2013).

34 *See* e.g., Serdar Yegulalp, *4 Reasons Why Google Joined OpenStack*, INFOWORLD (July 17, 2015); Nick Chase, *Brace Yourself: Google Joins OpenStack,* OPENSTACK: UNLOCKED (July 20, 2015).

35 *See* IBM, *Statement of Non-Assertion of Named Patents Against OSS*, http://www.ibm.com/ibm/licensing/patents/pledgedpatents.pdf. See also Appendix.

annual U.S. patent recipients for the twelfth consecutive year, and the pledge covered less than one percent of IBM's patent portfolio.[36] In its patent pledge IBM promised the public that:

> [w]e are pledging the free use of 500 of our U.S. patents, as well as all counterparts of these patents issued in other countries, in the development, distribution, and use of open source software. We believe that the open source community has been at the forefront of innovation and we are taking this action to encourage additional innovation for open platforms.

IBM's pledge includes a broad defensive termination provision allowing it to revoke the pledged license in the event of a lawsuit asserting any intellectual property rights against open source software. IBM's patent pledge, along with earlier pledges made by Red Hat and subsequent pledges made by other companies that rely on open source software as part of their business model, pledges discussed in more detail in Chapter 1, are designed to protect and promote the development and use of open source software, particularly the Linux open source operating system. In the same year that it made its unilateral patent pledge, IBM was also a founding member of Open Invention Network (OIN), a defensive patent pool intended to protect Linux and Linux-related open source software through defensive cross-licensing.[37]

IBM's interest in an open source software platform such as the Linux operating system extends to cloud computing, and the company advocates an open cloud architecture for cloud computing, one based upon open source and open standards. But IBM seems to have a specific approach to open cloud computing and a particular type of openness in mind.[38] IBM has moved away from its traditional focus on hardware and now earns much of its revenues from infrastructure software and IT services, including the provision of cloud facilities to business enterprises.[39] It has argued for industry-wide open standards for cloud computing and has pursued a strategy of building its cloud computing

---

[36] *See* Jeremy Geelan, *IBM Patent Bombshell: "The Windows Patent Strategy Is … Over," Says Groklaw*, ULITZER (Jan. 11, 2005), http://linux.sys-con.com/node/47749.

[37] *See* OPEN INVENTION NETWORK, http://www.openinventionnetwork.com. *See also* Contreras, Chapter 1.

[38] *See* IBM, *Open Cloud Architecture*, http://www.ibm.com/developerworks/cloud/library/cl-open-architecture/

[39] *But see* Quentin Hardy, *IBM: The Cloud Taketh Away,* N.Y. TIMES (Jan. 21, 2014); Steve Lohr, *A Closer Look Inside IBM's Cloud Challenge*, N.Y. TIMES (May 12, 2014).

offerings around the open source cloud operating system OpenStack.[40] IBM uses its vast patent portfolio in support of the open source operating system provided by OpenStack Foundation[41] in much the same way as it has supported the development, adoption and use of Linux as an industry standard open source operating system. The OpenStack Foundation has its own approach to patents, relying on a defensive licensing strategy to deal with patent threats to the use of OpenStack. Pursuant to this strategy, contributing members such as IBM and HP are required to agree to the terms of the Apache 2.0 open source license.[42] The Foundation considered but rejected alternative ways of handling patents such as the Google Open Patent Non-Assertion Pledge or the Open Invention Network patent cross license.

Rackspace, which promotes itself as the open cloud company, was instrumental in creating the OpenStack cloud computing platform and promoting it as an open source alternative to proprietary cloud technologies. Rackspace earns revenues from providing cloud computing and managed hosting services, emphasizing the high quality of its services and customer support.[43] Instead of relying solely on defensive patent strategies such as non-assertion patent pledges to protect OpenStack, Rackspace is known for its aggressive pursuit of patent trolls in its effort to promote and protect an open source cloud platform.[44] "At Rackspace," they explain on their web site, "we believe that an open cloud will create the best opportunities for developers and end users. We also know that most of the innovation around computer systems and software now happens in the open source community."[45] Rackspace, along with Microsoft, has also made prior art pledges – pledges to disclose technical information that will be accessible and useful for patent examiners in their prior art searches when evaluating patent applications.[46]

---

40 *See* e.g., Knorr, *supra* note 33.

41 *See* e.g., Chris Mellor, *OpenStack's Success Will Depend on IBM and HP's Tech Queens*, THE REGISTER (Nov. 6, 2014).

42 Pursuant to the terms of the Apache 2.0 license, anyone who contributes code to the OpenStack project also contributes a patent license covering what it has contributed. If it brings a patent suit, it loses the licenses provided by other contributors.

43 *See* e.g., Jordan Novet, *Rackspace Says So Long to Commodity Cloud Wars with Its New Pricing Model*, VENTUREBEAT (July 15, 2014).

44 *See* Rack Blogger, *Join Us in the Fight Against Patent Trolls*, RACKSPACE (Nov. 19, 2012).

45 Id.

46 *See* Van Lindberg, *Transparency: The Ultimate Weapon in the Fight Against Patent Trolls*, RACKSPACE (Mar. 6, 2014).

Google, one of Amazon's closest competitors, earns its revenue largely from advertising, and as a result has an interest in increasing the use of the internet by facilitating access to the internet and keeping the cost of information low. As described by *The Economist*, "almost everything the company [Google] does – building huge data centers, fighting copyright restrictions, digitizing the world's libraries, developing a new browser and, most recently, even helping to launch satellites – is aimed at increasing the use of the internet."[47] Google has been diversifying its revenue streams, however, including efforts to expand revenues from areas such as cloud platform technologies.[48] It has invested heavily in its own proprietary Google Cloud Platform as well as developing a suite of cloud applications. Google's interests remain focused on open source approaches to internet technologies and its patent pledges reflect this.

Google's patent pledge has taken the form of what it calls an "Open Patent Non-Assertion Pledge" made in support of open innovation.[49] The pledge is a promise not to sue any user, distributor or developer of free software or open source software on specified patents unless Google is attacked first. Google makes a point of indicating that it will require any subsequent assignee of the pledged patents to agree to abide by the pledge. Google's first non-assertion patent pledge, made in March 2013, covered ten patents relating to MapReduce and Hadoop programming models which have applications in cloud computing environments.[50] This pledge included a controversial patent covering a form of parallel processing utilized in tools like Hadoop that are important to a wide range of products and services relying on big data.[51] Google's senior patent counsel described Google's first patent pledge as a commitment to an open internet.[52] A later pledge included 79 patents relating to essential elements of "big data" that are important to the development of cloud

47 *See Highs and Lows*, THE ECONOMIST (Oct. 23, 2008).

48 *See* Conner Forrest, *Four Ways Google Makes Money outside of Advertising*, TECHREPUBLIC (Jan. 16, 2015).

49 *See Open Patent Non-Assertion Pledge*, GOOGLE, http://www.google.com/patents/opnpledge/pledge/. *See also* Contreras, Chapter 1. See also Appendix.

50 *See* e.g., Jeff Roberts, *Google Donate Patents to Protect Cloud Software from Lawsuits,* GIGAOM, March 28, 2013.

51 *See* e.g., Barb Darrow, *The Week in the Cloud: AWS Goes Mobile; Google Vows Patent Pledge; Cloud Wars Rage On*, GIGAOM (Mar. 31, 2013).

52 *See* e.g., Duane Valz, *Taking a Stand on Open Source and Patents*, GOOGLE OPEN SOURCE BLOG (Mar. 28, 2013).

computing.[53] Google acquired these patents from IBM and CA Technologies.[54] A further 152 patents relating to technologies that facilitate speed and security on the web and five patents relating to MapReduce data-processing technology were added to the list of patents pledged by Google in August 2014.[55]

Although Google received positive publicity for its patent pledge, its pledge has notable limits, both in terms of the number of patents pledged and the scope of the pledge. The pledge covers free software and open source software only, and it does not extend to any proprietary software or hardware that is used in combination with open source software. The patents pledged are a tiny fraction of Google's rapidly growing patent portfolio. The pledge includes a defensive termination provision that sweeps broadly to cover itself, its affiliates, and any third party based in whole or part on a product or service developed by or on behalf of Google or its affiliates. Coming from a company that has only recently become a patent aggressor, with its involvement in a high profile suit in which its subsidiary at the time Motorola Mobility sued Apple for patent infringement,[56] the patent pledge may signal a more rather than a less aggressive approach to patents. While Google continues to advocate publicly for patent reform to limit software patents, it has increased its patent filings exponentially over the last decade and is now among the largest winners of U.S. software patents and the owner of more than 51,000 patents.[57]

While Google leads the field in its commitment to, and interest in, maintaining an open source internet, and has directed its patent pledges towards promoting an open source internet, it has pursued development of its own proprietary cloud platform and cloud applications. But Google is keenly interested in attracting companies that have their own private clouds to Google's cloud platform by making it easy for them to integrate their private clouds with Google's public cloud, and many of these

---

53 *See* e.g., Frederic Lardinois, *Google Adds 79 Cloud and Big Data Patents to its Open Patent Non-Assertion Pledge*, TECH CRUNCH (Aug. 8, 2013).

54 *See* e.g., Jeff Roberts, *Google Donates 79 More Patents to Shield the Cloud from Lawsuits*, GIGAOM (Aug. 8, 2013).

55 *See Google Developers Announcement*, GOOGLE (Aug. 26, 2014), https://plus.google.com/+GoogleDevelopers/posts/eJFWj3VNG1L.

56 *But see*, Mike Masnick, *Why Google's "We Won't Sue" Patent Pledge May Actually Suggest a Greater Proclivity to Sue over Patents*, TECHDIRT (Mar. 28, 2013).

57 *See* Antonio Regalado, *Google's Growing Patent Stockpile*, MIT TECH. REV. (Nov. 29, 2013).

private clouds rely on OpenStack. It is thus no surprise that Google very recently joined as an official member of the OpenStack Foundation and committed to provide engineering resources to OpenStack.[58] Google's increased participation in OpenStack is likely fueled by its desire to influence the direction of the OpenStack platform. Google is particularly interested in establishing its own software container technology – technology useful in moving applications between platforms – as the standard container technology for OpenStack.[59] Google also recently announced that it would join Open Invention Network (OIN) and that OIN would cover OpenStack.[60]

While there is some level of cooperation among companies advocating for open clouds, there is also competition among alternative open source approaches and varying strategic alliances between competing open source groups and different market competitors. OpenStack, backed by IBM and now by Google, among others, faces competition from alternative open source operating systems such as Apache CloudStack.[61] CloudStack was originally a commercial system developed by a start-up company called Cloud.com and designed to be compatible with Amazon's proprietary platform. Cloud.com was acquired by Citrix in 2011, and Citrix turned around and donated CloudStack to the Apache Software Foundation in 2012. By doing so, Citrix put CloudStack into an open, committee-driven governance model and made the entire system open source. Citrix still benefits indirectly from CloudStack through the sale of support and complementary goods, and also uses CloudStack as part of its competition with VMware, which relies on a competing open source system called Eucalyptus.[62] Eucalyptus, mentioned earlier in connection with Amazon, is an open source cloud computing system compatible with Amazon's proprietary cloud computing platform.[63] OpenStack seems to be winning the competition against alternative open

---

58 Weinberger, *supra* note 5.

59 *See* e.g., Frederic Lardinois, *Google Signs on as OpenStack Sponsor, Will Contribute Container Tech*, TECHCRUNCH (July 15, 2015).

60 *See* e.g., Phipps, *supra* note 16.

61 *See* e.g., Lydia Leong, *Citrix, CloudStack, OpenStack, and the War for Open-Source Clouds*, GARTNER BLOG NETWORK (Apr. 3, 2012).

62 *See* e.g., Richard Tee & Jason Woodard, *Architectural Control and Value Migration in Layered Ecosystems: The Case of Open-Source Cloud Management Platforms*, Paper presented at Vienna Conference on Strategy, Organizational Design, and Innovation, Vienna, June 22–23, 2013. *See also* K. Boudreau, *Open Platform Strategies and Innovation: Granting Access vs. Devolving Control*, 56 MGMT. SCI. 1849, 1849 (2010).

63 *See* e.g., Brockmeier, *supra* note 22.

source operating systems, while also remaining a player to contend with in the cloud computing market. This is due at least in part to support, including not only technical and financial support but also patent cover in the form of patent pledges and defensive licensing practices, from cloud players such as IBM, Cisco and VMware, and now also Google, with significant patent holdings.[64]

Microsoft has made its own patent pledges in support of its desired form of open cloud platform, with a focus on promoting interoperability between Azure and alternative cloud platforms. Microsoft has made limited patent pledges in the form of an open specification promise and community promise that apply to developers and customers who want to implement specifications identified by Microsoft.[65] The promises are unilateral, voluntary promises to limit the assertion of Microsoft patents against the developers and users of certain specifications in order to facilitate the implementation and use of these specifications.[66] The focus of the pledges is on allowing interoperability with Microsoft products, and the pledges are carefully crafted to support this goal.[67] Although the impetus for efforts at promoting interoperability might have started as a response to European court directives in the wake of antitrust cases,[68] they appear to have become part of Microsoft's business strategy to promote its version of an "open" cloud as a cloud platform allowing for some level of interoperability with other cloud platforms.[69]

---

64 *See* e.g., Matt Weinberger, *Microsoft, Google, and Amazon Haven't Won the Cloud Wars Yet*, BUS. INSIDER (May 19, 2015).

65 *See Patent Promises and Patents*, MICROSOFT, https://msdn.microsoft.com/en-us/openspecifications/dn750984. *See also* Contreras, Chapter 1.

66 *See* e.g., Andy Updegrove, *Microsoft Releases New "Open Specifications Promise" on 35 Web Services Specifications*, THE STANDARDS BLOG (Sept. 12, 2006).

67 *See* Contreras, Chapter 1.

68 *See* e.g., Nicholas Economides & Ioannis Lianos, *A Critical Appraisal of Remedies in the E.U. Microsoft Cases*, 2010 COLUM. BUS. L. REV. 346, 355 (2010); *Microsoft Statement on European Commission Decision*, MICROSOFT (Dec. 16, 2009).

69 *See* e.g., Bill Gates, *Building Software that is Interoperable by Design*, MICROSOFT (Feb. 3, 2005); Heidemarie Hanekop & Patrick Feuerstein, *Institutional Foundations of Open Innovation and Field Dynamics in the Software Industry: From Antagonism to Contested Cooperation between Firms and Open Source Community* (working paper, 2014); M. Lange, *Interoperability and Microsoft* (Microsoft Whitepaper, Winter 2009).

One of the most recent patent pledges relevant to cloud computing was made by Panasonic in March 2015.[70] Panasonic pledged to "make available for royalty-free use mature and tested device-to-cloud software technology" and to provide "royalty-free access to software, patents and experience from its product ecosystem" to support the development of the Internet of Things (IoT) software and services.[71] This pledge provides yet another example of a company most likely hoping to make certain aspects of cloud computing open with an eye on extracting revenues from complementary products and services.

IV. PLEDGES AND PLATFORM COMPETITION

In this complicated intellectual property landscape patents seem to play multiple roles, including defensive roles, use to exclude competitors, and use to signal and commit to openness. But one dominant feature of this industry, and the role of patents and patent pledges in the industry, stands out. Major competitors in the field are interested in having their own respective approaches to cloud computing serve as the dominant industry platform. While their use of patent strategies varies with how open the platform they advocate for is and where the open and the proprietary features of cloud computing will be concentrated, the main players are using, or not using, patents and patent pledges as part of platform competition.

A platform technology refers to a technology or group of technologies that are used as a base upon which other technologies and applications can be developed. In the context of cloud computing, platforms are characterized by both direct and indirect network effects. Consumers may prefer cloud computing platforms that other consumers have adopted for reasons such as familiarity, ease of collaboration and likelihood of survival – thus creating direct network effects. Consumers may also prefer cloud computing platforms that have a large range of applications, while application providers want to develop applications for platforms with a large customer base – thus creating indirect network effects. The

---

[70] *See* e.g., *Panasonic to Share Intellectual Property to Spur Growth of Internet of Things*, PR NEWSWIRE (Mar. 23, 2015).

[71] *See* e.g., Panasonic press release, *Panasonic to Share Intellectual Property to Spur Growth of Internet of Things*, PANASONIC (Mar. 23, 2015).

presence and strength of these network effects will impact the nature of competition among platform providers.[72]

As discussed in Chapter 1, platform technologies, which are characterized by two-sided network effects, benefit from approaches to patents that attract and retain both customers and developers. The more customers, the more attractive the platform is for developers, and the more developers, the more attractive the platform is for customers. Patent pledges are used strategically to influence the attractiveness of the pledger's cloud computing platform for both developers of applications and customers. They are also used to control or encourage switching between platforms, and to impact the nature and type of openness of the platform.

Amazon, which has and wishes to retain a large market share attractive to both customers and application developers, has preferred a proprietary patent strategy that helps to lock its large customer base to its proprietary platform. Competing platforms that have entered the market, such as the Google Cloud Platform, Microsoft Azure and OpenStack, have all adopted more open approaches to their platforms. They range from limited openness, such as the interoperability offered by Microsoft and Google, to open source approaches such as that offered by OpenStack. Offering patents for free can be used strategically by competitors to make their platforms more attractive to customers and to developers by reducing dangers of lock-in and increasing the ability of customers to select among platforms and applications. Providers of complementary goods also seek to influence platform choice. They are interested in having an open source platform of their choice that will be compatible with their own products and services. These companies have an interest in pledging their patents as a way of promoting adoption of their favored open source platform. Patent pledges are playing important roles in this competition to be, or choose, the winning cloud computing platform(s).

CONCLUSION

This chapter has highlighted some of the ways in which patent pledges are being deployed as part of the competition to control the cloud. Patent strategies will continue to shape the evolution of the cloud computing industry. New business models and technologies will in turn influence the

---

[72] *See* e.g., Chaim Fershtman & Neil Gandal, *Migration to the Cloud Ecosystem: Ushering in a New Generation of Platform Competitio*n, 85 COMM. AND STRATEGIES 1 (2012).

evolution of patent strategies. Patent pledges seem to be playing important but poorly understood roles in this evolving intellectual property landscape. This chapter concludes that while the pledges may be royalty-free, their impact may not be. They are being used to reshape the relationships between patents, competition and innovation in ways that are deserving of further study.

16. Patent pledges and developing countries: the tryst with India's destiny

Tania Sebastian

I. INTRODUCTION: UNDERSTANDING THE DEBATE

The epoch-making speech of Shri Jawaharlal Nehru, the first prime minister of Independent India, on the eve of India's independence from the British empire, resonates true even today. Titled "Tryst with Destiny," his speech pledges, among other things "dedication to the service of India and her people and to the still larger cause of humanity." Nearly 60 years after independence, India's tryst with healthcare has arrived, Compulsory patent licenses in India have benefitted thousands of patients in a typical developing nation, beginning with *Natco Pharma Ltd.* v. *Bayer Corp.*[1] This case addressed the core issue of accessibility of life-enhancing drugs for cancer patients and its viability under the Indian Patent Act, 1970.[2] With a little over 2% of Indian cancer patients having access to the drug "Sorafenib Tosylate" (sold under the brand name "Nexavar" by Bayer), the exorbitantly priced medicine was made available at 97% less, well within the "reasonable affordable price" range of the population.[3] It is in light of this singular development that the stage for Patent Pledges is now set, with India now working to deliver low-cost drugs to the third world and under-developed countries, as part of a commitment to public benefit from innovation.[4] This chapter examines

[1] Compulsory License Application No. 1 of 2011, Application for Compulsory License Under Section 84(1) of the Patents Act, 1970 in Respect of Patent No. 215758, Natco Pharma Ltd. v. Bayer Corp. (Mar. 9, 2012).

[2] Indian Patents Act, 1970 (as amended in 2005), 27 India A.I.R. Manual 450, § 84, 90 (1979).

[3] Additional issues addressed are not central to this chapter.

[4] IANS, *India Pledges New Low-Cost Drugs to Developing Nations*, BUS. STANDARD (Mar. 10, 2014).

whether patent pledges can be implemented in a way that similarly serves the public interest in the context of a broad development-focused intellectual property system.

This chapter specifically frames these questions:

- Does ambiguity or uncertainty in the enforceability of patent pledges disadvantage smaller developing country firms with less leverage in negotiation and litigation?
- Do patent pledges, as compared to compulsory licenses, limit developing countries to working within an unbalanced patent system, rather than balancing IPR with other national interests such as healthcare, poverty alleviation, and climate change?
- Are enough high-value patents pledged as to provide real freedom to innovate for developing country firms to operate? Or do examples like the Eco-Patent Commons warn against this optimism?

Full answers are not available to these questions yet, but as the use of patent pledges continues, it is important to interrogate whether they are structured and enforced in a way that reduces barriers and provides benefits to developing countries to the same extent they do to companies in developed countries.

II. DO PATENT PLEDGES PROVIDE CERTAINTY TO DEVELOPING COUNTRY INNOVATORS?

While patent pledges offer great potential to increase access for developing country companies, there are also concerns surrounding the present regime of patent pledges and those pledges' potential impact on developing countries. Patent pledges by companies such as Tesla Motors and IBM[5] are examples of striking the balance between proprietary and open systems in a way that is focused on the United States context. However, such structures could potentially disadvantage developing countries. Concerns for a developing country about patent pledges are numerous, including consequences for a developing country with respect to the potential differing developed country understanding of vague terms (e.g., the "good faith" terminology of Tesla's pledge). Interpretation of imprecise pledges are entangled in a web of contract law, intellectual property

---

[5] *See* Appendix and Contreras, Chapter 1.

law, and *lex fori* issues along with the connected matters of arbitration and mediation.

While there is potential for patent pledges to benefit innovators in developing countries' companies, there remains ambiguity surrounding patent pledges and their enforceability. When that uncertainty leads to legal conflict, the power differential between companies making patent pledges and the companies relying on them in developing countries can lead to a disadvantage for smaller, less well-resourced firms. The enforceability of the pledge is paramount if acted upon by a developing country.

Concerns relating to the reasonableness of royalties under "FRAND" and similar pledges[6] also demand attention. In the specific case of a developing nation, "reasonableness" in royalty should mean royalties that the patent holder could obtain in open, up-front competition with other technologies, not the royalties that the patent holder can extract once other participants are effectively locked in to use technology covered by the patent.

Further, while the benefits from FRAND-type pledges are well established, the full benefits do not always accrue to developing country actors. One example is Microsoft's ActiveSync protocol for synchronizing calendar, emails, and other information between smartphones and PCs. This protocol was subject to a RAND pledge wherein all relevant patents were to form part of the licensing terms. However, it has been alleged that Microsoft refused to license its patents to Android Original Equipment Manufacturers on a standalone basis, insisting instead that they license the more expensive "Android Licensing program,"[7] which ties in the pledged patents with other non-essential patents. The result of this arrangement was a jump in royalty demands from $0.33 to $5–15, putting the burden of increased costs on the customers. Effects such as these may have serious disparate impacts in developing countries.

---

6 *See* Contreras, Chapter 1.

7 *See Licenses*, ANDROID, https://source.android.com/source/licenses.html.

III. PATENT PLEDGES AND COMPULSORY LICENSES: COMPLEMENTARY APPROACHES TO ACCESS TO INNOVATION?

Companies such as Google have pledged their patents in specific software sectors such as free and open source software.[8] However, there is a tension between applauding those patent pledges and critiquing the monopoly power that the patents granted in the first instance. Over time, remedies have been sought to mitigate the effect of patent thickets and monopoly power, of which patent pooling and FRAND commitments are the best cited examples and the most recent addendum to which is patent pledges. Developing countries can benefit from these pledges, if well implemented, but hurdles remain. India, for example, has a gross domestic product (GDP) that is a fraction of that of the U.S., a staggering population living in poverty,[9] and an ever-widening gap between the rich and the poor.[10] In that context patent pledges are just one piece of the effort to bring the benefits of innovation to alleviate the impact of poverty in developing countries, while other approaches such as compulsory licenses and limits on patentability are blunt instruments for limiting the impact of patent monopolies.

Ultimately, the patent pledge regime is modeled on the lines of the current developed country intellectual property enforcement model. While some patent pledges hold promise for developing economies, that remains a case-by-case determination, rather than an endorsement of the current regime of patent pledges remains writ large. For developing countries, such as India, there is the ongoing tension between working with the IP industry in developed countries through tools such as patent pledges, and working in development-focused models, such as through the use of compulsory licenses. India, though, has taken the first step in a dual manner, by the The Protection and Utilization of Public Funded

---

8 *See Open Patent Non-Assertion Pledge*, GOOGLE, http://www.google.com/patents/opnpledge/pledge/. See also, Appendix.

9 In 2012, the Indian government stated 21.9% of its population is below its official poverty limit. The World Bank, in 2011 based on 2005's Purchasing Power Parities International Comparison Program, estimated 23.6% of the Indian population, or about 276 million people, lived below $1.25 per day on purchasing power parity.

10 Press Trust of India, *Poor-Rich Gap Growing in India, Asia-Pacific: UNESCAP*, THE ECON. TIMES (Oct. 3, 2014).

Intellectual Property Bill, 2008[11] and by committing to make available to developing countries next generation life-saving drugs through compulsory licensing.[12]

IV. EXAMINING THE ECO-PATENT COMMONS AND OTHER GREEN TECHNOLOGY PLEDGES IN THE DEVELOPING WORLD – ARE HIGH-VALUE PATENTS BEING PLEDGED?

As discussed in Chapters 1 and 4, the Eco-Patent Commons (EPC) launched by IBM, Nokia, Pitney Bowes, and Sony in partnership with the World Business Council for Sustainable Development (WBCSD) was formed to "encourage collaboration for new innovation through an online collection of environmentally beneficial patents pledged by the member companies for free use by anyone."[13] In terms of developing countries, the impact of the EPC has been low.[14] Our present horizons of patent pledges need to be expanded so as to specifically include the dilemmas of the developing world. These patent pledges should also not amount to "patent dumping," thereby giving away patents that are effectively redundant or valueless to promote open innovation.

From the perspective of economies that are developing, there are two key requirements for patent pledges to benefit innovation: that "valuable" patents are pledged, and that those pledges are predictably and reliably enforceable. The need, hence, is to understand that firms should pledge valuable patents and not the outdated and invaluable ones, especially in

---

[11] The Public Funded IP Bill makes it mandatory for grant recipients to "make disclosure of public funded IP to the government within the time specified ..." (section 3 (3) (a)). "Time specified" is 60 days from the actual knowledge of the public funded IP (section 4). The Act was introduced with laudable objectives as: to ensure that benefits of public funded research reach the public, create an environment in which wealth can be generated from the university system and forge more close academia-industry partnerships etc. Though withdrawn, it was one of the first steps by the government to recognize the importance of IP in the public space.

[12] *India Pledges New Low-Cost Drugs to Developing Nations*, *supra* note 4.

[13] *See Eco-Patent Commons,* ECO-PATENT COMMONS, https://ecopatentcommons.org/. *See also* Contreras, Chapter 1.

[14] Bronwyn H. Hall & Christian Helmers, *Innovation and Diffusion of Clean/Green Technology: Can Patent Commons Help?*, 66 J ENVIR. ECON. & MGMT. 33, 33–34 (2013).

the context of a developing economy.[15] Cronin argues that the patents contained in the EPC are of little value as they protect outdated technologies. As a solution to this problem, Cronin suggests including novel non-patented inventions that have not been made public, presumably because they were protected via trade secrecy that may be done in the form of defensive publications.[16]

In a review of the EPC initiative, Srinivas identifies a number of problems with the initiative. He argues that the technologies protected so far by patents in the EPC "have a very limited application in the further development of technologies in key sectors." He is sceptical about providing royalty-free access to single green patents, as most technologies are covered by multiple patents which are not included in the commons.[17]

CONCLUSION

Patent pledges can be used as mechanisms to foster innovation between developed and developing economies and thereby build more holistic markets and relationships. The accomplishment of these aims, however, requires careful attention to the specific needs of users in developing countries.

---

[15] Id.; *see also* Oliver Alexy & Markus G. Reitzig, *Gaining It by Giving It Away: Capturing Value in "Mixed" Appropriability Regimes* (Feb. 24, 2010) (unpublished manuscript).

[16] Nancy Cronin, *Growing the Eco-Patent Commons to Truly Promote Green Innovation*, GREENBIZ (Apr. 15, 2008).

[17] Krishna Ravi Srinivas, *Sink or Swim: Eco-Patent Commons and the Transfer of Environmentally Sustainable Technologies*, BIORES (May 1, 2008).

PART V

Patent pledges moving forward

17. How to make and keep a patent pledge

Timothy S. Simcoe

As described in Chapter 1, there is a growing number of unilateral "patent pledges" made by individual patent holders outside of the standard setting process. These pledges are often similar to a typical Standard Setting Organization (SSO) disclosure. They identify a set of patents, and perhaps a specific field of use, and provide a commitment to potential infringers regarding the availability or terms of a license. The motivations behind a patent pledge are presumably quite similar to those of an SSO participant – the patent holder would like to see the underlying technology widely diffused. However, because pledges take place outside of the formal legal and institutional structure provided by an SSO, these decentralized commitments raise interesting questions about enforcement.

This short chapter will offer several observations about the motivations for patent pledging, the formal structure that underpins these licensing commitments, and the possibility of creating a public registry to record pledges that take place outside of SSOs.[1]

I. MOTIVATIONS

Patent pledges are an example of strategic commitment. Patentees give up some of their rights to influence the behavior of potential infringers. Farrell and Gallini describe the economics of this situation, and emphasize that a profit-maximizing seller can benefit from a commitment to increased competition if the reduction in unit margins is more than offset by an increase in quantity demanded.[2] This would be the case, for

[1] Contreras, Chapter 18.

[2] Joseph Farrell & Nancy Gallini, *Second-Sourcing as a Commitment: Monopoly Incentives to Attract Competition*, 103 Q.J. ECON. 673–94 (1988).

example, if the absence of a commitment would lead potential users to choose an alternative technology, or cause business partners to forgo investments in implementation.[3]

If sellers are profit maximizing, and pledges are designed to encourage adoption of the underlying technology, why do some patentees commit to a price of zero? One answer is that firms choose to forgo licensing opportunities in order to seek margins on the sale of complementary products. For example, IBM's pledges to the open source community may encourage the diffusion of open source technology, which is a complement to IBM's services and systems integration businesses.[4] Another potential explanation is that pledged patents have little or no expected value aside from any public relations benefit that the pledge itself provides.

Assuming that pledged patents have some value, why do patentees not just abandon their patents by declining to pay periodic renewal fees, thereby placing the underlying technology into the public domain? Some companies surely do. As of 2012, the holders of roughly 90 percent of US patents paid their first renewal fee, 70 percent paid the second renewal fee, and only 50 percent paid the third and final fee to keep the patent in force.[5] However, patentees that offer royalty-free commitments may still wish to reserve the rights to assert and license the same patent in other fields of use. For example, most SSO licensing commitments apply only to a particular standard, and some open source licenses are limited to non-commercial use. A second motivation for reserving rights is that they can be used to enforce the terms of a conditional commitment. For example, a firm might pledge to license its patent royalty-free, but only so long as the licensee offers a reciprocal commitment. Such reciprocity provisions are widespread among SSO licensing commitments.

---

[3] The literature on standard essential patents often argues that hold-up is the reason why patentees offer licensing commitments. This may be true, but hold-up problems are not a necessary condition for licensing commitments to be useful. Competition between technologies could also suffice.

[4] *See*, e.g., Wen Wen, Marco Ceccagnoli & Chris Forman, *Opening Up Intellectual Property Strategy: Implications for Open Source Software Entry by Start-Up Firms*, MGMT. SCI. (2016).

[5] Dennis Crouch, *Patent Maintenance Fees*, PATENTLYO (Sept 26, 2012).

II. FORMAL STRUCTURE

It is natural to view unilateral patent pledges as fundamentally different from SSO licensing commitments, and courts may well choose to enforce them in different ways. However, it is also useful to consider how SSOs and pledges might represent two poles along a continuum of methods for organizing access to shared technology. In the unified view, licensing commitments can take a variety of forms. As described in Chapter 1, some patent holders simply make a pronouncement on their web page.[6] Others establish a cross-licensing "club" or consortium that can have several tiers of paid and unpaid participation.[7] Such groups tend to focus on a single issue or technology, and have a largely static structure. The largest SSOs such as the Institute for Electrical and Electronic Engineers (IEEE) and the European Telecommunications Standards Institute (ETSI) typically have a well-defined process for offering several types of licensing commitment, as well as a process for changing the organization's overarching intellectual property policies.

A very simple economic model of the choice of formal structures for making voluntary licensing commitments could begin by comparing the fixed costs of creating a formal structure with the variable costs of an individual disclosure or licensing commitment. When a single firm wants to publicly "release" a few patents related to a specific technology, the fixed costs of setting up a formal structure are likely to exceed the potential benefits. In these cases, the public announcement on a corporate web site may suffice. However, as more technologies and participants are added to the picture, the fixed costs of creating a formal structure are often justified by the per-commitment (or per-participant) benefits of formalizing rules and procedures.

This observation is admittedly straightforward, and there are other economic models that emphasize different trade-offs, such as the selection of a "lenient" intellectual property policy that attracts patent-holding participants to the SSO while still encouraging users to adopt the technology.[8] Nevertheless, viewing SSO licensing commitments and patent pledges as two options along a continuum of possible choices encourages us to consider why a particular set of rules was adopted. And

---

6 *See*, e.g., *Microsoft's Open Specification Promise*, MICROSOFT, Appendix.

7 *See*, e.g., *LOT Agreement*, LOT NETWORK, http://lotnet.com/download-lot-agreement/; *Testing Policies*, HDMI CONSORTIUM, http://www.hdmi.org/manufacturer/testing_policies.aspx.

8 Josh Lerner & Jean Tirole, *A Model of Forum Shopping*, 96 AM. ECON. REV. 1091, 1091–113 (2006).

as courts and policy makers wrestle with questions of enforceability under these different structures, it would be wise to keep the underlying commonalities in mind.

III. RECORDATION

While SSOs often maintain a database of patent disclosures and licensing commitments, there is no comparable central record for most patent pledges. Consequently, pledges can feel impermanent.[9] I will conclude by discussing the question of whether and how pledges should be recorded, a question that is further discussed in Chapter 18.

As a threshold matter, it is important to ask whether there is a potential market failure to be addressed. Hal Varian provides an economic model of clearance and registries in the copyright setting, and suggests that there is a free-rider problem in the search process that matches buyers and sellers.[10] A second potential market failure could emerge if parties try to renege on commitments after removing them from public view, or work to "launder" pledges through patent transfers.

These concerns do not seem particularly important at the time a commitment is made. Patentees have every incentive to make it easy for prospective infringers to locate the pledge, and users who make large investments in reliance on the promise will have strong incentives to make a copy and hold onto it. This suggests that a public registry of commitments would have limited benefits.

However, if adoption of the underlying technology creates market power (e.g. because of network effects) and there is an effort to remove or obscure the commitment for *later* licensees, then a registry might have some value. This scenario offers a plausible explanation for many SSOs' public archives of patent disclosures and licensing commitments. Increasingly, these SSO policies also include mechanisms to ensure that commitments remain in force following the transfer or sale of a patent.[11]

A registry might also promote greater specificity about what *exactly* is being pledged. With both SSOs and pledges, patent holders sometimes provide a complete list of potentially infringed patents and other times

---

[9] One attempt to solve this problem is the Patent Pledge Database discussed in the Introduction.

[10] Hal R. Varian, *Copyright Term Extension and Orphan Works*, 15 INDUS. & CORP. CHANGE 965, 972 (2006).

[11] NATIONAL RESEARCH COUNCIL OF THE NATIONAL ACADEMIES, *supra* note 1 at Chapter 5.

simply allude to a particular standard or technology. Some observers have called for greater specificity in the SSO disclosure process.[12] However, any ban on so-called "blanket" disclosures, or requirements that a company conduct a formal patent search, could diminish incentives to make welfare-improving commitments in the first place.

So, is there a strong case for a public registry? At present, the majority of licensing commitments are made to SSOs, and most of those groups have a private registry. If there were a substantial demand for a pledge registry, private provision of this service (e.g. by an SSO that allows broader use of its disclosure database) would not be difficult. The natural home for a public registry would be the U.S. Patent and Trademark Office (PTO), which is quite good at tracking individual patents, but may find it difficult to track "blanket" commitments that indicate only a willingness to license any patents required to implement a particular standard or technology. On balance, the overall benefits of creating a public registry do not seem large.

On the other hand, the costs of creating a public registry might also be small. The U.S. Patent and Trademark Office (PTO) already has systems to track renewals and transfers of patent rights. While the information in these systems could certainly be improved and provided to the public in a more accessible manner, adding a field that notes the presence of a licensing encumbrance should not be technically challenging. Moreover, the availability of an "official" recordation process for licensing commitments could provide a low-cost mechanism for patentees to legitimate their commitments and perhaps distinguish "serious" pledges from potential scams.

The preceding discussion suggests that creating a registry should not be at the top of the PTO's list of information technology priorities. It is almost surely more important to focus on creating a transparent and easy-to-read record of all patent renewals and transfers of ownership, and to clean up the assignment data and technology classification system so that it is easier to identify all jointly owned patents in a particular technology area. However, if it is easy to create a simple registry of patent pledges and licensing commitments in the context of these larger efforts, that registry might become a useful tool in support of private efforts to organize open access to shared technology platforms.

---

12 *See*, e.g., Deanne E. Maynard, Sean P. Gates, John Thorne & Gail F. Levine, Verizon Commc'ns Inc., Written Comments of Verizon Communications Inc. for Federal Trade Commission Workshop on Standard- Setting Issues 4 (2011).

18. A registry for patent pledges[1]

Jorge L. Contreras

I. THE NOTICE FUNCTION OF PATENT PLEDGES

In order for a patent pledge to achieve the pledgor's desired effect, whether to induce the market to adopt a particular technology platform, to endorse an interoperability standard, or to portray the pledgor in a more favorable light, broad public dissemination or "notice" of the pledge is necessary. Likewise, in order to extend the benefit of the pledge to the intended category of beneficiaries, whether a promise not to enforce a patent, to charge a reasonable royalty rate, or not to seek injunctive relief, broad public notice is also desirable. Nevertheless, many patent pledges fail to achieve this notice function.

A. Obscurity: Where Are All the Pledges?

As discussed in Chapter 1, patent pledges may be made in a variety of ways, from formal documents submitted to standards development organizations (SDOs), to Congressional testimony, speeches, and corporate press releases. Pledges made through the formal disclosure processes of an SDO, coupled with public SDO publication of patent and licensing disclosures, are the most likely to give broad notice to the relevant marketplace. Technology developers that participate in SDOs should thus have a high degree of awareness of the patent-related disclosures made with respect to standards on which they are collaborating.

Manufacturers who intend to sell standards-compliant products may also have a high level of awareness of pledges made regarding relevant standards. That is, a firm that wishes to enter the market for USB hubs might reasonably be expected to research the status of patents covering the USB standard and pledges that exist with respect to such patents. On

[1] This chapter is based, in part, on Jorge L. Contreras, *Patent Pledges*, 47 ARIZ. ST. L.J. 543 (2015), with permission of the author.

the other hand, the manufacturer of a laptop computer that will implement more than 250 different standards[2] may not have the resources, time, or personnel to undertake an equivalent search, and could be unaware of particular pledges made with respect to patents claiming aspects of those standards.

Outside the regime of formal standard-setting, specific awareness of patent pledges may drop off further. While a corporate press release or speech containing a patent pledge may attract significant media and industry attention when it is made, both news cycles and corporate memories are short, and such pledges may be forgotten, or never noticed, by those who might potentially benefit from them. The lack of a tie to a particular technical standard may also make pledges more difficult to identify through searching. Thus, while the USB hub manufacturer wishing to find pledges relating to the USB standard could, with only modest effort, search for pledges relating to this well-known standard, the difficulty of locating relevant pledges increases dramatically when the product is a software application, a genetic test, or an energy efficient vehicle.

B. Impermanence

Closely related to the problem of *finding* patent pledges is the problem of *preserving* them after they are made. Even if a pledge is initially made in a public and widely observed manner, issues can arise if it is later taken down, modified, or moved to a new web address. In fact, it is nearly impossible to verify whether pledges made years ago have been altered, subtly or not, by their makers. And if pledges simply disappear from the web, what is their ongoing status? Should a patent holder be expected to honor a pledge that it took down years ago? Would it matter if the firm seeking to enforce the pledge did not exist when the pledge was made, or when it was taken down? These questions are far from hypothetical. Online content is notoriously volatile.[3] And numerous patent pledges

---

[2] *See* Brad Biddle, Andrew White & Sean Woods, *How Many Standards in a Laptop? (And Other Empirical Questions)*, 2010 INT'L TELECOMM. UNION SEC. TELECOMM. STANDARDIZATION KALEIDOSCOPE ACAD. CONF. PROC. 123, 123 (2010).

[3] *See* Raizel Liebler & June Liebert, *Something Rotten in the State of Legal Citation: The Life Span of a United States Supreme Court Citation Containing an Internet Link (1996–2010)*, 15 YALE J.L. & TECH. 273, 273 (2013) (finding nearly one-third of web links cited in Supreme Court opinions from 1996–2010 are dead).

have already been affected by ambiguities arising from the disappearance of online links and content.

For example, in 2011 the Eco-Patent Commons (EPC) announced that Hitachi pledged an unidentified patent relating to parts recycling.[4] By mid-2012, however, Hitachi was no longer listed as an EPC member, and its patent was not listed in the EPC's catalog of pledged patents.[5] And in 2016, the EPC itself ceased operations. In view of these changes, what happened to Hitachi's pledge? The Ground Rules of EPC provided that once a patent is pledged to EPC, that pledge cannot be revoked, even if the patent owner withdrew from EPC.[6] Thus, a Hitachi patent may still be pledged, but the identity of the patent and any other terms of the pledge can no longer be found. And without ongoing institutional support, the EPC's web sites and associated statements will disappear from public view. Though web archival services such as WayBackMachine. com can help, their results are ad hoc and cannot be relied upon to provide a complete picture of the worldwide web at every moment in the past.

C. Successor Obligations

In today's dynamic technology marketplace, patents are being transferred in larger numbers and with greater rapidity than ever before. Particularly in the ICT sector, patents transferred in large portfolio sales, corporate mergers, and other transactions are often subject to patent pledges. What happens to a patent pledge when the original pledgor transfers the underlying patent to a third party? Do such pledges travel with patents, binding their new owners, or are they personal commitments binding only on the original promisor?

This question was central to the FTC's 2008 action against Negotiated Data Solutions (N-Data), the successor to a patent essential to IEEE's fast Ethernet standard. Shortly after acquiring the patent, N-Data announced that it would not honor the original patent owner's commitment to license the patent to all implementers for a flat fee of $1,000.[7] The FTC alleged

---

[4] Press Release, World Bus. Council for Sustainable Dev., Hitachi, Ltd. joins Eco-Patent Commons (July 25, 2011).

[5] *E-PC ALL Pledged Patent*, Eco-Patent Commons (May 2011), http://ecopatentcommons.org/sites/default/files/docs/ecopatent-database.pdf.

[6] *Frequently Asked Questions*, Eco-Patent Commons, http://ecopatentcommons.org/frequently-asked-questions#QA19.

[7] Negotiated Data Solutions LLC, No. 051-0094, 2008 WL 4407246, at *4 (F.T.C. Sept. 22, 2008) [hereinafter N-Data Order].

that N-Data's disavowal of the original patent pledge amounted to an unfair method of competition in violation of the FTC Act. The action was settled with N-Data agreeing to honor the original owner's patent pledge.

The issue arose again in 2011, when bankrupt Nortel Networks, a major contributor to many telecommunications and computer networking standards, proposed the sale of its remaining assets, including approximately 4,000 patents, on a "free and clear" basis.[8] Several product vendors, together with IEEE, raised concerns that Nortel's "free and clear" sale could invalidate patent licensing commitments that Nortel had previously made to several SDOs. Ultimately, the purchaser of the patents, a consortium including several large product vendors, agreed to abide by Nortel's prior licensing pledges.

To address the transfer of patent pledges along with underlying patents, an increasing number of SDOs are requiring that purchasers of patents be bound by pledges made by prior owners. This approach has been endorsed almost universally by commentators and regulatory agencies that have considered it.[9] Nevertheless, problems can arise. Patent holders may fail to notify purchasers about long-ago pledges, or may fail to impose adequate contractual provisions binding the purchasers to abide by those pledges. Such contractual commitments may not be enforceable for one reason or another, and the original patent holder may have little incentive, if it is even still in existence, to enforce those provisions against the purchaser.

Moreover, the vast majority of SDOs have not yet implemented such requirements, leaving the enforcement of patent pledges against subsequent owners determined solely as a matter of law. And despite cases such as *N-Data*, which was settled prior to adjudication, it is not clear that either common law or antitrust law definitively bind the acquirer of a patent to honor a pledge made by a previous owner.

---

8 *In re* Nortel Networks Inc., No. 09-10138(KG), 2011 WL 4831218 at *6 (Bankr. D. Del., Jul. 11, 2011). Under Section 363(f) of the U.S. Bankruptcy Code, a bankruptcy trustee or debtor-in-possession may sell the bankruptcy estate's assets "free and clear of any interest in such property." Id. at 9.

9 *See* NAT'L RESEARCH COUNCIL, INTELLECTUAL PROPERTY CHALLENGES FOR STANDARD-SETTING IN THE GLOBAL ECONOMY 93–94 (Keith Maskus & Stephen A. Merrill eds., 2013).

II. CONSIDERATIONS REGARDING A PATENT PLEDGE REGISTRY

As observed by Abraham Bell and Gideon Parchomovsky, registries are "the most common means of conveying information about property rights."[10] Property registration systems increase public information about property rights and thereby enable a wide range of efficient and value-enhancing transactions to occur.[11] Bell and Parchomovsky add to this conventional account two additional functions of property registries: their tendency to frustrate illicit and non-consensual transactions in property and to give true property owners assurances regarding their title, thus enabling them to more fully enjoy their rights.[12] In view of these general benefits, it is worth considering whether the creation of a public registry of patent pledge information could help to address the challenges of notice, permanence, and transfer.

A. The Registration Regime for Patent Transfers and Licenses

Registration systems for real property transfers in the United States are generally traced to the Massachusetts Bay Colony's 1640 Recording Act,[13] though the practice of recording title deeds did not become widespread until the nineteenth century.[14] Title recording systems developed in order to create a public record of title transfers, good against both the parties to a transaction and third parties.[15] Similar title recording systems exist with respect to other forms of valuable personal property including automobiles, aircraft, ships, and even bicycles.[16]

In many jurisdictions, the sale or other transfer of a patent must be recorded in a governmental registry in order to have legal effect.[17]

---

10 Abraham Bell & Gideon Parchomovsky, *Of Property and Information*, __ COLUM. L. REV. __ (2016).

11 Douglas G. Baird & Thomas H. Jackson, *Information, Uncertainty, and the Transfer of Property*, 13 J. LEGAL STUD. 299 (1984).

12 Bell & Parchomovsky, *supra* note 10, at 19–23.

13 R. POWELL & P. ROHAN, 14 POWELL ON REAL PROPERTY § 82.01[1] (Michael Allan Wolf ed., 2015).

14 *See* BENITO ARRUÑADA, INSTITUTIONAL FOUNDATIONS OF IMPERSONAL EXCHANGE: THEORY AND POLICY OF CONTRACTUAL REGISTRIES 55 (2012).

15 Id.

16 *See* THOMAS W. MERRILL & HENRY E. SMITH, PROPERTY: PRINCIPLES AND POLICIES 912–17 (2d ed. 2012); Bell & Parchomovsky, *supra* note 10, at 24–25.

17 JAY DRATLER, JR., LICENSING OF INTELLECTUAL PROPERTY, VOL. 2, § 8.02[1] n.9 (2015 update).

Though the U.S. PTO offers a recording system for patent transfers, recording of a patent transfer is not required in order to make the transfer valid. Instead, the U.S. recording system for patent transfers is similar to so-called "notice" recording statutes for real estate, in which recording protects a purchaser against a subsequent purchaser of the same patent.[18] Section 261 of the Patent Act provides that: "an assignment, grant or conveyance shall be void as against any subsequent purchaser or mortgagee for a valuable consideration, without notice, unless it is recorded in the Patent and Trademark Office within three months from its date or prior to the date of such subsequent purchase or mortgage."[19]

The statute thus encourages recordation of patent transfers by making unrecorded transfers vulnerable to supersedure by subsequent transfers made without notice of the prior transfer. Nevertheless, because the recording of patent transfers remains voluntary in the U.S., many patent transfers go unrecorded, creating a level of ambiguity regarding the ownership of patents.

Like patent transfers, licenses of patent rights may be recorded at the PTO. However, unlike transfers, patent licenses need not be recorded in order to prevail against subsequent competing licenses.[20] Whereas an unrecorded patent transfer may not be recognized if the patent holder later transfers the patent to a buyer that lacks notice of the prior transfer, an unrecorded patent license *will* be recognized even if a later license is purported to be granted.[21] Accordingly, there are few reasons to record patent licenses, and doing so may actually disadvantage the parties to the license by disclosing confidential information contained in the license. Consequently, it is likely that only a small percentage of patent licenses are actually recorded at the PTO.

Against this backdrop, it may seem that recording patent pledges, which fall even below patent licenses in terms of formality and definiteness, would be inadvisable or, at best, of little value. However, such recording could have significant positive benefits.

---

18 *See* MERRILL & SMITH, *supra* note 16, at 916.

19 35 U.S.C. § 261 (2012).

20 *See* David J. Dykeman & Daniel W. Kopko, *Recording Patent License Agreements in the USPTO*, INTELL. PROP. TODAY, Aug. 2004, at 18, 18; DRATLER, *supra* note 17, § 8.02[1].

21 Dykeman & Kopko, *supra* note 20, at 18 n.7.

B. Potential Benefits of a Patent Pledge Registry

A centralized and comprehensive public patent pledge registry would address many of the notice issues raised by patent pledges. First, the recording of pledges in a public registry would provide broad and accessible notice of pledges when they are made. Although some SDOs already maintain registries of patent pledges, these registries relate solely to the SDO's standards and are not generally linked to or searchable with other SDOs' records. Moreover, many SDO registries are accessible only by SDO members, limiting their usefulness to the broader market. And, most importantly, there is no consolidated public record of patent pledges outside these few SDOs. The existence of a single, trusted public pledge repository could reduce the burden on SDOs to maintain public databases of their own, and would have the added benefit of imposing a needed level of consistency and convenience on disclosures that are today scattered across multiple websites and presented in a wide range of incompatible formats.

Second, a public registry of patent pledges could strengthen legal arguments regarding the reliance of intended beneficiaries on pledges. Under the U.S. Copyright Act, recording the transfer or exclusive license of a copyright "gives all persons constructive notice of the facts stated in the recorded document."[22] While no corresponding provision exists in the U.S. Patent Act, it is arguable, certainly by analogy to copyright law and many examples from the common law of real property conveyancing,[23] that third parties operating in the relevant marketplace should be aware of pledges when they are registered.

Third, a registry of patent pledges would preserve the content of pledges against subsequent alteration and disappearance. As previously discussed, patent pledges can be altered or taken down by the patent holder with ease and very few repercussions. A permanent public registry of patent pledges would create a historical record showing when pledges were made and on what terms.

Finally, a recording system could reliably notify patent acquirers of pledges made with respect to the patents they are acquiring, improving the odds that pledges will be honored by subsequent patent owners in the

---

[22] 17 U.S.C. § 205(c) (2012). *See also* DRATLER, *supra* note 17, § 8.02[2] n.17.

[23] *See*, e.g., MERRILL & SMITH, *supra* note 16, at 917.

first instance (i.e., without litigation), and increasing the odds, should litigation occur, that the subsequent owner will be required to honor the pledge.[24]

C. Promoting the Use of a Patent Pledge Registry

The public registry proposed above would be of little value if firms failed to use it to register their patent pledges. There are three usage regimes that could be implemented with respect to such a registry system: (1) an entirely voluntary system, (2) a mandatory system, and (3) a voluntary system with incentives to participate.

1. Voluntary registration

An entirely voluntary registration system, though probably easiest to implement, is not likely to yield significant benefits. As noted above, the PTO's current voluntary registration system for patent licenses is seldom used. Likewise, other voluntary disclosure/registration systems relating to patent pledges have had mixed success. On one hand, the Internet Engineering Task Force permits voluntary disclosure of patent licensing terms, with hundreds of pledges reported in its online database.[25] On the other hand, both the Institute of Electrical and Electronics Engineers and European Telecommunications offer participants a means for voluntarily disclosing licensing terms such as maximum royalty rates, but only a handful of firms have made disclosures over the past several years.[26] There are several possible reasons that firms fail to take advantage of voluntary registration systems: there is an inherent cost associated with marshaling, submitting, and managing registrations; firms may prefer, for competitive reasons, to keep as much information as possible regarding their patents confidential; and firms may fail to recognize value in participating in a registration system. Accordingly, it is not likely that a purely voluntary registration system would yield significant benefits.

2. Mandatory registration

Reporting systems that are governmentally mandated present numerous issues of implementation, administration, and enforcement. Such systems

---

[24] Bell & Parchomovsky, *supra* note 10, at 10.

[25] *See* IETF DATATRACKER, https://datatracker.ietf.org; Jorge L. Contreras, *Technical Standards and Ex Ante Disclosure: Results and Analysis of an Empirical Study*, 53 JURIMETRICS 163, 182–83 (2013) [hereinafter Contreras, *Ex Ante*].

[26] Contreras, *Ex Ante*, *supra* note 25, at 206 n.134.

require a motivated agency with adequate funding and authority to oversee the development and operation of the system and then to police compliance on an ongoing basis. Moreover, mandating registration of patent pledges would necessitate the development of clear rules delineating which pledges must be registered. While none of these obstacles is insurmountable, it seems that mandating the registration of patent pledges at a governmental level might not be optimal.

Registration of pledges in a public registry could, however, be mandated by SDOs and other private organizations. Imposing a registration obligation at the SDO level would have both advantages and disadvantages. A principal advantage of SDO-mandated registration includes the relative ease of defining which pledges to register (i.e., all pledges made with respect to the SDO's standards). In fact, many SDOs already require the registration and publication of pledges made with respect to SDO standards. Moving from a plethora of individual SDO repositories to a single, centrally managed public repository would represent a change in format, but not in the basic registration requirements that already exist at these SDOs.

There are, however, disadvantages in relying on SDOs to mandate the registration of patent pledges. First, SDOs generally operate by consensus voting, and to the extent that certain SDO members opposed a registration requirement (e.g., in order to facilitate the alteration or retraction of their pledges), the requirement might not be approved. Moreover, patent pledges made within the context of SDOs represent only a fraction of the pledges being made in the market, and a system that fails to address the large body of non-SDO pledges will remain substantially incomplete.

3. Voluntary registration with encouragement

Given the weakness of both voluntary and mandatory registration systems, it is possible that the optimal means for establishing a useful and complete patent pledge registration system is through a voluntary public repository, the use of which is encouraged by affirmative governmental incentives. Such incentives might include lessening antitrust penalties for allegedly anticompetitive conduct involving pledged patents, similar to the relief from antitrust liability offered to joint ventures under the National Cooperative Research and Production Act (NCRPA).[27] For example, firms engaged in standard-setting have been charged with violations of Section 2 of the Sherman Act for allegedly engaging in

[27] 15 U.S.C. §§ 4301–06 (2012).

exclusionary conduct through deception regarding their patents. Similar claims have been brought under Section 5 of the FTC Act, which prohibits unfair methods of competition. If a patent holder made and registered a pledge to grant licenses on FRAND terms, it could be immunized from these deception-based antitrust claims, while still facing potential liability under estoppel, contract, and other theories. The rationale for eliminating these deception-based claims in such cases is straightforward: the public registration of patent pledges improves public notice of pledges, lessening patent holder opportunities for deception.

D. Designing the Registry

Any public registry of patent pledges would require careful planning and design. The Patent Pledge Database[28] is a first step in this direction. It was created in order to provide a publicly accessible and stable repository of patent pledges. The database contains a PDF image of each patent pledge, made at the time the pledge was entered into the database, which provides some proof against subsequent changes.[29] This repository, however, only contains pledges that have been identified by the curators and other volunteers, and does not permit self-registration of pledges by patent holders. As such, it cannot claim to be definitive or comprehensive.

A preferable arrangement might be a truly public repository maintained by a governmental agency or a non-governmental organization (NGO). Such a repository should be open to all patent pledges and permit registration by patent holders. If the repository were hosted by a national patent office or offices, pledges could be linked directly to patent records, making them convenient to locate and providing notice to anyone reviewing the relevant patent records. The U.S. Patent and Trademark Office (PTO) and European Patent Office (EPO) already have searchable electronic databases, which could conceivably be modified to accommodate pledge information with a reasonable amount of effort. Moreover, both the PTO and EPO have already initiated programs of cooperation with leading SDOs to coordinate their efforts, including by incorporating

---

[28] Program on Info. Justice & Intell. Prop. – Am. Univ. Wash. Coll. L., Non-SDO Patent Statements and Commitments, http://www.pijip.org/non-sdo-patent-commitments/.

[29] In the six years that the Patent Pledge Database has been operational, it has already served to preserve numerous "disappearing" pledges. *See* id.

more standards-related information into existing prior art databases.[30] As a result, patent offices such as these would be logical agencies to host and maintain such public pledge repositories.

A key question to consider in the design of a public registry is the kind and quantity of information to include in it.[31] A public repository of patent pledges should, at a minimum, include information regarding the maker of the pledge, the patent(s) affected, and the features of the pledge itself. As far as format, patent holders should probably be permitted to describe their patent pledges in a manner of their choosing, but should also include some form of classification system to enable efficient searching and analysis of large numbers of recorded pledges.

Once a pledge is registered, it should be date-stamped and "frozen" to avoid ambiguity regarding its scope at the time made. Of course, if a patent holder later wishes to change or retract such a pledge, the registry should not prohibit it from doing so, provided that such changes and retractions are similarly date-stamped and recorded, and all prior versions of the pledge remain publicly accessible.

CONCLUSION

In order best to avoid the pitfalls of obscurity, impermanence, and transfer that may affect pledges made in today's environment, the establishment of a government-managed registry of patent pledges is recommended. While governmental mandating of registration presents numerous administrative and legal issues, and mandating registration by SDOs would address only a subset of the pledges being made, a voluntary registration system coupled with governmental incentives to registration could achieve significant beneficial results.

---

[30] *See* NAT'L RESEARCH COUNCIL, INTELLECTUAL PROPERTY CHALLENGES FOR STANDARD-SETTING IN THE GLOBAL ECONOMY 32 (Keith Maskus & Stephen A. Merrill eds., 2013).

[31] Bell & Parchomovsky, *supra* note 10, at 47–48.

19. Overcoming information asymmetry in patent pledge records

Nicole Shanahan

I. INTRODUCTION

There are several obstacles to overcome before patent pledges can achieve the most benefits within the larger context of a patent ecosystem that is characterized by a lack of transparency and information asymmetry. While the patent office is required by Congress to publish patents, understanding the content of a patent application still requires expert analysis. Furthermore, how the patented technology relates to the commercial goals of the patent holder is nearly always unknown. Some patent holders may wish to open access to their technology, but communicating this information to those who would benefit from it in a timely way remains a challenge.

The way patent pledges are publicized and made available today is not effective in reaching an optimal level of distribution of the underlying open access contained in these pledges. Additionally, the value of informal media pronouncements are, from a legal perspective, minimally understood.

II. WHAT WE NEED TO UNDERSTAND ABOUT PATENT PLEDGES

As discussed in Chapter 1, patent pledges often take the form of press or website announcements by patent holders that they will not enforce their patents under certain conditions. But in order to be most useful, and to achieve the greatest degree of legal enforceability and recognition, the intended market audiences for patent pledges must be informed about the details of these pledges.

Thus, in addition to bibliographic information concerning pledged patents (such as patent numbers, titles, application numbers, assignees, etc.), it is useful to understand the content of the patents for each respective pledge. This means understanding the practical use and application of patents based on claim language, a task that has been historically challenging due to the limitations of existing patent search technology.[1] However as the technical patent community progresses on its research in data structuring and relevancy metrics, the future of automated analysis will be more promising, as will the process that goes into mapping those patents to relevant commercial and research entities.

In the meantime, and without the benefit of readily available automation tools, manually listing pledges for browsing on the Internet is currently possible via basic keyword searching over a database table published to a public website. To date, Jorge Contreras and his researchers have provided the most comprehensive database of patent pledges.[2] At the current time, however, this database remains limited in what information is made available from the patent holders, and no database contains a real-time record of the applicable patent numbers. This means that, even though a pledge is made, the larger community must put forth the expenditure on expert hours to understand the relevance of the pledged patents. It generally requires a sophisticated party to conduct a thorough analysis of the contents of the pledged portfolios and make the determination whether the patents are useful for a particular application.

As discussed in Chapter 18, other proposals have been made regarding a more centralized, official registry of patent pledges. However, in order for any compilation of patent pledges to be most useful, it must offer more information than is currently available and provide means by which searches and other data gathering can be conducted efficiently and effectively. Improvements to the economics of acquiring patent rights can dramatically shift how individuals and companies interact with intellectual property. This is where designing a private ordering software system will become most useful: technology is the ultimate transaction cost economizer. The following section proposes informational fields designed to improve the information exchanged between patent pledge makers and the innovation sector.

---

[1] Ravi Mohan, *Analysis of the Entire Market Value Rule in Complex Technology Litigation: Arduous Royalty Base Determinations, Unjust Damage Rewards, and Empirical Approaches to Measuring Consumer Demand*, 27 SANTA CLARA COMPUTER & HIGH TECH. L.J. 639, 643 (2011).

[2] *Non-SDO Patent Statements and Commitments*, PROGRAM ON INFORMATION JUSTICE AND INTELLECTUAL PROPERTY, http://www.pijip.org/non-sdo-patent-commitments/.

A. Managing Relevant Metadata

Provided below is a suggested list of fields that patent holders contributing to a patent pledge database should publish in order to optimize the pledged IP's reach and use. The fields can be integrated from a variety of sources, ranging from government databases, subject matter annotations, patent portfolio management systems, and analytic systems.

1. Data that is accessed via URL links or API integration

The following data already exists in our current IT ecosystem and is actively being maintained by governments as well as companies that have a proprietary interest in these datasets such as Thomson Reuters and LexisNexis.

- USPTO (United States Patent and Trademark Office) PAIR bibliographic data
- Image file wrapper
- Transaction history
- Patent family tree
- Contact information for pledging party
- Assignee information

2. Data inputs from pledging party or subject matter experts

- Commercial summary of the invention (i.e. a 500-word abstract of the technology)
- List of parties that may receive benefits (or detailed description of the recipient group, i.e. "companies with less than 20 employees")
- Type of pledge (non-assertion, RAND, maximum royalty rate, and so on)
- Limitations to use, if any
- Duration of the pledge
- Any reporting requirements of the beneficiary of the pledge

3. Data inputs via big data analytics

The following data is largely machine maintained and produced. The machines generate algorithmic analysis of data using approaches such as natural language processing with latent semantic analysis and latent Dirichlet allocation, which are methods for extracting the meaning and representation of words using statistical computations, or logical rule-based processing, which uses declarative semantics and structured data to solve questions. These methods are used by artificial intelligence developers to solve higher order intellectual tasks.

- Semantic search of the patent database to provide a patent landscape analysis
- Patent validity ratings (i.e. algorithms that utilize several metrics to determine if a patent is "strong" or "weak")
- Mapping of patent claims to relevant products and services
- Claims analysis

Public availability of even a small subset of the above data would be a large improvement over the current pledge environment, which rarely includes even a patent application number.

B. Creating a Consistent Patent Ontology

Since the 1990s the software community has been working to overcome technical problems that stand in the way of shared, reusable knowledge-based software.[3] Core among these problems is the inconsistent representation of information. For example, an individual's name represented in the following formats will cause a software program to treat each entry as a unique individual when in fact the names all refer to a single individual:

John Smith
Smith, John
J. Smith
Smith, J.

The United States Patent and Trademark Office (USPTO) has been impacted by this very problem as it relates to the names of inventors. Searching the government's patent database by first and last name can often result in over-representation, by including others with a similar name, or under-representation, if the searched format of the name differs from the invention record. This problem of disambiguating inventor names has persisted into today, and in September 2015 the USPTO hosted a technical workshop to solicit a solution from six research teams who each presented a computational approach to defining and implementing unique identifiers.[4]

---

[3] Thomas R. Gruber, *Toward Principles for the Design of Ontologies Used for Knowledge Sharing*, 43 INT. J. HUMAN-COMPUTER STUDIES, 907, 907–28 (1995).

[4] The six teams represented were: the Centre for Transformative Innovation (CTI) at Swinburne University of Technology, InnovationPulse, Institute of

This is why database ontologies are not only useful for the patent system, but necessary if the patent system is to evolve. Database ontologies are used to logically organize information for distributed digital consumption. A computational ontology is an explicit representation of information. The term is borrowed from philosophy, where an Ontology is a systematic account of existence.[5] In modern times, database ontologies have played an important role in the evolution of automation and server-to-server communications. It is a tool for connecting distributed parties who may not know one another, but are engaged in the active exchange of information.

One good example of such improvements is the effect that the Gene Ontology has had in transforming the field of gene sequencing. Prior to the Gene Ontology, different molecular biology databases were using different naming conventions to describe important information about gene products. The discrepancies posed a large barrier to integrating the databases, which was the single largest obstacle to comparative genomic studies. The Gene Ontology was revolutionary within bioinformatics because it provided a controlled vocabulary that could be used to annotate database entries, allowing, for the first time, the databases to be combined to perform large-scale comparisons.[6]

For the patent system, such an industry-wide mapping of patent information to an ontological structure would be transformative and enable computer-readable formats to pass between parties, and expedite both the patenting process with the government, as well as the private ordering of patent rights. The uses would be expansive, from the early research and development of new ideas (i.e. mapping an inventor disclosure document to the government patent databases to return a qualified list of claims, which are pre-annotated), to searching for and identifying relevant patent pledges that would assist an organization to make valuable budgetary decisions on whether or not to invest in a specific product or service. The patent ontology would also assist in the transmission of information between the software systems of private parties who wish to engage in the private ordering of patent rights, such

---

Scientific and Technical Information of China (ISTIC), KU Leuven, University of Massachusetts at Amherst IESL, and Penn State University.

5 Gruber, *supra* note 3, at 908.

6 MIHAIL POPESCU & DONG XU, DATA MINING IN BIOMEDICINE USING ONTOLOGIES 10–12 (1st ed., 2009); Jorge L. Contreras, *Technical Standards and Bioinformatics*, in BIOINFORMATICS LAW: LEGAL ISSUES FOR COMPUTATIONAL BIOLOGY IN THE POST-GENOME ERA (Jorge L. Contreras & A. James Cuticchia, eds., 2013).

as cross-licenses, pledges, and patent pools. The ease, speed, and cost of patent rights distribution will drop if software is able to organize the core elements of each arrangement including the transmission of patent files, claim charts, existing encumbrances, key contractual terms, and the like.

C. Incentivizing Engagement and Monetizing the Exchange of Information

The question many pose is who should manage pledge data. Should it be the government? A private organization? An exchange? The reality is that the future of information technology may not require any single party to serve as the central holder of all the data. Instead, the future's computer networks will allow parties to treat information as a utility or commodity, thereby placing more value on the bits of information exchanged over bytes of bulk data.

The easy and incremental transaction of information matters because storing and maintaining high quality information is expensive. Today, datasets are currently sold in bulk to meet economies of scale. The patent system suffers from the same misalignment of economic incentives that has been holding back the Open Data movement for over a decade.[7] Engaging parties to open up their data to the public is virtually impossible without the correct financial motivators. The financial motivators for public access to proprietary data cannot exist if low-cost infrastructure for data transmission does not exist.

This brings us to an area of computer science research that has been theoretical until recent years, and is now possible due to decreases in the cost of data storage (Kryder's Law) and increases in computing speed (Moore's Law).[8] Kryder's Law considers the ongoing evolution of magnetic disk storage, and highlights the significance of the 50-million-fold increase of storage capacity occurring between 1956 and 2005.[9] The compressing of digital bits into ever-smaller storage devices (both magnetic and electronic) permits tools such as GPS software to exist in cars and phones, and allows developers to create and manage increasingly large of amounts of data affordably. The sister theory to Kryder's Law is Moore's Law, which contemplates the relationship between

---

7 *See*, e.g., Kevin Desouza & Kendra Smith, *Big Data for Social Innovation*, STAN. SOC. INNOVATION REV. (Summer 2014).

8 *See* Daniel Martin Katz, *Quantitative Legal Prediction—or—How I Learned to Stop Worrying and Start Preparing for the Data-Driven Future of the Legal Services Industry*, 62 EMORY L.J. 909, 913–15 (2013).

9 Chip Walter, *Kryder's Law*, SCI. AM. (Aug. 2005), at 32–33.

computer processing speed and the evolution of transistors. Moore's Law has evolved with the evolution of the semiconductor industry, and over the past 50 years meant the doubling of transistors (per die area) every two years.[10] Such doubling has allowed computers to perform more powerfully and more efficiently at lower costs. This means that computers can run programs with evermore sophistication, thereby completing increasingly rigorous tasks.

Thanks to this progress, web-based knowledge integration can achieve impressive results. This means that the ability to integrate a plurality of data sources over the web to produce new information products is economically and technically feasible. Most importantly, opening data for integration costs less to the database owner than it has ever before and they can more efficiently monetize information due to the speed and sophistication of web-based tools. Systems that allow, for example, the analytical processing of Hoover's data, a McKinsey report, and USPTO data to determine the commercial value of patents are technically plausible. Posting a patent pledge to a website could trigger the automatic production of a summary of the pledged assets, and inform relevant companies of the existence of that pledge. In today's paradigm, this might still require purchasing entire data sets from each data entity. However, in the future we can achieve this integration via a web-platform that permits the combining and analysing of specific parts of each dataset to produce higher levels of intelligence and users pay for the incremental use of just those parts as if consuming an information utility.

Advances in information technology can be utilized in achieving both the legal goals (i.e. 35 U.S.C. Sections 101, 102, and 103) and social goals (access to innovation) of the patent system. As a group from MIT and Harvard recently noted in a variant of Lessig's famous observation that "code is law," law is also code.[11] Software engineers are perpetually solving challenges related to complex collections of "instructions, directives, and conditional statements."[12] Like modern-day software engineering, our patent system involves the complex integration of rules emanating from a variety of sources. The *Manual of Patent Examining Procedure* currently contains nearly 2000 pages of substantive and

---

[10] Ethan Mollick, *Establishing Moore's Law*, 28 IEEE ANNALS OF THE HIST. OF COMPUTING 62, 62–75 (2006).

[11] William P. Li, Pablo Azar, David Larochelle, Phil Hill, and Andrew W. Lo, *Law Is Code: A Software Engineering Approach to Analyzing the United States Code* (Sept. 21, 2014).

[12] Id.

procedural requirements.[13] The government's many policy objectives often run in parallel and need to be prioritized, for example, "the promotion of innovation" and the "the regulation of frivolous lawsuits" can produce conflicting law in the eyes of the public. The Supreme Court produces laws that the federal courts interpret, producing an ensemble of complexity. However, applying software and database approaches to complex legal questions is possible and is occurring today.[14] It is proposed here as a method for solving informational issues relating to patent rights ordering.

While some datasets are readily available via the USPTO, economic or legal incentives are required for the patent holder to create, maintain, and provide that information. The economic impetus for producing structured, digital information will likely fall to existing business models relating to patent transactions, such as transactional attorney services, as well as third party intermediaries that perform brokerage and aggregator services. One piece of evidence supporting this theory is RPX Corporation's (a well-known patent aggregator) purchase of e-discovery company Inventus Solutions Inc. to assist its member companies in defending against lawsuits,[15] as well as the growing use of and demand for tools such as Lex Machina, which help law firms and companies analyse patent litigation trends.[16] In addition to private sector information providers, the government also plays an important role in making its own data more accessible, such as providing patent contents in machine readable formats, and correcting schema impediments impacting inventor disambiguation, classifications, and assignments.

D. Integrating Pledge Databases into Existing Search Tools

Bringing down the cost and barriers involved in communicating what is in a patent pledge, for example identifying the patents that have been pledged, will be key to the efficacy of pledges. One way to accomplish

---

13 THE MANUAL OF PATENTING PROCEDURE (MPEP) (9th ed., rev. July 2015), last revised Nov. 2015.

14 Id. *See also*, Frank J. Cavaliere, *Web-Wise Lawyer*, PRAC. LAW. (April 2016); Tom Bolt, *Tomorrow's Law Practice: Using Technology to Build Bridges*, LAW PRAC. (March/April 2016); Joshua Poje, *Understanding—and Balancing—Technology as a Tool*, LAW PRAC. (March/April 2016); *see also*, Tom Bolt, *Tomorrow's Law Practice: Using Technology to Build Bridges*, LAW PRAC. (March/April 2016).

15 Josh Beckerman, *Patent Clearinghouse RPX to Buy Discovery Management Provider Inventus*, WALL ST. J. (Dec. 15, 2015).

16 *About Us*, LEX MACHINA, https://lexmachina.com/about/.

these goals is by conducting a semantic relevancy patent search limited to the claims of patents that have been pledged. For example, Innography provides a front end to a database that users can input a large block of descriptive text.[17] See Figure 19.1 for an example of searching a block of text taken directly from the IEEE 802.22-2011 Standard for Wireless Regional Area Networks in TV Whitespaces materials.[18] The "semantic" search option is selected (versus "keyword" search, which is limited to individual words. The semantic search processes strings of text for their linguistic meaning).

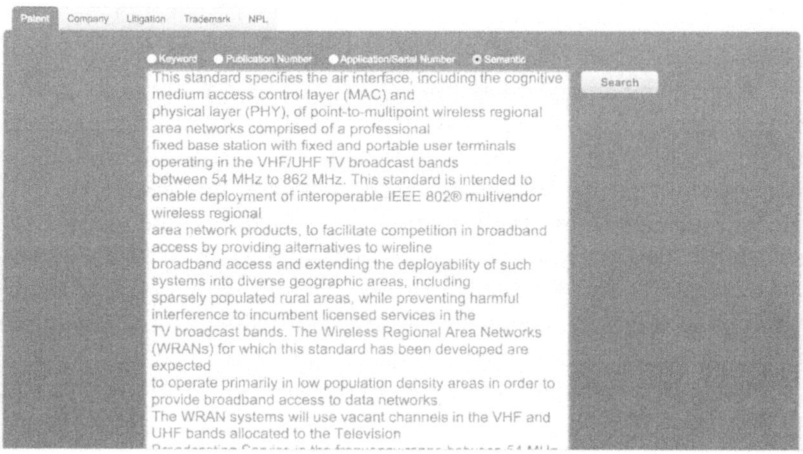

Figure 19.1

The ability to conduct this search and limit (filter) the results to patents with open-innovation characteristics would be immediately helpful to companies that are seeking to innovate in spaces with more relaxed patenting coverage (i.e. where companies operating in the space have made patent pledges). See Figure 19.2 for a proposed additional filter to the semantic search in the Innography interface.

---

[17] In 2010 Innography, a patent search tool, formed a strategic partnership with TextWise, the first commercial search system based primarily on natural language processing. *See* Kristen Whitman, *Innography: A Source for International Litigation Data*, INTELLOGIST (Nov. 17, 2010); *see also, History*, TEXTWISE, http://textwise.com/history.

[18] *Get IEEE 802®: Local and Metropolitan Area Network Standards*, IEEE STANDARD ASSOCIATION, http://standards.ieee.org/getieee802/download/802.22-2011.pdf.

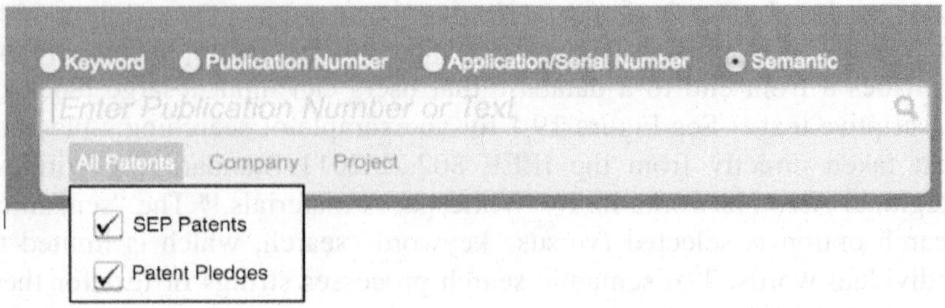

Figure 19.2

Parties interested in maximizing their access to IP should make patent pledge searching a regular habit of their IP strategy. There is no downside in understanding the value of available pledged patents, and the upside can be significant to product improvements and research and development (R&D) strategy. Whereas a patent generally inhibits the use of the patented invention by third parties—and therefore the need of the unlicensed third party to develop a work around or seek a license—a patent pledge signals the opposite: it is an opportunity and even an invitation to make commercial use of the patented invention. It also sends signals on where parties should be budgeting within their IP portfolio. If a company is spending a large budget on arguing the novelty of a patent application in prosecution, a patent pledge may signal to the company it need not invest in responding to rejected claims language.

Given the strategic value of patent pledges to users of patent search tools, there is commercial value for vendors of these systems to invest in maintaining the pledge data. The issue remains, however, that collecting the data requires either the cooperation of the pledging party to supply the information, or a third party committed to collecting and maintaining that information.

III. PROPOSED TECHNICAL METHODS FOR FORMALIZING PATENT PLEDGES

Today, lawyers, brokers, and non-practicing entities are responsible for the lion's share of information exchange in the marketplace for patent assets. Lawyers assist parties in the negotiation of patent transactions,[19]

[19] William F. Lee & A. Douglas Melamed, *Breaking the Vicious Cycle of Patent Damages*, 101 CORNELL L. REV. 385, 412 (2016) ("There is also broad

the preparation of claim charts, and patent validity analysis. Non-practicing entities often send cease and desist letters and settlement offers to collect license fees. Brokers prepare packages to encourage the purchase of patent and technology assets. These communications largely exist behind closed doors, and often do not have the benefit of pricing transparency or analytics to guide decisions.

While a handful of parties have attempted to create marketplaces for the bid and buy of patent licenses,[20] no single technology platform has successfully scaled this process. So long as a formalized technology fails to scale, the service intermediaries will continue to control transaction costs. As Professor Ron Gilson noted in his 1984 paper "Lawyers as Transaction Cost Engineers": "In a world in which assets are priced according to any version of capital asset pricing theory, there is little role for business lawyers."[21] It follows that if patent rights are priced accurately, based on such accepted metrics as patent validity, patent strength, and scope, there would be little need for patent intermediaries to debate fees, nor would there be a need to use the legal system to establish (or disprove) patent infringement. Ultimately, the goal of many patent holders is to establish a patent sale or license agreement. How they arrive at that goal today is complicated by a lack of transparency into key decision-making criteria.

This section contains proposals for two technical platforms to address three core parts of private ordering of patent pledge information: information exchange, transaction negotiation, and management overhead. Core to both proposals is an emphasis on the private ordering, or demarcation, of patent rights by the parties who participate.

---

agreement that a sound way of assessing the market value of the patented technology is to imagine a hypothetical ex ante negotiation between a willing licensee and a willing licensor—provided that the hypothetical negotiation framework is carefully and properly applied").

[20] *See* Jorge L. Contreras, *FRAND Market Failure: IPXI's Standards-Essential Patent License Exchange*, 15 CHI-KENT J. INTELL. PROP. 419, 419 (2016).

[21] Ronald J. Gilson, *Lawyers as Transaction Cost Engineers* (John M. Olin Program in Law and Economics Working Paper No. 147, 1997).

A. Recordation Techniques

1. Recordation of pledges from existing patent management tools: prosecution docketing, data management systems, invention disclosure repositories, and contract management

In-house legal departments and law firms have a variety of back office IT systems that help them manage and maintain the status of patents under management. These include systems that enable docketing, workflow, and contract management. Each of these systems could be enabled to provide an informational output for publicizing patent pledges.

For in-house departments, a docketing system, for example, could include an extension from a cloud-based management platform to the public via a public-facing URL. The interface would allow the in-house department to identify the assets they wish to pledge, construct a pledge information page for the specified patent numbers, insert the associated patent serial numbers, and publish the page or share it widely with a click of the button.

Figure 19.3 shows one such example of an interface developed by the author during a research fellowship at CodeX, the Stanford Center for Legal Informatics. In this example, a pledge is made for a portfolio that relates to flash memory controller technology.[22]

The metadata collected for such pledges can be used to connect the pledged assets to companies, sectors, open source blogs, and any other web community that might find the asset valuable for R&D, analytics, and business opportunity. Parties can manage a variety of pledges and disseminate that information widely using a platform that informs on both the details of the pledge, the related patent records and attach supporting files that are relevant to the technology.

2. Decentralized consensus technologies: block chain and the dawning of decentralized consensus protocols

Block chain is a protocol technology that has gained popularity with Bitcoin, a cryptocurrency whose highest market cap was $12.7B in January of 2014.[23] Block chain provides for the decentralized exchange of files, which can represent anything, from currency to contracts (and even marriages!). In a perfect block chain system, no central authority acts as an administrator for transactions. The community has provided

---

[22] CLEARACCESSIP, www.clearaccessip.com.

[23] *Market Capitalization*, BLOCKCHAIN.INFO, https://blockchain.info/charts/market-cap.

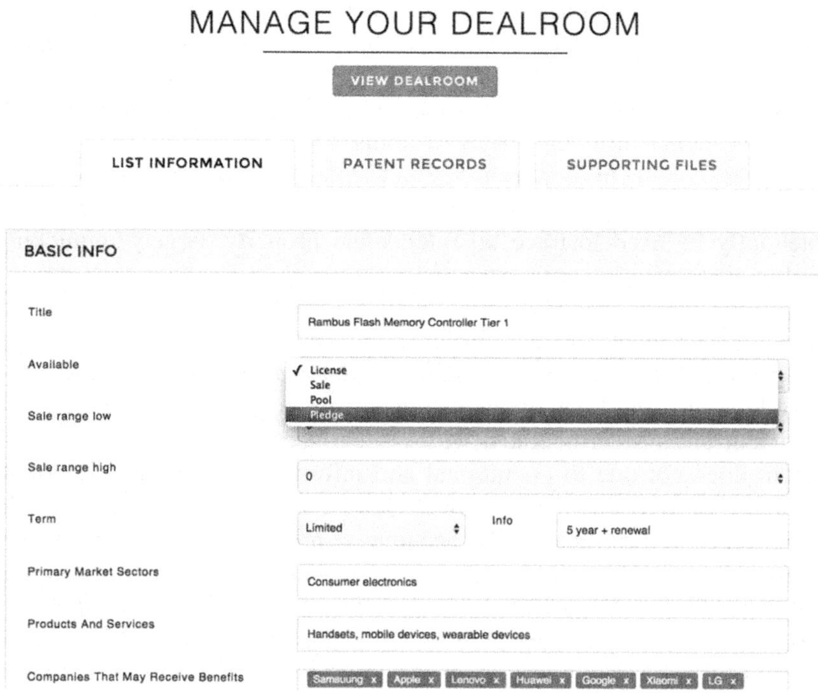

Figure 19.3

incentives for any party to perform a sequence of computations that validate the trustworthiness of each submitted transaction. This is known as Bitcoin mining.

In short, the block chain is a linked list of blocks of data.[24] It is a truncated method to achieve the integration of disjointed pieces of information. The method both communicates and validates the existence of all mutual parts and parties to the ledger, such that, for example, contributions from parties A-B can be validated by interested party D-F. There have already been talks within the cryptocurrency community of adapting block chain and decentralized consensus technology to intellectual property.[25] The motivation is to move away from the one-size-fits-all

[24] Interview with Jeremy Rubin, MIT Digital Currency Initiative (Sept. 17, 2015).

[25] *See*, e.g., Ben Guarino, *Next Generation Blockchain Applications Go Well Beyond Bitcoin*, INVERSE (Oct. 14, 2015) ("Patent protection without the public

patent system, to a robust system of recordation that can adapt and work with greater transparency, accuracy, and trust. The patent community currently operates in informational silos: patent prosecutors and examiners must both achieve the same objective under our statutory system but use significantly different means of doing so.

It does not seem unreasonably difficult to adapt the block chain protocol to record patent pledges. Taken further, the block chain could potentially be used to trace all intellectual property, largely mimicking the functions of a government patent system.

In some ways, the data infrastructure for this already exists in our current governmental patent systems. Information disclosure statements and prior art searches, for example, produce huge trees of knowledge about how one set of patent claims relates to other sets of relevant claims. If our current system operated with perfect accuracy (our current patent system does not due to operational and informational limitations), there would be no overlap of truly novel claims. The patented claims would string together and we could accurately map innovation within any industry in a time continuum of invention. Patent families would represent their structures in real-time, and all parties would have transparency into who owns what. It may also be possible to tie the existing patent system into a separate block chain system of proving novelty that is more robust than our current PTO examiner-applicant system. Ethereum's technology, for instance, could be used to define "prior art" by providing an accurate chronological ledger of the recordation of inventions. Individuals seeking to publish their invention as they create it could do so by using Ethereum, which is a distributed ledger technology that allows conditions to be embedded into the software code forming the ledger.[26] The invention would receive a unique hash embedded with the details of the invention.

---

patent: Proof of Existence is a service that, for a small Bitcoin fee, offers a blockchain-based proof that you, in fact, owned a document at a specific time. If you wanted to have retroactive evidence of an idea you created, you could point to the blockchain to show it was yours first").

26 *See* Michael Abramowicz, *Cryptoinsurance*, 50 WAKE FOREST L. REV. 671, 682 (2015) ("For example, Ethereum could be used to facilitate gambling contracts; so long as the code can determine the winner of a bet, it can ensure that winners are compensated. The founders of Ethereum have also argued that it could facilitate 'smart contracts,' with payments mechanistically determined by computer code"). *See also,* Guarino, *supra* note 25.

Take another recent development at Stanford Computer Science by Professor David Mazières. Mazières has developed "The Stellar Consensus Protocol" (hereinafter "SCP") which possesses four key properties: Decentralized Control, Low Latency, Flexible Trust, and Asymtotic Security.[27] The SCP is designed to reduce fraud, speed up consensus, and ensure security of information. The system also costs very little to run, and requires less computation compared to the block chain (which means less energy use—one of the largest pitfalls of Bitcoin). When compared to our current system of communicating patent data, an SCP operated system would be an improvement to transparency, access, control, and validation.

The SCP could be applied within and outside of national patent offices with similar effects. SCP requires the identification of trusted parties who then hold slots within the network. Each network forms a quorum. Nodes (programmatic pathways) then exchange messages asserting statements about the slots. For example, a slot could be allocated for Examiner Smith in Art Unit number 3301. The Art Unit would make one unique quorum, consisting of all examiners within Art Unit 3301. When a node hears a sufficient (i.e. a majority) set of nodes assert a statement, it assumes no other functioning node will ever contradict that statement. In this example, if a majority of examiners submit that a claim is valid, the system will automatically record the issuance of a patent. The process of examination could be dispersed between many examiners rather than resting on the responsibility of one examiner. The distribution of the examination process could be implemented by a "knowledge network engine" that places the application under review by the top 10% of all examiners with a background in the art unit (thus forming the requisite quorum.) The examiners could receive a computer-generated summary of the application, and assert based on their knowledge (and perhaps a machine-generated search report), whether or not they believe the application to be valid. Over time, this system would improve patent quality because the number of qualified examiners making decisions on patentability will increase manifold. The system is also scalable due to increases in operational efficiency provided by analytics and workflow software.

---

[27] David Mazières, *The Stellar Consensus Protocol: A Federated Model for Internet-Level Consensus* (Stellar Development Foundation, Working Paper, Apr. 2015). *See also* Henry Corrigan-Gibbs, Dan Boneh & David Mazières, *Riposte: An Anonymous Messaging System Handling Millions of Users*, in PROCEEDINGS OF THE 36TH IEEE SYMPOSIUM ON SECURITY AND PRIVACY 321–38 (2015).

In the patent pledge context, a block chain ledger could also provide a system for recording the existence of patent pledges. Today, patent pledges at best can be tied back to a website owned by a domain holder. However, if the website is taken down, or its contents retracted, the parties relying on the existence of that pledge may not have a way to prove their reliance. The block chain solves this issue, because a copy of the ledger is downloaded by all parties contributing to it. Any new party making a pledge would be making a pledge to a block chain containing all prior pledges. The ledger would be saved on a variety of servers (i.e. distributed), and those parties holding the ledger would each have indisputable proof of the existence of the pledge.

Each industry could have industry-specific branches on a single patent pledge block chain branch. For example, the wearable device industry could have an allocated branch where parties create new hashes that are tagged with a patent number. The hash would represent a unique patent pledge that would be traceable via the patent number to the registered assignee. The same would apply to other industries such as batteries or electrical aircraft: each would have a unique branch of hashes representing patent pledges.

Distributed ledgers may provide reasonably simple and low-cost methods of securely storing a variety of patent information. Without a doubt, it would provide a secure way to prove the existence of certain actions such as when an invention is made, or a party decides to pledge its patents.

CONCLUSION

Patent pledges represent an enormous opportunity to explore the potential of private ordering systems. At the center of ensuring their success is information, and we must look to technology and data structuring as core components. Patent pledges are a great starting point given their current flexibility and growing popularity among patent holders.

More significantly, however, is what will happen to the patent system once private ordering is widely adopted as regular intellectual property practice. In a world where we can operate a currency regime using online encryption technology, the idea that we could also record the existence of human innovation without a centralized PTO authority becomes a truly viable possibility. Patenting when paired with the decentralization of rights distribution could help society return to the constitutional root of patenting which is inevitably "to promote the progress of science and useful arts."

20. Best practices for making patent pledges

Meredith Jacob

I. WHY BEST PRACTICES ARE NEEDED

As discussed in the other chapters in this book, patent pledges exist across a broad spectrum of specificity, findability, and legal definiteness, resulting in a concomitantly broad range of usefulness and legal certainty for parties who would rely on those pledges. This chapter lays out a set of recommended best practices for making patent pledges that fulfills the potential interests of the pledgor in having the public rely on the pledge (and possibly induce some change in behavior) and the pledgee in reasonable legal predictability when acting in response to that pledge.

In Chapter 1, Contreras lays out a range of reasons why a pledgor may make a patent pledge: *inducement*, *collective action*, *voluntary restraint* and *philanthropy*. It is against those motivations, and the theories for enforcement in Chapter 5, that these best practices are drawn.

II. BEST PRACTICES

The following set of best practices is not a proscriptive list, and must be read in the context of the capacity and sophistication of the pledging entity, the benefits it will receive if the pledge is relied upon, and the risks posed to others relying on the pledge.

A. Clearly Identify the Patent(s) Being Pledged

1. Identify by patent number and field of art

The first requirement for a patent pledge to be useful is to identify unambiguously which patents are being pledged.[1] Failing to identify such patents specifically and clearly can lead to uncertainty among pledgees, who may risk liability if they incorrectly guess the pledgor's intent. Such uncertainty may chill the pledgee's and the market's willingness to rely on the pledge in making costly design, production and marketing decisions.

In an ideal pledge, patents covered by the pledge will be identified by patent number (and issuing nationality), in addition to the technology area covered. When a pledge refers or could refer to future patents, that should be made clear as well, and those patent numbers should be added when issued.

The specification of a field of art is useful when the pledgor is attempting to create freedom to operate, such as in the case of patent pledges for open source software. This provides the pledgee with two types of certainty: that a specific patent is covered by the pledge, and also that patents within the descriptive scope of the patent have not been intentionally excluded.

2. If identification by patent number is impracticable, provide mechanisms to improve certainty

In situations in which it is burdensome to provide patent numbers for all pledged patents (such as the pledge of a large portfolio or all of a company's patents as applied to a certain field), there are other reasonable steps that a pledgor can take. One useful step is to make clear statements about the inclusions and exclusions at the margins of a pledged field of patents. For example, a pledgor that pledged "all patents in the field of open source software" could specifically include or exclude patents for software or methods that could be integrated into open source software, but were not clearly a part of open source software at the time of invention.[2]

---

1 Many patent pledges, though well intentioned, fail to notify the market which patents are subject to the pledge. *See*, e.g., IBM OSS pledge in Appendix defining the scope of its pledge as covering "all patents pertaining to open source software."

2 Software or other related patents need not be operating system or programming language dependent. An older patent relating to a interface, a process or a piece of hardware may be a key part of current open sources

Additionally, pledgors who are unable to identify the patent numbers of pledged patents should consider establishing a process for potential users of the pledge to submit inquiries about the inclusion or exclusion of specific patent numbers.[3] If determinations about the status of an individual patent are made, those results should be made publicly available in the same manner as the original patent pledge.

B. Define the Scope of the Pledge

1. Specify the commitment

As noted in Chapter 1, patent pledges can cover different commitments with respect to pledged patents. Pledgors must be clear what type of commitment they are making, whether a primary access commitment such as non-assertion of the patent, a FRAND licensing commitment, or a non-royalty commitment, such as a "no NPE transfers" commitment.

2. Define ambiguous terms

When delineating the scope of the commitment made by a patent pledge, the pledgor should attempt to define any terms that could be ambiguous. For example, the original Tesla patent pledge contained the assertion that "Tesla will not initiate patent lawsuits against anyone who, in good faith, wants to use our technology."[4] In that pledge, the meaning of "good faith" was not clearly defined, and caused significant speculation in the marketplace and academia in the weeks and months following its

---

software implementation, but contain no reasonable way to identify that in the text of the patent.

[3] For example, a simple notice to direct inquiries regarding the pledge to a specific email address at the company, akin to the notices found in online privacy statements, would be helpful.

[4] *See*, e.g., Adam Mossof, *Tesla's New Patent Policy: Long Live the Patent System* (June 14, 2014), http://cpip.gmu.edu/2014/06/17/teslas-new-patent-policy-long-live-the-patent-system/, discussing the particular meaning of "good faith" within the context of the original Tesla Patent Pledge. "Fortunately, one intrepid reporter at the L.A. Times asked this question, and the answer from Musk makes clear that this new policy is not an abandonment of patent rights in favor of some fuzzy notion of the public domain, but rather it's an exercise of his company's patent rights: 'Tesla will allow other manufacturers to use its patents in "good faith" – essentially barring those users from filing patent-infringement lawsuits against [Tesla] or trying to produce knockoffs of Tesla's cars.' In the legalese known to patent lawyers and inventors the world over, this is not an abandonment of Tesla's patents, this is what is known as a cross license."

release.[5] Fortunately, and perhaps in response to this criticism, Tesla subsequently clarified its pledge substantially (see Appendix).

3. Identify exceptions and exclusions

Some pledges contain specific exceptions or exclusions. In the SDO context, for example, pledgors retain the right to assert pledged patents "defensively," when an infringement claim has been brought against them by a licensee or user of a pledged patent.[6]

C. Transfers, Revocability, and Notice

As discussed in Chapter 18, given that pledges are often made in the ICT field, where transfers of large numbers of patents are common, and also that pledgees may make significant investment in reliance on a pledge, it is important to limit the pledgor's ability to revoke a patent pledge.

1. Promise to condition future transfers on continuation of the pledge

As emphasized in Chapter 18, an effective patent pledge should "travel with" the patent. If patent pledges can be undone by changes in patent ownership, then there is a high risk for the public that the pledge is unreliable. Entities making patent pledges should thus explicitly promise to make those pledges binding on future transferees of the patents.

2. Patent pledges should be irrevocable

Chapter 18 also observes that some pledges appear to be fleeting and impermanent. The disappearance of a pledge from public view can affect both public knowledge of the pledge, but could also arguably relieve the pledgor of its obligations under the pledge. Patent pledges should thus be irrevocable.[7] Looking again at the theories underlying the making of patent pledges, there is a range of self-regarding motivations for such pledges. Nevertheless, most pledgors benefit (or intend to benefit) from the pledges they make. Conversely, the users of pledged patents will

---

[5] While "good faith" is defined in some contract law contexts, there is insufficient case law or secondary materials on the field of patent pledges for this term to have certainty here.

[6] *See* AM. BAR ASS'N, STANDARDS DEVELOPMENT PATENT POLICY MANUAL 52–67 (Jorge L. Contreras, ed., 2007). Such a defensive suspension clause is also an aspect of the Tesla patent pledge (see Appendix).

[7] As discussed in Section B.3 there are situations, such as defensive assertion of a patent, where a pledgor may later assert a pledged patent, though the pledge has not been revoked.

likely make some investment of effort and resources in reliance on such pledges. In order to maintain the balance of equities between the pledgor and the public, patent pledges should expressly be irrevocable once made.

3. Notice of transfer

While Chapter 5 lays out the theories under which patent pledges may be legally enforceable, the risk of relying on a patent pledge lies not only in the language and form on the pledge, but also in an analysis of the business interests and reliability of the pledgor. For that reason, it is important for companies to provide notice if they have transferred any patents previously covered by a patent pledge, and whether the transfer affected the pledge in any manner.

III. IMPLEMENTATION OF A PATENT PLEDGE

A. Make Pledges Findable

Often, patent pledges made outside of an SDO context are made in a transitory announcement, press conference, or blog. While these pledges may serve the public relations interests of the pledgor, they are not maximally useful for potential users of the pledged patents.[8]

1. Post pledges in a topical, permanent section of a public website

While patent pledges are findable in a news or press release section of a website for a searcher who already knows they exist, that format provides poor findability, and little linkage to any subsequent additions or notices regarding the pledge commitments. Pledges should be posted to a “Legal” or “Intellectual Property” section of the public website for the company making the pledge.

2. Document dates pledges were made or modified

Until a registry for patent pledges is formalized, public website postings are often the only documentation of a non-SDO patent pledge. For that

---

[8] While large competitors may be able to get clarification or documentation of pledges through other routes, public announcements are often the only available notice to small innovators.

reason, it is important that the pledge includes the date it was made or updated and the page that any patents were added to the pledge.[9]

3. Text of pledges should be searchable and crawlable

Patent pledges will be most useful if they can be found and relied upon by the entire relevant market. Accordingly, pledges that are posted on the Web should be fully text-searchable and accessible to web crawlers and search engines (i.e., not contained in image or video files).[10]

IV. CONCLUSION

The above best practices are intended to improve the usefulness and enforceability of patent pledges, whether or not more formal measures, such as the registry proposed in Chapter 18, are adopted. The progression of the Tesla patent pledge from a blog post to a full section on the corporate website provides one illustration of the increased certainty and value provided by a well-documented patent pledge. While these best practices are not exhaustive, it is hoped that they provide some common sense recommendations that will be adopted by patent pledgors worldwide.

---

9 For full transparency, it would be ideal for a pledgor to maintain an archive of previous pledges, when pledge terms are altered or updated.

10 Cf. Michael W. Carroll, *Why Full Open Access Matters*, 9 PLoS BIOLOGY (Nov. 29, 2011) (discussing need for fully searchable text of online scholarly articles). For an example of a patent pledge embedded in a video file, see Randy Milch, General Counsel, Verizon, Software Patents and Their Challenges Conference at Colorado Law: Panel 3 (Oct. 9, 2013), http://www.youtube.com/watch?v=j_jgV6UKnp8&list=PLwFq2GL-i5UjaeZNyVOGbSKaJ5rPmvVNc&index=3 (now fully accessible in the Patent Pledge Database, http://www.pijip.org/non-sdo-patent-commitments/).

Appendix

TEXT OF SELECTED PATENT PLEDGES

1. Tesla Motors
2. IBM
3. Google
4. Myriad Genetics
5. Monsanto
6. Red Hat
7. Microsoft

1. TESLA MOTORS

"All Our Patents Are Belong to You"
Elon Musk, CEO, Tesla Motors
June 12, 2014

Patent Pledge

On June 12, 2014, Tesla announced that it will not initiate patent lawsuits against anyone who, in good faith, wants to use its technology. Tesla was created to accelerate the advent of sustainable transport, and this policy is intended to encourage the advancement of a common, rapidly-evolving platform for electric vehicles, thereby benefiting Tesla, other companies making electric vehicles, and the world. These guidelines provide further detail as to how we are implementing this policy.

Tesla's Pledge

Tesla irrevocably pledges that it will not initiate a lawsuit against any party for infringing a Tesla Patent through activity relating to electric vehicles or related equipment for so long as such party is acting in good faith. Key terms of the Pledge are explained below.

Definition of Key Terms

"Tesla Patents" means all patents owned now or in the future by Tesla (other than a patent owned jointly with a third party or any patent that Tesla later acquires that comes with an encumbrance that prevents it from being subject to this Pledge). A list of Tesla Patents subject to the Pledge will be maintained at the following URL: https://www.teslamotors.com/about/legal#patent-list.

A party is "acting in good faith" for so long as such party and its related or affiliated companies have not:

> asserted, helped others assert or had a financial stake in any assertion of (i) any patent or other intellectual property right against Tesla or (ii) any patent right against a third party for its use of technologies relating to electric vehicles or related equipment;
>
> challenged, helped others challenge, or had a financial stake in any challenge to any Tesla patent; or

marketed or sold any knock-off product (e.g., a product created by imitating or copying the design or appearance of a Tesla product or which suggests an association with or endorsement by Tesla) or provided any material assistance to another party doing so.

Transfer of Tesla Patents

Should Tesla ever transfer a Tesla Patent to a third party, it will do so only to a party that agrees, by means of a public declaration intended to be binding on such party, to provide the same protection that Tesla provided under the Pledge and to place the same requirement on any subsequent transferee.

Legal Effect

The Pledge, which is irrevocable and legally binding on Tesla and its successors, is a "standstill," meaning that it is a forbearance of enforcement of Tesla's remedies against any party for claims of infringement for so long as such party is acting in good faith. In order for Tesla to preserve its ability to enforce the Tesla Patents against any party not acting in good faith, the Pledge is not a waiver of any patent claims (including claims for damages for past acts of infringement) and is not a license, covenant not to sue, or authorization to engage in patented activities or a limitation on remedies, damages or claims. Except as expressly stated in the Pledge, no rights shall be deemed granted, waived or received by implication, exhaustion, estoppel or otherwise. Finally, the Pledge is not an indication of the value of an arms-length, negotiated license or a reasonable royalty.

What this pledge means is that as long as someone uses our patents for electric vehicles and doesn't do bad things, such as knocking off our products or using our patents and then suing us for intellectual property infringement, they should have no fear of Tesla asserting its patents against them.

2. IBM

IBM Statement of Non-Assertion of Named Patents Against OSS
January 11, 2005

IBM is committed to promoting innovation for the benefit of our customers and for the overall growth and advancement of the information technology field. IBM takes many actions to promote innovation. Today, we are announcing a new innovation initiative. We are pledging the free use of 500 of our U.S. patents, as well as all counterparts of these patents issued in other countries, in the development, distribution, and use of open source software. We believe that the open source community has been at the forefront of innovation and we are taking this action to encourage additional innovation for open platforms.

The following is the text of our pledge. It is our intent that this pledge be legally binding and enforceable by any open source software developer, distributor, or user who uses one or more of the 500 listed U.S. patents and/or the counterparts of these patents issued in other countries.

IBM's Legally Binding Commitment Not To Assert the 500 Named Patents Against OSS

The pledge will benefit any Open Source Software. Open Source Software is any computer software program whose source code is published and available for inspection and use by anyone, and is made available under a license agreement that permits recipients to copy, modify and distribute the program's source code without payment of fees or royalties. All licenses certified by opensource.org and listed on their website as of 01/11/2005 are Open Source Software licenses for the purpose of this pledge.

IBM hereby commits not to assert any of the 500 U.S. patents listed below, as well as all counterparts of these patents issued in other countries, against the development, use or distribution of Open Source Software.

In order to foster innovation and avoid the possibility that a party will take advantage of this pledge and then assert patents or other intellectual property rights of its own against Open Source Software, thereby limiting the freedom of IBM or any other Open Source Software developer to create innovative software programs, the commitment not to assert any of these 500 U.S. patents and all counterparts of these patents issued in other countries is irrevocable except that IBM reserves the right to terminate this patent pledge and commitment only with regard to any party who files a lawsuit asserting patents or other intellectual property rights against Open Source Software.

IBM'S LEGALLY BINDING COMMITMENT NOT TO ASSERT THE 500 NAMED PATENTS AGAINST OSS

The pledge will benefit any Open Source Software. Open Source Software is any computer software program whose source code is published and available for inspection and use by anyone, and is made available under a license agreement that permits recipients to copy, modify and distribute the program's source code without payment of fees or royalties. All licenses certified by opensource.org and listed on their website as of 01/11/2005 are Open Source Software licenses for the purpose of this pledge.

Subject to the exception provided below, and with the intent that developers, users and distributors of Open Source Software rely on our promise, IBM hereby commits not to assert any of the 500 U.S. patents listed above, as well as all counterparts of these patents issued in other countries against the development, use or distribution of Open Source Software.

In order to foster innovation and avoid the possibility that a party will take advantage of this pledge and then assert patents or other intellectual property rights of its own against Open Source Software, thereby limiting the freedom of IBM or any other Open Source Software developer to create innovative software programs, or the freedom of others to distribute and use Open Source Software, the commitment not to assert any of these 500 U.S. patents and all counterparts of these patents issued in other countries is irrevocable except that IBM reserves the right to terminate this patent pledge and commitment only with regard to any party who files a lawsuit asserting patents or other intellectual property rights against Open Source Software.

3. GOOGLE

Open Source Pledge

Open Patent Non-Assertion Pledge
March 28, 2013

Google is committed to promoting innovation to further the overall growth and advancement of information technology and believes that Free or Open Source Software is a very important tool for fostering innovation. Google is therefore pledging the free use of certain of its patents in connection with Free or Open Source Software on the following terms:

Definitions

"Free or Open Source Software" means any software that is licensed or otherwise distributed to the public in such a way that satisfies any version of "The Open Source Definition" provided by the Open Source Initiative at opensource.org/osd or any version of "The Free Software Definition" provided by the Free Software Foundation at gnu.org/philosophy/free-sw.html.

"Pledged Patents" means the specific patents listed by Google at the following URL designated for purposes of this Pledge: www.google.com/patents/opnpledge/patents/. Google may supplement this list of patents from time to time in its discretion.

"Pledge" means the promise set forth in the first two paragraphs under "Our Pledge."

Our Pledge

Google promises to each person or entity that develops, distributes or uses Free or Open Source Software (a "Pledge Recipient") that Google will not bring a lawsuit or other legal proceeding against a Pledge Recipient for patent infringement under any Pledged Patents based on the Pledge Recipient's (i) development, manufacture, use, sale, offer for sale, lease, license, exportation, importation or distribution of any Free or Open Source Software, or (ii) internal-only use of Free or Open Source Software, either as obtained by Pledge Recipient or as modified by Pledge Recipient, in standalone form or combined with hardware or with any other software ("Internal-Only Use"). The preceding Pledge does not apply to any infringement of the Pledged Patents by hardware or by software that is not Free or Open Source Software, or by Free or Open Source Software combined with special purpose hardware or with software that is not Free or Open Source Software (except Internal-Only Use).

It is Google's intent that the Pledge be legally binding, irrevocable (except as otherwise provided under "Defensive Termination" below) and enforceable against Google and entities controlled by Google, and their successors and assigns. Thus, Google will require any person or entity to whom it sells or transfers any of the Pledged Patents to agree, in writing, to abide by the Pledge and to place a similar requirement on any subsequent transferees to do the same.

The Pledge is not an assurance that any of the Pledged Patents cover any particular software or hardware or are enforceable, that the Pledged Patents are all patents that do or may cover any particular Free or Open Source Software, that any activities covered by the Pledge will not infringe patents or other intellectual property rights of a third party, or that Google will add any other patents to the list of Pledged Patents. Except as expressly stated in the Pledge, no other rights are waived or granted by Google or received by a Pledge Recipient, whether by implication, estoppel, or otherwise.

Defensive Termination

Because our Pledge is a promise not to assert certain Google patents without requiring any payment from a Pledge Recipient, we think it is only fair that we condition the Pledge upon the Pledge Recipient (and its affiliates) not asserting or profiting from the assertion of patents against Google, its affiliates, or its products or services. Accordingly, Google reserves the right to terminate the Pledge, to the extent Google deems necessary to protect itself, its affiliates, or its products and services ("Defensive Termination") with respect to any Pledge Recipient (or affiliate) who files a lawsuit or other legal proceeding for patent infringement or who has a direct financial interest in such lawsuit or other legal proceeding (an "Asserting Party") against Google or any entity controlled by Google or against any third party based in whole or in part on any product or service developed by or on behalf of Google or any entity controlled by Google.

Any Defensive Termination by Google with respect to an Asserting Party shall have the same effect as if Our Pledge was never extended to such Asserting Party in the first instance. Google, in its sole discretion, shall determine the manner and terms, if any, by which rights under Pledged Patents may be extended to an Asserting Party after that Asserting Party's lawsuit or other legal proceeding is permanently dismissed, terminated or withdrawn in writing.

Mistaken Assertion

Should Google ever initiate a lawsuit or other legal proceeding for patent infringement based on software which is not the subject of a Defensive Termination, and then receive written notice from the party against whom such lawsuit or other legal proceeding has been filed providing sufficient information for Google to reasonably determine that such software in fact satisfies the requirements of the Pledge, then Google will use reasonable efforts to withdraw such lawsuit (or the applicable claims therein) or move to terminate such other legal proceeding (or the applicable portions thereof) within sixty (60) days after receiving such written notice.

4. MYRIAD GENETICS

The Myriad Pledge

Myriad is dedicated, above all else, to improving patient care through pioneering research and the development of innovative molecular diagnostic tests.

Since 1991, the Company has invested more than $1 billion to enhance the world's collective scientific understanding of disease through collaborative research, outreach and education and to translate that knowledge into molecular and companion diagnostic tools that save and improve the lives of the patients we serve.

Today – and everyday – we reaffirm our commitment to serving as both a trusted advisor to patients and healthcare professionals and a collaborator with the scientific community.

Our Pledge to Patients and the Research Community

Research is integral to scientific progress and the translation of these research discoveries into accurate, clinically actionable tools is essential to patient care.

The Myriad Pledge: Myriad has supported and continues to support research institutions in the advancement of scientific and technological knowledge, and we will not impede noncommercial, academic research that uses patented technology licensed or owned by us.

Every patient has the right to have a second opinion confirmation of test results before making medical management decisions.

The Myriad Pledge: Myriad will continue its practice of not interfering with laboratories that conduct genetic testing on patients for the purpose of confirming a test result provided by Myriad.

Molecular and companion diagnostic testing that saves lives and lowers healthcare costs must be broadly accessible.

The Myriad Pledge: Myriad will continue to offer our financial assistance program and free testing to help patients with the greatest need.

5. MONSANTO

Monsanto's Commitment: Farmers and Patents

Our farmer customers are always treated with a high level of integrity, respect and transparency, especially during investigations of potential seed patent infringement. This document describes our commitment to farmers when reviewing, evaluating and investigating these matters.

I. We shall conduct investigations with standards that adhere to our pledge of transparency and ethical behavior, that are reviewed by a professional third party.
II. We will properly introduce ourselves, prominently display identification and clearly state the purpose of our contact.
III. We always seek permission prior to entering farmers' cropland and always abide by all federal, state and local laws concerning individual property rights, inspections and sampling activities.
IV. We will treat all inquiries and information as confidentially as possible.
V. We understand the importance of planting and harvesting and always seek to minimize interfering with farmers' normal activities. We strive for all conversations and meetings with a farmer to be held at a mutually agreeable time and location.
VI. We strive to resolve all seed patent infringement inquiries on a timely basis. If it is determined that no infringement occurred, the inquiry is immediately considered to be resolved. In cases of confirmed seed patent infringement, farmers will be afforded every opportunity to seek resolution through settlement.
VII. We always conduct good faith settlement negotiations. Farmers may retain counsel for representation at any time.
VIII. We will always retain a third party to conduct field sampling. Farmers may ask a third party representative to accompany and observe the sample collection process. Farmers may also retain an independent laboratory of their choice to verify the seed sampling findings.
IX. We will participate in mediated settlement discussions through a third party representative or an agricultural mediator at the farmer's request, after field sampling is completed.
X. It has never been, nor will it be Monsanto policy to exercise its patent rights where trace amounts of our patented seed or traits are present in farmer's fields as a result of inadvertent means.

6. RED HAT

Statement of Position and Our Promise on Software Patents

Our Position on Software Patents

Red Hat has consistently taken the position that software patents generally impede innovation in software development and that software patents are inconsistent with open source/free software. Red Hat representatives have addressed this issue before the National Academies of Science, the U.S. Federal Trade Commission, and the U.S. Department of Justice. Red Hat is also a signatory to a petition to the European Union encouraging the EU not to adopt a policy of permitting software patents. We will continue to work to promote this position and are pleased to join our colleagues in the open source/free software community, as well as those proprietary vendors which have publicly stated their opposition to software patents, in that effort.

At the same time, we are forced to live in the world as it is, and that world currently permits software patents. A relatively small number of very large companies have amassed large numbers of software patents. We believe such massive software patent portfolios are ripe for misuse because of the questionable nature of many software patents generally and because of the high cost of patent litigation.

One defense against such misuse is to develop a corresponding portfolio of software patents for defensive purposes. Many software companies, both open source and proprietary, pursue this strategy. In the interests of our company and in an attempt to protect and promote the open source community, Red Hat has elected to adopt this same stance. We do so reluctantly because of the perceived inconsistency with our stance against software patents; however, prudence dictates this position.

At the same time, Red Hat will continue to maintain its position as an open source leader and dedicated participant in open source collaboration by extending the promise set forth below.

Our Promise with Respect to Software Patents We Hold

Definitions:

Approved License means any of the following licenses: GNU General Public License v2.0 and v3.0; GNU Lesser General Public License v2.1 and v3.0, IBM Public License v1.0; Common Public License v1.0; Q Public License v1.0; Open Software License v3.0; and any open source license granted by Red Hat. Red Hat may add to this list in its sole discretion by publication on this page.

Open Source/Free Software means any software which is licensed under an Approved License.

Patent Rights means any of the rights to make, use[,] sell, offer to sell, import or otherwise transfer software, in either source code or object code form.

Red Hat means Red Hat, Inc.

Our Promise:

Subject to any qualifications or limitations stated herein, to the extent any party exercises a Patent Right with respect to Open Source/Free Software which reads on any claim of any patent held by Red Hat, Red Hat agrees to refrain from enforcing the infringed patent against such party for such exercise ("Our Promise"). Our Promise does not extend to any software which is not Open Source/Free Software, and any party exercising a Patent Right with respect to non-Open Source/Free Software which reads on any claims of any patent held by Red Hat must obtain a license for the exercise of such rights from Red Hat. Our Promise does not extend to any party who institutes patent litigation against Red Hat with respect to a patent applicable to software (including a cross-claim or counterclaim to a lawsuit). No hardware per se is licensed hereunder.

Each party relying on Our Promise acknowledges that Our Promise is not an assurance that Red Hat's patents are enforceable or that the exercise of rights under Red Hat's patents does not infringe the patent or other intellectual property rights of any other entity. Red Hat disclaims any liability to any party relying on Our Promise for claims brought by any other entity based on infringement of intellectual property rights or otherwise. As a condition to exercising the Patent Rights permitted by

Our Promise hereunder, each relying party hereby assumes sole responsibility to secure any other intellectual property rights needed, if any.

7. MICROSOFT

Open Specification Promise

Published: September 12, 2006 | Revised: February 15, 2007

Microsoft irrevocably promises not to assert any Microsoft Necessary Claims against you for making, using, selling, offering for sale, importing or distributing any implementation to the extent it conforms to a Covered Specification ("Covered Implementation"), subject to the following. This is a personal promise directly from Microsoft to you, and you acknowledge as a condition of benefiting from it that no Microsoft rights are received from suppliers, distributors, or otherwise in connection with this promise.

If you file, maintain or voluntarily participate in a patent infringement lawsuit against a Microsoft implementation of such Covered Specification, then this personal promise does not apply with respect to any Covered Implementation of the same Covered Specification made or used by you.

To clarify, "Microsoft Necessary Claims" are those claims of Microsoft-owned or Microsoft-controlled patents that are necessary to implement only the required portions of the Covered Specification that are described in detail and not merely referenced in such Specification. "Covered Specifications" are listed below.

This promise is not an assurance either (i) that any of Microsoft[-]issued patent claims covers a Covered Implementation or are enforceable or (ii) that a Covered Implementation would not infringe patents or other intellectual property rights of any third party. No other rights except those expressly stated in this promise shall be deemed granted, waived or received by implication, exhaustion, estoppel, or otherwise.

Index

802.11 standard 8, 24

ActiveSync protocol and pledges 29, 221–2
Agere, injunction action 120–21
AirBnB, patent pledge 2
Alcatel-Lucent, pledge 15, 16
Allied Security Trust (AST)
  antitrust issues 159
  catch-and-release approach 158
Amazon.com 260–62, 263–4, 275
Android operating system 1, 9, 32, 43, 164, 279
anticommons theory 73–4, 84
antitrust and competition law
  Brazil 193–4
  China 201–3, 204–7
  domain position and abuse thereof 174–5
  and enforcement of patent pledges 106–12
  European Union 106, 168ff
  horizontal arrangements
    and OPAs and DPAs 158–60
  KFTC *see* Korean Fair Trade Commission
  Korea 213–16, 219–22
  monopolization 107–8
  open source software
    Germany 157–8
    U.S. 157
  predatory pricing 160
  price competition
    and OPAs and DPAs 160–61
  rule of reason 155
  TFEU *see* Treaty on the Functioning of the European Union
Apache web server 9
Apple
  involvement in EC enforcement actions 173
  ITC exclusion order 132
  litigation with Samsung
    Korea 210
    U.S. ITC 132–3
  as member of Rockstar Bidco 34
  pledges 7, 33–4
  v. Motorola *see Apple v. Motorola*
Apple v. Motorola 14, 17, 103, 172–3, 212, 271
application programmer interface (API) 264–5
AT&T 7

Bayh-Dole Act 65–6
Betamax standard 28–9
BioBrick licenses 254
BiOS initiative 255
biotechnology, pledges and 10–11, 34, 56ff
block chain technology 312–14, 316
Bluetooth standard 30
BMI v. CBS 166
Broadcom v. Qualcomm 109

CAMBIA 255
Canada's Oil Sands Innovation Alliance (COSIA) 94–5, 96
CDMA standard 15
Cisco, pledges 7, 12, 21, 23
clearinghouses for intellectual property 64–5
climate change 82–3
cloud computing 260–62
commercially essential technologies 37
community licensing *see* patent pools

Compact Disc (CD) standard 28, 176–7
competition law *see* antitrust and competition law
compulsory licensing
  in Brazil 194–5
  and patent pledges in the developing world 280–81
contract law and patent pledges
  German law 138–42
  Korean law 211–13
  U.S. law 101–4
Court of Appeals for the Federal Circuit (CAFC)
  policy levers 75
covenant not to sue *see* royalty-free licensing
  German law 141–2
Creative Commons licenses 249
CRISPR technology 58

de facto standards
  generally 28
  Korea 218, 220–22
Defensive Patent Aggregator (DPA) *see* Non-Practicing Entities
Defensive Patent License (DPL) 18, 32–3, 44, 154–5, 255–8
Dell 7
Department of Justice (DOJ), U.S.
  and ITC exclusion orders 125, 134
  joint DOJ-FTC 2007 intellectual property guidelines 157, 164
  and open source software 162
  as recipient of pledges 33–4
developing countries 84, 85, 96–7, 191, 278–9, 280–82
DMARC specification 12, 21
Dow Chemical 10, 21
Dropbox, patent pledge 2
DuPont 10, 21
DVD standard 24

eBay v. MercExchange see injunctive relief
Eco-Patent Commons (EPC)
  compared to GreenXchange 93
  developing world impact 281–2
  generally 10, 20, 21, 35, 36, 90–92, 96, 254, 292
equitable servitude and pledges 113
Environmental Law Institute 10, 20, 91
Ericsson
  as member of Rockstar Bidco 34
  pledges 7, 12, 15, 16, 27
essential facilities doctrine 109
estoppel *see* promissory estoppel
Ethernet standard
  generally 8
  N-Data case 110
European Telecommunications Standards Institute (ETSI) 8, 172, 173, 210, 211–12, 287
European Unitary Patent system 170, 187–8
exclusion orders *see* International Trade Commission
exhaustion of rights 51–4

Facebook, pledges 21
Fair, Reasonable and Nondiscriminatory (FRAND) licensing
  China regulation 204–5
  in developing countries 279
  and DPL 155
  enforceability of 101ff
  generally 12, 13, 14, 15–17, 26, 34, 37, 97, 242
  and injunctions 171
  as a remedy in Microsoft case 189
Federal Circuit *see* Court of Appeals for the Federal Circuit
Federal Trade Commission (FTC), U.S.
  and ITC exclusion orders 125
  joint DOJ-FTC 2007 intellectual property guidelines *see* Department of Justice
  N-Data case *see in re Negotiated Data Solutions LLC*
  Robert Bosch case *see in re Robert Bosch GmbH*
Federal Trade Commission Act
  Section 5 110–12
Firefox web browser 9

first sale doctrine *see* exhaustion of rights
Free and Open Source Software (FOSS) *see* Open Source Software
Fujitsu 16, 21

General Public License (GPL) *see* Open Source Software
German law
  contract law theories 138–42
  enforcement of patent pledges 138, 140–42
  good faith defense 145–6
  simple consent 144–5
  waiver of rights 143–4
Google
  acquisition of Motorola Mobility 34, 201–2
  Android *see* Android operating system
  cloud computing 260–62, 275
  cloud computing patents 263–4
  FTC order *see* Motorola Mobility, FTC order
  Open Patent Non-Assertion Pledge 43–5, 47, 142
  patent acquisitions 80–81
  patent purchase program 81
  pledges 9, 12, 33–4, 43–5, 270–72, 280, 328–30
government use rights 65
GNU software *see* Open Source Software
GPRS standard 172
GreenXchange 92–4, 96
Green Technology
  in China 200
  patents 84–5
  pledges 10, 11, 82ff
GSM standard 8

H.264 standard 8
Hewlett Packard Co.
  as member of EPC 10, 21, 91
Hitachi 21
hold-out 121
hold-up 25, 121, 125
HTTP 8, 24
Huawei 7
Huawei v. Interdigital (China) 201, 203–4
Huawei v. ZTE 115, 169, 171–3, 177–8, 180–81, 182–3

IEEE Standards Association 8, 120, 287
  policy amendments 16
IMS Health case 175–6
India 277–82
Information and Communications Technology (ICT) sector 6, 8, 199
injunctive relief
  eBay v. MercExchange 50, 120–24, 127–8, 169–70, 184
  Korea 213
  for NPEs 123
  pledges that limit 13, 17
innovation
  in developing countries 278
  encouragement of 161–7
  management of 249–52
  open innovation movement 252–3
  races 153
Intel Corp. pledges 7, 16
Intellectual Property Enforcement Directive (EU Directive 2004/48) 185–7
Interdigital Corp.
  China NDRC investigation 205–6
  Huawei v. Interdigital see Huawei v. Interdigital (China)
International Business Machines Corp. (IBM)
  antitrust 160
  cloud computing 260–62
  cloud computing patents 263–4, 266–7
  as member of EPC 10, 21, 91
  pledges 1, 7, 31, 38–9, 79, 267–9, 278, 286, 326–7
  services 31
International Organisation for Standardization (ISO) 8
International Telecommunications Union (ITU) 8

International Trade Commission (ITC)
exclusion orders 122–35
public interest factors 127–35
Internet Engineering Task Force (IETF) 8, 14, 20, 22
Internet Protocol (IP) 8
ISO 9000 standard 8
ISO 14000 standard 8

Korean Fair Trade Commission (KFTC)
IPR Guidelines 209, 216–18
as recipient of pledges 222

Letters of Assurance (LOAs) 19
License on Transfer (LOT)
network 45
and pledges 42, 154, 257
Linux operating system
antitrust challenges 156
commercial distribution 251
and innovation 162
pledges 1, 9, 31, 39–40, 41–2, 154
service-based revenue model 163, 251, 267
lock-in 25
Long Term Evolution (LTE) standard 2, 8, 15
Lumia *see* Microsoft Corp., purchase of Nokia handset business

Magill case 175, 176
MapReduce 43
market reliance theory 46, 114–15, 161
Massachusetts Institute of Technology (MIT) 11, 21
Matsushita
VHS standard *see* VHS standard
Max Planck Institute, pledges 21
Microsoft Corp.
ActiveSync *see* ActiveSync protocols
Android licensing 279
Brazilian antitrust action 190
cloud computing 260–62, 275
cloud computing patents 263–6
European antitrust litigation 189
Interoperability Principles 29–30
as member of Rockstar Bidco 34
open source software 251
pledges 7, 22, 29, 33–4, 236, 273
purchase of Nokia handset business 202–3 (China), 220–22
Microsoft v. Motorola 14, 15, 45, 101, 103, 172–3, 212
Mitsubishi Electric 16
Monsanto, pledge 1, 11, 332
Motorola Mobility
acquisition by Google 34
EC enforcement action 172–3, 177
FTC consent decree 111
FTC order 17
Microsoft v. *see Microsoft v. Motorola*
pledges 15
v. Apple *see Apple v. Motorola*
Myriad Genetics
BRCA gene patents 58
pledge 11, 34, 331

National Semiconductor pledge 110
NEC, pledges 15, 16
in re Negotiated Data Solutions LLC (N-Data) 110, 292–3
NextWave, pledges 15, 16
Nokia
as member of EPC 10, 21, 91
pledges 15, 16, 27
Nokia Siemens Networks, pledges 15, 16
Non-Practicing Entities (NPEs)
absence in biotechnology 71–3
Allied Security Trust *see* Allied Security Trust
business models 76
catch-and-release approach 158
defensive mechanisms 258–9
Defensive Patent Aggregators (DPA) 158
generally 67–8
injunctive relief 123
litigation 68–9, 167
pledges restricting transfers of patents to 13, 17–18

RPX Corp. *see* RPX Corp.
taxonomies 69–71
Nortel Networks, pledges in bankruptcy 34, 293
Novell, pledge 38
NTT DoCoMo, pledge 16, 27

Open Innovation (OI) movement *see* innovation, open innovation movement
Open Invention Network (OIN) 9–10, 21, 39, 41–2, 154, 255, 272
Open Patent Agreements (OPAs)
antitrust analysis of 156–7
defined 154
Open Patent Non-Assertion Pledge *see* Google
open science 57, 59
Open Source Software (OSS)
Antitrust analysis
Germany 157–8
U.S. 157
in China 199–200
enforcement of licenses in Germany 137, 139
General Public License (GPL) 156, 157, 162
and innovation 249–52
Jacobsen v. Katzer 165
Licenses 47, 59
movement 58
pledges relating to 8–9, 37–9, 326–7, 328–30, 333–5
service-based revenue model 163, 251
Open Web Foundation 12, 20
specifications 21
OpenStack platform 9, 266–7, 268–9, 272–3, 275
Oracle v. Google 265
Orange Book Standard case 176, 181

Panasonic, pledges 16, 274
Patent Assertion Entity (PAE) *see* Non-Practicing Entities
patent law
Brazilian patent law 190–93
in China 197
cloud computing patents 263–7
commercialization theory 229–30
compulsory licensing *see* compulsory licensing
disclosure requirements 229, 238–9, 243–4
European Unitary Patent *see* European Unitary Patent system
independent invention defense 243
informational value 227, 232–3, 244–5
misuse doctrine 112
moral opposition to 166–7
prior art 13, 299, 308–10, 315
prior user rights 241
prospect theory 229
registration system 294–5
renewals 286
right to exclude 228, 237–8, 241–3
Patent Pledge Database at American University 3, 299
patent pledges
beneficiaries 46, 102–3
in China 199–200
collective action 32–3, 151, 152–3
coordinated 18–20
defensive termination/suspension 327, 329–30, 334
disappearing 48–9, 290–92
distinguished from licenses 50
enforcement
EU 168ff
Germany 137ff
U.S. 101ff
identification of patents 11–12, 318–19
inducement 24–32, 36
informational value 232–3, 234–7, 239–40, 290–92, 301–2
interoperability 24–32
made in SDOs 18–19, 25–6
made outside of SDOs 26–7
made to government officials 22–3
market development 30–32
metadata 303–4
motivations 3, 24, 285–6

non-assertion commitments *see* royalty-free licensing
notice function 245, 290–93
ontology 304–6
open innovation 253
philanthropy 35, 78
platform leadership 27–30
public relations benefit 36, 78
public statements 23
recordation 288, 310–16, 321
registry 288, 294–300
relationship with patent theory 230–32
retractions 48–9
scope 12–18, 319–20
"the patent pledge" 35, 139
transfer of pledged patents 13, 292–3, 321, 325, 329
unilateral 20–23, 37ff, 287–8
valuation 50–51
voluntary restraint 33–4, 36
patent pools
antitrust analysis 157
in biotechnology 60–64
compared to OPAs 161
generally 152–3
Golden Rice pool 62–3
in green technology 89
relation to patent pledges 41–2
patent thicket 73
patent trolls *see* Non-Practicing Entities
Philips 28
platform technology 28, 274–5
privateering 44
promissory estoppel and patent pledges 45–6, 105–6, 212–13 (Korea)

Qualcomm, Inc.
China NDRC investigation 206–7
pledges 15

Rackspace 262, 266–7, 269
Rambus v FTC 108
Raymond, Eric S. 164
Reasonable and Nondiscriminatory (RAND) licensing *see* Fair, Reasonable and Nondiscriminatory (FRAND) licensing
Red Hat, Inc. 38, 40, 163, 251, 333–5
registries *see* patent pledges
reliance interests in patent pledges 45–6
Research in Motion (RIM)
as member of Rockstar Bidco 34
in re Robert Bosch GmbH 111, 161
Rockstar Bidco 34
royalties, patent
base 15–16
caps 13
maximum 14–15
royalty-free licensing
by OPAs 161
pledges 13, 14, 22, 26, 40
strategic considerations 286
RPX Corp.
antitrust issues 159
purchase of Inventus Solutions 308

Samsung
EC enforcement action 172, 177
pledges 7, 21
Siemens, pledges 16, 27
Sony
as member of EPC 10, 21, 91
as member of Rockstar Bidco 34
Betamax *see* Betamax standard
CD standard *see* Compact Disc (CD) standard
pledges 7, 16
Sony Ericsson, pledges 15, 16, 21
Southern California Edison, pledge 12
Standard-Spundfass case 176
Standards Development Organizations (SDOs)
Bylaws 19
FRAND commitments *see* Fair, Reasonable and Nondiscriminatory (FRAND) licensing
organizational structure 19
pledges made in 18–19, 25–6
policies 25

Standards-Essential Patents (SEPs)
and ITC exclusion orders 129–30
generally 37
standards wars
Betamax v VHS 28–9
Stellar Consensus Protocol (SCP) 315

Tesla Motors, pledge 1, 22, 30–31, 40, 79, 126, 197–8, 235, 239–40, 278, 324–5
Toyota, pledge 1
Transmission Control Protocol (TCP) 8
Treaty on the Functioning of the European Union (TFEU)
article 102, 178–80
generally 168–9
TRIPS agreement 194–5

UMTS standard 8, 172, 211
unfair methods of competition (FTC Act) 110–11
U.S. Trade Representative
disapproval of Apple ITC exclusion order 132–3

Verizon, pledges 7, 22
VHS standard 28

W-CDMA standard 15, 21, 27
Wi-Fi *see* 802.11 standard
Wikipedia 165
WiMax standard 15
Worldwide Web Consortium (W3C) 8, 14
Worldwide Web (WWW) protocol 8

Xerox Corp.
as member of EPC 10, 21, 91
XML 8

Yahoo!, pledges 21, 23

ZTE *see Huawei v. ZTE*